To Lillie
from Grandma
With lots of love x x x
March 5th 2000

To Claude
from Karen
with lots of love x
December 25th 2021

To Marie
FROM Claude
xxx
JUNE, 2022

# THE RING
# OF BRIGHT
# WATER
# TRILOGY

## Gavin Maxwell

*Edited, with an introduction by Austin Chinn*
*Foreword by Jimmy Watt*
*Afterword by Virginia McKenna*

VIKING

VIKING

Published by the Penguin Group
Penguin Books Ltd, 27 Wrights Lane, London w8 5tz, England
Penguin Putnam Inc., 375 Hudson Street, New York, New York 10014, USA
Penguin Books Australia Ltd, Ringwood, Victoria, Australia
Penguin Books Canada Ltd, 10 Alcorn Avenue, Toronto, Ontario, Canada m4v 3b2
Penguin Books (NZ) Ltd, Private Bag 102902, NSMC, Auckland, New Zealand

Penguin Books Ltd, Registered Offices: Harmondsworth, Middlesex, England

This trilogy edition first published in Great Britain by Viking 2000

1 3 5 7 9 10 8 6 4 2

Copyright © Gavin Maxwell Enterprises Ltd 2000
Introduction © Austin Chinn 2000
Foreword © Jimmy Watt 2000
Afterword © Virginia McKenna 2000

*Ring of Bright Water*
First published by Longmans Green & Co 1960
Copyright © Gavin Maxwell 1960

*The Rocks Remain*
First published by Longmans Green & Co 1963
Copyright © Gavin Maxwell 1963

*Raven Seek Thy Brother*
First published by Longmans Green & Co 1968
Copyright © Gavin Maxwell 1968

The moral right of the author has been asserted

Typeset in 12.25 on 14.25 pt Monotype Sabon
Set by Rowland Phototypesetting Ltd, Bury St Edmunds, Suffolk
Printed in England by Clays Ltd, St Ives plc

A CIP catalogue record for this book is available from the British Library

ISBN 0-670-88992-X

# Contents

# List of Illustrations

# Acknowledgements

The editor and publishers are grateful to the following for permission to reproduce the following material: Miss Kathleen Raine and Messrs. Hamish Hamilton Ltd for 'The Ring' from *Year One* from which the title of *Ring of Bright Water* is taken; the literary agents of the late Mr Ernest Thompson Seton for an extract from *Life Histories of Northern Animals*, published by Constable; Laurence Pollinger Ltd, Jonathan Cape Ltd and Holt, Rinehart and Winston Inc., for permission to quote from Robert Frost's poem 'Fire and Ice'.

The drawings in the text of *Ring of Bright Water* are all by Peter Scott with the following exceptions: pp. 10, 112 by Robin McEwan; p. 62 by Gavin Maxwell; p. 130 by Michael Ayrton.

The drawings in the text of *The Rocks Remain* are: pp. 173, 178, 192, 199, 233, 250 by Peter Scott; p. 181 by Gavin Maxwell and pp. 187, 207, 223, 237, 256 by Robin McEwan.

The drawings in the text of *Raven Seek Thy Brother* are all by Robin McEwan with the following exceptions by Peter Scott: pp. 266, 295, 300, 306, 407.

Most of the photographs are by Gavin Maxwell, with the following exceptions: Robin McEwen – Section 1, page 2, top; Jimmy Watt – Section 1, page 7, bottom; Section 2, page 7; Section 3, page 2, top and bottom; page 4, bottom; page 5, bottom; page 6, top.

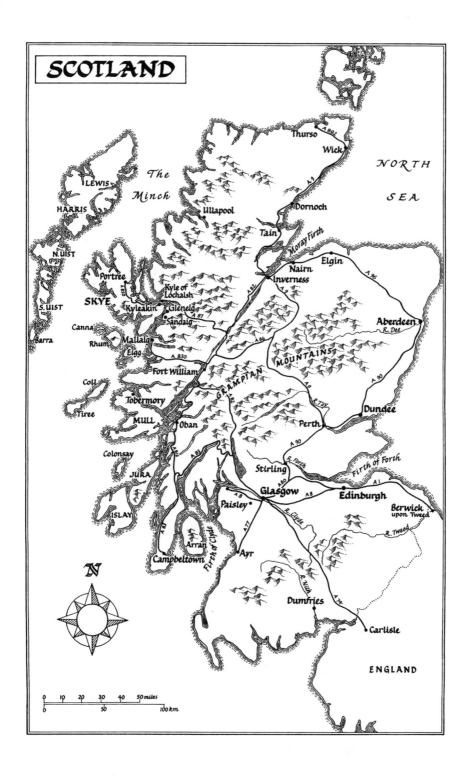

# Foreword

Camusfeàrna is the name Gavin Maxwell gave to what is really called Sandaig. Sandaig is near the village of Glenelg and means 'sand bay'. Gavin's ashes are buried there; a large boulder marks the spot, with a bronze plaque fixed to it saying *Gavin Maxwell b 15.7.14 d 7.9.69.* A few yards away the memorial to Edal stands under the rowan tree, now dead; in a year or two there will be no trace of it. On Edal's bronze plaque are the words *Whatever joy she gave to you, give back to nature.*

Many hundreds of people visit Sandaig every year; most of them feel it is a place of serenity and beauty with many echoes of the past. I lived there for seven years, and it wasn't all serenity then, but there were many happy times. Perhaps the most joyous was when we were on the green island (at low tide one can walk there). We heard the call of geese high in the clear autumn air and called up 'chck-chck-chck' at the tops of our voices; and the geese we had reared, and who had flown away in the spring, circled and lost height by dipping a wing as geese do, and with a huge clamour of greeting landed on the sand at our feet. It was a moment of overflowing joy that these wild creatures had chosen to return.

Gavin Maxwell is remembered as someone who brought to many an awareness of the need to take care of our fellow inhabitants of this vulnerable earth.

I now live within sight of Sandaig and on stormy days when the ebb tide meets the south-west wind, I can look through the spray to the bright white sand where the geese landed that memorable day.

Jimmy Watt
*Glenelg, September 1999*

xiii

# Introduction

'That was Camusfeàrna down there,' said John Pargeter. We were on the high backbone of Sleat, the southern peninsula of the Isle of Skye, looking down across the Sound of Sleat to a group of small islands and a little bay on the mainland shore of Scotland's west coast directly opposite.

I could see what appeared to be a miniature lighthouse on one of the islands and a low white house set back from the beach at the bottom of a steep coastal drop with a high mountain rising straight up behind it.

It was a shock of recognition, for unexpectedly I had come across the famous setting of Gavin Maxwell's *Ring of Bright Water*, and what had been for me, up to that moment, a literary landscape whose real location was unknown suddenly revealed itself before my eyes as an actual, physical landscape. And almost immediately I realized that we were standing on the ground from which Maxwell used to hear the stags roaring in the early autumn – 'I hear them first on the steep slopes of Skye across the Sound, a wild haunting primordial sound that belongs so utterly to the north . . .'

As if reading what might be in my mind John said, 'That croft you see is not the house – the house burned down.' Unexpected, too, this information about the later history of the place; I had read only *Ring of Bright Water*, and knew nothing beyond it. For some reason I did not ask John Pargeter when or how the house had burned down, or anything else about the story, but the question and the thought remained in the back of my mind.

And although we were on those steep slopes in pursuit of deer, and it was a marvellous bright day with tremendous scenery, a thrilling, if bloodless, stalk, and eagles and ptarmigan seen, it was the glimpse of Camusfeàrna from several miles away that remained my most vivid recollection.

Three years later, on a Highland moor, I chanced to mention something about the life of Gavin Maxwell to Colin McKelvie, and he said, 'Yes, there was the curse of the rowan tree, the house burned down, and the fire killed the otters.' More enigmatic pieces of information, hints, or rumours (I still had read only *Ring*), but strangely I did not pursue further enlightenment, again only letting this sit somewhere in my mind.

But not long after that I happened upon the two sequel books about Camusfeàrna, neither of which I had known existed, in a couple of second-hand bookstores, and I found them in the order of their publication – first *The Rocks Remain*, then *Raven Seek Thy Brother*. So I finally learned, through Maxwell's own writings, about the remaining story right up to its end.

The first book of this trilogy, *Ring of Bright Water*, has achieved the status of a classic. Its overwhelming reception in the early 1960s, which produced a readership of well over a million on both sides of the Atlantic, may owe something to the culture of that particular time which seized upon the compelling presentation of an attainable Eden in the world of the here and now.

Maxwell's notion of living in a paradise of nature in such a place has a precursor far back in time; the isolated location of Camusfeàrna on the edge of the sea, surrounded by rocks, trees and mountains, in a life of close proximity to wildlife hearkens back to an older tradition in the very same landscape. In the 9th and 10th centuries Celtic hermit monks lived in solitary dwellings on the coasts of Scotland and Ireland, especially on those coastal slopes facing (like Camusfeàrna) south and west, and they wrote Gaelic nature poetry of a very high order. Often they also described the wild creatures they lived near and wrote about as beloved friends.

Since the first publication of *Ring* forty years ago it has remained in print with a steadily growing number of later admirers (like myself), and its fame, while not as sensational and widespread as it was a generation and more ago, is remarkably undiminished. If it continues to be read in the future, as I believe it will, it may even be admired in quite a different way from the present, in a different time and by a different culture, for the permanent texts have a life of their own.

Gavin Maxwell once described *Ring of Bright Water*, perhaps slightly disingenuously, as 'no more than a kind of personal diary', which it decidedly is not; it is a carefully designed narrative that in some ways may be called a fiction. That is, he tells true things, but so selected, arranged, and concentrated through literary art that the narrative becomes a kind of fiction. This is not unlike another famous 'personal diary', Henry David Thoreau's *Walden*. (There are some interesting similarities between the two books, and it is only speculation on my part, but I believe that Maxwell may have had *Walden* partly in his mind when he wrote *Ring of Bright Water*.) The narrative may be true, but the art gives it the kind of intensity that only fiction possesses.

The present work contains the three books about Gavin Maxwell's life at Camusfeàrna from 1948 to 1968. Although he first took possession of the house in the autumn of 1948 he did not maintain residence there until the spring of 1949, and he kept up that residence until January 1968. This trilogy presents to the reading public for the first time the entire story by Maxwell, in a single, unbroken narrative, of his tenure at the place he called 'Camusfeàrna', a fictional name he gave to a real place in order to emphasize its symbolic topography.

*Ring of Bright Water*, which Maxwell finished writing in October 1959, chronicles roughly the first ten years of his life there (a little more than half the total), describing the simple, idyllic paradise existence that has enchanted a vast and uncountable number of readers throughout the world. *The Rocks Remain* (1963) and *Raven Seek Thy Brother* (1968), very different books from their predecessor, recount the last eight or nine years (slightly less than half the total).

It has been possible to combine these three books into one volume largely due to the content of *Rocks* and *Raven*, both of which contain much narrative material extraneous to the story of Maxwell's home, 'The Bay of the Alders', on the Scottish coast. Some of this writing set in Morocco, Majorca, Iceland, etc. is good in itself, but has no place in our story, and its inclusion in the published books is distracting to the tale set in Scotland. I suspect that it might have been slightly less painful to write a distressing account, the unravelling of the Camusfeàrna vision, in broken-up sections mixed in with other narratives than to give it all the undiluted form that it has in the present volume.

Despite the obvious exclusion of the 'outside' material, space requirements demanded further cuts in both books, some of which were regrettable even if necessary. And *Ring of Bright Water* has not been spared either, cut by about thirty per cent. Though at first I was dismayed at the violence such cutting did to the careful balance of that book, *Ring* plays a different and almost subordinate role here, being only the first chapter of a larger, more extensive, more personal, and entirely different story.

*Ring* is the first chapter, point of reference, and partly the cause of the failure of the single vision of simplicity and harmony told within its pages. Again and again in the dark chapters of *Rocks* and *Raven* Maxwell compares the before and after – with the changes brought about by the prosperity of the first book's huge success a manifest decline began in almost every happiness that Camusfeàrna had represented.

First, the telephone and electricity, then a second otter requiring extensive (and ugly) building construction to house both otters; boats and boat accidents, accidents in and out of the house, a dangerous breakdown in the relationships with both otters, huge expenses, growing swings of fortune and misfortune, anxiety about the management of an increasingly complicated life, mistakes and misjudgements, serious illnesses; all of this recounted by Maxwell as a downward spiral of his existence.

But despite the litany of disasters and the unrelenting march of calamitous adversity over a period of years, a moving redemption comes at the very end of this story with a restoration of the relationships with the otters and a momentary restoration of the feeling of the old life there.

At the end of this essay a mention might be made about Maxwell's effect upon an aspect of history, if that is not too grand a concept. Cyril Connolly (the previous owner of Maxwell's terrible pet lemur, Kiko) writes in the opening sentence of *The Unquiet Grave*, '. . . the true function of any writer is to produce a masterpiece and no other task is of any consequence'. We may grant Gavin Maxwell the accomplishment of a masterpiece with *Ring of Bright Water*, but there is even beyond this a significant consequence to his life and at least two other legacies that have been declared by two men who knew him:

Douglas Botting, Maxwell's biographer, has said, 'Gavin made his greatest impact through *Ring of Bright Water*, which marked the beginning of a groundswell of worldwide support for otter conservation that has continued to the present day. Gavin's contribution to saving the otter was immeasurable, and was probably the greatest achievement of his life.' And in an interview for a film about Gavin Maxwell that was shown on BBC Scotland in early 1999, John Lister-Kaye said, 'There is a legacy which relates to time and to place . . . and Gavin is very substantially responsible for interesting the wider public in the wild Highlands.'

The second of these tributes recalls the example of Sir Walter Scott, who through his writings in the first half of the 19th century brought Scotland, at that time neglected and dispirited, to the admiring attention of the whole world. Gavin Maxwell, on a smaller scale, through his writings in the second half of the 20th century, has brought the west coast of Scotland – 'sky, shore, and silver sea' – to the admiring attention of the people of today.

Austin Chinn
*October 1999*

# RING OF
# BRIGHT WATER

He has married me with a ring, a ring of bright water
Whose ripples travel from the heart of the sea,
He has married me with a ring of light, the glitter
Broadcast on the swift river.
He has married me with the sun's circle
Too dazzling to see, traced in summer sky.
He has crowned me with the wreath of white cloud
That gathers on the snowy summit of the mountain,
Ringed me round with the world-circling wind,
Bound me to the whirlwind's centre.
He has married me with the orbit of the moon
And with the boundless circle of the stars,
With the orbits that measure years, months, days, and nights,
Set the tides flowing,
Command the winds to travel or be at rest.

At the ring's centre,
Spirit, or angel troubling the still pool,
Causality not in nature,
Finger's touch that summons at a point, a moment
Stars and planets, life and light
Or gathers cloud about an apex of cold,
Transcendent touch of love summons my world to being.

# Foreword

In writing this book about my home I have not given to the house its true name. This is from no desire to create mystery – indeed it will be easy enough for the curious to discover where I live – but because identification in print would seem in some sense a sacrifice, a betrayal of its remoteness and isolation, as if by doing so I were to bring nearer its enemies of industry and urban life. Camusfeàrna, I have called it, the Bay of the Alders, from the trees that grow along the burn side; but the name is of little consequence, for such bays and houses, empty and long disused, are scattered throughout the wild sea lochs of the Western Highlands and the Hebrides, and in the description of one the reader may perhaps find the likeness of others of which he has himself been fond, for these places are symbols. Symbols, for me and for many, of freedom, whether it be from the prison of over-dense communities and the close confines of human relationships, from the less complex incarceration of office walls and hours, or simply freedom from the prison of adult life and an escape into the forgotten world of childhood, of the individual or the race. For I am convinced that man has suffered in his separation from the soil and from the other living creatures of the world; the evolution of his intellect has outrun his needs as an animal, and as yet he must still, for security, look long at some portion of the earth as it was before he tampered with it.

This book, then, is about my life in a lonely cottage on the north-west coast of Scotland, about animals that have shared it with me, and about others who are my only immediate neighbours in a landscape of rock and sea.

Gavin Maxwell
*Camusfeàrna, October 1959*

5

# I

I sit in a pitch-pine panelled kitchen-living room, with an otter asleep upon its back among the cushions on the sofa, forepaws in the air, and with the expression of tightly shut concentration that very small babies wear in sleep. On the stone slab beneath the chimney-piece are inscribed the words *Non fatuum huc persecutus ignem* – 'It is no will-o'-the-wisp that I have followed here.' Beyond the door is the sea, whose waves break on the beach no more than a stone's throw distant, and encircling, mist-hung mountains. A little group of greylag geese sweep past the window and alight upon the small carpet of green turf; but for the soft, contented murmur of their voices and the sounds of the sea and the waterfall there is utter silence. This place has been my home now for ten years and more, and wherever the changes of my life may lead me in the future it will remain my spiritual home until I die, a house to which one returns not with the certainty of welcoming fellow human beings, nor with the expectation of comfort and ease, but to a long familiarity in which every lichen-covered rock and rowan tree show known and reassuring faces.

I had not thought that I should ever come back to live in the West Highlands; when my earlier sojourn in the Hebrides had come to an end it had in retrospect seemed episodic, and its finish uncompromisingly final. The thought of return had savoured of a jilted lover pleading with an indifferent mistress upon whom he had no further claim; it seemed to me then that it was indeed a will-o'-the-wisp that I had followed, for I had yet to learn that happiness can neither be achieved nor held by endeavour.

Immediately after the war's end I bought the Island of Soay, some four thousand acres of relatively low-lying 'black' land cowering below the bare pinnacles and glacial corries of the Cuillin of Skye. There, seventeen miles by sea from the railway,

I tried to found a new industry for the tiny and discontented population of the island, by catching and processing for oil the great basking sharks that appear in Hebridean waters during the summer months. I built a factory, bought boats and equipped them with harpoon guns, and became a harpoon gunner myself. For five years I worked in that landscape that before had been, for me, of a nebulous and cobwebby romance, and by the time it was all over and I was beaten I had in some way come to terms with the Highlands – or with myself, for perhaps in my own eyes I had earned the right to live among them.

When the Soay venture was finished, the island and the boats sold, the factory demolished, and the population evacuated, I went to London and tried to earn my living as a portrait painter. One autumn I was staying with an Oxford contemporary who had bought an estate in the West Highlands, and in an idle moment after breakfast on a Sunday morning he said to me:

'Do you want a foothold on the west coast, now that you have lost Soay? If you're not too proud to live in a cottage, we've got an empty one, miles from anywhere. It's right on the sea and there's no road to it – Camusfeàrna, it's called. There's some islands, and an automatic lighthouse. There's been no one there for a long time, and I'd never get any of the estate people to live in it now. If you'll keep it up you're welcome to it.'

It was thus casually, ten years ago, that I was handed the keys of my home, and nowhere in all the West Highlands and islands have I seen any place of so intense or varied a beauty in so small a compass.

The road, single-tracked for the past forty miles, and reaching in the high passes a gradient of one in three, runs southwards a mile or so inland of Camusfeàrna and some four hundred feet above it. At the point on the road which is directly above the house there is a single cottage at the roadside, Druimfiaclach, the home of my friends and nearest neighbours, the MacKinnons. Inland from Druimfiaclach the hills rise steeply but in rolling masses to a dominating peak of more than three thousand feet, snow-covered or snow-dusted for the greater part of the year. On the other side, to the westward, the Isle of Skye towers across a three-mile-wide sound, and farther to the south the stark bastions of Rhum and the couchant lion of Eigg block the sea horizon. The descent to Camusfeàrna is so steep that neither the house nor its islands and lighthouses are visible from the road above, and that paradise within a paradise remains, to the casual road-user, unguessed. Beyond Druimfiaclach the road seems, as it were, to become dispirited, as though already conscious of its dead end at sea-level six miles farther on, caught between the terrifying massif of mountain scree overhanging it and the dark gulf of sea loch below.

Druimfiaclach is a tiny oasis in a wilderness of mountain and peat-bog, and it is a full four miles from the nearest roadside dwelling. An oasis, an eyrie; the windows of the house look westward over the Hebrides and over the Tyrian sunsets that flare and fade behind their peaks, and when the sun has gone and the stars are bright the many lighthouses of the reefs and islands gleam and wink above the surf. In the westerly gales of winter the walls of Druimfiaclach rock and shudder, and heavy stones are roped to the corrugated iron roof to prevent it blowing away as other roofs here have gone before. The winds rage in from the Atlantic and the hail roars and batters on the windows and the iron roof, all hell let loose, but the house stands and the MacKinnons remain here as, nearby, the forefathers of them both remained for many generations.

It seems strange to me now that there was a time when I did not know the MacKinnons, strange that the first time I came to live at Camusfeàrna I should have passed their house by a hundred yards and left my car by the roadside without greeting or acknowledgement of a dependence now long established. I remember seeing some small children staring from the house door; I cannot now recall my first meeting with their parents.

I left my car at a fank, a dry-stone enclosure for dipping sheep, close to the burn side, and because I was unfamiliar with the ill-defined footpath that is the more usual route from the road to Camusfeàrna, I began to follow the course of the burn downward. The burn has its source far back in the hills, near to the very summit of the dominant peak; it has worn a fissure in the scarcely

9

sloping mountain wall, and for the first thousand feet of its course it part flows, part falls, chill as snow-water even in summer, between tumbled boulders and small multi-coloured lichens. Up there, where it seems the only moving thing besides the eagles, the deer and the ptarmigan, it is called the Blue Burn, but at the foot of the outcrop, where it passes through a reedy lochan and enters a wide glacial glen it takes the name of its destination – Allt na Feàrna, the Alder Burn. Here in the glen the clear topaz-coloured water rushes and twitters between low oaks, birches and alders, at whose feet the deep-cushioned green moss is stippled with bright toadstools of scarlet and purple and yellow, and in summer swarms of electric-blue dragonflies flicker and hover in the glades.

After some four miles the burn passes under the road at Druim-fiaclach, a stone's throw from the fank where I had left my car. It was early spring when I came to live at Camusfeàrna for the first time, and the grass at the burn side was gay with thick-clustering primroses and violets, though the snow was still heavy on the high peaks and lay like lace over the lower hills of Skye across the Sound. The air was fresh and sharp, and from east to west and north to south there was not a single cloud upon the cold clear blue; against it, the still-bare birch branches were purple in the sun and the dark-banded stems were as white as the distant snows. On the sunny slopes grazing Highland cattle made a foreground to a landscape whose vivid colours had found no place on Landseer's palette. A rucksack bounced and jingled on my shoulders; I was coming to my new home.

I was not quite alone, for in front of me trotted my dog Jonnie, a huge black-and-white springer spaniel whose father and grandfather before him had been my constant companions during an adolescence devoted largely to sport. We were brought up to shoot, and by the curious paradox that those who are fondest of animals become, in such an environment, most bloodthirsty at a certain stage of their development, shooting occupied much of my time and thoughts during my school and university years. Many people find an especial attachment for a dog whose companionship has bridged widely different phases in their lives, and so it was with Jonnie; he and his forebears had spanned my boyhood, maturity, and the war years, and though since then I had found little leisure nor much inclination for shooting, Jonnie adapted himself placidly to a new role, and I remember how during the shark fishery years he would, unprotesting, arrange himself to form a pillow for my head in the well of an open boat as it tossed and pitched in the waves.

Now Jonnie's plump white rump bounced and perked through the heather and bracken in front of me, as times without number at night I was in the future to follow its pale just-discernible beacon through the darkness from Druimfiaclach to Camusfeàrna.

Presently the burn became narrower, and afforded no foothold at its steep banks, then it tilted sharply seaward between rock walls, and below me I could hear the roar of a high waterfall. I climbed out from the ravine and found myself on a bluff of heather and red bracken, looking down upon the sea and upon Camusfeàrna.

The landscape and seascape that lay spread below me was of such beauty that I had no room for it all at once; my eye flickered from the house to the islands, from the white sands to the flat green pasture round the croft, from the wheeling gulls to the pale satin sea and on to the snow-topped Cuillins of Skye in the distance.

Immediately below me the steep hillside of heather and ochre mountain grasses fell to a broad green field, almost an island, for the burn flanked it at the right and then curved round seaward in a glittering horseshoe. The sea took up where the burn left off and its foreshore formed the whole frontage of the field, running up nearest to me into a bay of rocks and sand. At the edge of this bay, a stone's throw from the sea on one side and the burn on the other, the house of Camusfeàrna stood unfenced in green grass among grazing black-faced sheep. The field, except immediately opposite to the house, sloped gently upwards from the sea, and was divided from it by a ridge of sand dunes grown over with pale marram grass and tussocky sea-bents. There were rabbits scampering on the short turf round the house, and out over the dunes the bullet heads of two seals were black in the tide.

Beyond the green field and the wide shingly outflow of the burn were the islands, the nearer ones no more than a couple of acres each, rough and rocky, with here and there a few stunted rowan trees and the sun red on patches of dead bracken. The islands formed a chain of perhaps half a mile in length, and ended in one as big as the rest put together, on whose seaward shore showed the turret of a lighthouse. Splashed among the chain of islands were small beaches of sand so white as to dazzle the eye. Beyond the islands was the shining enamelled sea, and beyond it again the rearing bulk of Skye, plum-coloured distances embroidered with threads and scrolls of snow.

Even at a distance Camusfeàrna house wore that strange look that comes to dwellings after long disuse. It is indefinable, and it is not produced by obvious signs of neglect; Camusfeàrna had few slates missing from the roof and the windows were all intact, but the house wore that secretive expression that is in some way akin to a young girl's face during her first pregnancy.

As I went on down the steep slope two other buildings came into view tucked close under the skirt of the hill, a byre facing Camusfeàrna across the green turf, and an older, windowless, croft at the very sea's edge, so close to the waves that I wondered how the house had survived. Later, I learned that the last occupants had been driven from it by a great storm which had brought

the sea right into the house, so that they had been forced to make their escape by a window at the back.

At the foot of the hill the burn flowed calmly between an avenue of single alders, though the sound of unseen waterfalls was loud in the rock ravine behind me. I crossed a solid wooden bridge with stone piers, and a moment later I turned the key in Camusfeàrna door for the first time.

# 2

There was not one stick of furniture in the house; there was no water and no lighting, and the air inside struck chill as a mortuary, but to me it was Xanadu. There was much more space in the house than I had expected. There were two rooms on the ground floor, a parlour and a living-kitchen, besides a little 'back kitchen' or scullery, and two rooms and a landing upstairs. The house was entirely lined with varnished pitch pine, in the manner of the turn of the century.

I had brought with me on my back the essentials of living for a day at two while I prospected – a bedding roll, a Primus stove with a little fuel, candles, and some tinned food. I knew that something to sit upon would present no problems, for my five years' shark hunting round these coasts had taught me that every west-facing beach is littered with fish-boxes. Stacks of fish-boxes arranged to form seats and tables were the mainstay of Camus-feàrna in those early days, and even now, despite the present comfort of the house, they form the basis of much of its furniture, though artifice and padding have done much to disguise their origin.

Ten years of going into retreat at Camusfeàrna have taught me, too, that if one waits long enough practically every imaginable household object will sooner or later turn up on the beaches within a mile of the house, and beachcombing retains for me now the same fascination and eager expectancy that it held then. After a westerly or south-westerly gale one may find almost anything. Fish-boxes – mostly stamped with the names of Mallaig, Buckie or Lossiemouth firms, but sometimes from France or Scandinavia – are too common to count, though they are still gathered, more from habit than from need. Fish baskets, big open two-handled baskets of withy, make firewood baskets and waste-paper baskets. Intact wooden tubs are a rarity, and I have found only three in my years here; it has amused me wryly to see cocktail bars in England whose proprietors have through whimsy put them to use as stools as I have by necessity.

A Robinson Crusoe or Swiss Family Robinson instinct is latent in most of us, perhaps from our childhood games of house-building, and since I came to Camusfeàrna ten years ago I find myself scanning every weird piece of flotsam or jetsam and considering what useful purpose it might be made to serve. As a beachcomber of long standing now I have been amazed to find that one of the commonest of all things among jetsam is the rubber hot-water bottle. They compete successfully – in the long straggling line of brown sea-wrack dizzy with jumping sand-hoppers – with odd shoes and empty boot polish and talcum powder tins, with the round corks that buoy lobster-pots and nets, even with the ubiquitous skulls of sheep and deer. A surprising number of the hot-water bottles are undamaged, and Camus-feàrna is by now overstocked with them, but from the damaged ones one may cut useful and highly functional table mats.

A surprising number of objects may be used to convert fish-boxes into apparent furniture. Half of one of the kitchen walls, for example, is now occupied by a very large sofa; that is to say it appears to be a sofa, but in fact it is all fish-boxes, covered with sheet foam rubber under a corduroy cover and many cushions. Next to it is a tall rectangle, draped over with a piece of material that was once the seat-cover of my cabin in the *Sea Leopard*, my chief shark-hunting boat; lift aside this relic and you are looking into a range of shelves filled with shoes – the whole structure is made of five fish-boxes with their sides knocked out. The same system, this time of orange-boxes from the shore and fronted by some very tasteful material from Primavera, holds shirts and sweaters in my bedroom, and looks entirely respectable. The art of fish-box furniture should be more widely cultivated; in common with certain widely advertised makes of contemporary furniture it has the peculiar advantage that one may add unit to unit indefinitely.

There came a time, in my second or third year at the house,

when I said, 'There's only one thing we really lack now – a clothes-basket,' and a few weeks later a clothes-basket came up on the beach, a large stately clothes-basket, completely undamaged.

Whether it is because the furnishings of these rooms have grown around me year by year since that first afternoon when I entered the chill and empty house, each room as bare as a weathered bone, or because of my deep love for Camusfeàrna and all that surrounds it, it is to me now the most relaxing house that I know, and guests, too, feel it a place in which they are instantly at ease. Even in this small matter of furniture there is also a continuous sense of anticipation; it is as though a collector of period furniture might on any morning find some rare and important piece lying waiting to be picked up on the street before his door.

There is much pathos in the small jetsam that lies among the sea-wrack and drifted timber of the long tide-lines; the fire-blackened transom of a small boat; the broken and wave-battered children's toys; a hand-carved wooden egg-cup with the name carefully incised upon it; the scattered skeleton of a small dog, the collar with an illegible nameplate lying among the whitened bones, long since picked clean by the ravens and the hooded crows. To me the most personal poignancy was in my search one morning that first year for a suitable piece of wood from which to fashion a bread-board. A barrel top would be ideal, I thought, if I could find one intact, and very soon I did, but when I had it in my hands I turned it over to read the letters ISSF, Island of Soay Shark Fisheries – the only thing the sea has ever given me back for all that I poured into it during those five years of Soay.

Some pieces of jetsam are wholly enigmatic, encouraging the most extravagant exercise of fantasy to account for their existence. A ten-foot-long bamboo pole, to which have been affixed by a combination of careful, seaman-like knots and the lavish use of insulating tape three blue pennants bearing the words 'Shell' and 'BP'; this has exercised my imagination since first I found it. A prayer flag made by a Lascar seaman? – a distress signal, pitifully inadequate, constructed over many hours adrift in an open boat surrounded by cruising sharks or tossed high on the crests of Atlantic rollers a thousand miles from land? I have found no satisfactory solution. Two broom handles, firmly tied into the form of a cross by the belt from a woman's plastic macintosh; a scrap of sailcoth with the words 'not yet' scrawled across it in blue paint; a felt Homburg hat so small that it appeared to have been made for a diminutive monkey – round these and many others one may weave idle tapestries of mystery.

But it is not only on such man-made objects as these that the imagination builds to evoke drama, pathos, or remembered splendour. When one is much alone one's vision becomes more extensive; from the tide-wrack rubbish-heap of small bones and dry, crumpled wings, relics of lesser lives, rise images the brighter for being unconfined by the physical eye. From some feathered mummy, stained and thin, soars the spinning lapwing in the white March morning; in the surface crust of rotting weed, where the foot explodes a whirring puff of flies, the withered fins and scales hold still, intrinsically, the sway and dart of glittering shoals among the tide-swung sea-tangle; smothered by the mad parabolic energy of leaping sand-hoppers the broken antlers of a stag re-form and move again high in the bare, stony corries and the October moonlight.

Comparatively little that is thrown up by the waves comes ashore at Camusfeàrna itself, for the house stands on a south-facing bay in a west-facing coastline, and it gains, too, a little shelter from the string of islands that lead out from it to the lighthouse. To the north and south the coast is rock for the most part, but opening here and there to long gravel beaches which the prevailing westerly gales pile high with the sea's litter. It is a fierce shoreline, perilous with reef and rock, and Camusfeàrna with its snow-white sand beaches, green close-cropped turf, and low white lighthouse has a welcoming quality enhanced by the dark, rugged coastline on either side.

It is a coast of cliffs and of caves, deep commodious caves that have their entrances, for the most part, well above the tides' level, for over the centuries the sea has receded, and between the cliffs the shingle of its old beaches lies bare. Until recently many of these caves were regularly inhabited by travelling pedlars, of whom there were many, for shops were far distant and communications virtually non-existent. They were welcome among the local people, these pedlars, for besides what they could sell they brought news from faraway villages and of other districts in which they travelled; they fulfilled the function of provincial newspapers, and the inhabitants of wild and lonely places awaited their coming with keen anticipation.

One of these men made his home and headquarters in a cave close to Camusfeàrna, a man who had been, of all improbable professions, a jockey. Andrew Tait was his real name, but as a deserter from the army he had changed it to Joe Wilson, and Joe's Cave his erstwhile home remains, even on the maps, though it is many years past since an angry people lit fires to crack the roof and banish him from that shore.

Joe was popular at first, for he was a likeable enough man, and if he and his cave consort Jeannie had never heard the wedding service a cave was perhaps safer than a glass-house if there were any stones to be thrown. Such pebbles that came his way seem mainly to have been on the question of his desertion. Jeannie was no slut nor Joe a slum-maker, and their troglodyte life was a neat and orderly affair, with a clean white tablecloth laid over the fish-box table for meals, meals that were of fish and crustaceans and every manner of edible shell. They walled in the front of their cave and built steps from it down to the sea, and even now the little runway where they drew up their boat is still free from boulders.

Only one thing marred their littoral idyll; both Jeannie and Joe were over-fond of the bottle. Jeannie held the purse-strings, and despite her own indulgence she was the wiser of the two. She would spend so much on drink and no more, but every time the two drank they quarrelled, and when Joe got past a certain point he would fight her for the money.

One night they had, as was their custom, rowed the four miles to the village pub, and there they began to drink in company with another pedlar, a simpleton, named John MacQueen, whom people called The Pelican. The Pelican was a player of the fiddle, and together they stayed late at the inn, bickering and drinking to the music of his strings.

What followed no one knows truly to this day, but it was the end of their Eden, the end of Jeannie and of Joe's Cave. Joe returned to the village in the morning proclaiming over and over again that Jeannie was 'Killt and droont, killt and droont.' Their boat was washed up ten miles to the south, half full of water, and in it was the dead body of Jeannie; the pocket of her skirt had been torn off and there was no money about her. Police came from the nearest township, but though local feeling ran high against Joe and The Pelican the details of Jeannie's death remained unsolved, and no charge of murder was brought against them. It seemed clear that Jeannie had been knocked out before she drowned; some, those who stood by Joe, said that she had fallen into the sea after a blow and then drowned; others that Joe and The Pelican had beaten her senseless in a drunken rage, had half-filled the boat with water, and then set Jeannie adrift to drown.

Whatever the truth, the people of the neighbourhood – if such it could be called, for Joe had no neighbours – believed that they had a monster in their midst; they came and built great fires in his cave, and set ablaze the heather of the hillside above it, so that the heat split the rock and the outer part of the cave fell, and Joe was left a homeless wanderer. He died years ago, but on the floor beneath the fire-blackened rock still lie small relics of his life with Jeannie, mouldering shoes, scraps of metal, a filigree tracery of rusted iron that was once a kettle. Above, on the ledges that formed the cornice of his dwelling, the rock-doves have made their homes, and their feathers float down upon the ruined hearth.

Pedlars of the traditional type were rare by the time I began to live at Camusfeàrna; their place had been taken by Indians, often importunate, who from time to time toured the roadside dwellings with small vans full of cheap materials. The local inhabitants, unused to high-pressure doorstep salesmanship, mistook these methods for affrontery; not all of the vendors were of savoury nature, but even the most innocuous were regarded with a wary suspicion. I met only one of Joe's lost tribe, and he has died since, hastened to the churchyard by a life-long predilection for drinking methylated spirits. He was, I think, in his early sixties when I first encountered him; he told me then that the perils of his preferred liquor were greatly exaggerated, for he had been indulging for forty years and only now was his eyesight beginning to suffer. He confided, however, that it was an inconvenient craving, for most ironmongers throughout the length and breadth of the West Highlands had been warned against supplying him, and he had been driven to the most elaborate of subterfuges to keep his cellar stocked. It was, perhaps, as well for him that he died before electricity came to the remote and outlying areas, for then, as I discovered to my cost, methylated spirits became virtually unobtainable.

The cave-dwelling pedlars had not always been the only inhabitants of the Camusfeàrna coastline, for before the Clearances in the early nineteenth century – whose cruelty and injustice are still a living ancestral memory in a great part of the West Highlands and Hebrides – there had been a thriving community of some two hundred people not far from where Camusfeàrna house now stands. The descendants of one of these families still live in California, where their forebears settled when driven from their homes, and of them is told one of the few local tales of 'second sight' that I have come across in the district.

The children of the old settlement at Camusfeàrna used to walk the five miles to the village school every morning and five miles home again at night; each child, too, had in winter to provide his contribution to the school fire, and they would set off before dawn for the long trudge with a creel of peats on their backs. One night this family had given shelter to an old pedlar, and as he watched the two sons of the house making ready their load in the morning he turned to their parents and said, 'Many a green sea they will go over, but many a green sea will go over them.' The boys came of a sea-faring line, and when they grew up they too followed the sea; one became a captain and the other a first mate, but both were drowned.

The tumbled, briar-grown ruins of the old village are scattered round the bay and down the shore, but the people are gone and the pedlars are gone and the house at Camusfeàrna stands alone.

Whereas the stories of 'second sight' are comparatively few, and refer most commonly to past generations, it should be realized that this bears no relation at all either to current credence in the faculty or to the number of people who are still believed to possess it. Quite contrary to general opinion, a person having or believing him or herself to have this occult power is extremely reticent about it, usually afraid of it, and conceals it from all but his most intimate friends. This is not because he is afraid of mockery or disbelief in the sense that his neighbour will say 'Behold this dreamer', but because men fear proof of a power beyond their own, and are uncomfortable in the company of one who claims or admits to it. These people who are convinced of being endowed with what is now more usually called extra-sensory perception are also frightened of what their own clairvoyance may show them, and it seems that they would willingly exchange their lot for that of the common man. Only when they are convinced that their gift can at that moment be turned to benign use are they prepared to call it voluntarily into play. My impression is that a deep, fundamental belief in the existence of 'second sight' is practically universal throughout the Western Highlands and the Hebrides, even among intelligent and well-read people, and that the few scoffers are paying lip-service to the sceptical sophistication they do not share. Circumstantial tales of other less controversial matters survive in the oral tradition with but little change in these districts to which literacy came late in history, and there is no reason to assume that those concerning 'second sight' should have suffered disproportionate distortion.

My nearest neighbour at Camusfeàrna, Calum Murdo MacKinnon, of whom I shall have more to say presently, comes of Skye stock, and tells a tale of his forebears which by its very simplicity is hard to ascribe to past invention. In the days of his great-grandfather a boy was drowned at sea, fishing in the bay before the village, and his mother became distraught with the desire to recover her son's body and give it Christian burial. Some half-dozen boats with grappling irons cruised to and fro all day over the spot where he had been lost, but found nothing. The talk of all the village was naturally centred on the subject, and in the late evening Calum Murdo's great-grandfather, over eighty years of age, infirm and totally blind, learned for the first time of all that had taken place. At length he said, 'If they will take me to the knoll overlooking the bay in the morning I will tell them where the body lies. They will need just the one boat.' The searchers obeyed him, and in the morning he was carried to the summit of the knoll by his grandson, who brought with him a plaid with which to signal at command. For more than half an hour the boat rowed to and fro in the bay below them with grapples hanging ready, but the old man sat with his blind head in his hands and said never a word. Suddenly he cried in a strong voice '*Tog an tonnag!* – Hoist the plaid!' His grandson did so and the grapples sank and returned to the surface with the body of the drowned boy.

Very little survives in legend from the early inhabitants of Camus-feàrna; surprisingly little when one comes to consider that in all likelihood the community existed for thousands of years. The earliest stories date, probably, from the Middle Ages, and one of these tells of a wild sea reiver, born in the bay, who harried the coast to the southward – notably the Island of Mull, with its many secret harbours and well-hid anchorages – in a galley, one of whose sides was painted black and the other white; an attempt, presumably, to refute description or to undermine morale by reports that in aggregate might give the impression of a pirate fleet. Whatever his tactics, they seem to have been successful, for he is said to have returned to Camusfeàrna and to have died, in old age, a natural death.

In the British Isles it is a strange sensation to lie down to sleep knowing that there is no human being within a mile and a half in any direction, that apart from one family there is none for three times that distance. Indeed few people ever have the experience, for the earth's surface is so overrun with mankind that where land is habitable it is inhabited; and whereas it is not

difficult to pitch a camp in those circumstances it is very rare to
be between four permanent walls that one may call one's home.
It brings a sense of isolation that is the very opposite of the
loneliness a stranger finds in a city, for that loneliness is due to
the proximity of other humans and the barriers between him and
them, to the knowledge of being alone among them, with every
inch of the walls wounding and every incommunicable stranger
planting a separate bandillo. But to be quite alone where there
are no other human beings is sharply exhilarating; it is as though
some pressure had suddenly been lifted, allowing an intense
awareness of one's surroundings, a sharpening of the senses, and
an intimate recognition of the teeming subhuman life around
one. I experienced it first as a very young man, travelling alone,
on the tundra three hundred miles north of the Arctic Circle, and
there was the added strangeness of nights as light as noon, so
that only the personal fact of sleep divided night from day;
paradoxically, for the external circumstances were the very opposite, I had the same or an allied sensation during the heavy air-raids
in 1940, as though life were suddenly stripped of inessentials such
as worries about money and small egotistical ambitions and one
was left facing an ultimate essential.

That first night as I lay down to sleep in the bare kitchen of
Camusfeàrna I was aware of the soft thump of rabbits' feet about
the sand dune warren at the back of the house, the thin squeak
of hawking bats, woken early by the warm weather from their
winter hibernation, and the restless piping of oyster-catchers
waiting for the turn of the tide; these were middle-distance sounds
against the muffled roar of the waterfall that in still weather is
the undertone to all other sound at Camusfeàrna. I slept that
night with my head pillowed upon Jonnie's soft fleece-like flank,
as years before I had been wont to in open boats.

The first thing that I saw in the morning, as I went down to the
burn for water, was a group of five stags, alert but unconcerned,
staring from the primrose bank just beyond the croft wall. Two
of them had cast both horns, for it was the end of the first week
in April, two had cast one, but the fifth stag still carried both,
wide, long and strong, with seven points one side and six on the

other, a far nobler head than ever I had seen during my years of bloodthirstiness. I came to know these stags year by year, for they were a part of a group that passed every winter low in the Camusfeàrna burn, and Morag MacKinnon used to feed them at Druimfiaclach – a little surreptitiously, for they were outside the forest fence and on the sheep ground. Monarch, she called the thirteen-pointer, and though he never seemed to break out to the rut in autumn I think he must have sired at least one stag-calf, for in the dark last year the headlights of my car lit up a partially stunned stag that had leapt at the concrete posts of the new forestry plantation fence, trying to get down to Camusfeàrna, and the head, though no more than a royal, was the very double of Monarch's wide sweep. I came near to killing him, for I thought that he was a stag wounded and lost by a stalking party from the lodge that day, but dazed as he was he managed to stagger out of the headlights' beam before I could get the rifle from its case.

I miss the stags that used to winter close to the house, for now there are young trees planted over the hill face between Camusfeàrna and Druimfiaclach, and the deer have been forced back behind the forest fence, so that there is none, save an occasional interloper, within a mile of the bay. In the first winter that I was at Camusfeàrna I would wake to see from the window a frieze of their antlers etching the near skyline, and they were in some way important to me, as were the big footprints of the wildcats in the soft sand at the burn's edge, the harsh cry of the ravens, and the round shiny seals' heads in the bay below the house. These creatures were my neighbours.

English visitors who have come to Camusfeàrna are usually struck inarticulate by the desolate grandeur of the landscape and the splendour of pale blue and gold spring mornings, but they are entirely articulate in their amazement at the variety of wild life by which I am surrounded. Many Englishmen are, for example, quite unaware that wildcats are common animals in the West Highlands, and assume, when one refers to them, that one is speaking of domestic cats run wild, not of the tawny lynx-like ferals that had their den, that and every other year, within two hundred yards of my door. They bear as much relation to the domestic cat as does a wolf to a terrier; they were here before our first uncouth ancestors came to live in the caves below the cliffs, and they are reputedly untameable. When I first came here the estate on whose land the house stood had long waged war upon the wildcats, and a tree by the deer-larder of the lodge, four miles away, was decorated with their banded tails hanging like monstrous willow catkins from its boughs. Now, since the estate has turned from general agriculture to forestry, the wildcats are protected, for they are the worst enemy of the voles, who are in turn the greatest destroyers of the newly planted trees. Under this benign regime the number of wildcats has marvellously increased. The males sometimes mate with domestic females, but the offspring rarely survives, either because the sire returns to kill the kittens as soon as they are born, and so expunge the evidence of his peasant wenching, or because of the distrust in which so many humans hold the taint of the untameable. It is the wild strain that is dominant, in the lynx-like appearance, the extra claw, and the feral instinct; and the few half-breeds that escape destruction usually take to the hills and the den life of their male ancestors. An old river-watcher at Lochailort, who for some reason that now eludes me was known as Tipperary, told me that one night, awoken by the caterwauling outside, he had gone to the door with a torch and in its beam had seen his own black-and-white she-cat in the fierce embrace of a huge wild tom. Thereafter he had waited eagerly for the birth of the kittens.

When the time came she made her nest in the byre, and all that day he waited for the first birth, but at nightfall she had not yet brought forth. In the small hours of the morning he became conscious of piteous mewing at his door, and opened it to find his cat carrying in her mouth one wounded and dying kitten. In the dark background he heard a savage sound of worrying and snarling, and flashing his torch towards the byre he saw the wild tom in the act of killing a kitten. There was a green ember-glow of eyes, the flash of a big bottle-brush tail, and then the torch lit up nothing more than a pathetic trail of mangled new-born kittens. The single survivor, whom the mother had tried to carry to the house for sanctuary, died a few minutes later.

Wildcats grow to an enormous size, at least double that of the very largest domestic cat; this year there is one who leaves close to the house Homeric droppings of dimensions that would make an Alsatian wolfhound appear almost constipated. It is comparatively rarely that one sees the animals themselves in the daytime, for they are creatures of the dark and the starlight. Once I caught one accidentally in a rabbit snare, a vast tom with ten rings to his tail, and that first year at Camusfeàrna I twice saw the kittens at play in the dawn, frolicking among the primroses and budding birch on the bank beyond the croft wall. They looked beautiful, very soft and fluffy, and almost gentle; there was no hint of the ferocity that takes a heavy annual toll of lambs and red-deer calves. Before man exterminated the rabbits they were the staple food both of the big leggy hill foxes and of these low-ground wildcats, and every morning I would see the heavily indented padmarks in the sand at the burrow mouths. But now the rabbits have gone and the lambs are still here in their season, and where there has been a strong lamb at dusk, at dawn there are raw bones and a fleece like a blood-stained swab in a surgery. Then come the ravens from the sea cliffs, and the hooded crows, the ubiquitous grey-mantled scavengers, and by nightfall there is nothing to show for those slow months in the womb but white skeleton and a scrap of soft, soiled fleece that seems no bigger than a handkerchief.

Among the mammals it is, next to the wildcats, the seals that surprise my southern visitors most. Right through the summer months they are rarely out of sight, and, being unmolested at Camusfeàrna, they become very tame. In the evenings they will follow a dinghy through the smooth sunset-coloured water, their heads emerging ever nearer and nearer until they are no more than a boat's length away. It is only a change in rhythm that frightens them; one must row steadily onwards as if intent on one's own business and unconcerned with theirs. The brown seals, with their big round skulls and short, dog-like noses, are everywhere, and I have counted more than a hundred in an hour's run down the shore in the dinghy; besides these, which breed locally, the Atlantic seals stay round the islands from May till early autumn, when they return to their scattered and comparatively few breeding rocks. The Atlantic seals that spend the summer at Camusfeàrna probably breed on the rocks west of Canna, by a long way the nearest to me of their colonies. They are never in large parties away from the breeding grounds; through the long still days of summer when the sea is smooth as silk and the sun is hot on the lichened rocks above the tide they loaf about the Camusfeàrna islands in twos and threes, usually bulls, eating largely of the rock fish and storing up energy to be used recklessly on their harems in the autumn, for during the rut the bulls may not feed for many weeks. To one who sees them for the first time the Atlantic seals seem vast; a big bull is some nine feet long and weighs nearly half a ton. They are splendid beasts, but to me they lack the charm of the little brown seal with its less dignified habits, inquisitive and dog-like. Once, on the rocks off Rhu Arisaig, I picked up a brown seal pup no more than a day or so old – he had the soft white baby coat that is more often shed in the womb, and he seemed for all the world like a toy designed to please a child. He was warm and tubby and not only unafraid but squirmingly affectionate, and I set him down again with some reluctance. But he was not to be so easily left, for as I moved off he came shuffling and humping along at my heels. After a few minutes of trying to shake him off I tried dodging and hiding behind rocks, but he discovered me with amazing agility. Finally I scrambled down to the boat and rowed quickly away, but after twenty yards he was there beside me muzzling an oar. I was in desperation to know what to do with this unexpected foundling whose frantic mother was now snorting twenty yards away, when suddenly he responded to one of her calls and the two went off together, the pup no doubt to receive the lecture of his life.

The red-deer calves, too, have no natural fear of man during their first days of life, and if in June one stumbles upon a calf lying dappled and sleek among the long green bracken stems one must avoid handling him if one wants to make a clean get-away. I used to pet them and fondle them before I knew better, and my efforts to leave led to more frenzied games of hide-and-seek than with the seal pup, while a distracted hind stamped and barked unavailingly. But while the calves during those first uninstructed days display no instinctive fear of humans, they are from the first terrified of their natural enemies, the eagles, the wildcats and the foxes. I have seen a hind trying to defend her calf from an eagle, rearing up with her ears back and slashing wickedly with her fore-hooves each time he stooped with an audible rush of wind through his great upswept pinions; if one hoof had struck home she would have brought him down disembowelled, but though she never touched more than a wingtip the eagle grew wary and finally sailed off down the glen, the sun gleaming whitely on the burnish of his mantle.

It is the helpless red-deer calves that are the staple food of the hill foxes in June, and the young lambs in April and May, but what they live on for the rest of the year now that the rabbits have gone and the blue mountain hares become so scarce, remains a mystery to me. Possibly they eat more seldom than we imagine, and certainly mice form a large part of their diet. Some years ago I went out with a stalker to kill hill foxes after lambing time. The foxes' cairn was some two thousand feet up the hill, and we left at dawn, before the sun was up over hills that were still all snow at their summits, silhouetted against a sky that was apple-green with tenuous scarlet streamers. The cairn, a big tumble of granite boulders in a fissure of the hillside, was just below the snowline, and by the time we reached it the sun had lifted in a golden glare over the high tops. The terriers went into the cairn and we shot the vixen as she bolted, and the dogs killed and brought out the five cubs; but of the dog fox there was no sign at all. We found his footprints in a peat hag a few hundred yards below, going downhill, and he had not been galloping but quietly trotting, so we concluded that he had left the cairn some time before we had reached it and was probably unaware of anything amiss. We sat down under cover to wait for his return.

We waited all day. The spring breeze blew fresh in our faces from where the sea and the islands lay spread out far below us, and we could see the ring-net boats putting out for the first of the summer herring. All day there was very little movement on the hill; once a party of stags in early velvet crossed the lip of the corrie on our right, and once an eagle sailed by within a stone's throw, to bank sharply and veer off with a harsh rasp of air between the quills as his searching eye found us. In the evening it became chilly, and when the sun was dipping over the Outer Hebrides and the snow-shadows had turned to a deep blue, we began to think of moving. We were starting to gather up our things when my eye caught a movement in the peat hags below us. The dog fox was trotting up hill to the cairn, quite unsuspicious, and carrying something in his jaws. The rifle killed him stone dead at fifty yards, and we went down to see what he had been carrying; it was a nest of pink new-born mice – all he had found to bring home in a long day's hunting for his vixen and five cubs.

At first sight it is one of the enigmas of the country around Camusfeàrna, this great number of predators surviving with so little to prey upon; in the air the eagles, buzzards, falcons, ravens, hooded crows, and on the ground the wildcats, foxes, badgers and pine martens. There is no doubt that a surprising number of the animal species spend much time during the off season – when there are no young creatures to feed on – in my own hobby of beachcombing. In the soft sand around the tide-wrack I come constantly upon the footprints of wildcats, badgers and foxes. Sometimes they find oiled seabirds, sometimes the carcase of a sheep, fallen from one of the green cliff ledges that throughout the West Highlands form such well-baited and often fatal traps, or of a stag that has tottered down from the March snowdrifts to seek seaweed as the only uncovered food, or they may creep upon sleeping oyster-catchers and curlews as they wait in the dark for the turn of the tide. But whatever they find it is to the shore that the fanged creatures come at night, and at times, perhaps, they find little, for I have seen undigested sand-hoppers in the droppings of both wildcats and foxes.

The ravens and hooded crows, though they will peck out the eyes of a living lamb or deer calf if he is weak, are in fact offal feeders for the greater part of the time. The hoodies spend much of their time about the shore in the late summer and midwinter, opening mussels by carrying them up to house-height and dropping them to smash on the rocks, but at most other seasons of the year there are routine harvests for them to gather elsewhere. In the back-end of winter, when the ground is as yet unstirred by spring, the old stags that have wintered poorly grow feeble and die in the snowdrifts and the grey scavengers squawk and squabble over the carcases; a little later, when the first warmth comes, and the hinds interrupt their grazing to turn their heads and nibble irritably at their spines, the hoodies strut and pick around them, gobbling the fat warble-grubs that emerge from under the deer-hides and fall to the ground. When the lambing season comes they quarter the ground for the afterbirths, and from then on there are the eggs and young of every bird lesser than themselves.

Of my human neighbours, the MacKinnons, I have so far said little. Calum Murdo MacKinnon is always given both his Christian names, for there are so many Calum MacKinnons in the district that Calum alone would be ambiguous; there are so many

Murdos as to make that name by itself ineffective too; and there are so many Murdo Calums, which is the true sequence of his names, that to retain his identity he has had to invert them. This was a common practice under the clan system, and is still the general rule in many parts of the West Highlands, where the clan names still inhabit their old territory. Sometimes he was abbreviated to 'Calum the Road' (in the same way I have known elsewhere a 'John the Hearse', a 'Duncan the Lorry', a 'Ronald the Shooter' and a 'Ronald Donald the Dummy' – the last not in any aspersion upon his human reality but because he was dumb). But the necessity for this strict taxonomy is a strange situation for one whose nearest neighbour other than myself is four miles distant.

Calum Murdo, then, is a small wiry man in middle age, who, when I first came to Camusfeàrna, had for long been the road-mender responsible for several miles of the single-track road on either side of Druimfiaclach. It might be expected that a Highlander living in this remarkable isolation would have few topics of conversation beyond the small routine of his own existence; one would not, for example, expect him to be able to quote the greater part of the *Golden Treasury*, to have read most of the classics, to have voluble and well-informed views on politics national and international, or to be a subscriber to the *New Statesman*. Yet these were the facts, and I fear it must have been a sad disappointment to Calum Murdo to find his new neighbour, of a supposedly higher educational level, to be on many subjects less well informed than himself. He would impart to me much fascinating and anecdotal information on a host of subjects, and would close every session with a rounded formula: 'And now, Major, an educated man like yourself will be fair sick of listening to the haverings of an old prole.' Over a period of ten years he has contributed much to my education.

With Calum Murdo's wife Morag, a woman of fine-drawn iron beauty softened by humour, I found an immediate common ground in a love of living creatures. One reads and hears much at second hand of the spiritual descendants of St Francis and of St Cuthbert, those who experience an immediate intimate communication with bird and beast, and of whom wild things feel no fear, but I had never encountered one of them in the flesh until I met Morag, and I had become a little sceptical of their existence. What little success I myself have with animals is due, I think, solely to patience, experience, and a conscious effort to put myself in the animal's position, but I do not think that any of these things have been necessary to Morag. She frankly finds more to like and to love in animals than in human beings, and they respond to her immediately as if she were one of themselves, with a trust and respect that few of us receive from our own kind. I am convinced that there exists between her and them some rapport that is not for the achievement, even by long perseverance, of the bulk of those humans who would wish it. It would not, perhaps, be difficult to find more understandable explanations for individual cases in which, with her, this rapport seems apparent, but it is the number of these cases, and the consistency with which the animals' behaviour departs from its established pattern towards mankind, that convinces me of something not yet explainable in existing terms.

A single instance will be enough for illustration. Across the road from the MacKinnons' door is a reedy hillside lochan some hundred yards long by fifty wide, and every winter the wild swans, the whoopers, would come to it as they were driven south by Arctic weather, to stay often for days and sometimes for weeks. Morag loved the swans, and from the green door of her house she would call a greeting to them several times a day, so that they came to know her voice, and never edged away from her to the other side of the lochan as they did when other human figures appeared on the road. One night she heard them restless and calling, the clear bugle voices muffled and buffeted by the wind, and when she opened the door in the morning she saw that there was something very much amiss. The two parent birds were at the near edge of the loch, fussing, if anything so graceful and dignified as a wild swan can be said to fuss, round a cygnet that seemed in some way to be captive at the margin of the reeds. Morag began to walk towards the loch, calling to them all the while as she was wont. The cygnet flapped and struggled and beat the water piteously with his wings, but he was held fast below the peaty surface, and all the while the parents, instead of retreating before Morag, remained calling at his side. Morag waded out, but the loch bottom is soft and black, and she was sinking thigh deep before she realized that she could not reach the cygnet. Then suddenly he turned and struggled towards her, stopped the thrashing of his wings, and was still. Groping in the water beneath him, Morag's hand came upon a wire, on which she pulled until she was able to feel a rusty steel trap clamped to the cygnet's leg, a trap set for a fox, and fastened to a long wire so that he might drown himself and die the more quickly. Morag lifted the cygnet from the water; he lay passive in her arms while she eased the jaws open, and as she did this the two parents swam right in and remained one on either side of her, as tame, as she put it, as domestic ducks; neither did they swim away when she put the cygnet undamaged on to the water and began to retrace her steps.

The swans stayed for a week or more after that, and now they would not wait for her to call to them before greeting her; every time she opened her door their silver-sweet, bell-like voices chimed to her from the lochan across the road. If Yeats had possessed the same strange powers as Morag, his nine and fifty swans would perhaps not have suddenly mounted, and his poem would not have been written.

It was not through childlessness that Morag had turned to animals as do so many spinsters, for she had three sons. The eldest, Lachlan, was thirteen when I came to Camusfeàrna, and he had twin brothers of eleven, Ewan and Donald. The twins were eager, voluble, and helpful, by intention if not in every case in result, and after the first weeks, when the family had become friends, it was they who would carry my mail down from Druimfiaclach in the evenings after school, and at weekends do odd jobs for me about the house. They painted the outside walls of the house with Snowcem for me – or as much of the walls as their diminutive statures and a broken ladder could compass. They carried the heavy white powder down from Druimfiaclach in paper bags, and one day I suggested that they would find it easier to use my rucksack. They were delighted with the suggestion, and returned the following day with the whole rucksack full to the lip with loose Snowcem powder, and not only the main well of the rucksack but every zip-fastening pocket that the makers had designed for such personal possessions as toothbrushes and tobacco. That was nine years ago, and the two are grown-up and out in the world, but in wet weather that rucksack still exudes a detectable whitish paste at the seams.

Gradually the MacKinnon household became my lifeline, my only link with the remote world of shops and post offices, of telegrams and anger, that I would so much have wished to dispense with altogether. It is not easy at any time to victual a house that has no road to it, and it becomes the more difficult when the nearest village with more than one shop is between thirty and forty miles distant by road. The mails themselves arrive at Druimfiaclach, once a day, by a complicated mixture of sea and road transport from the railhead at the shopping village. From it they are carried by motor-launch to a tiny village five miles from Druimfiaclach, where originally a vast old Humber and now a Land Rover takes over and distributes them among the scattered dwellings of the neighbourhood. I am, therefore, reasonably certain of receiving one post a day if I plod up the hill to Druimfiaclach to fetch it (though occasionally it is too rough for the launch to put out, and it is not unknown, this being the West Highlands, for the whole mailbag to be sent to Skye through oversight or petulance), but I can only leave a reply to that post at Druimfiaclach the following night, for collection by the Land Rover on the morning after that; so that if I receive a letter on, for example, a Tuesday evening, it will be Friday before the sender gets my reply. Newspapers reach me on the evening of the day after they are published, if I go to Druimfiaclach to fetch them. Because of the height of the surrounding mountain massifs no radio will emit more than a furtive whisper; by pressing one's ear to the set one may catch tantalizingly fragmentary snatches of news, too often of wars and rumours of wars, or of equally intrusive and unwelcome strains of rock 'n' roll, mouse-squeak reminders of far-off human frenzy, whose faintness underlines the isolation of Camusfeàrna more effectively than could utter silence.

In practice, the exchange of letters often takes a full week, and the frustrations inherent in this situation have led the more impatient of my friends to the copious use of telegrams. The only way in which a telegram can be delivered, other than by the Land Rover carrying the mail to Druimfiaclach in the evenings, is by five steep and weary miles' bicycling from the Post Office to Druimfiaclach, followed by a mile and a half of hill-track on foot. In all, ten miles bicycling and three miles walking. The village postmaster is a man of extreme rectitude and sense of duty; the first telegram I ever received at Camusfeàrna was when on a sweltering summer's day, the hills shimmering in the heat haze and the fly-tormented cattle knee-deep in the motionless sea, he stood exhausted before my door bearing a message which read 'Many happy returns of the day'. The mountains had travailed and brought forth a mouse; after that I persuaded him, with great difficulty, to exercise his own judgment as to whether or not a telegram was urgent, and to consign those that were not to the Land Rover for delivery to Druimfiaclach in the evening.

Telegrams between the West Highlands and England are often liable to a little confusion in transit, to the production of what the services call 'corrupt groups'. During my first stay at Camusfeàrna I realized that though the house had, as it were, dropped into my lap from heaven, I had no subsidiary rights; a diet composed largely of shellfish might, I thought, be suitably varied by rabbits, and I telegraphed to the owner of the estate to ask his permission. The telegram he received from me read: 'May I please shoot at Robert and if so where?'

The reply to this sadistic request being in the affirmative, I

35

shot at Robert morning and evening, with a silenced .22 from the kitchen window, and he went far to solve the supply problem both for myself and for my dog Jonnie. Alas, Robert and all his brothers have now gone from Camusfeàrna, and except by living entirely from the sea it is difficult to approach self-subsistence.

For a year or two there was goats' milk, for Morag had, characteristically, given asylum to four goats left homeless by their owner's demise; one of these, a dainty, frolicsome white sprite called Mairi Bhan, she presented to Camusfeàrna. It was but a token gesture, for the little nanny was unaware of any change in ownership, preferring the company of her co-concubines and her rancid, lecherous overlord. The herd, however, took to spending much of their time at Camusfeàrna, where they would pick their way delicately along the top of the croft wall to plunder and maim the old apple and plum trees by the bridge, necessitating strange high barriers that seem cryptic now, for the goats are long gone. Their cynical, predatory yellow eyes, bright with an ancient, egotistical wisdom, were ever alert for an open door, and more than once I came back to the house from an afternoon's fishing to find the kitchen in chaos, my last loaves disappearing between agile rubbery lips, and Mairi Bhan posturing impudently on the table.

In the end their predilection for Camusfeàrna was their undoing, for where a past occupier of the house had once grown a kitchen garden sprung rhubarb leaves in profusion; of these, one spring, they ate copiously, and all but the billy died. Never sweet to the nostrils or continent of habit, he became, deprived of his harem, so gross both in odour and in behaviour, that only the undeniable splendour of his appearance prevented my joining the ranks of his numerous enemies. He survived, a lonely satyr, a sad solitary symbol of thwarted virility, until the burden of his chastity became too great for him, and he wandered and perished.

The goats were not the only invaders of the house, for in those days there was no fence surrounding it, and a door left ajar was taken as tacit invitation to the most improbable and unwelcome visitors. Once, on my return to the house after a few hours' absence, I was warned of some crisis while as yet a quarter of a mile distant; a succession of mighty, hollow groans, interspersed with a sound as of one striking wooden boarding with a heavy mallet, conjured an image worse, if possible, than the bizarre reality. Halfway up the wooden stairway, where it turns at right angles to reach the small landing, an enormous, black, and strikingly pregnant cow was wedged fast between the two walls, unable to progress forward and fearful of the gradient in reverse. Her rear aspect, whose copious activity – whether under the stress of anxiety or from an intelligent desire to reduce her dimensions – covered the stairs below her with a positively Augean litter of dung, blocked both view and passage to any would-be rescuer; moreover she proved, despite her precarious foothold and elephantine fecundity, to be capable of kicking with a veritably faun-like flourish. It was, however, one of these moments of petulant aggression that brought, literally, her downfall; an attempt with both heels simultaneously collapsed her with a ponderous and pathetic rumble, and she lay on her great gravid belly with her legs trailing, mire-covered, down the stairs. When at the end of nearly an hour's haulage I had restored her to the outside world I feared for her calf, but I need not have worried. Not long afterwards I assisted at her delivery, not with forceps but with ropes attached to protruding hooves; the calf fell with a terrifying crash to a stone floor, and half an hour later was on his feet and suckling.

With the goats cut short, as I have said, in their connubial prime, Camusfeàrna has ever since been dependent upon tinned milk. General supplies reach me by the same three-stage route as the mail, with the assistance of the friendly, haphazard cooperation to be found in remote places. I leave my order for the grocer, the ironmonger, or the chemist at Druimfiaclach in the evening; the Land Rover collects it in the morning and hands it to the skipper of the mail launch, who delivers it to the shops and brings the goods back – if, that is, they are to be obtained at the 'shopping centre'. For though there are a surprising number of shops for what is really no more than a hamlet, there is also surprisingly little in them – the nearest place where such commonplace objects as, for example, a coat-hanger or a pair of blue jeans may be bought, is Inverness, nearly a hundred miles away on the opposite coast of Scotland, or Fort William, the same distance to the south. This is not due entirely to a somewhat characteristic lack of enterprise, but also to a Foolish Virgin attitude to the necessities of life that I had seen exemplified again and again during my ownership of the Island of Soay. It is only during my own time at Camusfeàrna that electricity has come to the district – though not to me – through the West of Scotland Hydro-Electric Board; before that all the houses were lit by paraffin lamps, and many of the people cooked by Primus stove. Yet, despite the notoriously capricious quality of the electric light in the north-west Highlands, every single shop in every single village immediately stopped stocking paraffin, methylated spirits, and candles. Last year, there was to my certain knowledge, no drop of methylated spirits for sale within a hundred miles. The friendly spirit of cooperation is, however, equal even to this situation: once I sent an SOS for methylated spirits to a distant village and received an odd-looking package in return. It did not look like methylated spirits, and I unwrapped it in puzzlement. Inside was a pencil note which I deciphered with difficulty: 'Sorry no methylated spirits but am sending you two pounds of sausages instead.'

# 3

I had been at Camusfeàrna for eight years before I piped water to the house; before that it came from the burn in buckets. During the first years there was a stout stone-piered bridge across the burn, and under it one could draw water that had not been fouled by the cattle at their ford a little lower; then, in 1953, the bridge was swept away by a winter spate, and there was none built again for five years. In the summer there is no more than a foot or so of water among the stones, deepening to three or four feet when it runs amber-coloured and seemingly motionless between the alder banks, but wedged high among the branches are wads of debris that show the level of its torrential winter spates. When the gales blow in from the south-west and the burn comes roaring down in a foaming peaty cataract to meet the invading sea, the alders stand under water for half their height, and in the summer blackened trailers of dry seaweed dangle from branches ten feet and more above the stream.

After the bridge had gone, the winter crossing of the burn to climb the hill to Druimfiaclach was always perilous, sometimes impossible. I stretched a rope between the alders from bank to bank, but it was slender support, for even when the water was no more than thigh deep the pure battering weight of it as it surged down from the waterfall would sweep one's legs from the bottom and leave one clinging to the rope without foothold, feet trailing seaward.

The purely natural changes that have taken place during my ten years at Camusfeàrna are astonishing. One is inclined to think of such a landscape as immutable without the intervention of man, yet in these few years the small alterations to the scene have been continuous and progressive. The burn has swept the soil from under its banks so that the alder roots show white and bare, and some of the trees have fallen; where there are none at the burn side the short green turf has been tunnelled under by the water so that it falls in and the stream's bed becomes ever wider and shallower. Farther down towards the sea, where the burn bends round to encircle Camusfeàrna, the burrowing of a colony of sand martins in the sand cliff that is its landward bank has had the same effect, undermining the turf above so that it gives beneath the sheep's feet and rolls down to the water's edge. Below the sand martins' burrows is now a steep slope of loose sand where ten years ago it was vertical. The sand dunes between the house and the sea form and re-form, so that their contour is never the same for two years, though the glaucous, rasping marram grass that grows on them imparts an air of static permanency. The whole structure of these dunes that now effectively block much of the beach from the house, and incidentally afford to it some shelter from the southerly gales, is in any case a thing of recent times, for I am told that when the present house was built fifty odd years ago the field stretched flat to the sea, and the seaward facing wall of the house was left windowless for that reason.

The beach itself, wherever the rock does not shelve straight into the sea, is in constant change too; broad belts of shingle appear in the sand where there was no shingle before; soft stretches of quicksand come and go in a few weeks; sandbars as white as snowdrifts and jewelled with bright shells rise between the islands and vanish as though they had melted under the summer suns.

Even the waterfall, to me perhaps the most enduring symbol of Camusfeàrna, has changed and goes on changing. When I am away from the place and think of it, it is of the waterfall that I think first. Its voice is in one's ears day and night; one falls asleep to it, dreams with it and wakens to it; the note changes with the season, from the dull menacing roar of winter nights to the low crooning of the summer, and if I hold a shell to my ear it is not the sea's murmur that comes to me but the sound of the Camusfeàrna waterfall. Above the bridge where I used to draw my water the burn rushes over stones and between boulders with the alders at its banks, and a wealth of primroses and wild hyacinths among the fern and mosses. In spring it is loud with bird song from the chaffinches that build their lichen nests in the forks of the alders, and abob with wagtails among the stones. This part of the burn is 'pretty' rather than beautiful, and it seems to come from nowhere, for the waterfall is hidden round a corner and the stream seems to emerge from a thirty foot wall of rock hung with honeysuckle and with rowan trees jutting from cracks and fissures. But looking up the burn from the foot of that rock the word 'pretty' becomes wholly inapplicable; the waterfall is of a beauty it would be hard to devise. It is not high, for the tall cataracts of eighty feet are some two hundred yards higher up its course; it emerges between boulders and sheer rock walls to drop some fifteen feet, over about the same breadth, from the twilight world of the deep narrow gorge it has carved through the hill face over thousands, perhaps millions, of years. It emerges frothing from that unseen darkness to fall like a tumbling cascade of brilliants into a deep rounded cauldron enclosed by rock walls on three sides, black water in whorled black rock, with the fleecy white spume ringing the blackness of the pool. Up above the black sides of the pot there are dark-green watery mosses growing deep and cushioned wherever there is a finger-hold for soil; the domed nest that the dippers build here every year is distinguishable from the other moss cushions by nothing but its symmetry. The sun reaches the waterfall for only a short time in the afternoon; it forms a rainbow over the leaping spray, and at the top of the fall between the boulders it gives to the smooth-flowing, unbroken water the look of spun green glass.

For most of the year the waterfall has volume enough for a man to stand on a ledge between it and the rock and remain almost dry; between oneself and the sky it forms a rushing, deafening curtain of milky brilliance through which nothing but light is discernible. If one steps forward so that the weight of water batters full on head and shoulders it is of the massiveness only that one is conscious, and it would be impossible to say whether the water were cold or hot. Only when one steps from it again, and the flying icy drops tingle on the skin, does the sensation become one of snow water.

It would seem that the waterfall could never change, yet year by year its form differs as a new boulder is swept down by the spates to lodge above its lip; or a tree falls from its precarious grip on the cliff faces above it and jams the doorway of its emergence; or a massive section of rock breaks away, split by the prising leverage of slow-growing tree roots.

In spring and autumn the natural decoration surrounding the waterfall surpasses anything that artifice could achieve; in spring the green banks above the rock are set so thickly with primroses that blossom almost touches blossom, and the wild blue hyacinths spring from among them seemingly without leaf; in late summer and autumn the scarlet rowanberries flare from the ferned rock walls, bright against the falling white water and the darkness of the rock.

It is the waterfall, rather than the house, that has always seemed to me the soul of Camusfeàrna, and if there is anywhere in the world to which some part of me may return when I am dead it will be there.

If it is the waterfall that seems the soul of Camusfeàrna, it is the burn and the sea that give its essential character, that sparkling silver that rings the green field and makes it almost an island. Below the house the beach is long and shelving, the tide running back at low springs for more than two hundred yards over alternate stone and sand. There is only one thing lacking at Camusfeàrna; within its narrow compass it contains every attraction but an anchorage. To look down from the hill above upon the bay and the scattered, intricate network of islands and skerries it would appear incredible that not one of those bights or niches should afford shelter, yet because of the long ebb of the tide each one of these seemingly tranquil miniature harbours dries out at low water. For years I had no boat at Camusfeàrna, and when at last I did buy a dinghy I was intimidated by the thought of those interminable hauls to and from the water's edge, and I bought a little nine-foot flat-bottomed pram that one could almost pick up. But to have a boat again at all, even that toy, brought a hankering to extend one's range up and down the coast and over to Skye, and now I have two dinghies with outboard motors, one of them a sturdy lifeboat's dinghy of fifteen feet, with decked-in bows. There are moorings laid in the bay where the burn flows out to the sea, and the pram is kept drawn up on the beach as ferry to and from the larger boat, but when the wind blows strong from the south it is always an anxious business. The suddenness and intensity of West Highland squalls, even in summer, has to be experienced to be understood; pale-blue satin water can become in a matter of minutes an iron-grey menace raging in white at the crests of massive waves. But the compensations outweigh the anxiety, for it was frustrating to live at the sea's edge and be unable to voyage upon it, to be unable to visit the distant islands, to fish in summer, to reach the nearest shop without the long climb to Druimfiaclach. The possession of the boats opened a whole new world around Camusfeàrna, a wide extension of its small enclosed paradise, and in summer the hours afloat drift by with work unheeded and the business of life seeming far off and worthless.

There is a perpetual mystery and excitement in living on the seashore, which is in part a return to childhood and in part because for all of us the sea's edge remains the edge of the unknown; the child sees the bright shells, the vivid weeds and red sea-anemones of the rock pools with wonder and with the child's eye for minutiae; the adult who retains wonder brings to his gaze some partial knowledge which can but increase it, and he brings, too, the eye of association and of symbolism, so that at the edge of the ocean he stands at the brink of his own unconscious.

The beaches of Camusfeàrna are a treasure house for any man whose eye finds wealth at the sea's edge. There are more shells than I have seen on any other littoral; a great host of painted bivalves of bewildering variety and hue, from coral pinks and primrose yellows to blues and purples and mother-of-pearl, from jewel-like fan shells no bigger than a little fingernail to the great scallops as big as a side-plate; nutshells and Hebridean ark shells and pearly top-shells and delicate blush-pink cowries. The sand-bars and beaches between the islands are formed of the disintegration of these myriad calceous houses, true shell sand that is blindingly white under the sun and crusted in deep layers at the tide's edge with tiny intact empty shells gaudy as multi-coloured china beads. A little above the shells, because they are heavier, lies a filigree of white and purple coral, loose pieces each of which would lie in the palm of a hand, but there are so many of them that they form a dense, brittle layer over the sand. On still summer days when the tide wells up the beaches without so much as a wrinkle or ripple of wavelet at its edge, the coral floats off on the meniscus of the water, so that the sea seems to be growing flowers as an ornamental pond grows water lilies, delicately branched white and purple flowers on the aquamarine of the clear water.

Where shells lie thick it is often those that are broken that have the greatest beauty of form; a whelk is dull until one may see the sculptural perfection of the revealed spiral, the skeletal intricacy of the whorled mantle. Many of the shells at Camusfeàrna, and the stones, too, have been embroidered with the white limy tunnels of the serpulid tube-worm, strange hieroglyphics that even in their simplest forms may appear urgently significant, the symbols of some forgotten alphabet, and when a surface is thickly encrusted it assumes the appearance of Hindu temple carving, or of Rodin's 'Gates of Hell', precise in every riotous ramification. Parts of the sculpture appear almost representational; a terrified beast flees before a pursuing predator; a well-meaning saint impales a dragon; the fingers of a hand are raised, like those of a Byzantine Christ, in a gesture that seems one of negation rather than benediction.

But above all it is the fantastic colouring of the beaches that as an image overpowers the minutiae. Above the tideline the grey rocks are splashed gorse-yellow with close-growing lichen, and with others of blue-green and salmon pink. Beneath them are the vivid orange-browns and siennas of wrack-weeds, the violet of mussel-beds, dead-white sand, and water through which one sees down to the bottom, as through pale green bottle-glass, to where starfish and big spiny sea urchins of pink and purple rest upon the broad leaves of the sea-tangle.

*

The beaches are rich, too, in edible shellfish. Besides the ubiquitous mussels, limpets and periwinkles, there are cockle beds, razor-shell beds, and even an oyster bed, though this last remains one of the mysteries of Camusfeàrna. The oysters were introduced many years ago by a former owner of the estate, in a little circular bay almost closed from the sea and no more than twenty yards across, where a trickle of fresh water comes down over the sand from an island spring. At the tideline above this bay arrives a constant litter of tantalizingly freshly emptied oyster shells that would not disgrace Wheeler's, and, very occasionally, a live oyster, but for all my searching year by year I have never discovered where the bed lies. This is as well, perhaps, for I suspect that by now the colony would have succumbed to my gluttony.

Below the tide around the islands the white sand alternates with a heavy rubbery jungle of sea-tangle or umbrella weed. The lobsters lurk in this dimness by day, and lobster-pots set in the sand patches between the weed are rarely unsuccessful. A variety of other life besides lobsters enters the pots, creatures couth and uncouth; sometimes the bait is covered with gigantic whelks, and almost always there are big edible crabs. Often there is a curious beast called the velvet swimming crab, with a shield of brown velvet and reproachful red eyes, and once I caught one of the most repulsive creatures I have ever come across, a spider crab. It was not only the enormously long legs and absence of pincers that were nauseating; he was grown over from head to foot, as it were, with a crinkly, purplish-red seaweed, lending him the same air of doubtful reality as a shroud traditionally imparts to a ghost. The weed is, in fact, grafted into position by the crab itself, for camouflage, and this implication of furtive cunning coming on top of the outrageous personal appearance is not reassuring.

# 4

Spring comes late to Camusfeàrna. More than one year I have motored up from the south early in April to become immobilized in snowdrifts on the passes twenty miles from it, and by then the stags are still at the roadside down the long glen that leads to the sea. By mid-April there is still no tinge of green bud on the bare birches and rowans nor green underfoot, though there is often, as when I first came to Camusfeàrna, a spell of soft still weather and clear skies. The colours then are predominantly pale blues, russet browns, and purples, each with the clarity of fine enamel; pale blue of sea and sky, the russet of dead bracken and fern, deep purple-brown of unbudded birch, and the paler violets of the Skye hills and the peaks of Rhum. The landscape is lit by three whites – the pearl white of the birch trunks, the dazzle of the shell-sand beaches, and the soft filtered white of the high snows. The primroses are beginning to flower about the burn and among the island banks, though all the high hills are snow-covered and the lambs are as yet unborn. It is a time that has brought me, in all too few years, the deep contentment of knowing that the true spring and summer are still before me at Camusfeàrna, that I shall see the leaf break and the ground become green, and all the snow melt from the hills but for a few drifts that will lie summer through.

It has its own orchestration, this little prelude to the northern spring; every year there is the sound of the wild geese calling far overhead as they travel north to their thawing breeding grounds, and sometimes the wild unearthly beauty of whooper swans' voices, silver trumpets high in the clear blue air. The eider ducks have arrived to breed about the shore and the islands; they bring with them that most evocative and haunting of all sounds of the

Hebridean spring and summer, the deep, echoing, wood-wind crooning of the courting drakes.

One by one the breeding bird species return to the beaches and the islands where they were hatched; the sand martins to the sand cliff at the burn foot, the wheatears to the rabbit burrows in the close-bitten turf; the black guillemots and the gulls to the Camusfeàrna islands. The herring gulls come first, to the biggest island, where the lighthouse stands, some two hundred and fifty pairs of them, and the air above the white-splashed rocks and sea pinks scattered with broken shellfish is vibrant with the clang of their calling and their wheeling white wings. Among them are two or three pairs of great black-backed gulls, massive, hoarse-voiced and vulturine. Then come the common gulls, delicate, graceful, segregated shrilly on to a neighbouring promontory, beadily mistrustful of the coarse language and predatory predilections of their neighbours; and, lastly, not until well into May, come the terns, the sea-swallows, to their own outlying skerry. They arrive in the same week as the swallows come up from Africa to nest in the old ruined croft across the field, and with the thin steel oar-beat of their wings spring has almost given place to summer.

By then the colour everywhere is green. The purple birch twigs are hidden in a soft cloud of new leaf; the curled, almond-bitter rods of young bracken have in those short weeks pushed up three feet from the earth and unfurled a canopy of green frond over the rust of last year's growth; the leaves of the yellow flag iris that margin the burn and the shore form a forest of broad bayonets, and the islands, that but for rank rooty patches of heather growing knee-deep seemed so bare in April, are smothered with a jungle-growth of goose grass and briar. To me there is always something a little stifling in this enveloping green stain, this redundant, almost Victorian, drapery over bones that need no blanketing, and were it not for the astringent presence of the sea I should find all that verdure as enervating as an Oxford water-meadow in the depths of summer.

Early in May comes the recurrent miracle of the elvers' migration from the sea. There is something deeply awe-inspiring about the sight of any living creatures in incomputable numbers; it stirs, perhaps, some atavistic chord whose note belongs more properly to the distant days when we were a true part of the animal ecology; when the sight of another species in unthinkable hosts brought fears or hopes no longer applicable. When the young eels reach the Camusfeàrna burn – no more than a uniform three inches long nor thicker than a meat-skewer, steel-blue when seen from above, but against the light transparent except for a red blob at the gills – they have been journeying in larval form for two whole years from their breeding grounds south-west of Bermuda, through two thousand miles of ocean and enemies. During that long, blind voyage of instinct their numbers must have been reduced not to a millionth but a billionth of those who set forth, yet it is difficult to imagine that there can have been vaster hordes than reach the Camusfeàrna burn; still more difficult to realize that these are but a tiny fraction of the hosts that are simultaneously ascending a myriad other burns.

Where the burn flows calm through the level ground their armies undulate slowly and purposefully forward towards the seemingly insurmountable barrier of the falls; on, above the bridge, into the stretch where the water rushes and stumbles over uneven stones; round the rock-twist to the foot of the falls. Here, temporarily daunted or resting before their assault upon the vertical, spray-wet rock-face, they congregate almost motionless in the rock pools, forming a steel-blue carpet inches deep; dip a bucket here, and it comes up with a greater volume of elvers than of water. Some mistake the true course of the burn, and follow steep trickles leading to cul-de-sac pools of spray water; to and from these (for the miraculous powers of their multitudes do not appear to include communication or deduction), there are simultaneous streams of ascending and descending elvers, while the spray-pool itself is filled to the brim with an aimlessly writhing swarm.

It is here, during the wait at the foot of the falls, that the last heavy toll is taken of their numbers; for a week or two the rocks below the waterfall are splashed white with the droppings of herons who stand there scooping them up by the bill-full, decimating yet again, on the verge of their destination, the remnants of the great concourse that has been travelling thus perilously for two years.

But one has not been witness to the long core, as it were, of that mighty migration, and so it is in the elvers' final ascent of the falls that the colossal driving power of their instinct becomes most apparent to the onlooker. At first, where at the edges of the falls the water splashes into shallow stone troughs among the horizontal ledges, the way is easy – a few inches of horizontal climb and the elver has reached the next trough. But after a foot or two of this ladder-like progression they are faced either with the battering fall of white water at their left or with a smooth black stretch of rock wall in front, hit every few seconds by heavy splashes of spray. For a few feet at the bottom of this wall grows a close slimy fir of waterweed, and among its infinitesimal tendrils the elvers twine themselves and begin, very slowly, to squirm their way upwards, forming a vertical, close-packed queue perhaps two feet wide. Sometimes a big gob of spray lands right amid their ranks and knocks a hundred of them back into the trough below, but slowly, patiently, they climb back again. I have never marked an elver so that it is recognizable, and for all I know this may happen to the same elver many, many times in a day or even in an hour. Perhaps it is something to do with the transparency of the creatures, besides their diminutive size and bewildering numbers, that makes the mind rebel both at the blind strength of their instinct and their inherent power to implement it, as though the secret power-house should be visible.

Once above the water-draggled weed there is no further incidental support for the climbing elvers; there is just sheer wet rock, with whatever microscopic roughness their transparent bellies may apprehend. They hang there, apparently without gravity, with an occasional convulsive movement that seems born of despair. They climb perhaps six inches in an hour, sometimes slithering backward the same distance in a second, and there are another twelve feet of rock above them.

It is not possible for more than a moment or two to identify oneself with any single one of this mass, but there is a sense of relief, of emotional satisfaction, in looking upward to the lip of the falls where they spill over from the hidden pool above, and seeing the broad band of glistening elvers that have accomplished the apparently impossible and are within an inch of safety.

Perhaps a few million out of billions top the Camusfeàrna falls; some, certainly, surmount the second and third falls too, and I have seen elvers of that size more than two thousand feet up the peak where the burn has its source. In perspective, the survival rate must be high when compared with that of spermatozoa.

Only once at Camusfeàrna have I seen any other living creatures in numbers to compare with those elvers, but I remember the occasion vividly. In the warm evenings of later summer, when the sun still flared a finger's breadth above the saw-tooth peaks of the Cuillin and glowed on the dense red berries of the rowans, the MacKinnon children would come down the hill from Druim-fiaclach to bathe at the white sand beaches of the islands. Long before I could hear them my dog Jonnie, growing a little corpulent and stiff now, would prick his ears and whine, and the feathery white stub of his tail would scuff softly on the stone floor. I would go to the open door and listen and Jonnie would sit very upright on the stone flags outside, staring up at the high skyline with his nose twitching and questing, and I would hear nothing but the sounds of ever-moving water and the faint, familiar bird-cries of the wilderness, the piping of shore birds and perhaps the mew of a buzzard wheeling overhead. There was the murmur of the dwindled waterfall and the trill of the burn among the boulders, and at the other side the muted sound of wavelets breaking in a small tumble of foam along the shore; there was the twitter of sand martins hawking flies in the still golden air, the croak of a raven, and gull voices from the sea that stretched away as smooth as white silk to the distant island of Eigg lying across the sea horizon. Sometimes there was the warning thump of a rabbit from the warren among the dunes behind the house.

But Jonnie always knew when the children were coming, and when at last I could hear them too, treble voices faint and far off and high above us, he would assume a sudden unconcern, walking with stiff indifference to lift his leg in a flourish over a nearby tuft of rushes or a post that guarded the small flower-bed. From the time that the boys' heads were bobbing small on the hill horizon it would be some five minutes before they had descended the last and steepest part of the track, crossed the bridge, and come up over the green grass to the door, and all the time I would be wondering what they had brought – longed-for or unwelcome letters, some supplies that I urgently needed, a bottle of goat's milk from their mother, or just nothing at all. When it was nothing I was at once relieved and bitterly disappointed, for at Camusfeàrna I both resent the intrusion of the outside world and crave reassurance of its continued existence.

One evening when the twins had brought me a bulky packet of letters I had been sitting reading them in the twilight kitchen for some time when I was roused by the urgent excitement of their cries from the beach. I went out to a scene that is as fresh in my mind now as though it were hours rather than years that lay between.

The sun was very low; the shadow of the house lay long and dark across the grass and the rushes, while the hillside above glowed golden as though seen through orange lenses. The bracken no longer looked green nor the heather purple; all that gave back their own colour to the sun were the scarlet rowanberries, as vivid as venous blood. When I turned to the sea it was so pale and polished that the figures of the twins thigh-deep in the shallows showed in almost pure silhouette against it, bronze-coloured limbs and torsos edged with yellow light. They were shouting and laughing and dancing and scooping up the water with their hands, and all the time as they moved there shot up from the surface where they broke it a glittering spray of small gold and silver fish, so dense and brilliant as to blur the outline of the childish figures. It was as though the boys were the central

décor of a strangely lit baroque fountain, and when they bent to
the surface with cupped hands a new jet of sparks flew upward
where their arms submerged, and fell back in brittle, dazzling
cascade.

When I reached the water myself it was like wading in silver
treacle; our bare legs pushed against the packed mass of little fish
as against a solid and reluctantly yielding obstacle. To scoop and
to scatter them, to shout and to laugh, were as irresistible as
though we were treasure hunters of old who had stumbled upon
a fabled emperor's jewel vaults and threw diamonds about us
like chaff. We were fish-drunk, fish-crazy, fish-happy in that
shining orange bubble of air and water; the twins were about
thirteen years old and I was about thirty-eight, but the miracle
of the fishes drew from each of us the same response.

We were so absorbed in making the thronged millions of tiny
fish into leaping fireworks for our delight that it was not for some
minutes that I began to wonder what had driven this titanic shoal
of herring fry – or soil, as they are called in this part of the world
– into the bay, and why, instead of dispersing outwards to sea,
they became moment by moment ever thicker in the shallows.
Then I saw that a hundred yards out the surface was ruffled by
flurries of mackerel whose darting shoals made a sputter of spray
on the smooth swell of the incoming tide. The mackerel had
driven the fry headlong before them into the narrow bay and
held them there, but now the pursuers too were unable to go
back. They were in turn harried from seaward by a school of
porpoises who cruised the outermost limit of their shoals, driving
them farther and farther towards the shore. Hunter and hunted
pushed the herring soil ever inward to the sand, and at length
every wavelet broke on the beach with a tumble of silver sprats.
I wondered that the porpoises had not long since glutted and
gone; then I saw that, like the fry and the mackerel that had
pursued them into the bay, the porpoises' return to the open
waters of the sound was cut off. Beyond them, black against the
blanched sunset water, rose the towering sabre fin of a bull killer
whale, the ultimate enemy of sea creatures great and small, the

unattackable; his single terrible form controlling by its mere presence the billions of lives between himself and the shore.

The sun went down behind the Cuillin and the water grew cold and the tide crawled grey up the beach, clogged with its helpless burden of fish, and long after the distance had become too dim to see the killer's fin we could hear the putter of the rushing mackerel as they moved in with the tide. When it was nearly dark we fetched buckets and dipped them in the sea's edge; they came up heavy in our hands, full not of water but of thumb-length fish.

In the morning it was dead low tide, and the sea, as still as a mountain tarn as far as the eye could reach, had gone back some two hundred yards. The tide-wrack of high-water mark lay right along the slope of white sand under the dunes, but that morning it was not dark like a tarry rope ringing the bay; it gleamed blue-grey and white with the bodies of millions upon millions of motionless minnow-sized fish. The gulls had gorged themselves when the sun rose; they sat silent, hunched and distended, in long rows on the wet sand a little to seaward, their shadows still long and formal under the low sun that glared over the hill.

I gathered a few more buckets of the fry, and kept them as cool as I could in the heat of that sunny September. But manna, like everything else, should be of at least fifty-seven varieties; when heaven sends bounty it too often sends monotony. The first meal of fried whitebait had the delight of novelty and of windfall, akin to the pleasure that for the first few days I take in some humble but new treasure harvested from the shore after gales; the second had lost little, but the sixth and seventh were cloying, while there were still three buckets full. Jonnie, who entertained an unnatural passion for fish of all kinds, ate more than I did, but the level in the buckets seemed never to diminish; a guest came to stay and we made them into fish-cakes and fish-pies, into kedgerees and fish-soups, into curries and savouries, until at last one merciful morning they began to smell. Then we used them to bait the lobster-pots, but after a while even the lobsters seemed to grow weary of them.

It so happened that about that time I made one of my rare shopping journeys to Inverness. The second item on the hotel luncheon menu was fried whitebait, and the dining-room was rich with the once-appetizing aroma. I left that hotel as might one who had perceived a corpse beneath his table, and it was some two years before I could eat whitebait again.

# 5

The smaller members of the whale tribe are a feature of every summer at Camusfeàrna. Sometimes the great whales, the blue and the rorquals, pass majestically through the Sound beyond the lighthouse, but they never came into the bay, for only at the highest tides would there be water enough to float their fantastic bulk.

Of all sea creatures whales hold for me a particular fascination, stemming, perhaps, from the knowledge of their enormously developed brains coupled with the unguessable, pressing, muffled world in which they pass their lives. So highly convoluted are those brains that it has been suggested that were it not for their frustrating limbless-ness they might well have outstripped man in domination of the earth's surface. Yet there are an incredible number of people who, because of the superficial similarities of bulk and habitat, confuse them with the great sharks whose brains are minute and rudimentary. Although from early times whaling men have had strange tales to tell of their quarry's extraordinary mental powers it is only comparatively recently that these things have become accepted fact. The American 'oceanariums' have allowed their porpoise and dolphin inmates to reveal themselves as highly intelligent, amiable, and playful personalities who evince an unexpected desire to please and cooperate with human beings. They will play ball games with their attendants, come up out of the water to greet them, and retrieve with obvious pleasure ladies' handbags and kindred objects that have accidentally fallen into their tank. They are also capable of unquestionable altruism to one another; like many animals, but perhaps even more than most, their behaviour compares very favourably with that of the human species. Yet for the oil in the blubber that insulates them from the cold of polar seas man has from the earliest days reserved for the whales the most brutal and agonizing death in his armoury, the harpoon buried deep in living flesh.

Until very lately zoologists held that whales were dumb, and both the system of communication that made possible concerted action by widely separated individuals, and the 'sixth sense' by which they could detect the presence of objects in water too murky for vision, remained undiscovered. We have long laboured under an obtuse presupposition that the senses by which other living creatures perceive their world must to a great extent resemble our own; but in fact we are, by scientific invention, only beginning to approach methods of perception that the whales always owned as their birthright. Not only can they hear sounds four times higher than the upper limit the human ear can detect, but they possess a highly developed system closely akin to our own recently discovered radar, sending out a constant stream of supersonic notes whose returning 'echoes' inform them of the whereabouts, size, and possibly much more as yet unguessed information, of all objects within their range. Underwater recording devices have now also established that members of the whale tribe keep up an almost continual conversational chatter among themselves, sounds that are seldom if ever uttered by a single whale with no other near him.

Because man could not hear them, man assumed that they were dumb. If a whale's cry of pain when struck with a harpoon had been audible it is just possible, but only just, that man would have felt more self-hatred in their slaughter; though the sight of two adult whales trying to keep the blow-hole of a wounded calf above water has failed to change the attitude of whaler to whale.

It is not, of course, easy for the casual shore visitor or boat passenger to deduce from the discreet, momentarily glimpsed fin of a porpoise all these complex and stimulating attributes of its owner; surprisingly few people, in fact, appear even to know that a porpoise is a whale.

The porpoises, six-foot lengths of sturdy grace, are the commonest of all the whale visitors to the Camusfeàrna bay. Unlike the rumbustious dolphins they are shy, retiring creatures, and one requires leisure and patience to see more of them than that little hooked fin that looks as if it were set on the circumference of a slowly revolving wheel; leisure to ship the oars and remain motionless, and patience to allow curiosity to overcome timidity. Then the porpoises will blow right alongside the boat, with a little gasp that seems of shocked surprise, and at these close quarters the wondering inquisitiveness of their eyes shows as plainly as it can in a human face, a child's face as yet uninhibited against the display of emotion. The face, like the faces of all whales but the killer, appears good-humoured, even bonhomous. But they will not stay to be stared at, and after that quick gasp they dive steeply down into the twilight; they go on about their own business, and will not linger to play as do the dolphins.

One summer a school of seventeen bottle-nosed dolphins spent a whole week in the Camusfeàrna bay, and they would seem almost to hang about waiting for the boat to come out and play with them. They never leapt and sported unless the human audience was close at hand, but when we were out among them with the outboard motor they would play their own rollicking and hilarious games of hide-and-seek with us, and a sort of aquatic blind-man's-buff, in which we in the boat were all too literally blind to them, and a target for whatever surprises they could devise. The beginning followed an invariable routine; they would lead, close-packed, their fins thrusting from the water with a long powerful forward surge every five or ten seconds, and we would follow to see how close we could get to them. When we were within fifty feet or so there would be a sudden silence while, unseen, they swooped back under the boat to reappear dead astern of us. Sometimes they would remain submerged for many minutes, and we would cut the engine and wait. This was the dolphins' moment. As long as I live, and whatever splendid sights I have yet to see I shall remember the pure glory of the dolphins' leap as they shot up a clear ten feet out of the sea, one after the other, in high parabolas of flashing silver at the very boat's side. At the time it gave me a *déjà vu* sensation that I could not place; afterwards I realized that it recalled irresistibly the firing in quick succession of pyrotechnic rockets, the tearing sound of the rockets' discharge duplicated by the harsh exhalation of air as each dolphin fired itself almost vertically from the waves.

In this school of dolphins there were some half a dozen calves, not more than four or five feet long as against their parents' twelve. The calves would keep close alongside their mothers' flanks – the right-hand side always – and I noticed that when the mothers leapt they kept their acrobatics strictly within the capabilities of their offspring, rising no more than half the height of those unencumbered by children.

The members of this school of dolphins spoke with voices perfectly audible to human ears; rarely when they were very close to the boat, but usually when they were heading straight away at a distance of a hundred yards or two. As they broke the surface with that strong forward-thrusting movement, one or more of their number would produce something between a shrill whistle and a squeak, on a single note held for perhaps two seconds. It seems strange that I can find no written record of any whale-sound as plainly and even obtrusively audible above water as this.

The Risso's grampus, or more properly Risso's dolphin, a few feet larger than the bottle-nose, visits Camusfeàrna bay in the summer too, but whereas in the shark fishery days I used to regard them as the sea's clowns, perpetually at play in uncouth and incongruous attitudes, the parties that come to Camusfeàrna have by comparison with the bottle-nosed been sedate and decorous, almost always cows with small tubby calves, intent on the serious business of feeding and avoiding danger. They would not allow the boat nearly as close to them as would the other dolphins, unlike whom they seemed to resent human presence, and would soon leave the bay altogether if frequently followed.

Contrary to information contained in the majority of text-books, in which Risso's dolphin is described as a rarity, it is in fact the commonest of all the lesser whales to visit the Hebrides in summer. During my years in the shark fishery, when our chief catcher the *Sea Leopard* would cruise day-long in search of a different shape of fin, it was a rare week in which we had not met with half a dozen schools of them. As with most other species of whale, the fishermen have their own names for them, names that they sometimes, to the confusion of an enquiring scientist, use to describe several separate species, so that it is only by the comparatively very rare strandings of individual whales that the presence of a species becomes established. The ring-net men call Risso's dolphin 'lowpers' or 'dunters', words deriving from the habit of seemingly aimless and random leaping. Neither Risso's nor the bottle-nosed dolphins travel, as do the white-sided and common dolphins, by a series of long leaps low over the waves; both seem to jump only when they are at leisure and frolicking.

In fact it is not easy for an eye with any practice to confuse the fin of Risso's dolphin with any other than that of a cow killer whale. 'Cow' is a strange feminine noun to give the most terrible animal in the sea; 'bull' is little better for her butcher mate, but the forms are fixed by long usage and must stand. Imaginations have strained to find a simile from land animals; the killer has been called the wolf of the sea, the tiger of the sea, the hyena of the sea, but none of these is really apt, and probably there is no other mammal of comparably indiscriminate ferocity.

Anyone writing of killer whales finds it necessary to quote the discovered contents of one killer's stomach, and indeed those contents produce so immediate an image that they will, perhaps, bear one more repetition. That particular killer was found to contain no fewer than thirteen porpoises and fourteen seals. A gargantuan meal, one would say, for a leviathan, yet by compari-son with the great whales the killer is a small beast, the bull no more than twenty-five feet overall and the cow a mere fifteen, while an adult porpoise is six feet long and the average among the seal species little less. Killers hunt in packs, and not even the great whales themselves are safe from them; the pack goes for the mighty tongue which in itself may weigh a ton, and when it is torn out the giant bleeds to death while the killers feed.

As I write there lies a few hundred yards down the shore the newly dead body of a brown seal. The forepart of the head has gone, where something has crunched through the skull in front of the eyes, and from one flank there has been ripped away a foot length of flesh and blubber, exposing the entrails. There are other possible solutions, though none of them likely; it is the typical work of a killer in killing mood. On Hyskeir the lighthouse men have told me how they have seen the killers slash seals for sport and not for food, and leave them maimed and dying among the skerries.

A killer or two comes every year to Camusfeàrna, but they do not linger, and if they did I would compass their deaths by any means that I could, for they banish the other sea life from my surroundings; also I do not care to be among them in a small boat. There are many tales, but few, if any, authenticated records, of their attacking human beings; however, I do not want to be the first. Last year a single bull terrorized the tiny harbour of the Isle of Canna the summer through; John Lorne-Campbell shared my aversion to being a guinea-pig for dietary research among killers, and wrote asking my advice about its destruction. I smugly advised him to shoot it, and gave reasoned instructions as to the precise moment and bull's eye, but I was thirty miles away, and I daresay my advice did not seem as sound and constructive on Canna as it did to me at Camusfeàrna.

My old quarry the basking sharks I have seen but seldom since they ceased to be my bread and butter, or rather my quest for bread and butter. The first basking shark with which I ever came to grips, sixteen crowded years ago was, by a strange coincidence, just out to sea from Camusfeàrna lighthouse, but in the ten years on and off that I have lived here since, I have only seen sharks on a bare half-dozen occasions, and most of them a long way off. No doubt they have often been showing at times when I was not there to see them. Only once have I seen them right close inshore, and then they were being hunted by my successors: I had been sitting up all night with my dog Jonnie, who was at the very edge of death, and I was too crushed with sadness and weariness to identify myself with that strange vignette of my past life.

The stages of Jonnie's illness have become blurred in my mind; the two crises from which he made miraculous but ephemeral recoveries seem no longer related in sequence. I had been in London, and travelled to Camusfeàrna in the last week of April. Morag had telephoned to me to tell me that Jonnie was not well, and by the time I arrived he had developed pneumonia; he was a dog of enormous strength, but he was growing old, and his heart was not a young dog's heart.

At the end of one despairing night sitting with him at Druimfia-clach, Morag relieved me after she had seen to her family's wants, and I set off down the hill for Camusfeàrna, dazed and unhappy and longing desperately to get into bed and sleep. When I came to the part of the track that looks down over the house and the sea I was startled by the unmistakable boom of a harpoon gun, and woke, as it were, to find myself staring straight into the past. Below me in the calm bay was a ring-net boat from Mallaig; there was a storm of thrashing spray about her bows, and from the gun in her stem drifted a thin haze of cordite smoke. A little farther out to sea were showing the vast dorsal fins of two more sharks. I saw the white water at the boat's bows subside as the harpooned shark sounded, and I sat and watched the whole familiar procedure as they got the winches started and hauled for half an hour before they had him back at the surface; I saw that great six-foot tail break water and lash and slam the boat's sides while they struggled, as I had struggled so often before, to lasso the wildly lunging target; I saw it captured and made fast – yet because of my own state of exhaustion and preoccupation the whole scene was utterly without meaning to me, and I had no moment of mental participation while the small figures of the crew scurried about the deck in pursuance of a routine that had once been my daily life. Yet at other times, when I have watched through the field glasses the cruising fins of sharks far down the

Sound, I have been possessed by a wild and entirely illogical unrest; the same sort of unrest, I imagine, that migratory creatures feel in captivity when the season for their movement is at hand.

Though Jonnie survived pneumonia to become seemingly as strong as before, the writing was on the wall. A few months later he developed cancer of the rectum, and while it was, I think, painless, he had always been a dog of great dignity and cleanliness, and he felt acutely the concomitant humiliation of an evil-smelling discharge over the white silk-and-wool of his coat. When I was away from Camusfeàrna he lived with Morag MacKinnon, to whom he accorded a devotion no less than to myself, but when I came back after months of absence he would go mad with joy like a puppy and lead the way down the path to Camusfeàrna as if I had never left it. But it was with Morag that he died at last, for I was too cowardly to travel north and watch my friend killed, as in all humanity he had to be.

Camusfeàrna is a very long way from a vet; the nearest, in fact, is on the Island of Skye, nearly fifty miles away by road and ferry-boat. When he visited Jonnie that winter of 1954 he said that the disease was progressing very rapidly, and that pain when it came would be sudden and acute, with a complete blockage of the rectum. He thought there was a fifty-fifty chance of Jonnie surviving what would now be a major operation, but he was insistent that action must be taken at once either to end Jonnie's life or to prolong it.

I had no car with me that year, so I hired one for the whole journey, to wait during the operation and to bring me back at night, either alone or with what I was warned would in any event be an unconscious dog. Jonnie loved car journeys, and he was enthusiastic to start on this one; as we bumped over the precipitous road to the ferry he stuck his head out of the window and quested the breeze with all the zest of his puppyhood long ago, and I was miserable to see in some sense his trust betrayed and to know that in the evening I might come back alone and leave him dead in Skye. All I could think of then and during the long wait while he was on the operating table was of past days spent with Jonnie, many of them seeming so long ago as to span a man's rather than a dog's lifetime. I stayed to help to give the anaesthetic; Jonnie was trusting but puzzled by the curious preparations, hating the stinking rubber mask that I had to hold over his face, but giving only one pathetic whimper of despair before he lost consciousness. Then for more than an hour I wandered aimlessly up and down the shore below that Skye village. The day was grey and heavy with coming snow, and a bitter little wind blew in from the sea and rustled the dead seaweed on the tideline. I thought of how I had nursed Jonnie through distemper twelve years before; of teaching that strangely woolly spaniel puppy to retrieve and to quarter the ground for game; of how once in his early prime he had, after an evening duck flight, swum out forty-one times through forming ice that skinned over behind him as he swam and returned forty-one times with a wigeon in his mouth; of how often his fleecy flank had formed a pillow for me in open boats; of the many times I had come back to Camusfeàrna knowing that his welcome was awaiting me.

I have more than once tried to analyse this apparently deliberate form of self-torture that seems common to so many people in face of the extinction of a valued life, human or animal, and it springs, I think, from a negation of death, as if by summoning and arranging these subjective images one were in some way cheating the objective fact. It is, I believe, an entirely instinctive process, and the distress it brings with it is an incidental, a by-product, rather than a masochistic end.

But Jonnie did not die then. When I was allowed to go into the surgery he was conscious but too weak to move; only his blood-stained tail fluttered faintly, and all through the cruelly long and jolting journey home he lay utterly motionless, so that again and again I felt for his heart to make sure that he was still living. It was night before we reached Druimfiaclach, and the snow had begun, piling in thick before an icy north wind. Morag, whose whole heart had gone out to Jonnie from the first day he had come to Druimfiaclach, had endured a longer suspense than I, but though Jonnie was living he yet seemed very near to death. For many days there was little change; either Morag or I would sit up with him all through the night and tend his helplessness. His very cleanliness provided the worst problem of all; while he was too weak to move he would yet endure agonies rather than relieve himself indoors, so that he had to be carried outside in that bitter weather and supported to keep him upright while one or other of us screened him with a blanket from the wind and the snow.

Jonnie recovered from the operation as only a dog of his tremendous physique could do, and for six months his prime was miraculously restored, but in the autumn the cancer came back, and this time it was inoperable. Morag wrote to tell me of this, and to ask my assent to his death before the pain should start and while he was as yet happy and active. I agreed with a heavy heart, not least because I knew that to make the arrangements for his death while he felt himself sound in wind and limb would be a torture to Morag; but, weighed down at the time by a bitter human loss, I lacked the courage to go north and take an active hand in things myself. Jonnie received the vet with enthusiasm, and Morag cuddled Jonnie while he received a lethal injection. He gave no sign of feeling the needle, and she only knew that he was dead by the increasing heaviness of his head in her hand. Morag had given her heart to Jonnie as she had to no other animal in her life, and for her that moment of betrayal must have been like death itself.

I have never had another dog since Jonnie; I have not wanted one, and shall not, perhaps, until I am of an age that would not be congenial to an active dog.

# 6

While I was quite clear that I did not want to own another dog, and that Jonnie's death had in some sense ended an overlong chapter of nostalgia in my life, it was, I think, autumn and winter's days at Camusfeàrna that with their long hours of darkness made me crave for some animal life about the house.

Autumn begins for me with the first day on which the stags roar. Because the wind is nearly always in the west, and because the fences keep the bulk of the stags to the higher ground above Camusfeàrna, behind the low mass of the littoral hills, I hear them first on the steep slopes of Skye across the Sound, a wild, haunting primordial sound that belongs so utterly to the north that I find it difficult to realize that stags must roar, too, in European woodlands where forests are composed of trees instead of windswept mountain slopes. It is the first of the cold weather that leads in the rut, and the milder the season the later the stag breaks out, but it is usually during the last ten days of September. Often the first of the approaching fall comes with a night frost and clear, sharp, blue days, with the bracken turning red, the rowan berries already scarlet, and the ground hardening underfoot; so garish are the berries and the turning leaves in sunshine that in Glengarry a post-office-red pillar-box standing alone by the roadside merges, for a few weeks, anonymously into its background.

When the full moon comes at this season I have sat on the hillside at night and listened to the stags answering one another from hill to hill all round the horizon, a horizon of steel-grey peaks among moving silver clouds and the sea gleaming white at their feet, and high under the stars the drifting chorus of the wild geese flying southward out of the night and north.

On such a night, before I ever came to Camusfeàrna, I slept

beside a lochan on the Island of Soay, and it was the wild swans that called overhead and came spiralling down, ghostly in the moonlight, to alight with a long rush of planing feet on the lochan's surface. All through the night I heard their restless murmur as they floated light as spume upon the peat-dark waves, and their soft voices became blended with my dreams, so that the cool convex of their breasts became my pillow. At dawn their calling awoke me as they gathered to take flight, and as they flew southward I watched the white pulse of their wings until I could see them no longer. To me they were a symbol, for I was saying good-bye to Soay, that had been my island.

Winters at Camusfeàrna vary as they do elsewhere, but at their worst they are very bad indeed. When one gets up in darkness to the lashing of rain on the window-panes and the roar of the waterfall rising even above the howl of wind and tide; when the green field is scattered with wide pools that are in part floodwater but in part the overspill of waves whose spray batters the house itself; when day by day the brief hours of light are filled with dark scudding clouds and blown spindrift from the crashing shore, one begins to know the meaning of an isolation that in summer seemed no more than an empty word.

The burn fills and runs ramping high through the trunks and limbs of the alders, carrying racing masses of debris that lodge among their branches, and through the roaring of its passage comes the hollow undertone of rolling, bumping boulders swept along its bed by the weight of white water pouring from the rock ravine. It was in such a spate as this that the bridge was washed away in 1953, and then for five years the only alternative when the burn was full, to braving that crazy crossing clinging to a stretched rope was the long route to Druimfiaclach by the near side of its course, more than two miles of steep ground and sodden peat bog. Since the gales tear in from the south-west, funnelling themselves between the Hebridean islands into demoniac fury, the wind is usually at one's back on the upward journey, but it is in one's face coming down, and there have been nights returning from Druimfiaclach, torchless and in utter darkness, when I have taken to my hands and knees to avoid being swept away like a leaf.

There is, of course, another side to the picture, the bright log fire whose flames are reflected on the pine-panelled walls, the warmth and nursery security of that kitchen sitting-room with the steady reassuring hiss of its Tilley lamps as a foreground sound to the tumult of sea and sky without; and, in the old days, Jonnie asleep conventionally on the hearth rug. But Jonnie was gone, and all too often the other pigments, as it were, for this picture were lacking too. The supply of paraffin would run out during the short dark days; candles became unobtainable within a hundred road miles; there was not space to store enough dry wood to keep the house heated. Until this year, when I installed a Calor gas stove, I cooked entirely by Primus, requiring both methylated spirits and paraffin, and when the house was without either and it would require an hour to coax a kettle to the boil over a fire of wet wood, there have been days when a kind of apathy would settle down upon me, days when I would rather creep back to bed than face the physical difficulties of life awake. When stores do arrive they have still to be lugged down the hill from Druimfia-clach, a long stumbling journey with an unbalancing load upon one's back and sleet slashing at one's face and eyes; and above all I remember in the past the chill, inhospitable familiarity of wet clothes, wet clothes hanging in rows above a barely-smouldering fire and with as much hope of drying as the sea itself.

Sometimes there is snow, though it rarely lies deep at Camus-feàrna itself, as the house can be no more than six feet above sea-level. But I remember one winter when it did, and it lay thick round the house and came swirling in gustily from the sea on the morning that I had to depart for the south. I left the house before dawn to catch the mail Land Rover at Druimfiaclach, the darkness only just relieved by the white wastes that ran right down to the waves. I remember that morning particularly because it was the worst, the most nightmarish climb that I have ever made to Druimfiaclach. The weather had been so bitter that the burn was low, frozen far up its course on the snow peak, and I had thought that with the aid of the rope I should be able to ford it in long seamen's thigh-boots. I saw my mistake when I reached it, but with a hundredweight or so of luggage on my back I preferred to try rather than to take the long route round through the bogs. Both my boots filled in the first couple of yards, but the house was locked and time was short, and I struggled across, soaked at last to the waist, hanging on to the rope with my legs swept downstream by the piling weight of snow water. At the far side of the burn I sat down and emptied my boots of a full two gallons apiece. I tried to wring out my trousers, but when, my teeth chattering like castanets, I got the boots back on again, the feet filled slowly with an icy trickle of water that still coursed down my legs. When I began the steep climb from the burn the burden on my shoulders seemed to have doubled its weight. I slipped and stumbled and panted up dim glaucous slopes that had lost all landmarks, and at the top of the first steep I was caught in a swirling, flurrying blizzard of wind and snowflakes, that spun me round in unsteady pirouettes and left me dizzy and directionless.

For all the hundreds of times that I had travelled this path in daylight and in darkness, I could recognize no curve nor contour in the merging grey pillows about me, and the snow was coming down so thick that it blanketed even the sound of the eighty-foot falls in the gorge. I had always been frightened of a stranger slipping down that precipice in the dark; now I was so hopelessly lost that I began to be afraid of it myself, and to avoid the ravine I began to climb upward over the steepest ground I could find. I reeled into snowdrifts and fell flat on my face, my feet slipped on boulders hidden by the snow and the weight on my shoulders threw me over backwards, and all the time the blizzard beat at me, slapping the wet snow into my eyes and ears, down my neck, and into every crevice of my clothing. Once I stumbled on a stag, snow-blanketed in the shelter of a rock; he was up and away and gone into snowflakes that were driving horizontally across the hill-side, and for some minutes I took his place under the rock, the stag smell pungent in my nostrils, wondering how I had ever thought Camusfeàrna a paradise. It took me an hour and a half to reach Druimfiaclach that morning, and when I got there it was more by accident than judgment. This was the prelude to an hour's travel by launch and four hours in the train to Inverness before starting the true journey south.

Yet it is the best and the worst that one remembers, seldom the mediocrities that lie between and demand no attention. At the end of struggles such as those there has always been the warmth and hospitality of the long-suffering MacKinnon house-hold, Morag's scones and gingerbread, and cups of tea that have tasted like nectar; and there have been fair winter days at Camusfeàrna, when the sea lay calm as summer and the sun shone on the snow-covered hills of Skye, and I would not change my home for any in the world.

But after Jonnie's death it seemed, as I have said, a little lifeless, and I began in a desultory way to review in my mind various animals, other than dogs, that might keep me company. Having been encouraged in my childhood to keep pets ranging from hedgehogs to herons, I had a considerable list available for screen-ing, but after a while I realized reluctantly that none of these creatures with which I was familiar would meet my present requirements. I put the idea aside, and for a year I thought no more of it.

Early in the New Year of 1956 I travelled with Wilfred Thesiger to spend two months or so among the little known Marsh Arabs, or Ma'dan, of southern Iraq. By then it had crossed my mind, though with no great emphasis, that I should like to keep an otter instead of a dog, and that Camusfeàrna, ringed by water a stone's throw from its door, would be an eminently suitable spot for this experiment. I had mentioned this casually to Wilfred soon after the outset of our journey, and he, as casually, had replied that I had better get one in the Tigris marshes before I came home, for there they were as common as mosquitoes, and were often tamed by the Arabs.

We spent the better part of those two months squatting cross-legged in the bottom of a *tarada* or war canoe, travelling in a leisurely, timeless way between the scattered reed-built villages of the great delta marsh both west of the Tigris and between the river and the Persian frontier; and towards the end of our journey I did acquire an otter cub.

It is difficult to find new words in which to tell of happenings that one has already described; if one has done one's best the first time one can only do worse on the second attempt, when the freshness of the image has faded; and that must be my excuse and apology for quoting here part of what I wrote of that otter cub, Chahala, soon afterwards; that and the fact that she is an integral and indispensable part of my narrative.

We were sitting after dark in a *mudhif*, or sheikh's guest house, on a mud island in the marshes, and I was brooding over the delinquency of the chatelaine, a bossy old harridan of a woman who had angered me.

'I felt an unreasonable hatred for that witless woman with her show of bustle and competence, and contempt that not even her avarice had mastered her stupidity. Thinking of these things, I was not trying to understand the conversation around me when the words "*celb mai*" caught my ear. "What was that about otters?" I asked Thesiger.

'"I think we've got you that otter cub you said you wanted. This fellow comes from that village half a mile away; he says he's had one for about ten days. Very small and sucks milk from a bottle. Do you want it?"

'The otter's owner said he would fetch it and be back in half an hour or so. He got up and went out; through the entrance of the *mudhif* I could see his canoe glide away silently over the star-reflecting water.

'Presently he returned carrying the cub, came across into the firelight and put it down on my knee as I sat cross-legged. It looked up and chittered at me gently. It was the size of a kitten or a squirrel, still a little unsteady on its legs, with a stiff-looking tapering tail the length of a pencil, and it exhaled a wholly delightful malty smell. It rolled over on its back, displaying a round furry stomach and the soles of four webbed feet.

'"Well," said Thesiger, "do you want her?" I nodded. "How much are you prepared to pay for her?"

'"Certainly more than they would ask."

'"I'm not going to pay some ridiculous price – it's bad for prestige. We'll take her if they'll sell her for a reasonable price, if not, we'll get one somewhere else."

'I said, "Let's make certain of getting this one; we're near the end of the time now, and we may not get another chance. And after all the prestige doesn't matter so much, as this is your last visit to the marshes." I saw this fascinating little creature eluding me for the sake of a few shillings' worth of prestige, and the negotiations seemed to me interminable.

'In the end we bought the cub for five dinar, the price to include the rubber teat and the filthy but precious bottle from which she was accustomed to drink. Bottles are a rarity in the marshes.

'Most infant animals are engaging, but this cub had more charm per cubic inch of her tiny body than all the young animals I had ever seen. Even now I cannot write about her without a pang.

'I cut a collar for her from the strap of my field-glasses – a difficult thing, for her head was no wider than her neck – and tied six foot of string to this so as to retain some permanent contact with her if at any time she wandered away from me. Then I slipped her inside my shirt, and she snuggled down at once in a security of warmth and darkness that she had not known since she was reft from her mother. I carried her like that through her short life; when she was awake her head would peer wonderingly out from the top of the pullover, like a kangaroo from its mother's pouch, and when she was asleep she slept as otters like to, on her back with her webbed feet in the air. When she was awake her voice was a bird-like chirp, but in her dreams she would give a wild little cry on three falling notes, poignant and desolate. I called her Chahala, after the river we had left the day before, and because those syllables were the nearest one could write to the sound of her sleeping cry.

'I slept fitfully that night; all the pi-dogs of Dibin seemed to bark at my ears, and I dared not in any case let myself fall into too sound a sleep lest I should crush Chahala, who now snuggled in my armpit. Like all otters, she was "house-trained" from the beginning, and I had made things easy for her by laying my sleeping bag against the wall of the *mudhif*, so that she could step straight out on the patch of bare earth between the reed columns. This she did at intervals during the night, backing into the very farthest corner to produce, with an expression of infinite concentration, a tiny yellow caterpillar of excrement. Having inspected this, with evident satisfaction of a job well done, she would clamber up my shoulder and chitter gently for her bottle. This she preferred to drink lying on her back and holding the bottle between her paws as do bear cubs, and when she had finished sucking she would fall sound asleep with the teat still in her mouth and a beatific expression on her baby face.

'She accepted me as her parent from the moment that she first fell asleep in my pullover, and never once did she show fear of anything or anyone, but it was as a parent that I failed her, for I had neither the knowledge nor the instinct of her mother, and when she died it was because of my ignorance. Meanwhile this tragedy, so small but so complete, threw no shadow on her brief life, and as the days went by she learned to know her name and to play a little as a kitten does, and to come scuttling along at my heels if I could find dry land to walk on, for she hated to get her feet wet. When she had had enough of walking she would chirp and paw at my legs until I squatted down so that she could dive head first into the friendly darkness inside my pullover; sometimes she would at once fall asleep in that position, head downward with the tip of her pointed tail sticking out at the top. The Arabs called her my daughter, and used to ask me when I had last given her suck.

'I soon found that she was restrictive of movement and activity.

Carried habitually inside my pullover, she made an *enceinte*-looking bulge which collected a whole village round me as soon as I set foot outside the door; furthermore I could no longer carry my camera round my neck as I did normally, for it bumped against her body as I walked.

'One evening Thesiger and I discussed the prospect of weaning Chahala. We both felt she should be old enough to eat solid food, and I felt that her rather skinny little body would benefit by something stronger than buffalo milk. However, I underestimated the power of instinct, for I thought that she would not connect flesh or blood with edibility and would need to be introduced to the idea very gradually. The best way to do this, I decided, was to introduce a few drops of blood into her milk to get her used to the taste. This proved to be extraordinarily naive, for while I was holding the bodies of two decapitated sparrows and trying to drip a little blood from them into her feeding bottle she suddenly caught the scent of the red meat and made a savage grab for the carcasses. I think that if I had not stopped her she would have crunched up bone and all with those tiny needle-like teeth, and we took this as evidence that she had already been introduced by her mother to adult food. I took the carcasses from her, much to her evident fury; and when I gave her the flesh from the breasts cut up small she wolfed it down savagely and went questing round for more.

'"Finish with milk," said Amara, our chief canoe-boy, with a gesture of finality, "finish, finish; she is grown up now." And it seemed so, but, alas, she was not.

'A week later we shot a buff-backed heron for her, and she wolfed the shredded flesh avidly. It was the last food that she ate.

'It was very cold that night. Over my head was a gap in the reed matting of the roof through which the stars showed bright and unobscured, but a thin wind that seemed as chill as the tinkle of icicles rustled the dry reeds at the foot of the wall, and I slept fitfully. Chahala was restless and would not stay still in my sleeping-bag; I did not know that she was dying, and I was impatient with her. In the morning I took her to a spit of dry land beyond the edge of the village to let her walk, and only then I realized that she was very ill. She would not move, but lay looking up at me pathetically, and when I picked her up again she instantly sought the warm darkness inside my pullover.

'We made an hour's journey through flower-choked waterways in low green marsh, and stopped at another big island village. It was plain to me when we landed that Chahala was dying. She was weak but restless, and inside the house she sought the dark corners between the reed columns and the matting walls. She lay belly downward, breathing fast and in obvious distress. Perhaps something in our huge medicine chest could have saved her, but we thought only of castor oil, for everything she had eaten the night before was still inside her. The oil had little effect, and though she sucked almost automatically from her bottle there was little life in her. I sat hopelessly beside her for a couple of hours when Thesiger came in from doctoring. "Better get out for a bit," he said. "I'll keep an eye on her. It's hell for you sitting in here all the time, and you can't do her any good. This is your last marsh village, and you may never see another."

'I went out, and remembered things that I had wanted to photograph and always postponed. Then I found that the shutter of my camera was broken, and I went back into the house.

'We left an hour later. When I felt the warmth of Chahala next to my shirt again I felt a moment's spurious comfort that she would live; but she would not stay there. She climbed out with a strength that surprised me, and stretched herself restlessly on the floor of the canoe, and I spread a handkerchief over my knees to make an awning of shade for her small fevered body. Once she called faintly, the little wild lonely cry that would come from her as she slept, and a few seconds after that I saw a shiver run through her body. I put my hand on her and felt the strange rigidity that comes in the instant following death; then she became limp under my touch.

' "She's dead," I said. I said it in Arabic, so that the boys would stop paddling.

'Thesiger said, "Are you sure?" and the boys stared unbelievingly. "Quite dead?" they asked it again and again. I handed her

75

to Thesiger; the body dropped from his hands like a miniature fur stole. "Yes," he said, "she's dead." He threw the body into the water, and it landed in the brilliant carpet of white and golden flowers and floated on its back with the webbed paws at its sides, as she had been used to sleep when she was alive.

'"Come on," said Thesiger. "Ru–hu–Ru–hu!" but the boys sat motionless, staring at the small corpse and at me, and Thesiger grew angry with them before they would move. Amara kept on looking back from the bows until at last we rounded the corner of a green reed-bed and she was out of sight.

'The sun shone on the white flowers, the blue kingfishers glinted low over them and the eagles wheeled overhead on the blue sky, but all of these seemed less living for me since Chahala was dead. I told myself that she was only one of thousands like her in these marshes, that are speared with the five-pointed trident, or shot, or taken as cubs to die slowly in more callous captivity, but she was dead and I was desolate. The fault lay with whoever, perhaps more than a million years ago, had first taken up the wild dog cub that clung to the body of its dead dam, and I wondered whether he too had in that half-animal brain been driven by the motives that in me were conscious.'

I fretted miserably over the death of Chahala, for she had convinced me utterly that it was an otter that I wanted as an animal companion at Camusfeàrna, and I felt that I had had my chance and wasted it. It was not until long afterwards that the probable cause of her death struck me. The Marsh Arabs drug fish with digitalis concealed in shrimp bait, and whereas the human system, or that of an adult buff-backed heron, might find the minute dose innocuous, the same quantity might be fatal to as young a creature as Chahala.

I had no more time in the marshes; Wilfred and I were to spend a few days in Basra before going on to pass the early summer among the pastoral tribes. But Chahala's death, which seemed to me like an end, was in fact a beginning.

# 7

The night that Chahala died we reached Al Azair, Ezra's tomb, on the Tigris. From there Wilfred Thesiger and I were both going to Basra to collect and answer our mail from Europe before setting off together again. At the Consulate-General at Basra we found that Wilfred's mail had arrived but that mine had not.

'I cabled to England, and when, three days later, nothing had happened, I tried to telephone. The call had to be booked twenty-four hours in advance, and could be arranged only for a single hour in the day, an hour during which, owing to the difference in time, no one in London was likely to be available. On the first day the line was out of order; on the second the exchange was closed for a religious holiday. On the third day there was another breakdown. I arranged to join Thesiger at Abd el Nebi's *mudhif* in a week's time, and he left.

'Two days before the date of our rendezvous I returned to the Consulate-General late in the afternoon, after several hours' absence, to find that my mail had arrived. I carried it to my bedroom to read, and there squatting on the floor were two Marsh Arabs; beside them lay a sack that squirmed from time to time.

'They handed me a note from Thesiger. "Here is your otter, a male and weaned. I feel you may want to take it to London – it would be a handful in the *tarada*. It is the one I originally heard of, but the sheikhs were after it, so they said it was dead. Give Ajram a letter to me saying it has arrived safely – he has taken Kathia's place . . ."'

With the opening of that sack began a phase of my life that in the essential sense has not yet ended, and may, for all I know, not end before I do. It is, in effect, a thraldom to otters, an otter fixation, that I have since found to be shared by most other people who have ever owned one.

The creature that emerged, not greatly disconcerted, from this sack on to the spacious tiled floor of the Consulate bedroom did not at that moment resemble anything so much as a very small medievally conceived dragon. From the head to the tip of the tail he was coated with symmetrical pointed scales of mud armour, between whose tips was visible a soft velvet fur like that of a chocolate-brown mole. He shook himself, and I half expected this aggressive camouflage to disintegrate into a cloud of dust, but it remained unaffected by his manoeuvre, and in fact it was not for another month that I contrived to remove the last of it and see him, as it were, in his true colours.

Yet even on that first day I recognized that he was an otter of a species that I had never seen in the flesh, resembling only a curious otter skin that I had bought from the Arabs in one of the marsh villages. Mijbil, as I called the new otter, after a sheikh with whom we had recently been staying and whose name had intrigued me with a conjured picture of a platypus-like creature, was, in fact, of a race previously unknown to science, and was at length christened by zoologists, from examination of the skin and of himself, *Lutrogale perspicillata maxwelli*, or Maxwell's otter. This circumstance, perhaps, influenced on my side the intensity of the emotional relationship between us, for I became, during a year of his constant and violently affectionate companionship, fonder of him than of almost any human being, and to write of him in the past tense makes me feel as desolate as one who has lost an only child. For a year and five days he was about my bed and my bath spying out all my ways, and though I now have another otter no whit less friendly and fascinating, there will never be another Mijbil.

For the first twenty-four hours Mijbil was neither hostile nor friendly; he was simply aloof and indifferent, choosing to sleep on the floor as far from my bed as possible, and to accept food and water as though they were things that had appeared before him without human assistance. The food presented a problem, for it did not immediately occur to me that the Marsh Arabs had almost certainly fed him on rice scraps only supplemented by such portions of fish as are inedible to humans. The Consul-General sent out a servant to buy fish, but this servant's return coincided with a visit from Robert Angorly, a British-educated Christian Iraqi who was the Crown Prince's game warden and entertained a passionate interest in natural history. Angorly told me that none of the fishes that had been bought was safe for an animal, for they had been poisoned with digitalis, which, though harmless to a human in this quantity, he felt certain would be dangerous to a young otter. He offered to obtain me a daily supply of fish that had been taken with nets, and thereafter he brought every day half a dozen or so small reddish fish from the Tigris. These Mijbil consumed with gusto, holding them upright between his forepaws, tail end uppermost, and eating them like a stick of Edinburgh rock, always with five crunches of the left-hand side of the jaw alternating with five crunches on the right.

It was fortunate that I had recently met Angorly, for otherwise Mijbil might at once have gone the way of Chahala and for the same reason. Angorly had called at the Consulate-General during the time that I had been waiting for my mail from Europe and had invited me to a day's duck shooting on the Crown Prince's fabulous marshes, an experience that nobody can ever have again, for now the hated Crown Prince is as dead as only a mob gone berserk could make him, and of my friend Angorly, whom I cannot believe ever to have taken much interest in anything political, there has been no word since the revolution.

The otter and I enjoyed the Consul-General's long-suffering hospitality for a fortnight. The second night Mijbil came on to my bed in the small hours and remained asleep in the crook of my knees until the servant brought tea in the morning, and during that day he began to lose his apathy and take a keen, much too keen, interest in his surroundings. I fashioned a collar, or rather a body-belt, for him, and took him on a lead to the bathroom, where for half an hour he went wild with joy in the water, plunging and rolling in it, shooting up and down the length of the bath underwater, and making enough slosh and splash for a hippo. This, I was to learn, is a characteristic of otters; every drop of water must be, so to speak, extended and spread about the place; a bowl must at once be overturned, or, if it will not overturn, be sat in and sploshed in until it overflows. Water must be kept on the move and made to do things; when static it is as wasted and provoking as a buried talent.

It was only two days later that he escaped from my bedroom as I entered it, and I turned to see his tail disappearing round the bend of the corridor that led to the bathroom. By the time I had caught up with him he was up on the end of the bath and fumbling at the chromium taps with his paws. I watched, amazed by this early exhibition of an intelligence I had not yet guessed; in less than a minute he had turned the tap far enough to produce a dribble of water, and, after a moment or two of distraction at his success, achieved the full flow. (He had, in fact, been fortunate to turn the tap the right way; on subsequent occasions he would as often as not try with great violence to screw it up still tighter, chittering with irritation and disappointment at its failure to cooperate.)

The Consulate had a big walled garden in which I exercised him, and, within it, a high-netted tennis court. In this enclosure I established after a few days that he would follow me without a lead and come to me when I called his name. By the end of a week he had accepted me in a relationship of dependence, and with this security established he began to display the principal otter characteristic of perpetual play. Very few species of animal habitually play after they are adult; they are concerned with eating, sleeping, or procreating, or with the means to one or other of these ends. But otters are one of the few exceptions to this rule; right through their lives they spend much of their time in play that does not even require a partner. In the wild state they will play alone for hours with any convenient floating object in the water, pulling it down to let it bob up again, or throwing it with a jerk of the head so that it lands with a splash and becomes a quarry to be pursued. No doubt in their holts they lie on their backs and play, too, as my otters have, with small objects that they can roll between their paws and pass from palm to palm, for at Camusfeàrna all the sea holts contain a profusion of small shells and round stones that can only have been carried in for toys.

Mij would spend hours shuffling a rubber ball round the room like a four-footed soccer player using all four feet to dribble the ball, and he could also throw it, with a powerful flick of the neck, to a surprising height and distance. These games he would play either by himself or with me, but the really steady play of an otter, the time-filling play born of a sense of well-being and a full stomach, seems to me to be when the otter lies on its back, and juggles with small objects between its paws. This they do with an extraordinarily concentrated absorption and dexterity, as though a conjuror were trying to perfect some trick, as though in this play there were some goal that the human observer could not guess. Later, marbles became Mij's favourite toys for this pastime – for pastime it is, without any anthropomorphizing – and he would lie on his back rolling two or more of them up and down his wide, flat belly without ever dropping one to the floor, or, with forepaws upstretched, rolling them between his palms for minutes on end.

Even during that first fortnight in Basra I learnt a lot of Mij's language, a language largely shared, I have discovered, by many other races of otter, though with curious variations in usage. The sounds are widely different in range. The simplest is the call note, which has been much the same in all the otters I have come across; it is a short, anxious, penetrating, though not loud, mixture between a whistle and a chirp. There is also a query, used at closer quarters; Mij would enter a room, for instance, and ask whether there was anyone in it by the word 'Ha!', uttered in a loud, harsh whisper. If he saw preparations being made to take him out or to the bath, he would stand at the door making a musical bubbling sound interspersed with chirps; but it was the chirp, in all its permutations and combinations of high and low, from the single querulous note to a continuous flow of chitter, that was Mij's main means of vocal communication. He had one other note unlike any of these, a high, snarling caterwaul, a sort of screaming wail, that meant unequivocally that he was very angry, and if provoked further would bite. He bit, in anger as opposed to nips in excitable play, four times during the year that I had him. Each of these occasions was memorable in the highest degree, though I was only once at the receiving end.

An otter's jaws are, of course, enormously powerful – indeed the whole animal is of strength almost unbelievable in a creature of its size – and those jaws are equipped with teeth to crunch into instant pulp fish heads that seem as hard as stone. Like a puppy that nibbles and gnaws one's hands because he has so few other outlets for his feelings, otters seem to find the use of their mouths the most natural outlet for expression; knowing as I do their enormous crushing power I can appreciate what efforts my otters have made to be gentle in play, but their playful nips are gauged, perhaps, to the sensitivity of an otter's, rather than a human, skin. Mij used to look hurt and surprised when scolded for what must have seemed to him the most meticulous gentleness, and though after a time he learned to be as soft mouthed as a sucking dove with me he remained all his life somewhat over-

excitably good-humoured and hail-fellow-well-bit with strangers.

The days passed peacefully at Basra, but I dreaded dismally the unpostponable prospect of transporting Mij to England, and to his ultimate destination, Camusfeàrna. BOAC would not fly livestock at all, and there was then no other line to London. Finally I booked a Trans-World flight to Paris, with a doubtful

Air France booking on the same evening to London. Trans-World insisted that Mij should be packed into a box of not more than eighteen inches square, and that this box must be personal luggage, to be carried on the floor at my feet.

Mij's body was at that time perhaps a little over a foot long and his tail another foot; the designing of this box employed many anxious hours for myself and the ever-helpful Robert Angorly, and finally he had the container constructed by craftsmen of his acquaintance. The box was delivered on the afternoon before my departure on a 9.15 p.m. flight. It was zinc-lined, and divided into two compartments, one for sleeping and one for the relief of nature, and it appeared to my inexperienced eye as nearly ideal as could be contrived.

Dinner was at eight, and I thought that it would be as well to put Mij into the box an hour before we left, so that he would become accustomed to it before the jolting of the journey began to upset him. I manoeuvred him into it, not without difficulty, and he seemed peaceful when I left him in the dark for a hurried meal.

But when I returned, with only barely time for the Consulate car to reach the airport for the flight, I was confronted with an appalling spectacle. There was complete silence from inside the box, but from its airholes and the chinks around the hinged lid blood had trickled and dried on the white wood. I whipped off the padlock and tore open the lid, and Mij, exhausted and blood-spattered, whimpered and tried to climb up my leg. He had torn the zinc lining to shreds, scratching his mouth, his nose and his paws, and had left it jutting in spiky ribbons all around the walls and the floor of the box. When I had removed the last of it so that there were no cutting edges left, it was just ten minutes until the time of the flight, and the airport was five miles distant. It was hard to bring myself to put the miserable Mij back into that box, that now represented to him a torture chamber, but I forced myself to do it, slamming the lid down on my fingers as I closed it before he could make his escape. Then began a journey the like of which I hope I shall never know again.

I sat in the back of the car with the box beside me as the Arab driver tore through the streets of Basra like a ricocheting bullet. Donkeys reared, bicycles swerved wildly, out in the suburbs goats stampeded and poultry found unguessed powers of flight. Mij cried unceasingly in the box, and both of us were hurled to and fro and up and down like drinks in a cocktail shaker. Exactly as we drew to a screeching stop before the airport entrance I heard a splintering sound from the box beside me, and saw Mij's nose force up the lid. He had summoned all the strength in his small body and torn one of the hinges clean out of the wood.

The aircraft was waiting to take off; as I was rushed through the customs by infuriated officials I was trying all the time to hold down the lid of the box with one hand, and with the other, using a screwdriver purloined from the driver, to force back the screws into the splintered wood. But I knew that it could be no more than a temporary measure at best, and my imagination boggled at the thought of the next twenty-four hours.

It was perhaps my only stroke of fortune that the seat booked for me was at the extreme front of the aircraft, so that I had a bulkhead before me instead of another seat. The other passengers, a remarkable cross-section of the orient and occident, stared curiously as the dishevelled late arrival struggled up the gangway with a horrifyingly vocal Charles Addams-like box, and knowing for just what a short time it could remain closed I was on tenterhooks to see what manner of passenger would be my immediate neighbour. I had a moment of real dismay when I saw her to be an elegantly dressed and *soignée* American woman in early middle age. Such a one, I thought, would have little sympathy or tolerance for the draggled and dirty otter cub that would so soon and so inevitably be in her midst. For the moment the lid held, and as I sat down and fastened my safety belt there seemed to be a temporary silence from within.

The port engines roared, and then the starboard and the aircraft trembled and teetered against the tug of her propellers, and then we were taxiing out to take off, and I reflected that whatever was to happen now there could be no escape from it, for the next stop was Cairo. Ten minutes later we were flying westwards over the great marshes that had been Mij's home, and peering downward into the dark I could set the glint of their waters beneath the moon.

I had brought a briefcase full of old newspapers and a parcel of fish, and with these scant resources I prepared myself to withstand a siege. I arranged newspapers to cover all the floor around my feet, rang for the air hostess, and asked her to keep the fish in a cool place. I have retained the most profound admiration for that air hostess, and in subsequent sieges and skirmishes with otters in public places I have found my thoughts turning towards her as a man's mind turns to water in desert wastes. She was the very queen of her kind. I took her into my confidence; the events of the last half hour together with the prospect of the next twenty-four had shaken my equilibrium a little, and I daresay I was not too coherent, but she took it all in her graceful sheer nylon stride, and she received the ill-wrapped fish into her shapely hands as though I were travelling royalty depositing a jewel case with her for safe keeping. Then she turned and spoke with her country-woman on my left. Would I not prefer, she then enquired, to have my pet on my knee? The animal would surely feel happier there, and my neighbour had no objection. I could have kissed her hand in the depth of my gratitude. But, not knowing otters, I was quite unprepared for what followed.

I unlocked the padlock and opened the lid, and Mij was out like a flash. He dodged my fumbling hands with an eel-like wriggle and disappeared at high speed down the fuselage of the aircraft. As I tried to get into the gangway I could follow his progress among the passengers by a wave of disturbance amongst them not unlike that caused by the passage of a stoat through a hen run. There were squawks and shrieks and a flapping of travelling-coats, and halfway down the fuselage a woman stood up on her seat screaming out, 'A rat! A rat!' Then the air hostess reached her, and within a matter of seconds she was seated again and smiling benignly. That goddess, I believe, could have controlled a panic-stricken crowd single-handed.

By now I was in the gangway myself, and, catching sight of Mij's tail disappearing beneath the legs of a portly white-turbaned

Indian, I tried a flying tackle, landing flat on my face. I missed Mij's tail, but found myself grasping the sandalled foot of the Indian's female companion; furthermore my face was inexplicably covered in curry. I staggered up babbling an inarticulate apology, and the Indian gave me a long silent stare, so utterly expressionless that even in my hypersensitive mood I could deduce from it no meaning whatsoever. I was, however, glad to observe that something, possibly the curry, had won over the bulk of my fellow passengers, and that they were regarding me now as a harmless clown rather than as a dangerous lunatic. The air hostess stepped into the breach once more.

'Perhaps,' she said with the most charming smile, 'it would be better if you resumed your seat, and I will find the animal and bring it to you.' She would probably have said the same had Mij been an escaped rogue elephant. I explained that Mij, being lost and frightened, might bite a stranger, but she did not think so. I returned to my seat.

I heard the ripple of flight and pursuit passing up and down the body of the aircraft behind me, but I could see little. I was craning my neck back over the seat trying to follow the hunt when suddenly I heard from my feet a distressed chitter of recognition and welcome, and Mij bounded on to my knee and began to nuzzle my face and neck. In all the strange world of the aircraft I was the only familiar thing to be found, and in that first spontaneous return was sown the seed of the absolute trust that he accorded me for the rest of his life.

For the next hour or two he slept in my lap, descending from time to time for copious evacuations upon the newspaper at my feet, and each time I had, with an unrehearsed legerdemain, to spirit this out of sight and replace it with fresh newspaper. Whenever he appeared restless I rang for fish and water, for I had a feeling that, like the story-teller of the Arabian Nights, if I failed to keep him entertained retribution would fall upon me.

Otters are extremely bad at doing nothing. That is to say that they cannot, as a dog does, lie still and awake; they are either asleep or entirely absorbed in play or other activity. If there is no acceptable toy, or if they are in a mood of frustration, they will, apparently with the utmost good humour, set about laying the land waste. There is, I am convinced, something positively provoking to an otter about order and tidiness in any form, and the greater the state of confusion that they can create about them the more contented they feel. A room is not properly habitable to them until they have turned everything upside down; cushions must be thrown to the floor from sofas and armchairs, books pulled out of bookcases, wastepaper baskets overturned and the rubbish spread as widely as possible, drawers opened and contents shovelled out and scattered. The appearance of such a room where an otter has been given free rein resembles nothing so much as the aftermath of a burglar's hurried search for some minute and valuable object that he has believed to be hidden. I had never really appreciated the meaning of the word ransacked until I saw what an otter could do in this way.

This aspect of an otter's behaviour is certainly due in part to an intense inquisitiveness that belongs traditionally to a mongoose, but which would put any mongoose to shame. An otter must find out everything and have a hand in everything; but most of all he must know what lies inside any man-made container or beyond any man-made obstruction. This, combined with an uncanny mechanical sense of how to get things open – a sense, indeed of statics and dynamics in general – makes it much safer to remove valuables altogether rather than to challenge the otter's ingenuity by inventive obstructions. But in those days I had all this to learn.

We had been flying for perhaps five hours, and must, I thought, be nearing Cairo, when one of these moods descended upon Mijbil. It opened comparatively innocuously, with an assault upon the newspapers spread carefully round my feet, and in a minute or two the place looked like a street upon which royalty has been given a ticker-tape welcome. Then he turned his attentions to the box, where his sleeping compartment was filled with fine wood-shavings. First he put his head and shoulders in and began to throw these out backwards at enormous speed; then he got in bodily and lay on his back, using all four feet in a pedalling motion to hoist out the remainder. I was doing my best to cope with the litter, but it was like a ship's pumps working against a leak too great for them, and I was hopelessly behind in the race when he turned his attention to my neighbour's canvas Trans-World travel bag on the floor beside him. The zipper gave him pause for no more than seconds; by chance, in all likelihood, he yanked it back and was in head first, throwing out magazines, handkerchiefs, gloves, bottles of pills, tins of ear-plugs and all the personal paraphernalia of long-distance air travel. By the grace of God my neighbour was sleeping profoundly; I managed, unobserved, to haul Mij out by the tail and cram the things back somehow. I hoped that she might leave the aircraft at Cairo, before the outrage was discovered, and to my infinite relief she did so. I was still grappling with Mij when the instruction lights came on as we circled the city, and then we were down on the tarmac with forty minutes to wait.

I think it was at Cairo that I realized what a complex and – to me at that time – unpredictable creature I had acquired. I left the aircraft last, and during all the time that we were grounded he was no more trouble than a well-behaved Pekinese dog. I put the lead on him and exercised him round the edge of the airfield; there were jet aircraft landing and taking off with an appalling din all around us, but he gave no sign of noticing them at all. He trotted along at my side, stopping as a dog does to investigate small smells in the grass, and when I went into the refreshment room for a drink he sat down at my feet as if this were the only life to which he was accustomed.

My troubles really began at Paris, an interminable time later. Mij had slept from time to time, but I had not closed an eye, and it was by now more than thirty-six hours since I had even dozed. I had to change airports, and, since I knew that Mij could slip his body strap with the least struggle, there was no alternative to putting him back into his box. In its present form, however, the box was useless, for one hinge was dangling unattached from the lid.

Half an hour out from Paris I rang for the last time for fish and water, and explained my predicament to the air hostess. She went forward to the crew's quarters, and returned after a few minutes saying that one of the crew would come and nail down the box and rope it for me. She warned me at the same time that Air France's regulations differed from those of Trans-World, and that from Paris onward the box would have to travel freight and not in the passenger portion of the aircraft.

Mij was sleeping on his back inside my jacket, and I had to steel myself to betray his trust, to force him back into that hateful prison and listen to his pathetic cries as he was nailed up in what had become to me suddenly reminiscent of a coffin. There is a little-understood factor that is responsible for the deaths of many wild animals in shipment; it is generally known as 'travel shock', and the exact causes have yet to be determined. Personally I do not question that it is closely akin to the 'voluntary dying' of which Africans have long been reputed to be capable; life has become no longer tolerable, and the animal *chooses*, quite unconsciously no doubt, to die. It was travel shock that I was afraid might kill Mijbil inside that box, which to him represented a circumstance more terrible than any he had experienced, and I would be unable even to give him the reassuring smell of my hand through the breathing-holes.

We disembarked in torrential rain that formed puddles and lakes all over the tarmac and had reduced my thin, semi-tropical suit to a sodden pulp before even I had entered the bus that was to take me and the three other London-bound passengers across Paris to Orly Airport. I clung to the unwieldy box all this time, in the hope of reducing Mij's unavoidable period of despair after I became separated from it; together with the personal impedimenta that I could not well lose sight of it rendered movement almost impossible, and I felt near to voluntary death myself.

After an hour's wait at Orly, during which Mij's cries had given place to a terrifying silence, I and my three companions were hustled into an aircraft. Mij was wrested from me and disappeared into the darkness on a luggage transporter.

When we arrived at Amsterdam instead of London the company was profusely apologetic. There was no flight to London for a further fifty-five minutes.

I had lost sight of Mij's box altogether and no one seemed to have a very clear idea of what had happened to any of the luggage belonging to the four London-bound passengers. A helpful official suggested that it might still be in Paris, as it must be clearly labelled London and not Amsterdam.

I went to the Air France office and let the tattered shreds of my self-control fly to the winds. In my soaking and dishevelled condition I cannot have cut a very impressive figure, but my anger soared above these handicaps like an eagle on the wind. I said that I was transporting to London a live animal worth many thousands of pounds, that unless it was traced immediately it would die, and I would sue the company and broadcast their inefficiency throughout the world. The official was under crossfire, for at my elbow an American business man was also threatening legal action. When the shindy was at its height another official arrived and said calmly that our luggage was now aboard a BEA plane due for take-off in seven minutes, and would we kindly take our seats in the bus.

We deflated slowly. Muttering, 'I guess I'm going to cast my personal eyes on that baggage before I get airborne again. They can't make a displaced person out of me', my American companion spoke for all us waifs. So we cast our personal eyes into the freight compartment, and there was Mij's box, quite silent in a corner.

It was the small hours of the morning when we reached London Airport. I had cabled London from Amsterdam, and there was a hired car to meet me. The box and all my luggage had been loaded on to the waiting car and we were on the last lap of the journey. What meant still more to me was that from the box there now came a faint enquiring chitter and a rustle of wood shavings.

Mijbil had in fact displayed a characteristic shared, I believe, by many animals; an apparent step, as it were, on the road to travel-shock death, but in fact a powerful buffer against it. Many animals seem to me to be able to go into a deep sleep, a coma, almost, as a voluntary act independent of exhaustion; it is an escape mechanism that comes into operation when the animal's inventiveness in the face of adversity has failed to ameliorate its circumstances. I have seen it very occasionally in trapped animals; an Arctic fox in Finmark, captive by the leg for no more than an hour, a badger in a Surrey wood, a common house mouse in a box trap. It is, of course, almost a norm, too, of animals kept in too cramped quarters in zoos and in pet stores. I came to recognize it later in Mijbil when he travelled in cars, a thing he hated; after a few minutes of frenzy he would curl himself into a tight ball and banish entirely the distasteful world about him.

On that first day that he arrived in England he had, I think, been in just such a barricaded state ever since the lid of the box was nailed down before reaching Paris; back, for all one may know, among the familiar scenes of his Tigris swamps, or perhaps in a negative, imageless world where the medulla had taken over respiration and the forebrain rested in a state bordering upon catalepsy.

He was wide awake once more by the time we reached my flat, and when I had the driver paid off and the door closed behind me I felt a moment of deep emotional satisfaction, almost of triumph, that I had after all brought back a live otter cub from Iraq to London, and that Camusfeàrna was less than six hundred miles distant from me.

I prised open the lid of the box, and Mijbil clambered out into my arms to greet me with a frenzy of affection that I felt I had hardly merited.

# 8

I lived at that time in a studio flat near to Olympia, one large room with a sleeping gallery that opened on to the garage roof, and penthouse premises at the back containing kitchen, bathroom and box-room, each of diminutive size and resembling a divided corridor. Despite the absence of a garden, these unconventional premises held certain advantages for an otter, for the garage roof eliminated the normal difficulties of keeping a house-trained animal in a London flat, and the box-room opening from the bathroom provided quarters in which at any time he might be left for short periods with all his essential requirements. But just how short those periods would be – a maximum of four or five hours – had never struck me until Mij had already become the centre point round which, eccentrically, revolved my life. Otters that have been reared by human beings demand human company, much affection, and constant cooperative play; without these things they quickly become unhappy, and for the most part they are tiresome in direct ratio to their discontent. They can be trying, too, out of sheer inquisitiveness and exuberance of spirits, but not in the seemingly calculated way that is born of deprivation.

The spacious tile-floored bedroom of the Consulate-General at Basra, with its minimum of inessential furniture or bric-a-brac, had done little to prepare me for the problems that my crowded and vulnerable studio would present in relation to Mijbil. Exhausted as he was that first night, he had not been out of his box for five minutes before he set out with terrifying enthusiasm to explore his new quarters. I had gone to the kitchen to find fish for him, expected by prearrangement with my charlady, but I had hardly got there before I heard the first crash of breaking china in the room behind me. The fish and the bath solved the problem temporarily, for when he had eaten he went wild with joy in the water and romped ecstatically for a full half hour, but it was clear that the flat would require considerable alteration if it was to remain a home for both of us. Meanwhile sleep seemed long overdue, and I saw only one solution; I laid a sleeping-bag on the sofa, and anchored Mij to the sofa-leg by his lead.

I have never been able fully to make up my mind whether certain aspects of otter behaviour merely chance to resemble that of human beings, or whether, in the case of animals as young as Mij was, there is actual mimicry of the human foster parent. Mij, anyway, seemed to regard me closely as I composed myself on my back with a cushion under my head; then, with a confiding air of knowing exactly what to do, he clambered up beside me and worked his body down into the sleeping-bag until he lay flat on his back inside it with his head on the cushion beside mine and his fore-paws in the air. In this position, such an attitude as a child devises for its teddy-bear in bed, Mij heaved an enormous sigh and was instantly asleep.

There is, in fact, much about otters that encourages humans to a facile anthropomorphizing. A dry otter at play is an animal that might have been specifically designed to please a child; they look like 'invented' animals, and are really much more like Giovannetti's 'Max' than anything else, a comparison that has instantly struck many people upon seeing my otters for the first time – the same short legs, the same tubby, furry torso, vast whiskers and clownish good humour. In the water they take on quite a different aspect and personality, supple as an eel, fast as lightning and graceful as a ballet dancer, but very few people have watched them for long below the surface, and I have yet to see a zoo that gives its otters a glass-sided tank – a spectacle that I believe would steal the show from the whole aquarium.

Mij and I remained in London for nearly a month, while, as my landlord put it, the studio came to look like a cross between a monkey-house and a furniture repository. The garage roof was fenced in, and a wire gate fitted to the gallery stairs, so that he could occasionally be excluded from the studio itself; the upstairs telephone was enclosed in a box (whose fastening he early learned to undo); my dressing-table was cut off from him by a wire flap hinging from the ceiling, and the electric light wires were enclosed in tunnels of hardboard that gave the place the appearance of a power-house.

All these precautions were entirely necessary, for if Mij thought that he had been excluded for too long, more especially from visitors whose acquaintance he wished to make, he would set about laying waste with extraordinary invention. No amount of forethought that I could muster was ever able to forestall his genius; there was always something that I had overlooked, something that could be made to speak with a crash for his mood of frustration, and it did not take me long to learn that prophylaxis was more convenient than treatment.

There was nothing haphazard about the demonstrations he planned; into them went all the patience and ingenuity of his remarkable brain and all the agility of his muscular little body. One evening, for example, after the contractors had departed for the third or fourth time, leaving, as I thought, an otter-proof situation at last, I had confined Mij to the gallery for an hour in deference to the wishes of a female visitor who feared for her nylons. He appeared, after a few moments, balancing adroitly on the top of the gallery railing, paying no attention either to us or to the formidable drop below him, for his plan was evidently already mature. At various points along the length of this railing were suspended certain decorative objects, a Cretan shepherd's bag, a dagger, and other things whose identity now eludes me. Purposefully, and with an air of enormous self-satisfaction, Mij began to chew through the cords from which these *objets d'art* or *de voyage* hung. After each severance he would pause to watch his victim crash to the parquet floor below, then he would carefully renew his precarious, straddling progress along the rail until he reached the next. We stood, my visitor and I, waiting to catch the more fragile items as they fell, and I remember that when the last fruit, as it were, had fallen from the bough she turned to me with a sigh and said, 'Don't you ever feel that this just simply can't go on?'

More usually, however, when he was loose in the studio, he

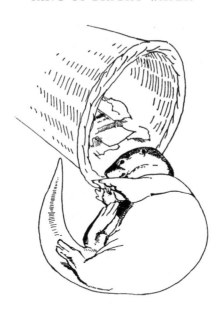

would play for hours at a time with what soon became an established selection of toys, ping-pong balls, marbles, india-rubber fruit, and a terrapin shell that I had brought back from his native marshes. The smaller among these objects he became adept at throwing across the room with a flick of his head, and with a ping-pong ball he invented a game of his own which would keep him engrossed for up to half an hour at a time. An expanding suitcase that I had taken to Iraq had become damaged on the journey home so that the lid, when closed, remained at a slope from one end to the other. Mij discovered that if he placed the ball on the high end it would run down the length of the suitcase unaided. He would dash around to the other end to ambush its arrival, hide from it, crouching, to spring up and take it by surprise as it reached the drop to the floor, grab it and trot off with it to the high end once more.

These games were adequate for perhaps half of all the time he spent indoors and awake, but several times a day he needed, as much psychologically as physically, I think, a prolonged romp with a human playmate. Tunnelling under the carpet and affecting to believe himself thus rendered invisible, he would shoot out with a squeak of triumph if a foot passed within range; or he would dive inside the loose cover of the sofa and play tigers from behind it; or he would simply lay siege to one's person as a puppy does, bouncing around one in a frenzy of excited chirps and squeaks and launching a series of tip-and-run raids. It was the 'tip' that was the trouble, for his teeth were like needles, and however gently he might try to use them, such games used, I am bound to say, to end with a certain amount of visible proof of his success in tactics left on the human hand. It did not hurt, but it made a bad impression upon visitors, many of whom were ready in any case to accord him the distrust appropriate to an alien upstart.

But I soon found an infallible way to distract his attention if he became too excitable, a way whose success was, I think, due to the refusal to be baffled by obstacles that is an otter characteristic. I would take the terrapin shell, wrap it in a towel, and knot the loose ends tightly across. He came to know these preparations, and would wait absolutely motionless until I handed him the bundle; then he would straddle it with his forearms, sink his teeth in the knots, and begin to hump and shuffle round the room in a deceptively aimless-seeming manner. Deceptive, because no matter how complex the knots he would have them all undone in five or ten minutes. At the end of this performance he liked, and seemed to expect, applause, and he would then bring the towel and the terrapin shell to be tied up again. He brought the towel first, dragging it, and then made a second trip for the terrapin, shuffling it in front of him down the room like a football.

At night he slept in my bed, still, at this time, on his back with his head on the pillow, and in the morning he shared my bath. With utter indifference to temperature he would plunge ahead of me into water still too hot for me to enter, and while I shaved he would swim round me playing with the soapsuds or with various celluloid and rubber ducks and ships that had begun to accumulate in my bathroom as they do in a child's.

Outside the house I exercised him on a lead, precisely as if he had been a dog, and, like a dog, he soon showed preference for certain streets and certain corners at which dogs of all sorts and sizes had left stimulating messages; messages that were, perhaps, the more fascinating for being, as it were, in a foreign language. Whether or not he could decipher their purport, whether or not they conjured up for him the various erotic, impudent or pugnacious images intended, he would spend minutes at a time sniffing these clearing-houses of local canine information, and would occasionally add to them some liquid comment of his own, tantalizingly cryptic, no doubt, to the next comer.

I was too timid of the result to allow him to meet any dog so to speak nose to nose, and I would pick him up if we met unattended dogs in the street, but for his part he seemed largely indifferent to them. The only time that I was conscious of some mutual recognition taking place, some awareness of similarity between canine and lutrine values, was one morning when, setting out for his walk, he refused to be parted from a new toy, a large rubber ball painted in gaudy segments. This ball was too big for his mouth, so that he could only carry it sticking out from one side of his jaws like a gigantic gum boil, and thus encumbered he set off briskly up the street, tugging at his lead. Rounding the first street corner we came face to face with a very fat spaniel, unattended and sedately carrying in its mouth a bundle of newspapers. The respective loads of otter and dog made it difficult for either of them to turn its head far as they came abreast, but their eyes rolled sideways with what appeared to me a wild surmise, and when they were a few paces past each other both suddenly stopped dead for a moment, as though arrested by some momentary mental revelation.

Mij quickly developed certain compulsive habits on these walks in the London streets, akin, clearly, to the rituals of children who on their way to and from school must place their feet squarely on the centre of each paving block; must touch every seventh upright of the iron railings, or pass to the outside of every second lamp-post. Opposite to my flat was a single-storeyed primary school, along whose frontage ran a low wall some two feet high separating a corridor-width strip of garden from the road. On his way home, but never on his way out, Mij would tug me in the direction of this wall, jump up on it, and gallop the full length of its thirty yards, to the hopeless distraction both of pupils and of staff within. There was more than one street of which he would use one pavement only, refusing with dug-in toes to be led to the other side, and there were certain drain grilles through which he would peer motionless for long seconds before he could be led away from them. On return to the flat he would scrabble frantically to be let in, and the moment his lead was unhitched he would roll on his back and squirm with eye-bewildering speed and vigour before returning to his toys.

Many of his actions, indeed, appeared ritual, and I think that comparatively few people who keep wild creatures realize the enormous security-value of routine in the maintenance of an animal's contentment. As soon as routine is broken a new element enters, in however minute and unrecognizable a trace – the fear of the unknown which is basic to the behaviour of all animals, including man. Every living creature exists by a routine of some kind; the small rituals of that routine are the landmarks, the boundaries of security, the reassuring walls that exclude a *horror vacui*; thus, in our own species, after some tempest of the spirit in which the landmarks seem to have been swept away, a man will reach out tentatively in mental darkness to feel the walls, to assure himself that they still stand where they stood – a necessary gesture, for the walls are of his own building, without universal reality, and what man makes he may destroy. To an animal these landmarks are of even greater importance, for once removed from its natural surroundings, its ecological norm, comparatively little of what the senses perceive can be comprehended in function or potentiality, and the true conditions for insecurity are already established. As among human beings, animal insecurity may manifest itself as aggression or timidity, ill-temper or ill-health, or as excessive affection for a parental figure; unfortunately this last aspect encourages many to cultivate insecurity in their charges, child or animal, as a means to an end.

It was about this time that Mij delivered his first serious, intentional bite. He was fed now upon live eels – which I had learned to be the staple food of many races of otter – supplemented by a mixture of raw egg and unpolished rice, a sticky concoction for which he evinced a gusto no doubt influenced by his early life among the Arabs. The eels I kept in a perforated bucket under the kitchen tap, and fed them to him in the bath; it had become an established way of quieting him when he was obstreperous, to shut him in with a full bath of water and three or four eels. On this occasion I had closed the bathroom door imperfectly, and Mij elected to bring his second eel through and eat it in the studio. To this, though he was sodden with water and the eel very slimy, there seemed no alternative, for it is folly to try to take away from a wild animal its natural prey; but when after a few mouthfuls he decided to carry it upstairs to the gallery I determined to call a halt, visualizing a soaking and eel-slimed bed. I put on three pairs of gloves, the outermost being a pair of heavily-padded flying gauntlets. I caught up with him halfway up the stairway; he laid down the eel, put a paw on it, and hummed at me, a high continuous hum that could break out into a wail. Full of euphoric self-confidence I talked away quietly to him, telling him that he couldn't possibly hurt me and that I was going to take the eel back to the bathroom. The humming became much louder. I bent down and put my heavily-gloved hand upon the eel. He screamed at me, but still he took no action. Then, as I began to lift it, he bit. He bit just once and let go; the canines of his upper and lower jaws passed through the three layers of glove, through the skin, through muscle and bone, and met in the middle of my hand with an audible crunch. He let go almost in the same instant, and rolled on his back squirming with apology. I still held the eel; I carried it back to the bath, where he refused to pay any further attention to it, fussing round me and over me and muzzling me with little squeals of affection and apparent solicitude.

There were two small bones broken in my hand, and for a week it was the size of a boxing glove, very painful, and an acute embarrassment to me in the presence of those who from the first had been sceptical of Mij's domesticity. I had been given a sharp and necessary reminder that though he might carry painted rubber balls through the London streets he was not a spaniel.

It was not lack of curiosity, so much as lack of time and opportunity, that made me delay for nearly three weeks before making any real effort to establish Mij's identity. It would, I thought, require a day's research in the library of the Zoological Society, and at that early stage Mij could not be left alone for more than a hour or so without fretting. But, as may be imagined, he caused no small stir in his walks through the streets of West Kensington, and it was increasingly borne in upon me that I could answer only in the most perfunctory and unsatisfactory terms the fire of questions with which our strolls were punctuated.

It is not, I suppose, in any way strange that the average Londoner should not recognize an otter, but the variety of guesses as to what kind of animal this might be came as no less of a surprise to me than the consistent accuracy with which a minority bracketed the bull's-eye without once touching it. Otters belong to a comparatively small group of animals called mustellines, shared by the badger, mongoose, weasel, stoat, polecat, marten, mink and others; an official at Cairo airport had set an early precedent of outer scoring when he asked whether Mij was an ermine – which is, of course, a stoat in winter coat. Now, in the London streets, I faced a continual barrage of conjectural questions that sprayed all the mustellines but the otter; wilder, more random fire hit on practically everything from 'a baby seal' to a squirrel. The seal heresy had deep root, and was perhaps the commonest of them all, though far from being the most bizarre. 'Is that a walrus, mister?' reduced me to giggles outside Harrods, and 'a hippo' made my day outside Cruft's Dog Show. A beaver, a bear cub, a newt, a leopard – one, apparently, that had changed his spots – even, with heaven knows what dim recollections of schoolroom science and a bewildering latinized world of sub-human creatures – a 'brontosaur'; Mij was anything but an otter.

But the question for which I awarded the highest score – a question evading with contemptuous dexterity any possible inaccuracy on the part of the speaker; putting the blame, as it were, for the creature's unfamiliarity squarely on my own shoulders; hinting, or doing more than hint, that someone had blundered, that the hand of the potter had shaken; containing, too, an accusation of unfinished work unfit for exhibition – came from a Herculean labourer engaged, mightily and alone, upon digging a hole in the street. I was still far from him when he laid down his pick, put his hands on his hips, and began to stare. As I drew nearer I saw that this stare held an outraged quality, one of surprise, certainly, but also of affront, as though he would have me know that he was not one upon whom to play jokes. I came abreast of him; he spat, glared, and then growled out, ' 'Ere, mister – *what is that supposed to be?*'

It was, I think, his question more than any other that reminded me of my own ignorance; I did not, in fact, know what Mij was supposed to be. I knew, certainly, that he was an otter, but I also knew that he must be one of a species which, if known to the scientific world, was at least not known to live in the delta marshes of the Tigris and Euphrates, for the scant zoological literature that had accompanied me to Iraq made it plain that the only known otter of the Mesopotamian marshes was the Persian sub-species of the common European otter, *Lutra lutra*. Chahala, the cub that had died, had clearly belonged to that race; she had longer fur with 'guard hairs' in place of Mij's sleek, darker velvet; she was lighter on her throat and belly than upon her back, whereas Mij's body seemed to have been slipped into an evenly dyed plush bag; the under side of her tail was not, as was Mij's, flat like a ruler.

In a village of the marshes between the Tigris and the Persian frontier I had bought two otter skins from the householder with whom we had been staying; both were, apart from any possible scientific interest, objects of fascination, for they had been 'case' skinned, the whole carcase having been removed, without a single incision, through the mouth. One of these skins belonged to Chahala's race; the other, contrast heightened by juxtaposition, was plainly of Mij's, a much larger and darker creature, whose fur was short and shiny and the colour of milkless chocolate. These two skins now reposed in my flat, pregnant with possibility and as yet unexamined by competent authority.

I telephoned to the Natural History Department of the British Museum, in Cromwell Road, and the same afternoon Mr Robert

Hayman arrived at my flat to examine the two skins and the living specimen. There is in the serious zoological world a dead-pan-ness, an unwillingness for committal, that must rival the most cautious of consulting physicians. Hayman was far too competent a zoologist, far too encyclopedic in his knowledge, to have been unaware in those first moments that he was looking at a skin and a living animal from a habitat that made the race quite unfamiliar to him, but he did not betray it. He took such measurements as Mij would permit, examined him closely, peered at his formidable array of teeth, and left bearing the two skins for comparison with museum series.

But in due course, after the slow, precise, painstaking processes of the taxonomic world, Mij's new race was proclaimed. Hayman summoned me to the museum to see the cabinets of otter skins from all over Asia, where the larger of mine lay, unlabelled and conspicuously differing from any other, in a drawer by itself, but in apposition to its nearest relatives. These, various sub-species of *Lutrogale*, a short-coated otter with a flat under side to the tail, ranged over most of Eastern Asia; according to their geographical race they were of a variety of hues from pale sandy to medium brown, but none had been recorded west of Sind, in India, and none resembled my specimens in colour.

There are very few people, and even fewer amateur zoologists, who stumble upon a sizeable mammal previously unknown to science; in the nursery world of picture-books of birds and beasts the few who had given their own names to species – Steller's eider and sea eagle, Sharpe's crow, Humboldt's woolly monkey, Meinerzthagen's forest hog, Ross's snow goose, Grant's gazelle, Père David's deer – had been surrounded for me with an aura of romance; they were the creators, partaking a little of the deity, who had contributed to the great panorama of bright living creatures in which, unshadowed and uncomplicated by know-ledge, my childish fancy wandered. Now, when Hayman sug-gested that the new otter should bear my name, I experienced a sharp, brief conflict; I felt that it should bear his, for he, not I, had done the work; but something small and shrill from the nursery days was shouting inside me that I could be translated into the hierarchy of my early gods and wear, however perilously, the halo of a creator. ('Can I have it for my own?' we used to ask when we were small. 'For my *very* own?' Here, surely, was an animal of my very own, to bear my name; every animal that looked like it would always bear my name for ever and ever, unless some odious taxonomist of the future, some leveller, some jealous, dusty scribe of the backroom and the skeletons, were to plot against me and plan the destruction of my tiny, living memorial.)

So Mij and all his race became *Lutrogale perspicillata maxwelli*, and though he is now no more, and there is no ostensible proof that there is another living specimen in the world, I had realized a far-off childish fantasy, and there was a Maxwell's otter.

# 9

It was now early May, and I had been in London for more than three weeks, three weeks of impatience and nostalgia for Camusfeàrna, and I felt I could wait no longer to see Mij playing, as I visualized him, under the waterfall, or free about the burn and the island beaches. I went by way of my family home in the south of Scotland, where Mij could taste a partial but guarded liberty before emancipation to total freedom in the north.

During his stay at Monreith, the home of my family, Mij's character began to emerge and to establish itself. At first on farm mill dams, then in the big loch over which the house looks out, and finally in the sea – which, though he had never known salt water, he entered without apparent surprise – he demonstrated not only his astonishing swimming powers but his willingness to reject the call of freedom in favour of human company. At first, guessing the urgency of the summons that his instincts would experience, I allowed him to swim only on the end of a long fishing line. I had bought a spring reel, which automatically took up the slack, and attached this to the butt end of a salmon rod, but the danger of underwater snags on which the line might loop itself soon seemed too great, and after the first week he ran free and swam free. He wore a harness to which a lead could be attached in emergency, but its function was as much to proclaim his domesticity to would-be human aggressors as one of restraint. The design of this harness, one that would neither impede movement nor catch upon submerged branches and drown him, was a subject that occupied my imagination for many months, and was not perfected for nearly a year.

This time of getting to know a wild animal on terms, as it were, of mutual esteem, was wholly fascinating to me, and our long daily walks by stream and hedgerow, moorland and loch were a source of perpetual delight. Though it remained difficult to lure him from some enticing piece of open water, he was otherwise no more trouble than a dog, and infinitely more interesting to watch. His hunting powers were still undeveloped, but he would sometimes corner an eel in the mill dams, and in the streams he would catch frogs, which he skinned with a dexterity seemingly born of long practice. I had rightly guessed that his early life in a Marsh Arab household would have produced an enlightened and progressive attitude towards poultry – for no Ma'dan would tolerate a predator among the sparse and scrawny scarecrows that pass in the marshes for chickens – and in fact I found that Mij would follow me through a crowded and cackling farmyard without a glance to right or to left. To most domestic livestock he was indifferent, but black cattle he clearly identified with the water buffaloes of his home, and if they gathered at the edge of water in which he was swimming he became wild with excitement, plunging and porpoising and chittering with pleasure.

Even in the open countryside he retained his passion for playthings, and would carry with him for miles some object that had caught his fancy, a fallen rhododendron blossom, an empty twelve-bore cartridge case, a fir-cone, or, on one occasion, a woman's comb with an artificial brilliant set in the bar; this he discovered at the side of the drive as we set off one morning, and he carried it for three hours, laying it down on the bank when he took to water and returning for it as soon as he emerged.

In the traces left by wild otters he took not the slightest interest. Following daily the routes for which Mij expressed preference, I found myself almost imperceptibly led by his instinct into the world in which the otters of my own countryside lived, a watery world of deep-cut streams between high, rooty banks where the leaves of the undergrowth met overhead; of unguessed alleys and tunnels in reedbeds by a loch's edge; of mossy culverts and marsh-marigolds; of islands tangled with fallen trees among whose roots were earthy excavations and a whisper of the wind in the willows. As one may hear or read a strange, unusual name, and thereafter be haunted by its constant coincidental recurrence, so, now that I had through Mijbil become conscious of otters, I saw all around me the signs of their presence where I had been oblivious to them before; a smoothed bank of steep mud which they had used for tobogganing; a hollowed-out rotten tree-stump whose interior had been formed into a dry sleeping place; the print of a broad, capable, webbed foot; a small tarry dropping, composed mainly of eel-bones, deposited upon a stone in mid-stream. In these last I had expected Mij to show at least an equal interest to that which he had displayed in their canine counterparts, but whether because otters do not use their excreta in an anecdotal or informative way, or because he did not recognize in these the product of his own kind, he treated them as if they did not exist.

During all the time that I had him he killed, so far as I know, only one warm-blooded animal, and then he did not eat it, for he seemed to have a horror of blood and of the flesh of warm-blooded animals. On this occasion he was swimming in a reedy loch when he caught a moorhen chick of a few days old, a little black gollywog of a creature half the size of a day-old chick. He had a habit of tucking his treasures under one arm when he was swimming – for an otter swimming underwater uses its forelimbs very little – and here he placed the chick while he went on in a leisurely way with his underwater exploration. It must have drowned during the first minute or so, and when at length he brought it ashore for a more thorough investigation he appeared disappointed and irritated by this unwarrantable fragility; he nuzzled it and pushed it about with his paws and chittered at it in a pettish sort of way, and then, convinced of its now permanent inertia, he left it where it lay and went in search of something more cooperative.

In the library at Monreith I explored what natural historians of earlier generations had to say about otters. There were no recent works, for the relevant section of the library had received no addition for many years past. The great American naturalist, Ernest Thompson Seton, writing soon after the turn of this century said, 'Of all the beasts whose lives I have tried to tell, there is one that stands forth, the Chevalier Bayard of the wilds – without fear and without reproach. That is the otter, the joyful, keen, and fearless otter; mild and loving to his own kind, and gentle with his neighbour of the stream; full of play and gladness in his life, full of courage in his stress; ideal in his home, steadfast in death; the noblest little soul that ever went four-footed through the woods.' In his writings I recognized the animal that I knew, 'the most beautiful and engaging of all elegant pets. There seems no end to its fun, its energy, its drollery, its good nature, and its postures of new and surprising grace'.[1]

We arrived at Camusfeàrna in early June, soon after the beginning of a long spell of Mediterranean weather. My diary tells me that summer begins on 22nd June, and under the heading for 24th June there is a somewhat furtive aside to the effect that it is Midsummer's Day, as though to ward off the logical deduction that summer lasts only for four days in every year. But that summer at Camusfeàrna seemed to go on and on through timeless hours of sunshine and stillness and the dapple of changing cloud shadow upon the shoulders of the hills.

When I think of early summer at Camusfeàrna a single enduring image comes forward through the multitude that jostle in kaleido-scopic patterns before my mind's eye – that of wild roses against a clear blue sea, so that when I remember that summer alone with my curious namesake who had travelled so far, those roses have become for me the symbol of a whole complex of peace. They are not the pale, anaemic flowers of the south, but a deep, intense pink that is almost a red; it is the only flower of that colour, and it is the only flower that one sees habitually against the direct background of the ocean, free from the green stain of summer. The yellow flag irises flowering in dense ranks about the burn and the foreshore, the wild orchids bright among the heather and mountain grasses, all these lack the essential contrast, for the eye may move from them to the sea beyond them only through the intermediary, as it were, of the varying greens among

[1] *Life Histories of Northern Animals* (Constable 1910).

which they grow. It is in June and October that the colours at Camusfeàrna run riot, but in June one must face seaward to escape the effect of wearing green-tinted spectacles. There at low tide the rich ochres, madders and oranges of the orderly strata of seaweed species are set against glaring, vibrant whites of barnacle-covered rock and shell sand, with always beyond them the elusive, changing blues and purples of the moving water, and somewhere in the foreground the wild roses of the north.

Into this bright, watery landscape Mij moved and took possession with a delight that communicated itself as clearly as any articulate speech could have done; his alien but essentially appropriate entity occupied and dominated every corner of it, so that he became for me the central figure among the host of wild creatures with which I was surrounded. The waterfall, the burn, the white beaches and the islands; his form became the familiar foreground to them all – or perhaps foreground is not the right word, for at Camusfeàrna he seemed so absolute a part of his surroundings that I wondered how they could ever have seemed to me complete before his arrival.

At the beginning, while I was still imbued with the caution and forethought that had so far gone to his tending, Mij's daily life followed something of a routine; this became, as the weeks went on, relaxed into a total freedom at the centre point of which Camusfeàrna house remained Mij's holt, the den to which he returned at night, and in the daytime when he was tired. But this emancipation, like most natural changes, took place so gradually and unobtrusively that it was difficult for me to say at what point the routine had stopped.

Mij slept in my bed (by now, as I have said, he had abandoned the teddy-bear attitude and lay on his back under the bedclothes with his whiskers tickling my ankles and his body at the crook of my knees) and would wake with bizarre punctuality at exactly twenty past eight in the morning. I have sought any possible explanation for this, and some 'feed-back' situation in which it was actually I who made the first unconscious movement, giving him his cue, cannot be altogether discounted; but whatever the reason, his waking time, then and until the end of his life, summer

'Nowhere in all the West Highlands and Islands have I seen any place of so intense or varied a beauty in so small a compass.'

Gavin Maxwell in the doorway of Camusfeàrna.

'On the stone slab beneath the chimney piece are inscribed the Latin words …"It is n will-o'-the-wisp that I have followed here." '

NON FATVVM H    ERSECVTVS IGNEM

t is the waterfall, rather than the house, that has always seemed to me the soul of Camusfeàrna.'

'Into this bright watery landscape Mij moved and took possession.'

# Mijbi

'With Kathleen, whose mere proximity would send him into ecstasies.'

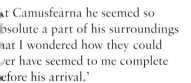

'At Camusfeàrna he seemed so absolute a part of his surroundings that I wondered how they could ever have seemed to me complete before his arrival.'

'I saw the long, unhurried beat of goose wings against the sky, and recognized, with an absurd surge of joy, my missing greylags.'

Calum Murdo Mackinnon – 'a small wiry man in middle age'.

'A stone's throw from the sea on one side and the burn on the other, the house of Camusfeàrna stood unfenced in green grass among grazing black-faced sheep.'

Gavin and Edal. 'There was once more an otter at Camusfeàrna, playing in the burn and sleeping before the hearth.'

Edal and her keeper, Jimmy Watt

'By the end of June she was swimming as an otter should, diving deep to explore dim rock ledges at the edge of the sea tangle.'

or winter, remained precisely twenty past eight. Having woken, he would come up to the pillow and nuzzle my face and neck with small attenuated squeaks of pleasure and affection. If I did not rouse myself very soon he would set about getting me out of bed. This he did with the business-like, slightly impatient efficiency of a nurse dealing with a difficult child. He played the game by certain defined and self-imposed rules; he would not, for example, use his teeth even to pinch, and inside these limitations it was hard to imagine how a human brain could, in the same body, have exceeded his ingenuity. He began by going under the bedclothes and moving rapidly up and down the bed with a high-hunching, caterpillar-like motion that gradually untucked the bedclothes from beneath the sides of the mattress; this achieved he would redouble his efforts at the foot of the bed, where the sheets and blankets had a firmer hold. When everything had been loosened up to his satisfaction he would flow off the bed on to the floor – except when running on dry land the only appropriate word for an otter's movement is flowing; they pour themselves, as it were, in the direction of their objective – take the bedclothes between his teeth, and, with a series of violent tugs, begin to yank them down beside him. Eventually, for I do not wear pyjamas, I would be left quite naked on the undersheet clutching the pillows rebelliously. But they, too, had to go; and it was here that he demonstrated the extraordinary strength concealed in his small body. He would work his way under them and execute a series of mighty hunches of his arched back, each of them lifting my head and whole shoulders clear of the bed, and at some point in the procedure he invariably contrived to dislodge the pillows while I was still in mid-air, much as a certain type of practical joker will remove a chair upon which someone is in the act of sitting down. Left thus comfortless and bereft both of covering and of dignity, there was little option but to dress while Mij looked on with an all-that-shouldn't-really-have-been-necessary-you-know sort of expression. Otters usually get their own way in the end; they are not dogs, and they co-exist with humans rather than being owned by them.

His next objective was the eel-box in the burn, followed, having breakfasted, by a tour of the water perimeter, the three-quarter circle formed by the burn and the sea; shooting like an underwater arrow after trout where the burn runs deep and slow between the trees; turning over stones for hidden eels where it spreads broad and shallow over sun-reflecting scales of mica, tobogganing down the long, loose sand slope by the sand-martin colony; diving through the waves on the sand beach and catching dabs; then, lured in with difficulty and subterfuge from starting on a second lap, home to the kitchen and ecstatic squirming among his towels.

This preamble to the day, when Mij had a full stomach and I had not, became, as he established favoured pools and fishing grounds which had every morning to be combed as for a lost possession, ever longer and longer, and after the first fortnight I took, not without misgiving, to going back indoors myself as soon as he had been fed. At first he would return after an hour or so, and when he had dried himself he would creep up under the loose cover of the sofa and form a round breathing hump at the centre of the seat. But as time went on he stayed longer about the burn, and I would not begin to worry until he had been gone for half the day.

There were great quantities of cattle at Camusfeàrna that year, for the owner of the estate was of an experimental turn of mind, and had decided to farm cattle on the lines of the Great Glen Cattle Ranch. The majority of these beasts were black, and, as at Monreith in the spring, Mij seemed to detect in them an affinity to his familiar water buffaloes of the Tigris marshes, for he would dance round them with excited chitterings until they stampeded. Thus massed they presented too formidable an appearance for him, and after a week or two he devised for himself a means of cattle-baiting at which he became a past master. With extreme stealth he would advance *ventre à terre* towards the rear end of some massive stirk whose black-tufted tail hung invitingly within his reach; then, as one who makes a vigorous and impatient tug at a bell-rope, he would grab the tuft between his teeth and give one tremendous jerk upon it with all his strength, leaping backward exactly in time to dodge the lashing hooves. At first I viewed this sport with the gravest alarm, for, owing to the structure of the skull, a comparatively light blow on the nose can kill an otter, but Mij was able to gauge the distance to an inch, and never a hoof so much as grazed him. As a useful by-product of his impish sense of humour, the cattle tended to keep farther from the house, thus incidentally reducing the number of scatological hazards to be skirted at the door.

I had a book to write during those summer months at Camusfeàrna, and often I would lie for hours in the sun by the waterfall; from time to time Mij would appear from nowhere, bounding up the bank from the water, to greet me as though we had been separated for weeks.

The manuscript that I was writing became blurred and stained as though by tears; I would lie, as I have said, sunbathing and writing in the grass by the burn, and every now and again Mij's busy quartering of the stream's bed from the falls to the sea and back again would bring him to the point above which I lay. With delighted squeaks and gurgles he would rush through the shallows and come bounding up the bank to deposit his skin-load of water indiscriminately upon myself and my manuscript, sometimes adding insult to injury by confiscating my pen as he departed.

In the sea, Mij discovered his true, breath-taking aquabatic powers; until he came to Scotland he had never swum in deep waters, for the lakes and lagoons of his native marshes are rarely more than a fathom or two deep. He would swim beside me as I rowed in the little dinghy, and in the glass-clear waters of Camusfeàrna bay, where the white shell sand alternates with sea tangle and outcrops of rock, I could watch him as he dived down, down, down through fathom after fathom to explore the gaudy sea forests at the bottom with their flowered shell glades and mysterious, shadowed caverns. He was able, as are all otters and seals, to walk on the bottom without buoyancy, for an otter swims habitually under water and does not dive with full lungs, depending for oxygen – we must presume in the absence of knowledge – upon a special adaptation of the venous system. The longest that I ever timed Mij below the surface was almost six minutes, but I had the impression that he was in no way taxing his powers, and could greatly have exceeded that time in emergency. Normally, however, if he was not engrossed, he would return to the surface every minute or so, breaking it for only a second, with a forward diving roll like that of a porpoise. Swimming at the surface, as he did if he wanted to keep some floating object in view, he was neither very fast nor graceful, a labouring dog-paddle in amazing contrast to his smooth darting grace below water. For hours he would keep pace with the boat, appearing now on this side and now on that, sometimes mischievously seizing an oar with both arms and dragging on it, and from time to time bouncing inboard with a flurry of water.

Only when I was fishing did I have to leave Mij shut up in the house, for he was a creature who must test everything with his mouth, and my worst nightmare was the vision of a mackerel hook in his jaw. At first I fished little, having no great liking for the lythe and coal fish that are all one may depend upon in early summer round the Camusfeàrna skerries. Though by mid-June there are all the signs of summer; the teeming, clangorous bird life of the islands established for many weeks and the samphire and goose-grass alive with downy chicks, it is not until July that with the coming of the mackerel the sea appears to burst into life; for following them come all the greater creatures that prey upon them, and the mackerel in their turn force up to the surface the lesser fishes upon which they feed, the small, glittering, multitudinous fry of many species, including their own. When far out on the blank face of the summer sea there are screaming patches of gulls that dip and swoop, half running, half flying, alighting with wings still open to grab and to swallow, one may guess that somewhere beneath them lies a great shoal of mackerel, who are pushing up to the surface and the waiting gulls the little fish fleeing in panic from, perhaps, their own parents. Sometimes there are curiously local patches of fry at the surface, and at sunset when the sea is really as smooth as glass – a much misused simile, for it rarely is – I have seen, miles from shore, little dancing foot-wide fountains of blue and silver mackerel no longer than a man's thumb, and have found no predator below them.

After the mackerel had arrived I fished for a few minutes in the cool of every evening; for them Mij, though he never caught one himself, so far as I knew, had an insatiable passion, as had Jonnie before him; and I too welcomed them, perhaps because of childhood associations. When I was a child in Galloway we used to fish for mackerel by trolling from a sailing-boat a single hook baited with bright metal, or with a sliver of flesh and skin sliced from a mackerel's flank (how well I recall the horror of seeing for the first time this operation performed upon the living fish; the tears, the reassurance, all among the blue waves and the spindrift and the flapping brown sail). We caught our fish singly and re-baited the hook each time, and if we caught twenty or thirty fish in an afternoon we chattered about it for weeks. It was not, I think, until shortly before the war that the murderous darrow came into general use in the West Highlands, and at Camusfeàrna, where there is no means of disposing of surplus fish but dumping them, it has the disadvantage of limiting fishing time to a few minutes. A darrow consists of a twelve-foot cast carrying up to twenty-two flies of crudely dyed hen's feathers, weighted at the bottom with a two-pound sinker. The boat is stationary in anything from six to twenty fathoms of water, and the darrow and line are allowed to run out until the sinker bumps the bottom. By that time, as often as not in Camusfeàrna bay, there are half a dozen or so mackerel on the hooks. If there are not, it is simply a question of hauling in two fathoms of line and letting it run out again, and repeating this process until either the boat drifts over a shoal or a moving shoal happens to pass beneath the boat. Sometimes the mackerel are in shallower water, clear water where one can see fathoms down to pale sand and dark sea-tangle and rushing shoals of aquamarine fish as they dart at the bright feathers. Quite often every single fly is taken at once; then at one moment the line is lead-heavy, tugging and jerking, and at the next light as floating string as the mackerel swim upward carrying the sinker with them. There is a great art in dealing with a full darrow, for twenty-two large fish-hooks flipping wildly about the hold of a small boat catch more than fish. In the days of the Soay Shark Fishery I saw many barbs sunk deep in hands and legs of mackerel fishers; there was only one way of extraction, and a very painful one it was – to push the hook clean through, as opposed to pulling on it, then to snip off the barb with wire cutters and work the hook all the way back again.

It is not always mackerel that take the darrow flies; there are saith and lythe and the strangely heraldic gurnards, so fantastically armoured with spikes and thorns as to make their capture by anything but man seem nothing short of impossible, yet I have watched, with the same sensations as a man might view a big snake swallowing an ox whole, a shag swallow a large gurnard tail first – against the grain, as it were. This extraordinary and surely gratuitously painful feat took the shag just over half an hour of grotesque convulsion, and when the stunt was at last completed the bird had entirely changed its shape. From being a slim, graceful, snake-like creature with a neck like an ebony cane, it had become an amorphous and neck-less lump – its crop so gigantically distended as to force the head far back down the spine and flush with it – unable to rise or even to swim without danger of ridicule.

Mij himself caught a number of fish on his daily outings; and week by week, as his skill and speed grew, their size and variety increased. In the burn he learned to feel under stones for eels, reaching in with one paw and averted head; and I in turn learned to turn over the larger stones for him, so that after a time he would stand in front of some boulder too heavy for him to move, and chitter at me to come and lift it for him. Often, as I did this, an eel would streak out from it into deeper water and he would fire himself after it like a brown torpedo beneath the surface. Near the edge of the tide he would search out the perfectly camouflaged flounders until they shot off with a wake of rising sand-grains like smoke from an express train – and farther out in the bay he would kill an occasional sea trout; these he never brought ashore, but ate them treading water as he did so, while I thought a little wistfully of the Chinese who are said to employ trained otters to fish for them. Mij, I thought, with all his delightful camaraderies, would never offer me a fish; I was wrong, but when at last he did so it was not a sea trout but a flounder. One day he emerged from the sea on to the rock ledge where I was standing and slapped down in front of me a flounder a foot across. I took it that he had brought this for congratulation, for he would often bring his choicer catches for inspection before consuming them, so I said something encouraging and began to walk on. He hurried after me and slammed it down again with a wet smack at my feet. Even then I did not understand, assuming only that he wished to eat in company, but he just sat there looking up and chittering at me. I was in no hurry to take the gesture at its face value, for, as I have said, one of the most aggressive actions one can perform to a wild animal is to deprive it of its prey, but after perhaps half a minute of doubt, while Mij redoubled his invitation, I reached down slowly and cautiously for the fish, knowing that Mij would give me vocal warning if I had misinterpreted him. He watched me with the plainest approval while I picked it up and began a mime of eating it; then he plunged off the rock into the sea and sped away a fathom down in the clear water.

Watching Mij in a rough sea – and the equinoctial gales at Camusfeàrna produce very rough seas indeed – I was at first sick with apprehension, then awed and fascinated, for his powers seemed little less than miraculous. During the first of the gales, I remember, I tried to keep him to the rock pools and the more sheltered corners, but one day his pursuit of some unseen prey had taken him to the seaward side of a high dry reef at the very tide's edge. As the long undertow sucked outward he was in no more than an inch or two of marbled water with the rock at his back, crunching the small fish he had caught; then, some forty yards to seaward of him I saw a great snarling comber piling up higher and higher, surging in fifteen feet tall and as yet unbreaking. I yelled to Mij as the wave towered darkly towards him, but he went on eating and paid no heed to me. It curled over and broke just before it reached him; all those tons of water just smashed down and obliterated him, enveloping the whole rock behind in a booming tumult of sea. Somewhere under it I visualized Mij's smashed body swirling round the foot of the black rock. But as the sea drew back in a long hissing undertow I saw, incredulously, that nothing had changed; there was Mij still lying in the shallow marbled water, still eating his fish.

He rejoiced in the waves; he would hurl himself straight as an arrow right into the great roaring grey wall of an oncoming breaker and go clean through it as if it had neither weight nor momentum; he would swim far out to sea through wave after wave until the black dot of his head was lost among the distant white manes, and more than once I thought that some wild urge to seek new lands had seized him and that he would go on swimming west into the Sea of the Hebrides and that I should not see him again.

As the weeks went by his absences did grow longer, and I spent many anxious hours searching for him, though as yet he had never stayed away for a night. When I had drawn blank at the falls and at all his favourite pools in the burn or among the rock ledges by the sea, I would begin to worry and to roam more widely, calling his name all the while. His answering note of recognition was so like the call of some small dowdy bird that inhabits the trees by the waterside that my heart would leap a hundred times before I knew with certainty that I had heard his voice.

The first time that I found him in distress was in the dark ravine above the waterfall. The waterfall divides, in some sense, the desert from the sown; the habitable world from the strange, beautiful, but inhospitable world of the dark gorge through which the burn flows above it. In summer, when the water is low one may pick one's way precariously along the rock at the stream's edge, the almost sheer but wooded sides rising a hundred feet at either hand. Here it is always twilight, for the sun never reaches the bed of the stream, and in summer the sky's light comes down thin and diffused by a stipple of oak and birch leaves whose branches lean out far overhead. Here and there a fallen tree-trunk spans the narrow gorge, its surface worn smooth by the passage of the wildcats' feet. The air is cool, moist, and pungent with the smell of wild garlic and watery things such as ferns and mosses that grow in the damp and the dark. Sometimes the bed of the stream widens to deep pools whose rock flanks afford no foothold, and where it looks as though the black water must be bottomless.

Once Morag asked me, in an offhand way behind which I sensed a tentative probing, whether I felt at ease in that place. It was a question that held a tacit confession, and I replied frankly. I have never been at ease in it; it evokes in me an unpleasant sensation that I associate only with the unfurnished top floor of a certain house, a sensation which makes me want to glance constantly over my shoulder, as though, despite the physical impossibility, I were being followed. I catch myself trying to step silently from stone to stone, as though it were important to my safety that my presence should remain undetected. I should have been abashed to tell Morag of this had she not given me the lead, but she told me then that she had had a horror of the place ever since she was a child, and could offer no explanation.

To conform to the spirit of my confession the gorge ought, of course, to be shunned by bird and animal alike, but it has, in fact, more of both than one might expect. There are foxes' and badgers' and wildcats' dens in the treacherous, near-vertical walls of the ravine; the buzzards and hooded crows nest every year in the branches that lean out over the dark water; below them there are the dippers and grey wagtails (a crass ornithological misnomer for this canary-yellow creature), and, for some reason, an unusual number of wrens that skulk and twitter among the fern. Whatever makes the gorge an unpleasant place to some people does not extend its influence beyond human beings.

The deep pools spill in unbroken falls a few feet high, and after two hundred yards or so there is the second real waterfall, dropping fifty feet interrupted by a ledge pool halfway down. That is the upper limit of the 'haunting', though the physical details of the gorge above the second falls differ little from those of the stretch below it; then, a further hundred yards up the burn's course, the way is blocked by the tall cataract, eighty feet of foaming white water falling sheer.

Mij, certainly, found nothing distasteful in the reach where my ghosts walked, and he had early used his strength and resource to scale the Camusfeàrna waterfall and find out what lay beyond. Thereafter this inaccessible region had become his especial haunt, and one from which his extraction presented, even when he was not in difficulties, almost insuperable problems. The clamour of the falling water effectively drowned the calling human voice, and even if he did hear it there was little chance of the caller perceiving his faint, birdlike response. On this occasion there was more water in the burn than is usual in summer, and there had been, too, a recent landslide, temporarily destroying the only practicable access from above. I lowered myself into the ravine on a rope belayed to the trunk of a tree, and I was wet to the waist after the first few yards of the burn's bed. I called and called, but my voice was diminished and lost in the sound of rushing water, and the little mocking birds answered me with Mij's own note of greeting. At length one of these birds, it seemed, called so repeatedly and insistently as to germinate in me a seed of doubt, but the sound came from far above me, and I was looking for Mij in the floor of the burn. Then I saw him; high up on the cliff; occupying so small a ledge that he could not even turn to make his way back, and with a fifty-foot sheer drop below him; he was looking at me, and, according to his lights, yelling his head off. I had to make a long detour to get above him with the rope and all the while I was terrified that the sight of me would have spurred him to some effort that would bring tragedy; terrified, too, that I myself might dislodge him as I tried to lift him from his eyrie. Then I found that the trees at the cliff-top were all rotten, and I had to make the rope fast to a stump on the hill above, a stump that grew in soft peat and that gave out from its roots an ominous squelching sound when I tugged hard on it. I went down that rock with the rope knotted round my waist and the feeling that Mij would probably survive somehow, but that I should most certainly die. He tried to stand on his hind legs when he saw me coming down above him, and more than once I thought he had gone. I had put the loop of his lead through the rope at my waist, and I clipped the other end to his harness as soon as my arm could reach him, but the harnesses, with their constant immersion, never lasted long, and I trusted this one about as much as I trusted the stump to which my rope was tied. I went up the rope with Mij dangling and bumping at my side like a cow being loaded on to a ship by crane, and in my mind's eye were two jostling, urgent images – the slow, sucking emergence of the tree roots above me, and the gradual parting of the rivets that held Mij's harness together. All in all it was one of the nastiest five minutes of my life; and when I reached the top the roots of the stump were indeed showing – it took just one tug with all my strength to pull them clean out.

But the harness had held, though, mercifully, it broke the next time it was put to strain. Mij had been missing, that day in the ravine, for nine hours, and had perhaps passed most of them on that ledge, for he was ravenously hungry, and ate until I thought he must choke.

There were other absences, other hours of anxiety and search, but one in particular stands out in my mind, for it was the first time that he had been away for a whole night, the first time that I despaired of him. I had left him in the early morning at the burn side eating his eels, and began to be uneasy when he had not returned by mid-afternoon. I had been working hard at my book; it was one of those rare days of authorship when everything seemed to go right; the words flowed unbidden from my pen, and the time had passed unheeded, so that it was a shock to realize that I had been writing for some six hours. I went out and called for Mij down the burn and along the beach, and when I did not find him I went again to the ravine above the falls. But there was no trace of him anywhere, though I explored the whole dark length of it right to the high falls, which I knew that even Mij could not pass. Just how short a distance my voice carried I realized when, above the second falls, I came upon two wildcat kittens at play on the steep bank; they saw me and were gone in a flash, but they had never heard my voice above the sound of the water. I left the burn then and went out to the nearer islands;

it was low tide, and there were exposed stretches and bars of soft white sand. Here I found otter footprints leading towards the lighthouse island, but I could not be certain that they were Mij's. Later that summer his claws became worn so that his pad-marks no longer showed the nails, but at that stage I was still unsure of distinguishing his tracks from those of a wild otter, unless the imprints were very precise. All that evening I searched and called, and when dusk came and he still did not return I began to despair, for his domestic life had led him to strictly diurnal habits, and by sundown he was always asleep in front of the fire.

It was a cloudy night with a freshening wind and a big moon that swam muzzily through black rags of vapour. By eleven o'clock it was blowing strong to gale from the south, and on the windward side of the islands there was a heavy sea beginning to pile up; enough, I thought, for him to lose his bearings if he were trying to make his way homeward through it. I put a light in each window of the house, left the doors open, and dozed fitfully in front of the kitchen fire. By three o'clock in the morning there was the first faint paling of dawn, and I went out to get the boat, for by now I had somehow convinced myself that Mij was on the lighthouse island. That little cockleshell was in difficulties from the moment I launched her; I had open water and a beam sea to cross before I could reach the lee of the islands, and she was taking a slosh of water over her gunwale all the way. If I shipped oars to bale I made so much leeway that I was nearly ashore again before I had done, and after half an hour I was both wet and scared. The bigger islands gave some shelter from the south wind but in the passages between them the north-running sea was about as much as the little boat would stand, and over the many rocks and skerries the water was foaming white and wicked-looking in the half light. A moment to bale and I would have been swept on to these black cusps and molars; the boat would have been crunched on them like a squashed matchbox, and I, who cannot swim a stroke, would have been feeding the lobsters. To complete my discomfort, I met a killer whale. In order to keep clear of the reefs I had rowed well north of the small islands that lie to landward of the lighthouse; the water was calmer here, and I did not have to fight to keep the nose of the boat into the waves. The killer broke the surface no more than twenty yards to the north of me, a big bull whose sabre fin seemed to tower a man's height out of the water; and, probably by chance, he turned straight for me. My nerves were strung and tensed, and I was in no frame of mind to assess the true likelihood of danger; I swung and rowed for the nearest island as though man were a killer's only prey. I grounded on a reef a hundred yards from the tern island, and I was not going to wait for the tide to lift me. Slithering and floundering in thigh-deep water over a rock ledge I struggled until I had lifted the flat keel clear of the tooth on which it had grated; the killer, possibly intent upon his own business and with no thought for me, cruised round a stone's throw away. I reached the tern island, and the birds rose screaming around me in a dancing canopy of ghostly wings, and I sat down on the rock in the dim windy dawn and felt as desolate as an abandoned child.

The lighthouse island was smothered in its jungle-growth of summer briars that grip the clothing with octopus arms and leave trails of blood-drops across hands and face; on it I felt like a dream-walker who never moves, and my calling voice was swept away northwards on gusts of cold, wet wind. I got back to the house at nine in the morning, with a dead-weight boat more than half full of water and a sick emptiness in my mind and body. By now part of me was sure that Mij too had met the killer, and that he was at this moment half digested in the whale's belly.

All that day until four o'clock in the afternoon I wandered and called, and with every hour grew the realization of how much that strange animal companion had come to signify to me. I resented it, resented my dependence upon this subhuman presence and companionship, resented the void that his absence was going to leave at Camusfeàrna. It was in this mood, one of reassertion of human independence, that about five in the evening I began to remove the remaining evidence of his past existence. I had taken from beneath the kitchen table his drinking bowl, had returned for the half-full bowl of rice and egg, had carried this to the scullery, what the Scots call the back kitchen, and was about to empty it into the slop pail, when I thought I heard Mij's voice from the kitchen behind me. I was, however, very tired, and distrustful of my own reactions; what I thought I had heard was the harshly whispered 'Hah?' with which he was accustomed to interrogate a seemingly empty room. The impression was strong enough for me to set down the bowl and hurry back into the kitchen. There was nothing there. I walked to the door and called his name, but all was as it had been before. I was on my way back to the scullery when I stopped dead. There on the kitchen floor, where I had been about to step, was a large, wet footprint. I looked at it, and I thought: I am very tired and very overwrought; and I went down on my hands and knees to inspect it. It was certainly wet, and it smelled of otter. I was still in a quadrupedal attitude when from the doorway behind me I heard the sound again, this time past mistaking – 'Hah?' Then Mij was all over me, drenched and wildly demonstrative, squeaking, bouncing round me like an excitable puppy, clambering on my shoulders, squirming on his back, leaping, dancing. I had been reassuring myself and him for some minutes before I realized that his harness was burst apart, and that for many hours, perhaps a day or more, he must have been caught like Absalom, struggling, desperate, waiting for a rescue that never came.

I knew by that time that Mij meant more to me than most human beings of my acquaintance, that I should miss his physical presence more than theirs, and I was not ashamed of it. In the penultimate analysis, perhaps, I knew that Mij trusted me more utterly than did any of my own kind, and so supplied a need that we are slow to admit.

When I missed Mij from his accustomed haunts I would go first to the waterfall, for there he would spend long hours alone, chasing the one big trout that lived in the big pool below the falls, catching elvers, or playing with some floating object that had been washed down. Sometimes he would set out from the house carrying a ping-pong ball, purposeful and self engrossed, and he would still be at the waterfall with it an hour later, pulling it under water and letting it shoot up again, rearing up and pouncing on it, playing his own form of water polo, with a goal at which the human onlooker could but guess. Once, I remember, I went to look for him there and at first could not find him; then my attention was caught by something red in the black water at the edge of the foam, and I saw that Mij was floating on his back, apparently fast asleep, with a bunch of scarlet rowan berries clasped to his chest with one arm. Such bright objects as these he would often pick up on his walks, and carry them with him until some rival attraction supplanted them. I never performed any tests to define his degree of colour vision, but whether by chance or selection his preferred playthings were often of garish hue.

I was watching him at the waterfall one day, trying to take photographs of him as he frolicked with his ping-pong ball in the deep pool, when I lost my footing on the sloping rock and found myself in beside him, camera and all. I had just started back for the house to change my clothes when I heard voices. A dry-stone wall runs between the waterfall and the house, and when I reached this with Mij at my heels I saw a figure approaching me whom I recognized with difficulty as the literary editress of the *New Statesman*; with difficulty, because her clothes were far from conventional, and I had not previously seen her away from city surroundings. We exchanged greetings over the wall, and began to talk. Mij climbed on to the wall top beside me and watched.

Now Mij had an especial vice that I have not yet mentioned; a vice that I had been unable to cure, partly, anyway, because I did not understand its cause or motivation. To put it bluntly, he bit the lobes of people's ears – not, certainly, in anger nor in spite; not, apparently, as a conscious act of aggression or ill-will, but simply because he liked doing so. He collected them, so to speak, not as David collected the foreskins of the Philistines, in enmity, but as an amiable hobby. He just nipped through them like an efficient ear-piercer, and apparently felt the better for it. It was now so long since he had met strangers and had the opportunity to add an ear to his list that I had momentarily forgotten this deplorable proclivity. My visitor leaned an arm on the wall as she talked, with her head a mere foot from Mij's, and

Mij reached out, without comment, and pierced the lobe of her left ear with surgical precision.

It was her finest hour. I had seen many lobes pierced by Mij; I was a connoisseur of reaction to the situation, ranging from the faint shriek, through gabbling reassurance, to the ominous flushed silence: I thought I knew them all, but I was wrong. Not by the smallest interruption in her flow of speech, not by so much as a hint of an indrawn breath did she betray that she had perceived the incident; only her eyes, as she continued her sentence, assumed an expression of unbelieving outrage entirely at variance with her words.

One of the few people who escaped this hallmark, as it were, of Mij's acquaintance, was Morag. I myself had had both ears pierced early in my association with my namesake, and now enjoyed immunity. To only two other people did he extend the tempestuous attention that he accorded to me, to Morag and to Kathleen Raine; but though the degree of demonstrative love to each of us did not greatly differ it was quite unlike in kind – with each, that is to say, he formed an entirely different relationship. With Kathleen, whose mere proximity would send him into ecstasies, he was rough and rumbustious, fiercely possessive, and he took advantage of her whenever and however he could; she in turn found some strange community with him, and was pre-pared to put up uncomplainingly with his most exuberant horse play. With Morag he was gentler, less bullying, in his love, and with me more deferential, more responsive to the suggestion of command. But it remained around us three that his orb revolved when he was not away in his own imponderable world of wave and water, of dim green depths and tide-swayed fronds of the sea-tangle; we were his Trinity, and he behaved towards us much as Mediterranean people do towards theirs, with a mixture of trust and abuse, passion and irritation. In turn each of us in our own way depended, as gods do, upon his worship; I, perhaps, most of all, because he belonged to the only race of living creature that was ever likely to bear my name.

# IO

I returned to London with Mij in the autumn, and with his usual good humour he adjusted himself quickly to the absence of his beloved burn and foreshore. During the car journey from Camusfeàrna to Inverness he seemed, in a long deep sleep, to shed his wild nature and to awake metamorphosed as a domestic animal. In the station hotel he lay beside my chair while I had tea, and when a waitress brought him a saucer of milk he lapped it as delicately as any drawing-room cat, spilling never a drop. He entered his first-class sleeper as one long used to travel, and at the studio next morning he seemed actively pleased to be among his old surroundings. He settled quickly, too, in his earlier routine; eels in the bath; walks round the grubby London streets; even, not without trepidation on my part, an afternoon's shopping in Harrods. By one local shop he was allowed to make his own selection before purchase; he had, as I have mentioned, a passion for rubber toys, more especially such as would squeak or rattle when manipulated. Near by to my flat was a shop devoted entirely to such oddities; india-rubber fruit and buns, explosive cigars, apparently full glasses from which no drop of liquid could escape, even papier mâché imitations of dog and cat excrement – the whole practical joker's compendium. Here I was hesitating one day between a chocolate éclair that whistled and an india-rubber mackerel that wheezed when the assistant said, 'Why not let him make his own choice, sir?' and placed both on the floor. Mij plumped for the éclair, to the assistant's surprise, and thereafter Mij chose his own toys and himself bore them home in triumph. It was a very realistic éclair, and as we passed the door of the pub on the corner a figure emerged swaying slightly, focused on Mij, and stood riveted. 'Good God!' he said, quite quietly, and behind him a voice shouted, 'You've got 'em again, Bill – you've got 'em again!'

Mij seemed in those days to possess a quality of indestructibility, an imperviousness to physical hurt, that was little short of miraculous. He succeeded, despite all my precautions, in falling from the gallery to the parquet floor below, but he might, for all the notice he took of the incident, have fallen upon a feather bed; his head was caught, without protest, in a slamming door; and, finally, he chewed a razor blade into fragments. I had been out for the evening, and had left him the premises beyond the kitchen, the bathroom, that is to say, with a full bath, and beyond it the box-room where he had a tattered armchair of his own and an electric fire that shone down upon it from the wall. When I came in I opened the bathroom door and called him, but there was no response. I went in and saw that the bath was empty of water, at the bottom of it my safety razor was in two pieces, lying among splintered pieces of the blade. It did not at that instant strike me that the total absence of blood indicated, however improbably, an intact otter; I went through into the box-room expecting to find a corpse in the chair beneath the warm glow of the fire. But there among the cushions he was squirming with self-satisfaction, as though conscious of having carried out a difficult task with initiative and acumen, and there was not, as far as I could discover, so much as a scratch on him.

I cannot now remember whether, when I had been in Iraq, I had ever seriously considered what was to be done with an otter during such times as I was unable to look after him myself; when, for example, I was again abroad, or even when I wanted to be away from my own premises for a day or two. Perhaps I had thought that at any rate in the latter case he could accompany me, for I had not yet learned that an otter is not at its best as a guest in a strange house – or rather that the house would be very strange indeed at the end of the visit. Mij was content to be alone for four or five hours, but for no longer unless those hours began in the evening, and now I found my activities so hamstrung by this dependence that I was forced to take the problem seriously.

In November I had to be away from London for three days, to lecture in the Midlands, and this was Mij's first and only imprisonment away from the people and surroundings that he knew. I arranged for him to be boarded for those three days at the zoo sanatorium, and took him up to Regent's Park in a taxi. Once inside the gardens he plodded sturdily ahead at the end of his lead, and for all his reaction the teeming animal voices and smells around him might not have existed. Only when he passed by the aviaries containing the great birds of prey did he cower and tug his lead the other way; a memory, perhaps, of his native marshes where, winter long, the eagles wheel above the wastes of water, and where they must be the otter's only natural enemy; or perhaps an inborn instinct that his race's foes came from the skies. I left him in a grim cage whose last occupant had been a sick wart-hog, and when the door was closed on him and he found himself alone his wails went to my heart. I could hear him long after I had closed the gate of the sanatorium yard.

On the evening of the next day I telephoned from the north to enquire if he had settled down. Too much, I was told; in fact he had insulated himself from the world by the same deep coma into which he had sunk when shut into a box on the air journey. He had refused all food, and after digging at the iron and cement that enclosed him until his feet bled he had curled up in my sheepskin coat and refused to be roused. I was advised to come back for him as soon as possible; not rarely pet animals in such surroundings would pass almost imperceptibly from such a coma into death.

I left for London very early the next morning, but there was a dense white fog which slowed me to a bicycle's speed for the first hundred miles. Then it furled up suddenly to reveal a bare blue sky and bright autumn sunshine. My car was a ferocious vehicle, converted from a single-seater Grand Prix racing car, and in her distant prime speeds in excess of 160 m.p.h. had been claimed for her, but at this moment I was running-in a set of new pistons that she seemed to require about as often as more modest conveyances need refilling with petrol. With that last hundred miles the running-in distance was, on the milometer, completed, but in my anxiety to reach London and my pining otter I left out of account that they had been covered so slowly as to be valueless for the purpose. I came out on to the long straight north of Grantham, and unfortunately there was not another car in sight to slow me down. I had been driving at about 90 m.p.h.; now, I thought, I would go very much faster, and, for a short time I did. The supercharger screamed, dial needles moved with incredible rapidity towards red zones; I had a glimpse of the speedometer hovering at 145 m.p.h., and I was still accelerating briskly. Then there was a rending sound, the cockpit filled with a great puff of blue smoke, and in the mirror I saw a thin black trail of oil stretching away behind me. I came to rest opposite to a farmhouse, and all I could think of was whether a train could get me to London before the staff of the zoo sanatorium went off duty in the evening. The farm had a telephone; the only possible train left Grantham in thirty-eight minutes, and I caught it as it was moving out of the station.

Back at the zoo sanatorium, I could not at first even see Mij in his cage. There were a lot of dead fish lying about untouched and a big basin the size of a hip bath had been slopped about so that there was water everywhere; the sheepskin jacket was lying in a huddle in the middle of this, and there was no movement anywhere. I came in through the steel-barred door and called his name, but nothing stirred. I put my hand into the jacket and I felt him warm and breathing, as far into the arm hole as he could push himself. Only when I thrust my hand in beside him until I could touch his face did he begin to awaken, with a slow, dazed air as if he were emerging from a trance; then suddenly he was out and leaping in a frenzy of joy, clambering over me and inside my coat, and rushing round and round that barren cage until he threw himself down panting in front of me.

In those two days he had taken on the sour small-cat-house odour of stale urine and dejection and indignity that is the hallmark of the captive; he had lost his self-respect and fouled his own bed, so that his usually sweet-smelling fur stank like an ill-kept ferret. It was not an experiment that I ever repeated, but his boarding was clearly a problem to which I had to find a solution.

He paid one more visit to the zoo, but this time not as a captive. I had for long wanted to have a clear, eye-level view of his performance under water, and to this end I was allowed by the Zoological Society to erect in the back premises of the Aquarium a large glass tank that I had hired for the day. Had I known that there was never to be another opportunity I would have arranged for a cinema camera, but as things were I asked Michael Ayrton to come and make drawings of him. With the tank I was provided with a number of goldfish for Mij to catch and consume; I could have wished that there had been something of more feral appearance, something associated less in the mind's eye with the parlour and the aspidistra and the loving care of an old maid, or with the cosy, unpredatory world of the nursery, where only in fiction was nature permitted to be red in tooth and claw. Mij, however, was untroubled by any such connotations, and set about their destruction with a zeal and a display of virtuosity for which even my long hours of watching him from above had left me unprepared. His speed was bewildering, his grace breath-taking; he was boneless, mercurial, sinuous, wonderful. I thought of a trapeze artist, of a ballet dancer, of a bird or an aircraft in aerobatics, but in all these I was comparing him to lesser grandeurs; he was an otter in his own element, and he was the most beautiful thing in nature that I had ever seen.

As with his toys, he was not content to be in possession of only one fish at a time; having captured the first he would tuck it under one arm, and, apparently utterly unhandicapped by this awkward parcel, would swoop, sometimes 'looping the loop' as he did so, upon another; at one moment he had fish under both arms and a third in his mouth. At the conclusion of this display, which had cost me in hire charges some ten shillings a minute, I felt that I had seldom been so richly rewarded for financial outlay on visual experience, and I determined that I must have a glass tank of my own for him in London.

I began my own search for emancipation by inserting an advertisement in *Country Life*, the *Field*, and *The Times*, requesting

in gist a temporary home for Mij where he could be left for anything from days to months as necessity demanded. Altogether I received some forty replies to this somewhat egregious demand, and conscientiously followed up every one of them, but one by one the prospective guardians were weighed and found wanting. Few of them had any idea of what they would be taking on; fewer still had premises in any way suitable; some turned out to be schoolchildren applying without their parents' knowledge. At the end of two months I was no further on than on the day I had drafted the advertisement.

Then I began to interview retired zoo keepers, but a few weeks of this convinced me that a retired zoo keeper has an implacable intention to remain retired. Meanwhile the book that I had been writing was finished, and I should in the normal course of events have begun again to travel. It seemed an impasse. Though I found a temporary solution – to return to Camusfeàrna in the spring and there to write a book about Mij – these were clearly no more than delaying tactics, and with friends in the zoological world I left an urgent plea to find me, by hook or by crook, a whole-time otter-keeper. But by the time he was found and engaged, Mij was dead.

What little there remains to tell of his story I shall write quickly, for anyone who in reading it has shared a little of my pleasure in his life must share, too, a little of my unhappiness at his death.

I had arranged to go to Camusfeàrna to spend the spring and summer alone in his company, and there to write the book about him that I had projected. I was to leave London early in April but I needed a fortnight's freedom from his incessant demands upon my time, and I arranged that he should precede me to Scotland in the charge of a friend. I packed his 'suitcase', a wicker basket whose essential contents seemed ever to become more and more elaborate – spare harnesses, leads, tins of unpolished rice, cod-liver oil, toys partially disintegrated but long favoured, and I travelled with him in the hired car from my flat to Euston station. It was a big Humber, with a broad ledge between the top of the back seat and the rear window; here, I recall with a vividness that is still in some sense painful, he sprawled upon his back and rolled my fountain pen to and fro between his forepaws, or held it clasped with one of them against his broad, glossy belly. I called my companion's attention to the rich sheen of his coat reflecting the neon lights. He was in his most domesticated mood.

At the station he tugged purposefully at the lead all the way up the astonished platform to the sleeper, where he made straight for the wash basin and accommodated his plastic body to the curves. His left hand reached up and fumbled vaguely with the tap. That was the last I ever saw of him.

During the next ten days I received letters telling me of Mij's delight in his renewed freedom, of the fish that he had caught in the river and in the sea; of how he would come in dog-tired and curl up before the fire; of anxious hours of absence; of how it had been decided at last that he would be safer without his harness, which, despite the care and experiment that had gone to its design, might still catch upon some underwater snag and drown him.

On 16th April I had packed my own luggage, and was to be at Camusfeàrna myself the following afternoon, when I received a telephone call from the estate agent of the property to which Camusfeàrna belonged. It was rumoured, he told me, that an otter had been killed at the village four miles north of Camusfeàrna, and Mij was missing. There was, however, a discrepancy; the otter that had been killed was said to have been so mangy and scabby that the killer had not thought it worthwhile to preserve the skin. There was no detailed information.

Nor was there to be any yet; no tidy end, no body to identify, no palliative burial at the foot of the rowan tree; no human kindness that would spare those who had been fond of him the day-long search, the door standing open all through the night.

I arrived at the village the following afternoon. I had heard conflicting tales at the railhead station, on the launch that took me to the village, at the village pier. Some said that a very old wild otter had been killed, but that Mij was already safely returned, others that he had been seen in a village miles to the south of Camusfeàrna. I did not believe them; I knew that Mij was dead, but I was driven by a compulsive desire to know by whom and how he had been killed.

A roadman, I was told in the village, had been driving his lorry past the church when he had seen an otter on the road where it bordered the sea, and had killed it. The skin was partly hairless and he had not kept it.

I found out where this man lived, and drove some four miles inland to see his family. I arrived furtively, for I expected to find Mij's pelt nailed out to dry somewhere in the environs of the house – a thing I should not be allowed to see if I made my enquiry first. For me it would have felt like finding the skin of a human friend, but I had to know.

The family denied all knowledge of it. The skin, they said, had been so mangy that the killer, Big Angus, had thrown it away before reaching home. No, they didn't know where. Big Angus was not back yet – he would come riding on the pillion of a motor-cycle; if I was to wait in the village I might see him.

I waited. The motor-cycle came at last. Yes, it was true that he had killed an otter yesterday, but it was also true that the skin was half bald, and he had not thought it worth keeping. He was soft-spoken and ingenuous.

I asked him to show me where it had happened. I walked back with him some two hundred yards to a sharp bend where a little churchyard lay between the road and the sea. He had come round the corner with his lorry, and the otter had been there, just above the road, in the ditch. He had stopped his lorry.

I could see it desperately plainly. 'How did you kill him?' I asked. 'With a stick?' 'No, Major,' he said, 'I had a pick-head in the back of the lorry.' He thought that a wild otter would wait in the road while he went to fetch the instrument of its death. He stuck to his story; by his account the otter he had killed could not have been mine. 'He was very old and skinny,' he said again and again. 'I threw the carcase in the river, and I don't remember where.' He had been well briefed and well rehearsed, as I learned much later, when he had gone in panic to seek advice. Brave murderer; for his lies and deceit I could have killed him then as instinctively and with as little forethought as he had killed the creature I had brought so many thousands of miles, killed him quickly and treacherously, when he was expecting it no more than Mij had, so that the punishment would fit the crime.

Instead, I appealed foolishly to the quality he lacked; I pleaded with him to tell me; I tried to make him understand what it would be like for me to remain at Camusfeàrna waiting day after day for the return that I did not believe possible. He did not give way an inch.

I learned later, from someone else with more humanity.

'I felt I couldn't sit by and see you deceived,' he said. 'It's just not a decent action in a man, and that's the truth. I saw the body of the beast on the lorry when it stopped in the village, and there wasn't a hair out of place on the whole skin – except the head, which was all bashed in. If he didn't know fine it was yours he knew then, because I told him: "You want to get your head seen to," I said, "if you think that's a wild otter, or if you think a wild one would wait for you to kill it in broad daylight." It's just a pack of lies he's telling you, and I couldn't think of you looking and calling for your pet up and down the burn and by the tide every day, and him dead all the while.'

I got the story little by little. Mij had been wandering widely for some days past, and though he had always returned at night he must have covered great distances, for he had turned up one day at a hamlet some eight miles south by sea. There he had been recognized and gone unmolested; the next day he had journeyed north up the coast to the village where he was killed. Earlier in the day he had been recognized there too; a man who saw an otter in his hen run had fetched his gun before he was struck by the otter's indifference to the chickens, and made the right deduction. Mij had been on his way home when he had met Big Angus, and he had never been taught to fear or distrust any human being. I hope he was killed quickly, but I wish he had had one chance to use his teeth on his killer.

He had been with me for a year and a day on the night he had left London.

# II

I missed Mij desperately, so much that it was a year before I could bring myself to go to Camusfeàrna again. I mourned for my fallen sparrow; he had filled that landscape so completely, had made so much his own every yard of the ring of bright water I loved, that it seemed, after he had gone from it, hollow and insufficient; for the first time all the familiar things in which I had taken joy appeared as a stage backcloth against which no player moved. I did not stay there after I knew that he was dead; instead, I returned at once to Sicily, and resumed a work that had by now been long interrupted. As the slow summer months passed under that scorching sun, the year during which I had had an otter for a companion, and even Camusfeàrna itself, seemed at times like a dream. I could not deny to myself how much I had been affected by the death of one wild animal, but some part of me stood aside and questioned the validity, the morality, perhaps, of such an attitude in face of the human misery surrounding me. Like my occupancy of the Isle of Soay, that year now appeared to me episodic, sharply defined at beginning and end, and without possible extension; but, as in that other instance, I was wrong.

I came back from Sicily in the autumn, and moved house to Chelsea, partly, I must confess, because I found the elaboration of otter-proofing devices that now composed my premises to be too constant and nagging a reminder of my failure to keep alive an animal to which I had given so much attention. But I had grown accustomed to the continual proximity of an animal, and when one day in Harrods I found a ring-tailed lemur, lately the property of Cyril Connolly, not even the price of seventy-five pounds could discourage me from my folly. Kiko, as she was called, came to live in my new flat. Kiko was an exceedingly beautiful animal rather larger than a very large cat, an *haute couture* creation in soft blue-grey fur, with a foxy black-and-white face, a great bushy tail of alternating black and white rings, golden eyes, monkey hands with straight needle-pointed claws, and habits that were both insanitary and obscene. For the greater part of the time she remained almost perpetually on heat; what was noticeable, however, was not so much the heat as the humidity. For the rest, she had some deep-seated psychosis that made her about as suitable a pet as a wild-caught leopard. For nine hundred and ninety-nine minutes out of every thousand she was as loving and gentle as any child might wish; for that remaining minute she was a killer, attacking without warning or *casus belli*, and always from behind. Her technique of inflicting grievous bodily harm was to spring from some high bookcase to one's shoulder – she could leap twenty feet without apparent effort – and claw for the eyes with the rending pins on her fingers. Whatever the early traumatic experience responsible for this hideous treachery, it was, I deduce, concerned in some way with windows, for each of her three attacks was launched when I was standing at a window, and, for one purpose or another, touching it; at the moment of the third and final outrage I was talking through the window to someone on the pavement outside.

I think I was fortunate not to have been killed by Kiko, for I ignored the danger signs for far too long. I chose to regard my slit eyelid as an accident, thinking that she had lost her balance and clawed without intent. The next time I defended my eyes with my hands, and as a result bear scars that I shall never lose, for her teeth were slashing instruments with razor-sharp edges. I excused this on the ground that she had interpreted my movement as a gesture of aggression. The next time I used my arms rather than my hands to cover my eyes, and Kiko lost balance and fell to the floor. She seemed to me to be making angry feints at my legs, but I was unaware of any actual contact before I noticed, with something very like panic, that I was standing in a large and rapidly widening puddle of blood. I knew that nothing but an artery could have produced that astonishing volume; I got out of the room somehow, and made for the bathroom, leaving behind me a trail of blood that appeared appropriate to a slaughterhouse. There I found that my tibial artery was sticking out of my calf like a black cigarette end, and spouting blood to a distance of more than a foot. I soaked a handkerchief and tried to apply a tourniquet, but my knowledge had deserted me; I could not remember the pressure point. At the end of several minutes trying here and there I estimated that I had by now lost something like two pints of blood, and I wasted several more seconds trying to calculate how soon I should lose consciousness, for I was already beginning to feel weak and shaky. I made out that at the present rate of loss I had a little over five minutes, and I was searching wildly for some thread to tie the artery when I suddenly had a perfect mental picture of a huge wall chart showing the venous system in red and the arterial in blue. The tibial artery, of course, only surfaced at the groin. I got the tourniquet on and a cigarette lit and began to think about Kiko. The psychoanalysis of a lemur, I realized, would present insuperable problems. She now shares spacious accommodation with three other ring-tailed lemurs in the Chester Zoo. She is still mine, and once I hoped that she would breed and I might rear her offspring well sheltered from trauma, but now I feel that lemurs, sharing as they do a common ancestor with man, might require as careful choosing as do human friends.

After Kiko came a bush baby, who, apart from the wholly misleading blood-curdling shriek with which he would nightly challenge the sleeping jungle of Chelsea, turned out to be a really crashing bore; his hobbies, moreover, were solitary and embarrassing. Later, after he had moved on to less exacting ownership than mine, I was offered another with the curious but most appropriate name of Hitchcock; though he proved, in fact, to have been christened by the surname of his owners, it was a reminder, and I declined.

I did not experiment with any other animals; none of these creatures had, anyway, the least affinity with Camusfeàrna. I acquired, instead, a baker's dozen of small, brilliant tropical birds, who flew at liberty about my sitting-room; they proved to be both less insanitary and less dangerous than Kiko.

*

137

In the early spring of the following year I made up my mind to go back to Camusfeàrna. There, with the cold, bright March weather shining on the landscape that had long become my real home, I found myself assailed again by echoes of the emptiness that I had experienced when Mij was killed; dimly at first, and then clear and undisguised, came the thought that the place was incomplete without an otter, that Mij must have a successor; that, in fact, there must always be an otter at Camusfeàrna for as long as I occupied the house.

Having at last made up my mind, I turned all my attention to this end. With vivid recollection of my slavery to Mij's exigence, I wrote first to the zoological friends who had offered to find an otter-keeper for me, and then began a systematic examination of all the holts I knew up and down the coast from Camusfeàrna. One of the chain of islands leading out from the bay is called Otter Island, and on it is a tumbled cairn of big boulders forming a system of low caves much used by otters; in an earlier year, before I had become as it were otter-conscious, there had been a litter of cubs there. But now, though several of the inner chambers had been well ordered and lined with fresh bedding, there was no sign of young, and the public lavatory was little used. There is a lavatory at every otter holt, and the excrement (which is known as 'spraint', and has no offensive odour, being composed almost entirely of crunched fish bones, or, in the case of shore-living otters, of fragments of crab carapace) often forms a high pyramidal pile; on the very top of one such I remember seeing, in that year when the cubs were on Otter Island, a tiny caterpillar of spraint whose deposition must have been an acrobatic feat for the tottering cub.

One by one I visited all the holts of which I knew, but there seemed no otters breeding in the Camusfeàrna area. I did not despair of acquiring a cub locally, for otters have no 'breeding season', and cubs have been found in every month of the year, but as a second string I wrote to Robert Angorly in Basra, and asked if he could arrange with the Marsh Arabs to get me another of Mij's species.

In response to Angorly's request the Marsh Arabs brought in a succession of cubs, three of which were *Lutrogale perspicillata maxwelli,* but each in turn died within a few days of arrival. This he at last put down to the fact that for days before arrival they had been tended by ungentle and inexpert hands; now he said flatly that he would accept no cub that had been more than twelve hours captive. As a result, the next cub lived, and in late June he wrote to tell me that I could arrange her transport to England when I liked. She was not, he said, a Maxwell otter, but he personally believed her to belong to yet another undiscovered race. She lived in the house, and was as playful and friendly as any dog.

With this apparent certainty of a successor to Mij, I began to make elaborate preparations, for I was anxious to make the fullest use of my hard-earned experience. My early enquiries for an otter-keeper had at last borne fruit, and now I was able to engage Jimmy Watt, a boy leaving school, who, though without firsthand knowledge of otters, had a profound natural feeling for animals and a desire to work with them. In London I had a large glass tank erected in the garden.

I had arranged for the otter to be flown from Basra to London on Thursday, 10th July, but the glazing of this tank was still uncompleted on the preceding Monday, and I telegraphed to Angorly asking him to postpone dispatch until the same flight on Tuesday the 15th.

On Monday, 14th July, revolution swept Iraq, and on that Tuesday they were playing football with the Crown Prince's head in the streets of Baghdad. Of Robert Angorly, who by nature of his office as chief game warden numbered as one of the tyrant's personal entourage, I have heard no word since.

Then I made up my mind to rear a cub in Scotland, and with that end in view I returned to Camusfeàrna, for a prolonged stay, in the spring of 1959.

I had been there for no more than a week when there occurred by far the strangest episode in the saga of my efforts to replace Mijbil, a coincidence so extravagant, partaking so insolently of the world of fiction, that had it been unwitnessed or in another land I should hesitate to record it.

On 19th April I motored to the station, thirty-odd miles away, to meet an arriving guest, a foundation guest, as it were, who over many visits had constructed much of the Camusfeàrna furniture, and who with me had watched the house grow from an empty shell. I arrived very early in the village, to do some necessary shopping, and had lunch in the hotel, a large and exceedingly glossy hotel that caters for the most moneyed element of the tourist trade; in the summer it is loud with Cadillacs and transatlantic accents. Now, however, it was comparatively empty; and on falling into conversation with the hall porter I found that we had many acquaintances in common. He remembered my shark-fishing boat the *Sea Leopard*; we shared affectionate memories of Captain Robertson of the island steamer *Lochmor*, who, because of a voice pitched in an almost supersonic key, had been commonly known as Squeaky.

We exchanged stories about Squeaky, and it transpired that I knew one that he had never heard. It dated from the war years; Squeaky had been sailing northwards from Barra in a thick white mist, and there was among his passengers a certain admiral spending his leave in the Hebrides. Peering from the boat-deck into the enveloping white screen, the admiral thought the ship was on a course to lead her into a minefield, and as the minutes passed and the *Lochmor* churned on unheedingly he grew more and more apprehensive. At length his alarm became so acute that he decided to beard the captain on the bridge. The two had never met, and Squeaky was quite unaware that he was carrying a high-ranking naval officer. Gazing glassily ahead with his remarkably protuberant blue eyes, and dreaming perhaps of happy deals in coupon-free Harris tweed at the northern extremity of his run, he was suddenly outraged to observe standing at his elbow a stocky little man in a raincoat and a Homburg hat. Squeaky was an habitually irascible man, and he exploded.

'Ket off my plutty pridge, you pugger!' he shouted in a voice like that of an angry wren.

The admiral remembered that he was in civilian clothes, apologized, and introduced himself. Squeaky, though by nature no respecter of persons, was impressed.

'An Atmiral, is it? And what could I be toing for you, Atmiral?'

'Well – Captain Robertson – I wondered whether you would be kind enough to give me our position.'

'Position? Ach, well, we're chust here or hereabouts.'

'No, no, Captain, I meant our position on the chart.'

'Is it a chart?' shrilled Squeaky. 'I haven't seen a chart for forty years!'

The admiral was insistent. 'Ach, well, Atmiral, if you're so keen to be seeing a chart, come down to my capin and have a wee tram, and we'll see what we can find you.'

The two went below to the captain's cabin, and after the 'wee tram' Squeaky began to rout about in his chart drawer. There were charts of the Indian Ocean and the China Sea, charts of polar seas and of the Caribbean, of the English Channel and the Skagerrak; at last, seemingly at the very bottom of the drawer, he discovered a chart of the Minch. He spread this on the table, adjusted his spectacles, and at length planted a stubby forefinger a few miles north of Eriskay.

'Well, Atmiral, it's hereabouts we are, and this is our course northwards.'

The admiral stared ominously at a sprinkling of black dots right in the ship's path. 'What,' he asked bleakly, 'are these?'

Squeaky peered. 'Those plack tots? Well, if they're rocks we're puggered for sure, but if they're what I *think* they are, which is fly-shit, we're right as rain!'

I have digressed to recount the whole of this anecdote, partly because it is irresistible, and partly because the sharing of this joke and of other memories with the hall porter had a direct bearing upon the dream-like happenings of two hours later. Had we not in those few minutes discovered the bond of mutual friends and recollections, those extraordinary events would never have taken place.

I met my guest on the station platform, and we returned to the hotel for what Squeaky would have called a 'wee tram' before setting off for Camusfeàrna. We sat in the sun-lounge that over-looks the sea, but we were well back from the window, and out of sight of the gravel sweep beyond the glass. Suddenly the hall porter came running over to us from the hall.

'Mr Maxwell!' he called. 'Mr Maxwell! Come quick to the door and tell me what's this strange beast outside – quick!'

I have an open mind on the subject of so-called telepathy and extra-sensory perception in general; I have had one or two curious experiences, but none quite as strange as the overwhelming and instant certainty that I felt then of what I was going to see. Whether that certainty communicated itself from me to my guest, or whether he had a separate moment of clairvoyance, he too had a sudden and vivid knowledge of what was outside the door.

Four people were walking past the hotel, making for a car parked near to the jetty. At their heels lolloped a large, sleek otter, of a species that I had never seen, with a silvery-coloured head and a snow-white throat and chest. I had a deep feeling of unreality, of struggling in a dream.

I rushed up to the party, and began to jabber, probably quite incoherently, about Mijbil and how he had been killed, and about how time and time again my efforts to find a successor had been frustrated at the eleventh hour. I must have been talking a great deal, because what they were saying in reply took a long time to sink in, and when it did the sense of dreaming increased almost to the point of vertigo.

'. . . only eight months old and always been free, house trained, comes and goes as she likes . . . brought her up myself with a bottle. In six weeks we've got to go back to West Africa, so it looked like a zoo or nothing – what else could we do? Everyone admires her, but when they come to the point of actually owning her they all shy off . . . Poor Edal, it was breaking my heart . . .'

We were sitting on the steps of the hotel by this time and the otter was nuzzling at the nape of my neck – that well-remembered, poignant touch of hard whiskers and soft face-fur.

By the time I had taken in what her owners, Dr Malcolm Macdonald and his wife, from Torridon, were saying, the party had dwindled by two; it transpired that the only reason why they had been in the village at all was to give a lift to two foreign girl hikers whose destination it was. And the only reason that I was there was to meet my guest, and the only reason that the Macdonalds and I had met at all was that two hours earlier I had made the acquaintance of the hall porter and exchanged reminiscences about Squeaky Robertson. I had not sat near enough to the window to see the otter for myself, and if he had not called me they would have passed by the hotel and gone home to Torridon, and I should have finished my drink ten minutes later and gone home to Camusfeàrna.

It had been a strange climax of our meeting, the meeting of the only man in the British Isles who was trying desperately to find a home for a pet otter with the only man who was searching, with equal desperation, for an otter.

Ten days later Edal became mine, and there was once more an otter at Camusfeàrna, playing in the burn and sleeping before the hearth.

# 12

Nothing was decided at that first meeting; Edal's owners not unnaturally wanted to satisfy themselves that this extraordinary coincidence was all it seemed on the surface, and that she would find with me the home they wanted for her. They promised to write during the next few days; Edal jumped into their car with the ease of familiarity, and as they drove away she appeared leaning far out of the passenger window, one hand delicately shielding her windward ear.

A week later she visited Camusfeàrna for an afternoon; then, after an interval of ten days Malcolm and Paula came to stay for a weekend, to leave Edal with me when they went. I had not been idle during those ten days; I was determined to repeat none of the mistakes that had led, directly or indirectly, to Mij's death. I sent to Malcolm Macdonald a harness that had been made for Mij just before he was killed; with the help of Jimmy Watt I enclosed the house with a fence that might not, perhaps, have foiled Mij, but which would, I thought, be barrier enough to baffle this apparently more docile, less self-willed creature if she should think in the first days to seek her late foster parents; within these confines we dug a pool and piped to it water that rose in a fountain jet appropriate to more formal surroundings. The entrance to this enclosure, and thus to the house, we guarded by a double gate, the lowermost wood of which met a sheet of metal sunk into the ground against digging. I did not think that these precautions would be necessary for long; they were to make certain that during the period when she would inevitably fret and believe herself to belong elsewhere I should not lose her through any fault of my own.

Even during that first weekend, while I was still a stranger to her and her surroundings were unfamiliar, I was so enchanted by Edal that I found it difficult to believe my own good fortune. Because she did not feel herself to be in her own home I was able to see in those first days only a fraction of her fascination, a mere corner of the piquant personality I came to know later, but I saw enough to know that if I had searched the world over I could have found no more perfect successor to Mijbil.

On the third day, while Edal was sleeping soundly on the sofa, Paula and Malcolm left silently. Our good-byes were hushed, almost tacit, both because we did not want to awaken that softly-breathing ball of fur, and because something of their own feeling of unhappiness and betrayal had communicated itself to me, and in my long-postponed moment of triumph I felt not jubilation but sadness for the sundered family.

After they had gone Jimmy and I sat beside Edal on the sofa, waiting miserably for her awakening and the panic that we thought would follow the realization of her abandonment. An hour passed, two, and still she slept on. Presently Morag arrived; the Macdonalds had called at Druimfiaclach as they left, and told her that Edal might feel less lost and despairing in feminine company. So we three sat silently and anxiously, as around a sick bed, and my thoughts wandered between the sleeping animal and her late owners, for I had recognized in them the same obsessional feeling for their otter as I had experienced for Mij, and for nothing in the world would I have changed places with them as they drove home desolate now.

When Edal awoke at last she appeared to notice little amiss. Paula's jersey lay beside her on the sofa, her own towel and toys were on the floor, and if she was aware of her owners' absence she was too well-mannered a guest to comment upon it so early. Also, as was to be expected, she got on extremely well with Morag.

It is time to give a more detailed description of Edal as she was when she came to me early in May 1959.

By far the strangest and most captivating aspect of her was that of her hands. Unlike Mij, whose forepaws were, despite the

dexterity he contrived with them, true paws with wide connecting webs between the digits, hers were monkey-hands, unwebbed, devoid of so much as a vestige of nail, and nearly as mobile as a man's. With them she ate, peeled hard-boiled eggs, picked her teeth, arranged her bed, and played for hours with any small object that she could find.

Once in a hospital in Italy I watched a crippled child practising the use of artificial hands. She had before her a solitaire board and a numbered set of marbles; the holes were numbered too, but the marbles had been wrongly placed, and her task was to transpose them until each ball and socket corresponded. She worked with complete absorption, oblivious of onlookers, and with each passing minute she discovered new powers. Once, too, I had watched a ball juggler practising his act with the same withdrawn, inturned eye, the same absence of irritation or impatience at failure, the same apparent confidence of ultimate success.

Of both these Edal reminded me as she juggled with such small objects – marbles, clothes-pegs, matches, Biro pens – as could be satisfactorily contained within her small, prehensile grasp; she would lie upon her back passing them from hand to hand, or occasionally to the less adept grip of her webbed but almost nail-less hind feet, working always with two or more objects at a time, gazing fixedly at them all the while, as though these extremities of hers were in some way independent of her and to be watched and wondered at. At moments it was clearly frustrating for her to require four feet upon which to walk, for she would retrieve a lost marble clutching it firmly in one hand – usually the right – and hobbling along upon her other three limbs.

Because, it seemed, of her delight in her own dexterity, it was her practice to insert her plaything of the moment into some container from which it had then to be extracted, a boot or a shoe for choice, and it mattered little to her whether this receptacle already contained a human foot. She would come hobbling across the room to me with some invisible treasure clenched in her right fist and thrust it into my shoe just below the ankle bone; on more than one occasion the foreign body thus introduced turned out to be a large and lively black beetle. She was also an adept, if not entirely imperceptible, pickpocket; with impatiently fumbling fingers she would reach disconcertingly into the trouser pockets of any guest who sat down in the house, hardly waiting for an introduction before scattering the spoils and hurrying away with as much as she could carry. With these curious hands she could, too, throw such playthings as were small enough to be enclosed by her fingers. She had three ways of doing this; the most usual was a quick upward flick of her arm and forepart of the body as she held her clenched fist palm downward, but she would also perform a backward flick which tossed the object over her shoulder to land at her other side, and, on occasion, usually when in a sitting position with her back supported, she would throw overarm.

Like Mij, she was an ardent footballer, and would dribble a ball round the room for half an hour at a time, but here she had an additional accomplishment that Mij had not learned, for when she shot the ball wide or over-ran it she would sweep her broad tail round with a powerful scoop to bring it back within range of her feet.

For the rest she was a small, exceedingly heavy body inhabiting a rich fur skin many sizes too large for her. It cannot be described as a loose fit; it is not a fit at all. The skin appears to be attached to the creature inside it at six points only: the base of the nose, the four wrists or ankles, and the root of the tail. When lying at ease upon her back the surplus material may be observed disposed in heavy velvety folds at one or other side of her, or both; a slight pressure forward from the base of her neck causes the skin on her forehead to rise in a mountain of pleats like a furled plush curtain; when she stands upright like a penguin the whole garment slips downwards by its own inertia into heavy wrinkles at the base of her belly, giving her a non-upsettable, pear-shaped appearance.

She is thus able to turn, within surprisingly broad limits, inside her own skin, and should one attempt to pick her up by the scruff of the neck one is liable to find oneself gripping a portion of skin rightly belonging to some quite different part of her body, merely on temporary loan, so to speak, to the neck. The colour of the fur is the best guide to what really belongs where; her chest and throat are of yellow-tinged white – not pure white as I had thought when seeing her first in the sunshine – and here the pelt hangs in such positive bags of redundancy that she has a habit of gathering up this bib in her two hands and sucking it with an enjoyment that the fine plush texture makes wholly understandable. The bib is divided from a silvery, brocade-texture head by a sharp line of demarcation immediately below the ears; the body and the enormous tail are pale mauvish-brown, velvet above and silk below. Beyond the points of attachment at the four wrists the fur is of an entirely different character; it changes from velvet to satin, tiny, close-lying hairs that alter colour according to how the light falls upon them. The tightly gloved hands and the enormous fullness above the wrists give her the appearance of wearing heavy gauntlets; watching her lolloping out for her morning walk with Jimmy Watt I have thought that she resembled nothing so much as a very expensive woman taking no chances on the weather at a point-to-point meeting.

Her comparative babyhood, and her upbringing by human beings, had left some strange gaps in her abilities. To start with, she could not lap water or milk, but only drink from a dish as does a bird, lifting her head to allow the liquid to trickle down her throat, or sucking it noisily with a coarse, soup-drinking sound punctuated with almost vocal swallowing. She possessed, however, an accomplishment probably unchallenged among wild animals – that of drinking milk from a spoon. One had but to produce and exhibit a cup and spoon for her to clamber on to one's lap and settle herself with a heavy and confiding plump, head up and expectant. Then she opened her mouth and one poured the spoonfuls into it, while the soup noises reached a positive crescendo. At the end of this performance she would insist upon inspecting the cup to make certain that it was indeed empty; she would search into it with enquiring fingers and abstracted gaze; then, belching and hiccuping from time to time, she would lift the spoon out in one clenched hand and lie upon her back, licking and sucking it.

It came as a shock to me to discover that she was the most precarious of swimmers. Even in the wild state otter cubs have little if any instinct for water, and their dam teaches them to swim against their better judgment, as it were, for they are afraid to be out of their depth. In the water Edal preferred to keep her feet either in surreptitious contact with the bottom or within easy reach of it, and nothing, at that time, would tempt her into deep water. Within these self-imposed limits, however, she was capable of a performance that even Mij might have envied; lying on her back she would begin to spin, if that is the correct word, to revolve upon her own axis, to pirouette in the horizontal plane, like a chicken on a spit that has gone mad. In this, as in the novelty of new aquabatic powers that she quickly learned, she took a profound delight, and if she had not yet apprehended that otters should swim under water and only return to the surface for refreshment, she knew all the joys of a great disturbance upon it.

Her language was at first an enormous problem to me. While she shared a certain number of notes with Mij they were, whether by reason of her different species or because she had not been taught to speak by parent otters, used in so utterly different contexts as to produce, at the beginning, acute misunderstanding. Thus the singing hum that had proclaimed Mij's extreme anger she employed to ask for food that a human was holding, and she later learned to do this at request. Mij's interrogatory 'Hah?' was, with her, also a request for some piece of food held in the human hand, a confirmation that she had smelled it and found it acceptable. The high, snarling wail that had, very rarely, marked the end of Mij's patience and the probability of a bite, she produced in response to any stranger who came near her, and appeared apprehensive rather than aggressive, for she never bit, but only ran to the safety of her friends. All through the first two nights I suffered, intermittently, from this terrifying din screeched into my very ear-holes. She had been wont to share a bed with her late owners, and to pass most of the night upon the pillow; now she chose the foot of my bed, and, heavy and forgetful with sleep, came ambling up every half hour or so to take her accustomed position. At the discovery of a strange head on the pillow, one that seemingly never lost its dismaying novelty, she put her mouth against my ear and vented her feelings in wails and screams of abandoned anguish. I could not, perhaps, be blamed for finding this alarming; I also was recalled each time suddenly to consciousness, and to me those sounds had in the past been precursors to a bite like a leopard's.

Her call note was basically the same as Mij's, but less resonant and assertive, more plaintive and feminine. Beyond these similarities, she had a whole range of then unfamiliar expressions denoting affection, pleasure, greeting or casual conversation; notes strongly reminiscent of the human infant; most of these might, unflatteringly, fall into the category of squeals rather than chirps – unflatteringly, for they had none of the ugliness that the word connotes. Like the other otters I had owned she had a note used only when suddenly and extremely alarmed; I had heard it first from Chahala in the Tigris marshes, when the door of the reed-hut was suddenly darkened by a human figure. The sound was exactly like that produced by a human being who fills his cheeks with air and expels it violently through half-closed lips. I heard it once from Mij and once from Edal.

From the very first she formed an entirely different relationship with Jimmy Watt from that which she established with me; it was, with him, a violently vocal friendship on her side, while with me, though she quickly became deeply affectionate and demonstrative, much remained tacit. Jimmy she would greet, crow over, harangue, nag, scold, caress and croon to, yell at if he disturbed her while she was sleeping, squeal with pure joy when he first appeared in the morning; with me, while she would perform the same actions, she spoke hardly a word. 'It's youth,' said Morag. 'She thinks he's another otter.' A little later other differences between the two relationships were evident, for on her daily walks she would come anywhere with me, but would not follow Jimmy if he appeared to her to be setting off in a dull or distasteful direction.

We had intended that for a full fortnight Edal should remain within the confines of the fence that enclosed the house and the pool. At first this did not seem difficult, for the pool was a new delight to her, and her moments of fretting were rare, mainly in the evenings. Then one day our attention strayed from her for a moment or two and she was gone. Where the wire joined the little shed at the north end of the house, nearest to the bridge and the route by which she had arrived with Malcolm and Paula, she had found that she could force the barrier. By the time we had made sure of her absence she had perhaps ten minutes' start.

We guessed rightly the route that she had taken; when we reached Druimfiaclach she had already been there for five minutes. Morag was away, and her husband had been unable to establish rapport with this preoccupied creature all of whose thoughts were suddenly for the past. She lay at the top of the stairs (I have found that if there is a stairway an otter is possessed of an inalienable instinct to ascend it) and wailed piteously. She seemed pleased to see us, and greeted Jimmy with notes almost as loud as those of her distress, but she did not want to come back to Camusfeàrna. We had never put the lead on her before, but now there seemed no alternative.

The return journey took more than an hour. She would trot happily ahead for perhaps fifty yards; then she would sit down, dig in her toes, and wail. I did not realize that it would have been the easiest thing in the world to have picked her up and carried her home, with no inconvenience beyond the weight of her ponderous person, for I was still under misapprehension as to the threat contained in this item of her repertoire. As it was, the nervous strain was more exhausting than any load could have been.

A few days later she repeated this escape for the second and last time; but on that occasion Jimmy, unhampered by my conditioning to other otter language, caught her up half-way and carried her home round his neck like a lead-weighted fur collar.

At the end of a fortnight there was no further danger of her straying. We had provided her with so many distractions, so many novelties – and the greatest of these was certainly constant access to running water – that she had been suborned. It was, perhaps, fortunate for us that this period of acclimatization coincided with the migration of the elvers. For these transparent morsels, who swarmed and wriggled in the rock pools below the waterfall and formed a broad snail-paced queue up the vertical rock beside the white water, she discovered a passion that obscured every other interest. Hour after hour she would pass about these pools where Mij had hunted before her, scooping and pouncing, grabbing and munching, reaching up the rock face to pluck the pilgrims as they journeyed, and from these lengthy outings she would return surfeited to play and to sleep in the kitchen as if she had known no other home.

These elvers, however, proved no small embarrassment to us, for over a period of several weeks they intermittently blocked our water supply and reduced us once again to carrying water in buckets from the burn. In our anxiety to keep Edal occupied and amused during her period of acclimatization we scooped buckets-full of the elvers and tipped them into her pool. The pool was fed by a branch of the same alkathene piping that carried our water from the top of the falls to the house; the elvers, quick to discover the only upstream exit from the pool, took up their interrupted migration with the same inflexible determination that had inspired them for the past two years, ascending the hundred-and-twenty-yard length of pipe until they reached the perforated 'rose' at the top. The perforations in the metal were, however, just too small to allow passage to their bodies, and there they stuck and died, each hole blocked by the protruding head of an elver, a pathetic and ironic end to so long and brave a journey. The 'rose' in the pool above the waterfall was accessible to us only by rope descent into the ravine; a dozen times a day we would go there and extract the dead elvers, but it was like sniping at a swarm of locusts, for behind them there were ever more of the journeying host to strangle on the very verge of liberty.

Routine is, as I have explained, of tremendous importance to animals, and as soon as we saw that Edal was settled we arranged a daily sequence that would bolster her growing security. She had her breakfast of live eels, sent, as they had been for Mij, from London, and then one or other of us took her for a two-hour walk along the shore or over the hills. During these walks she would remain far closer at hand than Mij had done, and we carried the lead not so much as a possible restraint upon her as a safeguard against attack by one of the shepherds' dogs, for Edal loved dogs, regarded them as potential playmates, and was quite unaware that many dogs in the Western Highlands are both encouraged and taught to kill otters.

On one of these morning outings with her I had a closer view of a wild otter than ever before. Edal was hunting rock-pool life on a ledge two or three yards from the sea's edge and a few feet above it; she had loitered long there among the small green crabs, butter-fish and shrimps, and my attention had wandered from her to an eagle coasting over the cliffs above me. When I turned back to the sea I saw Edal, as I thought, porpoising slowly along in the gentle waves just beyond the pool where she had been. I could have touched her with, say, the end of a salmon rod. I whistled to her and began to turn away, but as I did so the tail of my eye perceived something unfamiliar in her aspect; I looked back, and there was a wild otter staring at me with interest and surprise. I glanced down to the pool at my feet, and saw Edal, out of sight of the sea, still groping among the weed and under the flat stones. The wild otter stayed for a longer look, and then, apparently without alarm, resumed his leisurely progress southward along the edge of the rocks.

In those rock pools along the shore Edal learned to catch gobies and butter-fish; occasionally she would corner a full-grown eel in the hill streams, and little by little she discovered the speed and the predatory powers of her race. Her staple diet was of eels sent alive from London, for probably no otter can remain entirely healthy without eels, but she was also fond of ginger nuts, bacon fat, butter, and other whimsical hors d'oeuvres to which her upbringing by humans had conditioned her. Among local fish she disdained the saith or coal fish, tolerated lythe and trout, and would gorge herself gluttonously upon mackerel. We put her eels alive into her pool, where after early failures in the cloud of mud that her antics stirred up, she proved able to detect and capture them even in the midst of that dense smoke-screen. This is achieved, I think, by the hypersensitive tactile perception of her hands, for when in the shallow end of the pool she would appear deliberately to avert her gaze while feeling round her in the opaque water; the palms, too, are endowed with a 'non-slip' surface, composed of a number of round excrescences like the balls of fingers, which enable her to catch and hold between them an eel that would slither easily through any human grasp.

By the end of June she was swimming as an otter should, diving deep to explore dim rock ledges at the edge of the sea tangle, remaining for as much as two minutes under water, so that often only a thin track of bubbles from the imprisoned air in her fur gave guide as to her whereabouts. (This trail of bubbles, I have noticed, appears about six feet behind an otter swimming a fathom or so under water at normal speed; never, as the eye subconsciously expects, directly above the animal.) But though she lost her fear of depth she never felt secure in great spaces of water; she liked to see on at least one side of her the limits of the element as she swam, and when beyond this visual contact she was seized with a *horror vacui*, panicking into an infantile and frenzied dog-paddle as she raced for land.

Hence our first experiments with her in the rowing boat were not a success; the boat was to her clearly no substitute for terra firma, and in it, on deep water, she felt as insecure as if she were herself overboard – more so, in fact, for she would brave a wild rush for the shore rather than remain with us in so obvious a peril.

Edal was not the only newcomer to Camusfeàrna that summer. Years ago I had formed, at Monreith, a great collection of wild geese; after the war they represented the only major collection of rare wildfowl left in all Europe, and in 1948 they went to form the nucleus of Peter Scott's Wildfowl Trust at Slimbridge. By then, however, the commoner varieties had bred in such numbers and were so elusive to the pursuer that they were not thought worth the trouble of transporting; and the flock of full-winged greylags remained about Monreith Loch, intermittently harried for sport or as vermin to the grazing parks, semi-feral, and unwary only in the breeding season, for ten years after the collection was a thing of the past. By 1959 there were still some two or three pairs nesting at the loch, and I arranged for one brood to be hatched under a hen at Monreith and sent up to Camusfeàrna. After a long and circuitous journey by train and boat five goslings arrived, feathered but not fledged, gawky, uncouth and confiding, displaying a marked predilection for human company at variance with the traditional characteristics of their race. This paradox was pleasing to me, for like many others I had come to a fondness for wild animals and birds by way of bloodthirstiness; in my youth I had been an ardent wildfowler, and these five goslings were the direct descendants of birds I had shot and wing-tipped or otherwise lightly wounded at the morning flight years before. It had, in fact, been the keeping and taming of a few wounded greylags shot in blustering winter dawns on the salt marsh and mud-flats of Wigtown Bay that had initiated my attempt at a living collection of all the wild geese of the world, and these gabbling flat-footed five who tried so persistently to force their way into the house at Camusfeàrna were the twelfth generation, or so, in descent from the victims of my gun. Perhaps it was from some obscure part of the guilt under which, unrecognized, we labour so often, that I wanted these birds to fly free and unafraid about Camusfeàrna, wanted to hear in the dawn and the dusk the wild music of those voices that long ago used to quicken my pulse as I waited shivering in the ooze of some tidal creek with the eastern horizon aflame.

As a daily delight and as an ornament to Camusfeàrna these particular wild geese exceeded my most optimistic expectations. To begin with they were, as I have said, as yet unable to fly; only the very tips of their sprouting pinion feathers peeped out of the casing of blue blood-quill, but day-long they would stand flapping hopefully and grotesquely, lifting themselves a foot or so into the air and progressing in a series of ill coordinated and ungainly hops. As it had fallen to Jimmy Watt and myself, neither of whom can swim, to teach an otter to do so, so now as the geese grew and their wing feathers became long enough for flight, but their imagination remained too small to compass the attempt, it was we who taught the wild geese to fly. Jimmy would run in front of them wildly flapping his arms in a mime of flight, until one day the goslings, performing much the same action as they hurried after him, found themselves, to their consternation, to be airborne. The immediate result was a series of most undignified crash landings, but in those few seconds they had found their powers; within a week they were strong and certain on the wing, and in answer to a call from the house they would come beating up the wind from the beaches of the distant islands.

At night we kept them shut up in a wire enclosure, wire floor and roof, too, as a safeguard against wildcats and foxes, and when we let them out in the morning they would rise with a great clamour and wing their way down the burn to the sea, twisting and turning in the air, 'whiffling' as wildfowlers call it, in the pure joy of their flight.

I must admit that for all their charm and beauty these five wild geese displayed, in some matters, a truly astonishing want of intellect, a plain stupidity, indeed; the very opposite of the sagacity usually ascribed to their race. Even after months of familiarity with the precincts of the house it was doubtful whether they could enter the garden gate without one or other of their number getting left behind; a goose would as often as not find himself on the wrong side of the open gate, and instead of walking round it to rejoin his companions, would concentrate upon moronic attempts to penetrate the wire that divided them from him.

More striking still was their behaviour in the pen which confined them at night. Every morning I would go to open the wire-netting door and release them; as soon as I appeared they would set up a gabble of greeting which reached crescendo as I lifted the barrier and they stalked out. One morning in September, being up at first light, I opened their door (which formed the whole of one side of the enclosure) some two hours earlier than the time to which they were accustomed. They greeted me as usual but did not immediately emerge, and I went back to the house thinking that they would move only when the sun was up, and pondering afresh on the role of routine in animal behaviour. It was nearly three hours later, and thus long past the time when they would normally have flown down to the sea, that I caught sight of them from the kitchen window. They were still inside the pen, chattering irritably, and walking up and down in front of the open door as if some invisible barrier separated them from the grass outside. Deciding that they could only be liberated by some symbolic gesture, I went out to them exactly as if we had not met that morning; I closed the door and then re-opened it with a flourish, talking to them the while as I was wont. With profound relief apparent, one would have said, in their every action, they came trooping out at my heels and almost at once took wing for the shore.

From the last days of May until early September the summer, that year, took leave of absence; while England panted in equatorial heat and the coast roads from London were jammed by twenty-mile queues of motionless cars, Camusfeàrna saw only sick gleams of sunshine between the ravings of gale and rain; the burn came down in roaring spate, and the sea was restless and petulant under the unceasing winds. The bigger dinghy dragged her moorings and stove a plank, and there were few days when the little flat-bottomed pram could take the sea without peril. Because of this, and because, perhaps, I welcomed Edal's fear of the open sea as a factor in favour of her safety, it was not until the first of September that we renewed experiments with her in the boats.

She had gained much confidence meanwhile, both in us and in her proper element, and she gambolled round us in the warm sunshine as we dragged the pram across the sand into a still blue sea that reflected the sky without so much as a ripple. The geese, ever companionable and anxious to share activity, followed us in a chuckling procession down the beach, and the whole strange convoy set off from the tide's edge together; Edal shooting through the clear, bright sea, grabbing and clasping the oar blades or bouncing inboard with a flurry of aerated water, the geese paddling along a few yards astern with mildly disapproving eyes behind their orange bills. We rowed for a mile down the coastline, with the glorious ochres and oranges of tide-bared weed as a foreground to the heather, reddening bracken, and the blue distances of mountain heights. All the magic of Camusfeàrna was fixed in that morning; the vivid lightning streak of an otter below water; the wheeling, silver-shouldered flight of the geese as they passed to alight ahead of us; the long, lifting, blue swell of the sea among the skerries and the sea tangle; the little rivers of froth and crystal that spilled back from the rocks as each smooth wave sucked back and left them bare.

Edal, finding herself from time to time swimming above an apparently bottomless abyss, would still panic suddenly and rush for the boat in a racing dog-paddle, her head above water and not daring to look down; her instinctive memories, it seemed, alternated between those of the dim mysterious depths and forests of waving weed, and the security of the hearth rug, lead, and reassuring human hands. So she would turn suddenly for the boat (of which she had now lost all fear and felt to be as safe as the dry land), a small anxious face above furiously striking forefeet, cleaving the surface with a frothing arrow of wave, and leap aboard with her skin-load of water. Then she would poise herself on the gunwale, webbed hind feet gripping tensely, head submerged, peering down on the knife edge between sea and terra firma, between the desire for submarine exploration and the fear of desertion in the deep unknown. Sometimes she would slide, soundlessly and almost without ripple, into deep water, only to panic as soon as she had submerged and strike out again frantically for the boat. Yet in the moments when her confidence had not yet deserted her, when the slim torpedo of her form glided deep below the boat's side, weaving over the white sand between tall, softly waving trees of bright weed, or darting in sudden swift pursuit of some prey invisible from above, it seemed as if the clock had been set back and it was Mijbil who followed the dinghy through the shining water.

After the first of these paradise days among the islands the geese failed for the first time to return at nightfall. In the morning I called for them, but there was no greeting chorus in reply. It was as yet early for them to have felt any migratory instinct, which I thought would in any case have probably been extinguished by some generations of static forebears, and when I had seen no sign of them by the afternoon I feared that they had wandered too far and fallen prey to some tourist with a .22 rifle. I had, indeed, given up all hope of them when in the early evening I landed with Edal upon one of the white-sand beaches of the islands, drawn there by the desire to make the acquaintance of some visitors who had landed from a sailing dinghy. I was talking to them when I saw, half a mile or so to the northward, the long unhurried beat of goose wings against the sky, and recognized with an absurd surge of joy, my missing greylags. I called to them as they made to pass high overhead in the sunshine, and they checked in mid air and came spiralling down in steep, vibrant descent, to alight with a flurry of pinions on the sand at our feet.

It never ceased to give me delight, this power to summon wild geese from the heavens as they passed, seemingly steady as a constellation upon their course, or to call to them from the house when the sun was dipping behind the hills of Skye, to hear far off their answering clangour, and see the silhouette of their wings beating in from the sea against the sunset sky. I found more enjoyment in that brood of humble greylags than ever I had in the great collection of exotic wildfowl of which their ancestors had been the discarded dregs, the lees, not worth removal; more pleasure, perhaps, in their peaceful, undemanding coexistence than had any medieval nobleman in the hawk who at his bidding rose to take the wild duck as they flew or hurl the heron from the sky.

Though the greylags gave little trouble and much reward, they produced on occasion, as do all creatures for whom one is responsible, moments of acute anxiety. The worst of these was the sight of one of their number, out of my reach, doing its utmost to swallow a fish hook. Edal, as I have said, was fed upon live eels sent from London; this was a costly procedure, and as she grew and her consumption of eels rose beyond the original order for six pounds a week, I had begun experiments to supply her from the Camusfeàrna burn, in which eels abounded. But despite much advice I had failed signally to devise a satisfactory eel trap, and one afternoon we set a number of short lines from the bridge, baited with worms. This proved effective, and we had several eels in a few hours, but I had forgotten the geese. They were not often at the bridge, and I had not thought, in any case, that they would be inquisitive enough to investigate the almost invisible lines. Some two hours later, nevertheless, they chose perversely to fly in there from the sea, and by the time that I saw them one had a foot-length of trout cast dangling from its bill. At the end of the cast was the hook, a small hook taken from a stripped trout fly, and the goose, unaware of danger, was trying hard to swallow what remained. The fineness of the cast was all that impeded the intention, but while I watched in an agony of suspense another two or three inches disappeared from view. The other geese gathered round my feet, but this one, intent upon its personal problem, kept obstinately to the centre of the pool, while the hook, in response to the gobbling movements of the bill, mounted steadily higher. In the nick of time we lured it to the bank with an offer of food, and when I gripped the cast and pulled I found myself hauling it out hand over hand, for the bird had some five feet of line in its crop. The incident put a temporary full stop to my efforts to supply Edal with eels from the burn.

For the same reason the geese became an embarrassment, too, to fishing expeditions at sea; when they did not actually accompany the boat out from the beach they would discern it from afar, long after we thought to have eluded their pursuit; they would come winging out over the waves and alight, gabbling, alongside, pressing in close round the darrow line, fascinated by the fish-hooks and the dancing blue-and-silver glitter of fish hauled in over the gunwale, so that often it became necessary to control a darrow full of mackerel with one hand and fend the geese from danger with the other. It was at such moments that I understood how difficult life would be if all wild animals and birds were unafraid of man; how complicated the everyday business of living must have become to St Francis.

# 13

The house had been much transformed since Edal's arrival. While there had been no otter at Camusfeàrna I had concentrated upon improving the décor and comfort of the rooms; now that the whole premises were once more, as it were, in a state of siege this aspect had perforce to be abandoned for more practical considerations. Every table and shelf had somehow to be raised above the range of Edal's agile inquisition; every hanging object upon the walls moved upward like the population of a flooded town seeking sanctuary upon the rooftops. No longer could there be a paper-table at the end of the sofa, for this recently constructed innovation she appropriated for her own on the first day, tearing and crumpling the effete reading matter until it formed a bed suited to her exacting taste. There she lay upon her back and slept, her head pillowed across a headline describing traffic jams on the roads out of London.

It was exceedingly difficult to elevate every vulnerable object above her reach, for by standing on tiptoe she could already achieve three foot six inches. When wet she would pull down a towel, or several towels, upon which to dry herself; when bored she would possess herself of any object that caught her wayward fancy, and, deeply absorbed, set about its systematic disintegration. These moods would come and go; there were days when she was as sedate as a lap dog, but there were days, too, when there simply was not room enough on the walls for the fugitives from her depredations. By nature of its surroundings Camusfeàrna is heavily stocked with rubber boots, both wellingtons and sea-boots; many of these have over a period of years been patched with red-rubber discs, and Edal early found a fiendish delight in tearing these off and enlarging the holes they hid.

Thus the rooms to which she had access acquired the look of

country-house parks whose trees display the 'browsing line' so much deplored by late eighteenth-century writers on landscape gardening. From the height above ground to which the trees were branchless it was, in those parks, possible to deduce whether the owner kept fallow deer, cattle, or horses, and by much the same process I was able to compare the relative sizes of Edal and Mij. If there was any doubt at first, at the end of her first month with me she was certainly a much larger creature, and yet she was still a full six months younger than he had been when he was killed. Her growth was almost visible. In May Malcolm Macdonald had estimated that she was some forty-two inches long and weighed twenty-five pounds; by August she was close on fifty inches, and I estimated her weight as not far short of forty pounds. She was then a year old, and since she had not yet come into season it was clear that her growth was far from complete. In equatorial America there are otters the size of seals; if they have ever been domesticated the rooms of their owners must present a most curious appearance.

Because of the limitations of wall space in the kitchen–living-room it was not advisable to leave Edal quite alone there for long periods. She was more accommodating in this matter of being left alone than Mij had been, and if she had been exercised and fed she was content for five hours or more. When we went by boat to the village or over to Skye we would leave her shut into a room given up entirely to her, the unfurnished room over the kitchen, that had served the same purpose in Mij's day. Here she had her bed, made from a motor tyre covered with rugs; her lavatory in a corner, composed of newspapers laid on American cloth (to this somewhat remote convenience she would dutifully ascend from the kitchen whenever necessary); a host of miscellaneous toys; and dishes of water. This room had one great disadvantage: it had a single-plank floor and it was directly above the living-room. Though her water bowls were of the non-upsettable variety made for dogs, they were far from non-upsettable to her, for having tried and failed to tip them by leverage she would simply pick them up in both hands and overturn them; and the ceiling was, as I have indicated, far from waterproof. In the early days, too, her marksmanship at her lavatory was none too accurate, and this was unfortunately situated at a point roughly above the chair where any casual guest would normally sit.

Water multiplies its value to an otter as soon as it is falling or otherwise on the move, and Edal discovered that having overturned her bowl upstairs it was possible to scamper down to the kitchen and receive the double dividend of the drops falling through the ceiling; I have seen her on the kitchen floor, head up and mouth wide open, catching every drip as it pattered down from above.

The otter and the five greylag geese were the resident familiars of Camusfeàrna, though during the course of the summer there were other, more transient visitors; a young Slavonian grebe that from all the multitudinous waters of that landscape chose to alight upon the tiny pool that we had dug behind the house for Edal, and found the surrounding wire-netting too high to permit take-off; a miserable blind young vole dropped by its parent as she carried it in torrential rain from the suddenly flooded ditches of forestry drainage, and which survived for four days fed from a laborious replica of a mouse's teat; a wounded and scarcely fledged herring gull, picked up near to the house, dying in deluge and gale, who recovered to develop both flight and a degree of dependence upon household scraps; and a water rail, that arrived from the village in a cardboard box on the back of whose label was written, 'What bird is this, and is it usually found perched by the fire-side?' It had, inexplicably, been discovered squatting by the empty hearth when the householder came down in the morning. It was a great surprise to me, this bird of which a more usual view is in short flimsy flight low over the rushes of some snipe bog, the most unambitious of aerial enterprises, ending abruptly in a landing that, though invisible, one feels can only be ungraceful and inept. A thoroughly undistinguished bird, one would say, nondescript in plumage, gauche in action, and in habits retiring to the point of nonentity. Yet the specimen in the cardboard box, thus forced as it were into propinquity and social contact with mankind, revealed itself as dapper, even dressy, in personal appearance, with irascible ruby-red eyes and an aggressive, choleric temperament. He flew like a fighting cock at any hand that approached him, and the deceptively slender red bill had a grip like a pair of pliers. He clearly resented every detail of his ignominious captivity, but he had arrived in the evening and I did not want to set him free until I was sure that he was uninjured; he spent the night in my bedroom, whose floor was for the occasion littered with earthworms and other unsavoury offerings; either in pursuit of these or in simple self-assertion he stamped about all night making, as the occupant of the room beneath put it, a noise like a mouse in hob-nailed boots. Daylight showed him to be sound in wind and limb, and he resumed anonymity in a larger landscape.

Finally, producing a more lasting impression, came a wildcat kitten. Late one afternoon we had discovered that the Calor-gas cylinder (an innovation that year) was almost exhausted, and we decided to take the boat up at once to the village five miles away. It was a blue-and-gold September afternoon, with the sea between the islands as smooth as the face of a cut and polished stone. The tide was ebbing and the tops of the sea tangle showing between the skerries, so that had we not been pressed for time before the village shop would close we should have passed outside the lighthouse point; now the possible saving of ten minutes seemed a worthy gamble against the danger of running aground, and we decided to try the channel between the lighthouse island and its neighbour. I was at the tiller, and Jimmy Watt was kneeling in the bows, directing me between the rocks. Suddenly he called my attention excitedly to something at the surface on our port bow.

There, fifteen yards away, was a half-grown wildcat kitten, swimming uncertainly in the direction of the farther island. (I have since learned that it is no rarity for wildcats to take to the water, even when they are not pursued, but at the moment it seemed as strange as would a fish progressing over land.) The cat was in about two fathoms of water, and swam slowly and very high, so that the whole back and tail were above water and dry. I tried to turn towards it, but at that precise moment the outboard engine bracket, which in our hurry to set off had not been tightened securely on the transom, came adrift on one side and left me without steering. To our amazement the cat then appeared to turn towards the boat as if towards rescue, and by forcing the engine into the water with one hand I was able to bring the bows alongside it. I had never handled a living wildcat, and I thought the least that Jimmy was in for was a bad scratching, but there was not so much as a snarl as he grasped it round the body, lifted it from the sea, and dumped it into a wicker hamper. It was difficult to associate this meek, fluffy, lost kitten with the untameable ferocity of all reports, and I thought that here was the opportunity to test the rumours at first hand. But it was difficult to see how Camusfeàrna could contain with any placidity both a wildcat and an otter, and my thoughts turned to Morag; she, I thought, would welcome this ghost of her childhood days, for long ago she had kept, and mourned the loss of, a hybrid with a wildcat sire. She was at that time housekeeping, during the daylight hours, for the lodge by the river four miles up the coast, so we abandoned our idea of replenishing the Calor-gas supplies and headed for the river. Morag, however, had already left by the mail Land Rover for Druimfiaclach; at the lodge we were lent a car, and continued to her home by road. The calm of the cat within the hamper had by now given place to a low but almost continual growl, a menacing sound that suggested a curbed ferocity hardly held in rein.

When I learned that Morag felt herself too cramped by household duties to commit herself to the care of a wildcat, I should, no doubt, have released it, but despite all that I had heard and read of the untameable nature of wildcats I had met no one who could personally contribute to the picture; I knew, too, that it was very rare to capture an undamaged kitten, and I felt that an opportunity to test the validity of the myth was not to be thrown away. I returned to the lodge, and from there telephoned to Dr Maurice Burton, a zoologist who at his home in Surrey keeps and observes a great variety of wild creatures, and who had in the course of a lifetime devoted to the study of animal behaviour acquired experience of most British fauna. Curiously, however, he proved never to have kept a wildcat, and knew no one who had ever tried to tame one, though he did know someone whose lifelong ambition it had been to acquire a healthy kitten for the experiment. He proposed telephoning to this friend, who would in turn telephone to me during the next half hour, and in due course I spoke to Mr William Kingham, who was prepared to leave London by car at dawn the next morning to collect the cat. It was then Friday evening; he expected to complete the seven-hundred-mile journey by Sunday morning.

I carried the now distinctly vocal hamper back by boat to Camusfeàrna. There was only one way of bridging the next thirty-six hours: to evacuate my bedroom in favour of the kitten and to sleep in the kitchen. This I did with some reluctance, not because I envisaged the shambles to which my room would be reduced, but because it had been but three nights before that I had returned to it after the departure of my last guest.

It was already dark when we beached the boat below the house, and there was no means of obtaining any suitable food for a wildcat that night. I left the hamper open in my bedroom beside a saucer of tinned milk and some sea-trout roes. As an afterthought

I blocked the chimney with a screwed-up ball of wire-netting.

In the morning, after a far from novel night in a sleeping-bag by the kitchen fire, a cursory inspection of the bedroom discovered no cat. One of the trout roes and all the milk had disappeared, and there was an odoriferous mess in the centre of my bed, but of the perpetrator of this outrage there was no sign whatever. Just so, I remember, would we as children incarcerate hedgehogs in rooms that would not have offered exit to a mouse and yet find on awakening, eager and unwashed, not so much as a single spine to tell us that it had not been a dream. I have since suspected the adult world of some nocturnal interference in the matter, but in those days we were both fatalistic and ingenuous.

A more detailed examination revealed the cat, in the chimney. It had pulled out the inadequate cork of wire mesh, and was ensconced, owl-like, on a ledge some two feet above and to one side of the grate. My first tentative fumblings drove it up higher into the dim funnel, into regions accessible only to weapons of remote control such as chimney brushes.

I was distressed by this, for recapture was clearly necessary, and equally clearly would be a traumatic experience for the subject of an experiment in domestication. But there was no alternative, and Jimmy Watt, armed with a long string and a weight, scaled the roof while I waited, heavily gloved, to grasp the kitten when it should descend within range.

The gloves proved, in fact, to be encouragingly unnecessary; there was a certain amount of snarling and spitting, but no retaliation whatsoever. Liberated, the cat made one bound for the darkest corner of the room, and remained there, eyes glowing dully, while I made the chimney impregnable.

Sunday morning came and there was devastation in every corner of my bedroom, but there was no sign of any relief party from the south. During the night, it seemed, my captive had enjoyed the greatest of high spirits; it had concentrated not upon escape but destruction, tearing up letters, playing ball with ink-bottles, ascending with airy grace to remote shelves beyond the wildest dreams of any otter. It had dined well upon the carcase of an oyster-catcher, of which nothing but the wing feathers and the bill remained. The insult on the centre of the bed had been repeated, louder and clearer, so to speak, than before. The cat had taken up daylight quarters in a peat creel, a wicker pannier designed to be carried by a pony, that we had found washed up on the beach, and which now hung on the wall as a wastepaper basket beyond the reach of otters.

The necessity for shooting birds locally in order to feed this creature worried me. Many of the birds in the immediate vicinity of Camusfeàrna were tamer, more trusting, than in areas where someone or other was constantly on the prowl with a gun; not only was I reluctant to disturb this tranquillity, but I felt, as I set out from the house with a loaded weapon, like a deliberate traitor to the small sanctuary that I had long respected. The situation was made no easier for me by the geese, who insisted on accompanying me, sometimes on foot, sometimes locating me from afar and flying in to join me as I crouched, camouflaged, on the rock of some outlying skerry; by them I was embarrassed, obscurely ashamed that they should witness this predatory side to my nature. I found myself, as I crouched there in the salt wind and spray, repeating a childish little litany: 'I am only doing this so that the kitten may live'; this, by some absentminded transposition, reshaped itself into the words and tune of a forgotten hymn 'He died that we might live'; and then I realized that my subconscious mind had jumped a gap at which my intellect had jibbed – for after all Christians do eat the body and blood of their God.

So, with distaste, I kept the wildcat supplied with birds that I would rather have seen alive: a turnstone, a shag, an oyster-catcher, and a curlew, and my unwilling guest consumed them all with relish and went on defecating squarely in the middle of my bed. I put a box of earth on the floor, but though it was much dug by morning and smelled strongly of ammonia the bed remained the major receptacle.

On the Monday a telegram arrived explaining that Mr Kingham had reached Glasgow a day earlier, only to be overtaken by sickness that had compelled him to turn back. Unaware that the number from which I had spoken to him was five miles by sea, he asked me to telephone to him in Surrey that evening.

The relief that I had hourly awaited being thus indefinitely postponed, I set off again for the village with a faltering outboard motor which completed the northward but not the return journey. By intermittent use of the oars I got home late at night, with the promise of an immediate telegram about the future of the wildcat.

There were further delays and misunderstandings, but a week after the original capture an emissary arrived at the railhead twelve miles north by sea, and dispatched a hired launch to Camusfeàrna. He did not accompany it himself; I had assumed that he would arrive to stay for the night and receive such information as I could give him about the wildcat's habits, so that I was quite unprepared for boxing the animal at once with the launch waiting outside on an ebb tide. However, though the human escort was absent he had sent a stout and commodious crate filled with straw, at the back of which lay a plump unplucked pullet.

To the cat this third and necessarily hurried capture was still further trauma. He – for excremental reasons I vaguely supposed it to be a male – was crouched on a high shelf in the shadow of my typewriter (already knocked down and smashed by the otter), and the first advance of a gloved hand produced a tigerish and highly intimidating snarl of warning. On the second attempt he bounded from the shelf to a table in the window and crouched there growling with his back to the glass.

At this point Jimmy, who had been out in the boat fishing for mackerel when the launch came, arrived and demanded to take control. He put on the gloves and entered the arena with all the confidence of inexperience. At his first near approach the cat became transformed; almost, I had said, transfigured. The last trace of resemblance to a fluffy domestic Persian kitten vanished utterly; in its place was a noble, savage wild animal at bay before its ancestral enemy. Laying his ears not back but downward from the broad flat skull, so that the very tips and the tufts of hair that grew from within them were all that turned upward, baring every fang and gum in his head so that the yellow eyes became slits of rage and hate, swelling his ringed tail to twice its previous girth, he reared himself back against the glass of the window pane. But while one paw was lifted high with extended talons, the other still rested on the table, for the forelegs seemed to have elongated like telescopes; those velvet limbs had in an instant changed from instruments of locomotion into long-reaching weapons to rake and to slash. As an image of primordial ferocity I had seen nothing to equal it; it was splendid, it was magnificent, but it was war.

Jimmy, as yet accustomed only to handling creatures whose

bluff was easily called, was undismayed by this display of *fucht-barkeit*, but retired after an instant with a bite clean through glove and thumb-nail.

It seemed as if deadlock had been reached, until it occurred to us that we could as it were bottle the cat between the open of the crate and the window glass; this manoeuvre was instantly successful, and he bolted to the dim interior behind the straw and was silent. That was the last I saw of him; it is, however, not improbable that we shall meet again, for his new owner undertook that if the cat followed the pattern of legend and proved untameable it should be returned to Camusfeàrna and freed where wildcats enjoy the privilege of protection.

It is October, and I have been for six unbroken months at Camusfeàrna. The stags are roaring on the slope of Skye across the Sound, and yesterday the wild swans passed flying southwards low over a lead-grey sea. The ring of tide-wrack round the bay is piled with fallen leaves borne down the burn, and before a chill sea wind they are blown racing and scurrying up the sands. The summer, with its wild roses and smooth blue seas lapping white island beaches, is over; the flower of the heather is dead and the scarlet rowan berries fallen. Beyond are the brief twilit days of winter, when the waterfall will thunder white over flat rocks whose surface was hot to bare feet under summer suns, and the cold, salt-wet wind will rattle the windows and moan in the chimney. This year I shall not be there to see and hear these things; home is for me as yet a fortress from which to essay raid and foray, an embattled position behind whose walls one may retire to lick new wounds and plan fresh journeys to farther horizons. Yet while there is time there is the certainty of return.

Camusfeàrna
*October 1959*

# THE ROCKS
# REMAIN

# Foreword

To the most turbulent of lives come unforeseen periods of calm and tranquillity, as though some river running perpetually over rapids broadened suddenly into a deep, still pool of silence. Such a season of fair weather, an idyll belonging more properly to childhood or to old age, I described in *Ring of Bright Water*, the story of the West Highland cottage that I have called Camusfeàrna and of the otters that shared it with me. The time that this narrative covered represented perhaps the most placid period of my adult life; but without knowing it I had drifted nearer and nearer to the tail of the pool (for, I think, I had been in no backwater but in one of the main stream's many and various reaches), nearer to the rock lip where the water falls in cascade and spume before rushing on towards the sea. I was caught again in the full strength of a shallower current, whirled as a *bateau ivre* back into its familiar confusion, striking greater and lesser boulders as I had done before, and more closely aware of the other human beings who were swept along with me.

Thus this book, though a true sequel to its precursor, will have little of its flavour; it is the partial story of the succeeding years, their difficulties, disasters and delights; and if disaster either so minor as to be comic or so major as to appear tragic seems to predominate, it is, like the rocks that remain, in the eye of the beholder.

# I

# Return to Camusfeàrna

When I was away in Morocco in March 1960, I learned one day of a minor tragedy in my Chelsea house.

The houses of the square where I live when in London are of small rooms, in four floors. After Chelsea squares became fashionable the ground-floor back and front of these houses were, in most cases, knocked into one, giving a single long room of some twenty-five feet, with the structural supports of the old division projecting some eighteen inches from each wall. In the garden end of this room I was wont to work when I was in London, and in the other I had accumulated, slowly and almost by chance it seemed, a small collection of brilliant tropical birds, who flew at liberty and fed upon fruit suspended from natural branches. This collection had begun with an unwanted gift of two gem-like mites that I had for a time kept in a large and elaborate Victorian birdcage; eventually, having a dislike for the concept of caged birds, I liberated them in the room, and was so struck by their beauty in flight that I added another pair of a different species. The first had been tanagers, a South American group which contains some of the most brilliantly coloured birds in the world, and soon the addition of new tanager species became a minor, dilettante hobby. Certainly it was one mainly of sensory titillation, for we arranged concealed spotlamps to light the jewels in their wings as they flew, and papered the walls above the bookcases black so that none of the iridescence of the feathers should be lost by silhouette. By the spring of 1960 there were some fourteen of these birds, including one species that had rarely been kept successfully before. Most of them would fly down and take food from the hand.

The necessary temperature in this room was maintained by an

oil stove, and one night a week or so before my return to London from Morocco, some irregularity of wick or paraffin feed had started a fire. The circumstances that caused this never became clear, but it was a slow, smouldering fire giving off a dense smoke and covering walls and ceiling with an oily black soot. Jimmy Watt, who had spent the winter in London with Edal the otter (for Camusfeàrna was not yet a place of permanent residence), had not been awoken by the fumes until too late, and all the birds were dead.

Edal, however, was unharmed. She occupied a basement room of her own, with a tunnel through the wall into the garden, and she slept peacefully even through the pandemonium of the fire brigade's arrival; considering, perhaps, that the unseemly din above her was some typically tiresome human prank of no concern to her. So I returned, sad at the death of my birds whose wings seemed to have borne along so many sentences that without their inspiration would have been lumberingly pedestrian; as yet unquestioning that I should find Edal ready to return to Camusfeàrna and renew the idyll, unquestioning that the refuge, the pool of silence, could go on and on for ever.

When we had been separated in the past she had been used to greet me as does a dog after its master's prolonged absence, and when I walked into her room now I expected a demonstrative welcome. She was curled up on the bed, and when I called her name she barely lifted her head. She looked at me vaguely and immediately curled up again. At first I thought she was sleepy and had not recognized me; only slowly did I begin to understand that she was very ill. She had eaten nothing, I was told, for two full days.

It was the beginning of a three weeks' struggle, the first of two in six months, to save her life. Immediate veterinary tests showed

the presence of liver fluke; it was not generally suspected then, as it is now, that this parasite with its curious multi-stage life cycle is probably endemic in otters and causes no damage to function unless present in vast numbers, and Edal was therefore treated for liver fluke as being the root cause of her symptoms. Under this treatment, which made her constantly sick, her condition deteriorated rapidly, and she became extremely emaciated. When further tests showed the presence of shigella dysentery, we decided to abandon interest in the flukes altogether.

Her treatment was not easy. In her own room she would not allow the vet to examine her or to inject her, and he suggested that from the psychological viewpoint her submission would be much more probable in the alien atmosphere of his surgery. In this he proved right, as he did also in suggesting a method of restraint that appeared to me wholly impracticable. It was necessary to give her three separate injections in quick succession every day, besides taking her temperature rectally, and granted that no wild animal could be expected to undergo these painful indignities without protest, we had somehow to restrain her head from turning. Edal wore a harness, not a collar, because an otter's head is so little wider than the neck that a collar can always be slipped; now the vet suggested that if she wore two collars, with the lead attached to the hindmost one, the bunching up of the skin would keep them in position. This idea proved entirely successful, and every day Edal was immobilized on the operating table by three separate leads strained in different directions. It was strange that, as the drive to the surgery and the repetition of this ordeal became a daily routine, she showed no antipathy either to the waiting-room or the surgery; she never shied away from its door and she would sit on one of our laps, among the dogs, cats, parrots and other household pets that form the bulk of a city vet's practice. When the time came for her to be carried down to the surgery and laid upon the operating table she made no protest.

For a fortnight or so there was little change. At best she had an even chance of living, and though we tempted her with every kind of dainty she would eat nothing of her own free will; we had all this time to feed her forcibly with concentrated liquids.

At last one morning I noticed, as we drove down the King's Road on our daily visit to the surgery, that she seemed for the first time to be taking a little of her old interest in the traffic and the passers-by; she even hauled herself up to put her paws against the glass and peer, a little myopically, out of the passengers' window. In the waiting-room she was restless, and in the surgery she eyed the vet with distinct disfavour. He looked at her and said: 'I do believe we've done the trick. This morning she looks for the first time like a truly viable animal.' The same afternoon I opened her door quietly and looked round it, half expecting to find her inert upon the bed as she had been for so long, but she was engaged in guzzling a plate of scrambled eggs, stuffing her mouth full with those curious little simian hands just as she used to do. It was the first solid food, indeed the only food that she had eaten voluntarily, for sixteen days.

From then on she made a steady recovery; by 14th April she was her usual high-spirited and inquisitive self, and greeted a TV unit with all her old enthusiasm for novelties. She was, moreover, extremely patient with the constant retakes requisite to the threadbare story scripted for her by the BBC. (Mr Macdonald Hastings, the viewing public were asked to believe, had been astonished to see in the King's Road an otter at the heels of Jimmy Watt and myself. Fortunately, having a whole television unit with him, he and it followed us home unobserved and noted the number on our door. By what embodiment he was then assumed to have passed through that door it is difficult to imagine, for the next scene showed him peering, unannounced, round the door of my sitting-room and registering delighted surprise at the sight of Edal sitting on my lap.)

A few days later she travelled up to Camusfeàrna by train with Jimmy. As in the past with other otters, I contrived that she should share his first-class sleeper, but as before she required a dog ticket. This time, instead of leaving blank the space for description of the dog, I indulged a flight of fancy, and wrote 'Illyrian Poodle'.

Before Edal and Jimmy had left for Scotland there had taken

place a further one of those coincidences that make my experiences with otters read like fiction rather than fact. To appreciate the extent of the coincidence it should be understood that the West African species of otter to which Edal belongs has very rarely been brought to this country at all, and never, so far as I know, had there been a specimen bottle-reared from blind helplessness as Edal had been by Dr Malcolm Macdonald. Now a Mr and Mrs Davin, on short leave from Sierra Leone, telephoned to me to say that they had brought to England with them a male otter cub that they had acquired unweaned in Africa and had reared on a bottle. The cub had already been promised to a country gentleman whom they had met on the boat, but they would like me at least to see it.

Presently their car was at the door. I did not want to bring the cub into the house, for fear that some trace of Edal's infection might linger there: this was doubly important, as his owners explained to me, for not only did he eat with his fingers as did Edal, but he also had a baby habit of sucking them, especially when confronted with unfamiliar surroundings. Mr Davin reached into the travelling-box in the back of the car, and emerged with a superb ball of dark chocolate-coloured, almost black, plush; this in his arms uncoiled and re-formed as a small, stout otter lying on its back. It put three fingers of its right hand into its mouth and began to suck noisily, looking about with interest.

This otter seemed more completely domesticated than even Edal had been. It was the hour when the local school empties, and the children began to crowd round, screaming and laughing and calling to their distant companions, the bolder ones trying to touch him. To most animals, and more particularly to most wild animals, a surrounding crowd of vocal children and advancing hands would constitute a situation of fear, but this otter seemed in no way disconcerted; indeed it was clear that he considered them as potential playmates from whom he was being unjustly withheld. I coveted this creature; already in my mind's eye I could see him and Edal gambolling together under the waterfall at Camusfeàrna or porpoising after each other in the calm blue waters of the bay below the house; already I was mentally enlarging the size of the otter bed in the cottage kitchen.

Teko (he had been named after an up-country veterinary station in Sierra Leone, without his owners being aware that 'Tek' is in fact an Old English word for otter) was not content in the Surrey home to which, after our meeting, he had been taken, and when I learned that Mr and Mrs Davin intended anyway to visit the West Highlands during their holiday, bringing Teko with them, I felt that the warmth of his welcome would be so great both from humans and from Edal as to leave his owners no room for choice about his future. As in the case of Dr Malcolm Macdonald, they would have somehow to find a home for him before returning to West Africa, and I knew that few households were allowed to revolve round the life of otters as mine did at that date. I reckoned, however, without Edal's highly developed sense of property.

I arrived at Camusfeàrna a few days after Jimmy and Edal; I watched her revel anew in the freedom of stream and sea after her long winter sojourn in the drab confines of her London quarters, and in the fair golden weather that in those days seemed never to desert Camusfeàrna for long – it seemed to be the beginning of just such another summer idyll as the last. But there was to be no idyll, then or thereafter, for I had left the calm reaches of the river.

I had been at Camusfeàrna a fortnight or so when Mr and Mrs Davin arrived in the neighbourhood and found themselves lodgings some twelve miles away. By now they had more or less made up their minds that if Camusfeàrna seemed a suitable home for Teko they would leave him with me. I had provided them with a harness for him, so that his introduction to Edal could be carried out with the greatest caution and both animals under restraint. This policy paid dividends, for without our forethought there would have been little left of the unfortunate Teko. A year before, when Edal first arrived, any other animal was a welcome playmate; then, I am sure, she would have taken Teko to her heart with delight, but by now I entertained a suspicion that jealousy and possessiveness played no small part in her make-up, and I was determined that this first meeting should leave nothing to chance.

On the green sward of the field in which Camusfeàrna stands Mr and Mrs Davin waited with Teko on a lead, while I went upstairs, clipped Edal's lead to her harness and led her out. At first she did not see him, for the group stood among scattered clumps of rushes, but she saw strangers, and stood on her hind legs like a penguin to get a better view, for otters are myopic, and of their five senses trust their eyesight perhaps the least. Then she advanced a few paces and stood up again. She was then no more than ten or fifteen yards from the group, and this time she saw Teko. Her nostrils wiggled frantically, and at last she caught a whiff of his scent. She uttered a shriek of anger, and made a dash for him that almost pulled me off my feet. It was not an encouraging start. For a quarter of an hour we walked the two otters along the beach and about the field, always at a respectful distance from each other, while Edal kept up a running commentary of rage in that high, screaming wail which of all the animal cries I have heard sounds the most vindictive. Then I took her back to her room in the house, and Teko's owners and I conferred, as do generals when they have reluctantly to agree that they are attacking an unassailable position.

It seemed to us that the place of their meeting might affect her attitude, for otters are territorial animals, and that she might be more willing to accept him if the encounter were to take place on neutral ground over which Edal did not feel herself to reign supreme. The following day we made a second attempt, on the road above Camusfeàrna, but there was no noticeable improvement. Then we took Edal to the vicinity of the house where Mr and Mrs Davin were lodging twelve miles away. Here it seemed to me that she had begun to tolerate his presence a little, and her hymn of hate was not quite so continuous. There were, to use a printer's metaphor, more white spaces in the previously unbroken text of vituperation. She was, consciously, I think, lulling us into a sense of false security, hoping all the while for an opportunity which when it came left no doubt of her intentions. We were at the moment in single file, and she was walking beside me quite silently a few paces behind Teko and his owners, when he lagged a little behind them and gave her the chance for which she had been waiting so patiently. With a bound and a scream she had him by the tail and was worrying it like a dog trying to kill a rat. I contrived to haul her off almost in the same instant as it happened, and Teko fled whimpering pathetically to the consoling hands of his foster parents, while Edal's voice rose to a positive paean of hate and triumph.

The following day I watched Teko's departure with profound disappointment; Edal's intransigent attitude to the question of consorts had posed a problem to which I could see no solution. Time was short and Teko's owners were wasting their leave in searching for a home for him; while they did so I offered them the use of my London house with its otter room and tunnel to the garden.

Suitable homes for otters are not, however, easy to find, and it was no very great surprise to me when, little more than a fortnight later, they approached me again to ask how long it would take us to prepare separate quarters for Teko, who, they pointed out, had never been accustomed to freedom, and was conspicuously easy to entertain. I did not yet fully believe in Edal's permanent hostility towards him. Teko seemed to me an infinitely desirable creature, and I disliked the thought of his being placed in hands less tender and experienced than my own. I replied that it would take between a fortnight and three weeks.

In the event, however, no more than a week was available, and though fortunately most of the necessary materials were to hand, Jimmy and I had to work far into every night and begin again at dawn. I had foreseen that after the publication of *Ring of Bright Water* more and more uninvited visitors would find their way to the house, and visualizing that these might be accompanied by dogs unfriendly to otters I had decided to enclose a small piece of land surrounding the house with a continuous five-foot-high wooden paling. The wood for this formidable undertaking had been delivered by sea (the twine tying the planks into bundles of forty had in many cases broken as the cargo was lowered overboard and the whole bay had been bobbing with timber as difficult to round up as had been my Shetland sheep on Soay years before), and now lay above the tide-line on the beach below the house. With this wood we decided to construct for Teko a separate enclosure at one end of the cottage, where was also a small lean-to outhouse that might be converted to his use. Even in the early days storage space at Camusfeàrna had always been a problem, and over the years the contents of this modest building had become an inextricable jumble of lobster pots, ropes, paint tins, tools, boxes of nails and every imaginable form of junk, so that to extract any desired object from it had long since become a major task, necessitating both time and patience. Below this entangled miscellany the floor was covered several inches deep in coal-dust and debris.

Teko was an animal accustomed to living in human houses, and to lodge him in accommodation that did not in some sense resemble a human room would have been as inappropriate as to chain a drawing-room Pekinese to a barrel of straw in the open. In that week, then, we were required to reclaim, repaint and furnish the outhouse; to enclose a piece of land with wooden paling; to sink wire-netting deep into the ground against the possibility of Teko digging his way out; to construct some form of lavatory for him that would be easy to keep clean (the specialist would have been hard pressed to do better), to dig and cement a pool in which he could play, and to lead running water to it. With these basic conditions as his background, Teko could then be entertained in the living-room at any time when Edal was confined to her own quarters, and he could accompany us for walks or swims behind the dinghies after she had been exercised. The keeping of these two otters did, it is true, appear likely to become a full-time job; but as a visitor remarked, not without malice, this was perhaps as good a way of earning an anti-social living as any other.

All this work we completed in the week at our disposal, and though the cement was still damp enough to take the imprint of Teko's feet as he entered, and the paint was barely dry upon the walls of his house, he appeared entranced with his new quarters; never once did he whimper or call or behave otherwise than as if the place had always been his home. I put a camp-bed in his house and for the first few nights I slept there myself, for sharing sleeping quarters with an animal is the most certain way of establishing mutual confidence. It was not, in this case, an entirely comfortable procedure, for no sooner had I manoeuvred myself into the sleeping-bag than he would begin to explore my face with his simian fingers, pushing mobile digits between my lips and into my nostrils and ears, uttering the while a curious snuffle that led me to believe he had contracted a cold; only after the first few days did I discover that this was a sound of pleasure and contentment, like the purring of a cat. After some half-hour of this demonstrative affection he would squirm down into the warmth of the sleeping-bag and slumber peacefully through the night. Or so I had thought, but on the third morning I awoke to find myself engulfed in a smother of liberated kapok, blocking my nose, eyes and ears; Teko had spent the greater part of the night happily chewing holes in the lining of the sleeping-bag. I have contended, and continue to do so, that otters have a keen sense of humour, almost in the way that these words are used of human beings; the action equivalent to human laughter is for the otter to lie on its back and wriggle while keeping its mouth wide open.

Teko clearly found the result of his handiwork extremely funny.

Teko at that time was a weighty ball of very soft dark brown fur and fat and *bonhomie*; in character he was like neither Mijbil nor Edal, for he was (and still is) basically a clown. It is now nearly three years since he came to Camusfeàrna, and in that time he has grown to be the largest otter that I personally have seen, weighing perhaps fifty pounds. But his character is *au fond* unchanged, despite the two acts of violence with which his record is now stained. He has always been content to play by himself for hours at a time; in those days, when he had only a small pool, he would adapt any floatable object, a stick or an empty tin, for his water games, dragging it under water and pouncing on it as it rose again, and occasionally leaping with it on to terra firma and racing round and round the pool in circles; later, when he had a large and deep fibreglass swimming-pool of his own, he spurned all other toys in favour of a football, and with this he elaborated techniques to which Edal had never aspired. At the beginning the basic game was to try to keep the football under water; the impossibility of this project fascinated him, and round the original theme he wove a host of variations. He would shoot out of the water like a dolphin and land upon the football, trying to bear it under with him; release it suddenly so that it shot up high in the air; stalk it from the back and perform a thunderous belly-flopper upon it with clasping arms; dribble it round the grass enclosure using nose, four feet and tail – it was his mascot, his totem, his *alter ego*, and without it he seemed lost. His most surprising feat I should not have believed had I not witnessed it many times. The edges of the fibreglass pool were on all sides at the top of a small bank, so that from them led down a grass declivity of two or three feet. When, therefore, his antics shot the football out of the pool, it would inevitably roll down this slope; in the early stages he was content to try to push it and manhandle it back by any means he could. This was necessarily a slow and frustrating process, and quite suddenly he discovered that he could just clasp it in his arms and walk upright on his webbed hind feet. Almost always, however, either balance or the ball would begin to slip before he reached the top of the incline, and watching him from the window one morning as this began to happen I was astonished to see him actually throw the ball up into the pool, with a swinging, upward motion of both arms.

His most popular indoor parlour trick, in those days when he was allowed to meet visitors freely, was to play with the dancing beam of a torch shone upon the floor. Finding this to be elusive, intangible to nose or paws, he seemed to conceive of his tail as possessing some magic power for the capture of will-o'-the-wisps;

thus he would reverse towards the spot of light, trying to scoop at it with his tail, executing the while a quick jig step to keep pace with its movement, a highly individual step that came to be known as the *pas de loutre*.

Like Edal when she first arrived, Teko was at the outset an indifferent, barely adequate swimmer, but he lost his fears more quickly than she had done, and soon he was at home in the deepest of waters or the wildest of waves. His first day with bathers appeared utterly fascinating to him; it had not apparently crossed his mind that this curious upright foster-race who tended him could upon occasion be aquatic too. When Raef Payne, who had restored and occupied the old croft opposite to mine, accompanied him to the sea with snorkel and flippers, Teko was wild with delighted amusement. At first he was content to dive when Raef dived, and perform intricate aquabatics around him deep under water; then he discovered that he could ride the swimmer's back and go down with him; lastly, he found that he could embarrass the human considerably by removing the snorkel mask when it was least expected. After such a joke he would porpoise round and round the swimmer with the rhythmic grace of a ballet dancer; he seemed to laugh at his own antics and all those of all the world around him. I am glad that one coloured film was made of Teko that summer, before anyone had any cause to fear him.

Alas, Edal's only reaction to this splendid beast remained one of violent jealousy against an interloper. Like the Marquis of Montrose, her heart did evermore disdain a rival to her throne, as it was plainly as such rather than a consort that she viewed him.

Exercising the two animals separately occupied much time, and I found my writing falling sadly behind. I decided to engage a second otter keeper, and in July Terry Nutkins arrived by way, so to speak, of the London Zoo. He was not employed there, but spent much of his free time about the Elephant House; his ambition was to be a *mahout*. This project presenting patent difficulties, he was inclined to accept any employment involving the care of animals outside an urban area. He came to Camusfeàrna as Teko's keeper, and the two established immediate rapport.

# 2

# Peace Dropping Slow

In the autumn of 1959, soon after the narrative of *Ring of Bright Water* had been brought to a close, my mother had undergone a serious operation in London, and it was clear that the timelessness of Camusfeàrna, its isolation from the outside world, must be regarded as an essentially egotistical aspect of my life. Camusfeàrna was a haven and refuge, but with the necessity of spending an ever-increasing part of each year so far from responsibility came, too, the necessity for communication. I had expected the telephone to be beyond my means, brought, as it would have to be by a separate line of posts all the weary distance from the road at Druimfiaclach; I was unfamiliar with the whimsical vagaries of the Postmaster-General's office, and the quotation of a mere five pounds installation fee I took at first sight for an unusually crass clerical error. In this I was wrong, and beyond a slightly increased rent for the instrument, the miracle was unqualified.

For some time before the installation of the actual telephone itself the effect was that of being under siege from a slowly approaching army. The advance began out of sight, far away up the hill, with a series of muffled but menacing explosions that grew daily heavier; the attackers themselves remained as yet invisible, though after the fourth day their hoarse and seemingly ferocious cries drifted down to us on the wind between distant detonations. Then one morning they were upon us; a mighty bang and a patter of falling rock-chips brought us bounding from our beds early one morning to see their heads upon the horizon three hundred yards away. They stood motionless in a group, regarding our defencelessness; one of them held before him a small uprooted birch tree.

'Birnam Wood,' I said.

'Don't worry, these people only attack at dusk.'

How often I have wished that were true of the telephone itself. The large outside bell above the door of the house jangles arrogantly at all hours, and often at what Terry Nutkins might, with unusual aptness, have termed 'the most undignified moment of the day'.

The first incoming telephone call was received at Camusfeàrna on 11th April 1960, and in retrospect the bell seems seldom to have been silent since. While the presence of the telephone has removed from Camusfeàrna a little of our sense of security, it has substituted another, for as a place of permanent residence it is a house of crisis, particularly in the winter; and in the frequent emergencies of human and animal health, of shipwreck and the accidents of fire and flood, there is the knowledge that help, however remote, can be summoned. Now, too, we could telephone for the household food supplies, as opposed to ordering them by letter two days in advance; it brought, in however small a quantity, relief from the exigence of a routine that left ever less time either to write or to enjoy Camusfeàrna. The next logical step towards buying back a little of the leisure I had lost by treating the house as a permanent home rather than a temporary haven, seemed the installation of electricity to take over at least a few of the endless chores which kept us house-bound during long days of summer, or cold and comfortless in the twilight of winter. Like the telephone line, the power wires also followed the roadside at Druimfiaclach; the distance was the same, and in my innocence it even appeared to me possible that the same poles might carry both lines. I knew little of departmentalism. Not only was it impossible for the North of Scotland Hydro-Electric Board to use the same poles but even to use the same route of approach. The telephone line branches to Camusfeàrna from Druimfiaclach – now I received a plan showing the proposed electrical supply starting from a full half-mile farther to the southward, and an estimate for installation into which that for the telephone would have divided nearly two hundred times. But I was determined upon it, determined to avoid the transport of ponderous Calor-gas containers and paraffin drums through the winter hurricanes; in my mind, too, were shining, ill-defined images of labour-saving devices; visions of placid hours of writing uninterrupted by the recurrent oppression of household tasks undone. So there came again the distant din of an advancing army, and at length a new group reached the southern horizon and stood looking down upon us with, it seemed, a wild surmise. On 4th July a party of the raiders approached the house itself, staggering across the green field under the weight of what appeared to be an enormous battering-ram; to complete the

illusion of warfare they began immediately and feverishly to dig slit-trenches. At length the battering-ram was hoisted upright and revealed itself as the feed-post to stand beside the house, the slit-trenches as recipients of vast baulks of timber to anchor its guy-wires.

When Teko was plainly settled into his new home we tried again, with all the caution born of experience, to introduce him to Edal. Some part of our difficulty lay in the fact that we did not know whether Edal had a greater affection for her keeper, Jimmy Watt, or for myself; Edal, it was clear, considered herself polyandrously married to both of us, and apparent infidelity by either of us towards another otter could touch off the full fury of a *Lutra cornuta*. The question posed itself simply as to who should lead which animal on these trial walks; nor did her behaviour do much to elucidate the problem, for she was furious if either of us led Teko, and even more furious if he stopped for a second to pick up some shell or other piece of jetsam that struck him as a desirable toy. Habituation by proximity had already proved a failure; we had constructed a small window in the wall of Teko's enclosure, a mere six inches square and formed of two thicknesses of fine-mesh wire netting two inches apart, through which they could see and smell each other but could inflict no damage. But soon we had to close this hatch in order to preserve reason. Daylong Edal would stand at the grill and with all the force contained in her small frame she projected the unearthly ear-splitting expression of her enmity; no other sub-human sound that I know is so baring to the nerves, unless it be the screaming of a falcon that has been mishandled in transference to its foster-parents. But while Edal's screaming window was an unqualified failure as a factor in her acclimatization to Teko, I did, as the weeks passed, begin to entertain some small hope for their future; when exercised together on leashes her attention was not so perpetually concentrated upon him, nor, when Jimmy and I separated and unleashed our respective otters, did she seem so keenly inclined to pursue Teko and put him to rout.

Then, early in August, all experiments stopped together, for it became not a question of whether we could save this situation but, for the second time that year, whether we could save Edal's life. Edal, who had for so long played marbles on the kitchen floor, slept on our pillows, and displayed all the intense affection of which an otter is capable, developed an infection of the brain arising from a septic tooth. In twenty-four hours she became a mad, savage, half-paralysed but unapproachable creature, recognizing no one, as dangerous as a wounded leopard yet to me as pathetic as a child mortally sick. I can still see her crazed head weaving in search of something to attack, her useless hindquarters dragging behind her before she would collapse in a twitching rigor. Perhaps I may not be blamed too much for having hoped that each of these might be the end of an animal that now bore no resemblance to Edal.

It had started, as I have said, with a septic tooth, and as soon as we saw that she was in pain we arranged to have the tooth extracted on the following day. This involved taking her by car to a far-distant town, and, as always upon such emergency occasions, the next day was a Sunday. The vet was, however, prepared to perform the operation at any time, and we arranged by telephone that Edal should be at his surgery by eleven o'clock in the morning. (A long succession of crises such as this and worse than this have made me wonder how Camusfeàrna was ever supportable without the telephone; Parkinson's Law that expenditure rises to meet income may evidently be extended to the theorem that crises rise to meet communication.)

Early in the morning we set off up the hill on foot, for there is no road to Camusfeàrna. At this stage Edal seemed normal, though once or twice it struck me fleetingly that there were moments when she found balance difficult. This suggested to me a derangement of her cerebellum, the hind part of the brain responsible for controlling movement, and with my limited knowledge it appeared no more than sensible to take some precaution against a similar disturbance of the cerebrum, the fore-brain controlling behaviour. I insisted, therefore, that Jimmy, in whose charge she would be while I drove, should wear thick gloves.

The car was a hard-top Land Rover, with a full division between front and rear. We had not as yet any precise reason to be afraid of her, and with a sheepskin coat we made for her a bed on the centre seat of the front cab, so that she was between us. Trouble started within the first half mile. Without any warning she flew at Jimmy's hands, and had they not been heavily gloved the damage would have been great. Again and again she repeated these attacks, and I thought my own ungloved hands would be her next target, for she seemed to resent movement, and I had to reach directly in front of her in order to use the gear lever. But in her confused brain it was Jimmy that she hated at that moment, and she treated me as if I did not exist. After three miles of acute nervous tension it became plain that the situation was untenable, and that one or other of us would be seriously hurt long before we had completed the eighty miles in front of us.

In her present condition it was not easy to see how to transfer her to the rear compartment, much less close the door upon her. We had to dangle her down out of the front cab on the end of her lead, taking care all the while that she could not come within range of us, and then to hoist her over the rear drop-board, a very much more difficult procedure. When, after some ten minutes of effort, we had at last completed the task and closed the door upon her we argued that her behaviour might in fact be no more than the effect of the tranquillizers we had given her before we started; they had, it is true, been of a variety that we had not tried before, but in all my previous experience tranquillizers administered to otters had produced the reverse of the desired and expected effect. They seemed to act much as alcohol affects the majority of human beings, leading to breakdown of all inhibitions and the collapse of learned behaviour; a wild animal in acute pain and without inhibitions could hardly be expected to display tranquillity and good humour.

At the surgery, two hours later, we were confronted with fresh difficulties, for there was no anaesthetic chamber, and we were forced to improvise with a large tea chest. Into this we lowered her as we had lowered her into the rear compartment of the Land Rover, and then air-sealed the top with heavy towels before pumping in the anaesthetic. Edal took what was for me an almost intolerable time to lose consciousness, for all the while she wailed like a wounded hare, a sound so utterly piteous and abandoned that I found my hands unsteady and a cold sweat coming out on my forehead. Jimmy was unable to bear it, and took refuge in the Land Rover outside.

When at last these dreadful cries had ceased we removed the towels and lifted her limp body out of the box and on to the operating table. Two vets worked upon her, but found it impossible to shift the molar. No ordinary practitioner could be expected to know the precise jaw and skull structure of an otter, much less of a foreign species; this tooth resisted every normal means of extraction, and, not knowing how high the roots were planted in the skull, they were afraid of inflicting fatal damage if they used greater force. Seeing Edal lying there limp upon the operating table, her mouth full of blood and her fur foul with her own excreta, I did not believe in her recovery. The one slender chance was that the mauling the tooth had received might have provided some drainage for the septic fluids.

We carried her back into the Land Rover no more than seconds before she came round from the anaesthetic; through the rear window I could see her, dazed and blood-stained, walking round and round the narrow floor space in stumbling circles. The part of me that remains a child was very near to tears.

At the end of the two-hour journey home I felt a small spark of hope, for she was able to walk down the hill, and though she was noticeably off balance I supposed this to be the after-effects of the anaesthetic. She would not eat, but in the circumstances this seemed no great cause for surprise. We contrived, again by dangling her from the end of a lead, to hoist her upstairs into her own quarters; there she appeared to go to sleep in her bed, and we left her for the night.

Early the next morning Mr Donald MacLennan, the local vet, came – I use the word local for want of a better, for he lives at Broadford in Skye, more than fifty miles away by road and sea-ferry. I was totally unprepared for the rapid overnight deterioration in Edal's condition, and I opened her door to bring her downstairs. She was partially paralysed and wholly mad. She fell rather than walked down the stairs, and stumbled out into the garden, where she toppled over on her side, kicking and twitching. I took this first convulsion for a death-agony, but after perhaps a minute she recovered from it, raised herself unsteadily, and looked around her with mad eyes for something to attack. Finally, for despite the paralysis she seemed enormously strong, she struggled into the living-room and dragged herself up into a low wooden armchair with a slot back. Here she was unapproachable, screaming and literally gnashing her teeth at the least sign of movement in the room.

The vet looked at her and said nothing; I was unused then to the painstaking deliberation of his diagnoses, and I took his silence for a death-warrant. Yet I did not want him to shoulder the responsibility; I knew that in a month's time, when *Ring of Bright Water* was to be published, Edal would become a famous animal, more famous, perhaps than Elsa the Lioness, and I felt it unfair to this young man to leave the decision to him alone. I telephoned to London, and the advice I received was unequivocal.

Jimmy and Edal next to the house . . .

. . . and on the heather hillside above the bay.

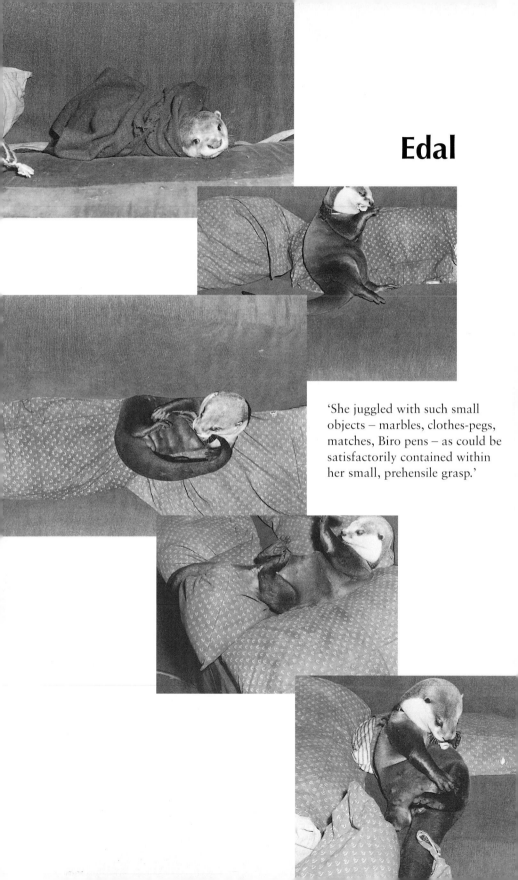

# Edal

'She juggled with such small objects – marbles, clothes-pegs, matches, Biro pens – as could be satisfactorily contained within her small, prehensile grasp.'

'She was a small, exceedingly heavy body inhabiting a rich fur skin many sizes too large for her . . . When lying at ease upon her back the surplus material may be observed disposed in heavy velvety folds at one or other side of her, or both.'

Edal at the waterfall.

Installing the otter pool 'looking like a giant's washing-up basin'.

Edal in her new quarters.

'At a range of two hundred yards or so from the citadel, the single word PRIVATE, in foot-high red letters.'

Mossy and Monday had discovered their unrivalled powers of escape from any enclosure.

. . a ring of bright water whose ripples travel from the heart of the sea'.

The winter of 1961-62.

'... the burn froze over and finally the waterfall itself'.

Camusfeàrna seen from the nort
Between the house and the bur
to the right of the Norway fir, ca
be seen the rowan tree, 'the mag
tree that stands beside every o
Highland cottage

Had I got a gun in the house? I had a pistol and only one remaining round; I searched for it and found it before returning to the living-room. It seemed to me now only a question of how Edal's execution could be carried out with the least possible distress to herself and to the humans who had made a pet of her. But the young vet, with his soft, deliberate Highland speech, said: 'It is not fair to consult a practitioner six hundred miles from the patient; he is not on the spot, and he has no opportunity to form an opinion as he would like. A bullet will prove nothing, and also it would spoil the body for post-mortem. I think there is a very faint chance, and if you are willing to try I am. We shall have to give her very massive injections of antibiotics daily for five days, and if there is no improvement then she will go into a coma and die quietly.' I felt, and I expect looked, helpless; I could not see how we might approach Edal closely enough to touch her, let alone restrain and inject her.

We had one small help – the slotted back to the chair on which she was sitting. While I distracted her attention from the front, Jimmy contrived somehow to clip a lead on to her harness through the gaps in the woodwork. Then, by using a shepherd's crook, I managed to lift the lead through until it was on the same side of the chair-back as she was. Down this lead we slipped the hand loop of another, so that she could be held from two different directions; in this way we moved her slowly off the chair until we could take a turn of one lead round a table leg. Then we drew the other lead tight too, from a direction at right-angles to the first, and I took hold of her tail. Even when she was held from three points and could not turn her head she managed to lash her body like a wounded snake. It must have been little easier than injecting a flying bird, but that vet did it, as I was to see him do it so often in the future. Then we put on rubber thigh-boots, and half hoisted, half dangled her back upstairs and into her own room, leaving attached to her the two leads that would make further injections possible.

For the following four days we repeated the same procedure, and each day Donald MacLennan showed the same extraordinary legerdemain in injecting his moving target. We entered that room only in thigh-boots – we did not know then how little protection these would have offered had Edal reached and attacked us with purpose – and always as we went about the daily routine of cleaning the floor and changing her water she would drag her paralysed hindquarters after her in pathetic attempts to attack.

Then at last came a day when as I entered the room I seemed to sense something different in her appearance. She was curled up in her bed in the corner, so that only her head protruded from the blankets, and she seemed to look at me questioningly, as though I had been away for a long time and she was not sure whether it could be me. I came nearer to her, and suddenly she gave a little whimper of recognition as she had been used to when she was pleased to see Jimmy or myself. With great hesitation I gave her the back of my bare hand to sniff and the greeting sounds redoubled. I knew then that, however long her physical paralysis might remain, she was now mentally normal. I knelt down on the floor beside her and put my face down to her and stroked her, and she rubbed her whiskers over my cheeks and pushed her nose into my neck while all the time she whimpered her welcome and affection for someone who had been away for so long.

Physically, her convalescence and recovery were protracted, but they progressed in precisely the sequence that the vet had hoped for; a returning power in her fore-quarters, then her hind limbs and, last of all, the ability to move her tail. It was early October before I was able to take her out of the house for the first time; that she had locomotive power was all that could be said, for her movements were awkward and ill-coordinated, each front foot raised high on the forward pace as if she were striking at something, and even in the hundred yards or so that I took her she lay down several times with a look of bewilderment and despair on her face. Very slowly, over a period of months, she regained the full use of all her muscles, began to play again, and to gallop and swim and dive. One day early in November I found her playing on the floor with a new toy that she had somewhere discovered; it was the single round of pistol ammunition with which I had been about to end her life on 8th August 1960.

*

A little before Christmas 1960 I left Camusfeàrna for North Africa. Jimmy and Terry were in charge of the otters, and a friend who wanted sanctuary in which to write of an expedition from which he had recently returned had undertaken to run the household and deal with any emergency that might arise. I knew that I should not see Camusfeàrna again for several months.

# 3

# All the Wild Summer Through

With that spring following the publication of *Ring of Bright Water* the privacy of Camusfeàrna came abruptly to an end. A great number of people who read the book accepted the disguise of place names as a challenge, and were determined to locate and visit the place; they came by their hundreds, and because at first we did not wish to appear churlish the once orderly routine of the house became chaotic. As spring turned to summer and the tourist season reached its height we became desperate, for the inroads upon our time meant that I was able to work only sporadically and without concentration. We erected *Private* notices on the two tracks by which the house may be approached, but these had little effect, and gradually our days became almost wholly occupied with warding off uninvited visitors. The number of notices that these had to pass before reaching Camusfeàrna was formidable; at the distance of more than a mile all gates already carried estate notices at the entry to the forestry ground, reading *Strictly Private*; after a further half-mile the hardy encountered the first of my own signboards – *This Is A Private Footpath To Camusfeàrna – No Unannounced Visitors Please*; then, for those who had penetrated all the outer defences, came an elaborate signboard with a drawing of a beseeching otter and the words: *Visitors: There Are Pet Otters Here – Please Keep Dogs On Leash*; and finally, at a range of two-hundred yards or so from the citadel, the single word PRIVATE, in foot-high red letters. Despite all these precautions, a steady stream of rubbernecks arrived daily, often with loose and undisciplined dogs, to bang on the single door of the house and demand, as if it were their right, to see the otters and all that had figured in the story.

One of the most extraordinary and revealing aspects of this

unconcerted invasion was the conviction of each that he or she, and he or she alone, was the pioneer; that it could not have been possible for any other to have discovered the true location of Camusfeàrna, or for any other to have wished to do so. Each claimed to have established the position by hours of labour with charts and deductive power worthy of Hercule Poirot; by a long past familiarity with the coastline that had yielded a sudden and vital clue; by private information given by a friend of a friend of an acquaintance; by some recognized piece of landscape in a published photograph – always, in sum, by some feat of mental or imaginative agility of which no other could be capable. After one long day, when we had wrestled many hours with such well-disguised angels, and when we were at last sitting down to eat for the first time since the previous evening, there came an authoritative rap on the door and a murmur of perceptibly transatlantic voices. I refused to move, and sent one of the boys to deal with the situation. The message he brought back was that the gentleman (the name eludes me) had travelled three thousand miles to see Camusfeàrna, and could not believe that I would be so inhospitable as to refuse him entry. For the first time since the beginning of the siege my temper broke; I replied that if indeed he had wished to travel three thousand miles to visit a total stranger he might have shown more courtesy than to arrive unannounced at half past nine in the evening. This churlish outburst set a precedent, and when a few days later I looked out from my window to see a party of five people leaning over the wooden palisade and baiting (I can find no other word) Teko, I found the instinct for battle strong in me. I went out and asked them with hostile civility from where they came. Manchester, I was told. 'And in Manchester,' I asked, with what coolness my rage could master, 'is it the custom to treat your neighbour's house and garden as a public exhibit?' There was a shocked silence; then the paterfamilias said plaintively: 'But this is not Manchester; in Scotland we've been told there's no law of trespass!'

This extraordinary situation does, in fact, obtain; in Scotland there is nothing but the unwritten rule of common civility to prevent any stranger entering the garden of a suburban or other house and making himself thoroughly at home. If he picks the flowers or otherwise damages the garden it is possible to secure an injunction against his future entry, but if he has a hundred friends lined up to repeat the performance it will be necessary to take out an injunction against each of them severally and in succession. An Englishman's home is his castle, but not a Scotsman's. Scottish law contains many such whimsical quirks; for example, a homicidal maniac may not be reincarcerated on the original findings if after escape he succeeds in remaining at liberty for three weeks. Research into the origins of such legal curiosities might be rewarding but not, one cannot help feeling, edifying.

As month succeeded month we became, in self-defence, more and more ruthless, because the very life of the place was at stake. If one of the boys was at Druimfiaclach collecting the mail and happened there to encounter a party of prospective visitors, he would give elaborately misleading directions as to how to arrive at Camusfeàrna; by these ruses I suspect, our household has forfeited the sympathy of a section of the public, but in order to survive we had no alternative. To not one of these victims of our seeming misanthropy had it occurred, apparently, that they were on holiday and we were not, that each of us had a full day's work to get through as much as, or more than, if we had been holding down an urban office job. We became, in the broadest sense, xenophobes, and resented any intrusion, because each day ended with work undone and a gradually increasing sense of handicap in earning our livings.

There were more precise, definable irritations. Those who were deterred by our final, flaming PRIVATE notices diverted their routes to the surrounding hilltops overlooking Camusfeàrna from a distance of perhaps three hundred yards; from these vantage-points they would scrutinize the house and its environs with field-glasses, telescopes and long-focus ciné-camera lenses, and on one Sunday morning when it was possible to count the heads of five such parties a female guest came to me almost in tears. 'Look,' she said, 'you told me you'd got no sanitation and I said I didn't mind using the countryside – but it's a different thing when four pairs of field-glasses and a ciné-camera are trained on you from all angles.'

What angered me perhaps more than anything else was an incident during the summer of 1961. A very smart small yacht came to anchor in the bay below the house, flying some pennant that was to me unrecognizable. There were three or four very fat men and women aboard. One of the men settled himself in some sort of deck chair in the stern, with a .22 rifle across his knees. His companion began to throw bread to the gulls, and as they alighted on the water in response to this invitation he shot them. We sat at the edge of the sand-dunes and watched. At the end of five minutes I began to grow exceedingly angry; as a blood sport this particular exercise seemed to me despicable. It is academically true that for the protection of other species the greater gulls should be kept within numerical limits, but the method of procedure outraged in me some quite illogical approach to the subject; it seemed wanton and destructive. I sent Jimmy to the house to fetch the .350 big game rifle. When he returned I waited until the fat man had shot a herring gull, and as it drifted away from his yacht, I shot at the dead bird. The noise of that rifle is considerable; the scene dissolved, figures hurried about the deck, the anchor was aweigh, and the yacht's auxiliary engines started almost before I had made up my mind to fire another shot astern of her.

The acquisition of my own present motor vessel *Polar Star* was one of the many minor follies with which my life has been sprinkled. When I began to find myself comparatively prosperous it was agreed by my new company, who took over the running of Camusfeàrna, that we had a strong case for a substantial and fast boat. High speed was an absolute necessity, for because of the otters we could never be absent for very long from the house, and distances in the West Highlands are great. Such a boat would, we felt, solve many of our transport and supply problems, and could also be used as emergency accommodation for guests, whose numbers seemed always to increase. The expenditure agreed for this project clearly precluded the purchase of a high-speed luxury yacht; in fact there seemed few craft that would satisfy our requirements for sale at any price. At length an advertisement from a Yorkshire shipyard caught my eye: it read, 'Ex-R.A.F., T.S.D.Y. 1945. 40 × 9.5 × 3 ft. draught, diagonal mah. hull, Transom stern, modern bow, twin Perkins 100 h.p. 1952, 20 knots, accommodation four, large cockpit, stated in very good condition, £2000.' The fact that this miracle was within our agreed price limit should have warned me; I had once before, in the shark fishing years, bought a boat unseen on the strength of the surveyor's report, and I should have remembered the deplorable results. It is aggravating to repeat a stupid mistake, and thus to demonstrate that one is slower to learn than many an animal. However, as I could not at the time leave Camusfeàrna I decided to rely upon an independent surveyor's report, together with advice from expert friends as to the suitability of the type of craft. By them I was advised that no hard chine boat could be expected to stand heavy seas, but that round-bilge construction of equivalent size and speed would be very far beyond the agreed expenditure. I therefore decided to buy the *Polar Star*, subject to a satisfactory survey; apart from a misleading attention to unimportant details, the report was excellent, and on 14th July Jimmy Watt left Sandaig for Bridlington to accompany the boat north with her two Yorkshire crew.

The *Polar Star* sailed from Bridlington on 16th July, to pass through the Edinburgh–Glasgow Canal, then the Crinan Canal, through the Mull of Kintyre, and so up the West Coast to Camusfeàrna. The voyage had an inauspicious beginning. The boat was no more than half an hour out from Bridlington when Jimmy saw fierce flames leaping from the stern between the diesel tanks and the Calor-gas cylinders. The crew were in the wheelhouse. When Jimmy raised the alarm, 'they started charging about all over the ship looking for fire extinguishers, cursing and swearing and expecting an explosion any minute. I had a look myself and there was an extinguisher in the wheelhouse all the time, so I took it and got the fire out myself.' After this mishap she made remarkable progress during the earlier stages of her voyage.

On the third day I was sitting writing at my desk at Camusfeàrna when I found my mind wandering to the probable position of the *Polar Star* at that moment. She must, I decided, be in the

Crinan Canal itself – and then a thought came into my head that sent a sharp shock of fear through me. A boat emerging from the Crinan Canal finds itself in the Sound of Jura, almost landlocked, and with only two northward passages to the open sea, those to the north and south of the Island of Scarba. To any uninformed person looking at a chart, the southern passage, between Scarba and Jura, would appear very much the more direct route to clear the southern end of Mull and reach the open sea. That passage, however, is a death-trap, the famous Gulf of Corryvreckan where many, many a boat bigger than the *Polar Star* has met her end in savage whirlpools or the roaring wall of water that is the main overfall. On board the *Sea Leopard* I had watched it from a respectful distance years before, a mad leaping confusion as if the tides of all the world had met in that one place. The CCC Sailing Directions call it 'the worst in the West Highlands . . . at any time there is such risk that it is inadvisable to attempt it'. Now it struck me as just conceivable, but conceivable enough to bring out a fine cold sweat, that the East Coast crew aboard the *Polar Star* had not heard of Corryvreckan and were sailing without proper written directions.

I grabbed the telephone and spoke to the canal authorities at Crinan. The *Polar Star*, they told me, had left the canal some minutes before; I explained my fears, and they offered to try to call her on her radio and telephone back to me. The next quarter of an hour passed slowly at Camusfeàrna, the slower for two incoming calls unconnected with my predicament, in the course of which I was barely able to remain civil. The third time the bell rang it was Crinan and they were reassuring. They had been unable to contact the *Polar Star* because, like much else about her, the radio was out of order, but they had talked with a fishing boat who had seen the *Polar Star*. She had passed, this boat reported, at about twenty-five knots, and appeared to be on course for the northern channel, not for Corryvreckan. I returned, a little uneasily, to my work. Jimmy had agreed to telephone from Mallaig, and that could not be for some hours.

It was late in the evening before he telephoned, and his voice sounded odd and strained. 'Are you in Mallaig?' I asked.

'No, we're in Tobermory.'

'Tobermory! But you left Crinan hours ago – is everything all right?'

'Well, not exactly. We ran into some trouble. There's no glass left in the wheelhouse, for example, and its hatch flaps have gone too. We ran into a sort of wall of water – like a head-on collision. Nobody was hurt – much.'

The *Polar Star*'s English crew had indeed steered straight into the Gulf of Corryvreckan, at its most dangerous of all tides, half ebb springs, and had charged the main overfall at maximum speed.

It was not until after Jimmy's arrival that I heard the full story of this adventure that might so easily have proved tragic. He had not seen the actual impact, for he had been making tea in the galley just aft of the wheelhouse. The *Polar Star* was travelling at full speed, slamming from wave top to wave top as hard chine boats do, when she seemed to Jimmy to ram something solid. The teapot was thrown from his hand and he himself was flung violently against the bulkhead; as this happened a wave of water some four feet deep swept through the double doors leading into the wheelhouse. Entrance for'ard thus effectively blocked, Jimmy made his escape aft. The roll hatch separating the cabin from the after hold was pulled down against the wind; raising it, he looked out upon a chaotic sea. It had, he said, no real form or shape beyond an impression of confused violence, for so many things appeared to be happening at once; there were fierce down-sucked whirlpools, waterspouts and waterfalls, and towering waves truncated at their ends. He climbed out on to the narrow unrailed side-deck and began precariously to make his way for'ard to the wheelhouse. While he was doing so the helmsman put the *Polar Star* about, still at full speed, and she came round in a wide arc, with seas coming up at her from all sides, from ahead and astern, from port and starboard all at the same time. Once clear of the worst of it Jimmy and one of the two Yorkshiremen worked furiously at the pumps, for the boat was half full of water. Jimmy asked what had happened. 'Dunno – something to do with the wind against the tide, I suppose.'

The *Polar Star* made Tobermory harbour three hours later, and there, past caring for rigid etiquette, her crew picked up the first vacant moorings that held a dinghy, and rowed it ashore.

I was reassured by one thought only; there could be very few vessels of the *Polar Star*'s size that could have attempted that folly and survived it.

The following afternoon the *Polar Star* came up on the southern horizon. Watching her through the field-glasses I could see little but the enormous bow wave she was throwing up; whatever her defects, twenty knots seemed a very conservative estimate of her speed, for from the moment at which she was first visible some ten miles away until she hove to and dropped anchor in the bay was no more than twenty-five minutes.

Terry and I rowed the dinghy out. This was my first sight of my new acquisition, and once aboard her I found it difficult to conceal my disappointment. Potentially, she was all that I had expected, but everything about her reeked of neglect and indifference, from the rusted and functionless instruments on her fascia board, to her uncaulked decks and damp-stained cabin.

As with so many other 'bargains' she required an enormous amount of expenditure before at last she became both trustworthy and socially presentable. At the outset she had, like some aboriginal woman, little but speed and a sound hull; for the rest she was dirty, neglected, squalid in appearance both inside and out, and with a highly unreliable transmission system from the wheel-house to the two big motors in her stern. These were controlled, if the word may be applied to any operation so imprecise, by two throttles on the fascia board, and two gigantic and rusty gear levers not less than four feet high. The neutral position in the forward and backward travel of these monstrosities was exceedingly difficult to achieve, and when found remained, so to speak, an armed neutrality, for the vessel would still creep ahead until the engines were finally stopped. The system was obsolete, and had in recent models been replaced by two small levers on the fascia board, operating a hydraulic gearbox and acting simultaneously as throttle and gear levers. This innovation, we discovered, could only be fitted to the more modern type of engine. In every sphere of life I have always found that one of the most difficult decisions for me has been to determine the moment at which to cut my losses; now, rightly or wrongly, we decided to replace both engines and transmission. We should then have a sound hull and sound engines, and during the winter months we could work at bringing the interior woodwork and fittings up to the same high standard.

This decision, however, we did not take until the autumn; and immediately after her first arrival at Camusfeàrna she had perforce to be sent to the nearest shipyard to remove the evidence of her encounter with Corryvreckan. There she spent some weeks, and we had little use from her that summer; none, in fact, beyond shopping runs to the village, a journey that we found she could accomplish in twelve minutes as opposed to our usual forty by foot-track and road.

August 1961 stands out with a terrible vividness in my mind. Before I began to write this book I wondered whether in the narrative that month should be omitted, whether people who through *Ring of Bright Water* had become vicariously fond of us and of our animals could take even at secondhand the shocks and blows that we sustained, for they came near to bringing about the disintegration of Camusfeàrna as we had known it. The shattering chain of events began with a single episode which, though alarming, did not prepare me for the nightmare that was to follow.

We had staying with us Caroline Jarvis from the London Zoo, who, the previous year, had arranged Terry's employment as an otter-keeper. At that time Edal had the run of the house for most of the day; she would go for her walk in the morning and sleep and play in the living-room; only if there were very many people, or if she was particularly obstreperous would we shut her up in her own quarters, a part of Jimmy's bedroom that he had divided by a four-foot high plasterboard partition. Caroline, who has enormous experience and love of animals of all kinds, got on extremely well with Edal; they had gone for walks together, and only the evening before Edal had gone to sleep on her lap. There was no tension in the atmosphere, nothing to warn us of what was coming.

The next morning Caroline, Jimmy and I set off for a walk with Edal. We had crossed the burn and were walking up the green slope beyond it when I saw Edal, who was close to Caroline, stop suddenly, almost like a pointer, and direct a malevolent glare at Caroline's foot. There was something so unfamiliar in Edal's expression that I called to Caroline to stand still, and hurried towards them. But it was already too late – Edal gave one piercing scream of rage and buried her teeth in Caroline's ankle. Jimmy and I pulled her off and attached a lead to her while Caroline limped home, making light of her injury. Jimmy and I went on with Edal to the islands, discussing all the way the possible reasons for her outrage. At first we were inclined to think that there might be some brain damage remaining from her long illness, but on the veterinary evidence we were forced to discard this theory as untenable. If the nerve itself had been damaged she could never have recovered the full use of her limbs and tail; it must have been the nerve sheath and that could not affect her present behaviour. It was, we concluded, some sort of explosion of jealousy; Edal considered herself polyandrously married to Jimmy and myself and had put Caroline in the position of a rival. We made up our minds not only that she should not meet Caroline again, but that we should be very careful about letting her meet any woman at all. Caroline left two days later; I did not know then that she had given to Terry the thick woollen sweater she had been wearing. I went to London on business for a week, drove north in the Mercedes, and did not get back until after dark on a Monday night.

It was so late that I was surprised, as I approached the village pier, to see in the headlights of my car the figures of Jimmy and of Raef Payne, an old friend who had taken over the holiday occupancy of the empty croft adjoining Camusfeàrna. They both looked grave and worried; I knew at once that some sort of disaster had taken place at Camusfeàrna.

It did not take long to say; Terry had been very badly bitten by Edal, and had been taken the previous day to Broadford Hospital on the Isle of Skye. The local doctor had stitched him up as well as she could, but there was the possibility that one finger would have to be amputated. No one seemed to have any very clear idea of how it had happened; Edal had been in her own room, and Terry had gone up to play with her as he often would. He had been entirely alone in the house – Jimmy was out, and Raef had been in his own house a hundred yards away. Both hands were badly damaged. Terry had run over to Raef's house more or less holding on a finger that would otherwise have dropped off.

There was no way for me to get to Skye that night, for it was hours past the time of the last ferry-boat; I would have to wait for the morning. I do not think any of us slept very much.

I went first to see the hospital doctor, so that when I went on from his house to the hospital I was not quite unprepared, for I had been told that Terry might lose one finger on each hand – it depended on how much deterioration there had been overnight. We had agreed that in any case I should bring Terry from the hospital to the doctor's house for a confirmatory examination, that I should bring him home to Camusfeàrna, and that the following day I should drive him to Glasgow for plastic surgery.

When I reached the little hospital I could at first find nobody; the place seemed deserted. I peered this way and that, and at length found myself looking down a corridor to the open door of a ward where a patient was visible sitting up in bed. He was not only sitting up, he was semaphoring wildly with his discarded pyjama-top – suddenly I realized that it was Terry, and that the signals were directed at me. I hurried down the corridor.

There were only two other patients in the ward, an old man and a child, and both were somnolent. Terry could hardly keep his voice down as he demanded over and over again: 'Do I get out of here? Are you going to take me away? You won't leave me here?' At close quarters the smell of gangrene was overpowering; its implications made my voice unsteady as I reassured him.

Back in the doctor's house, I tried to persuade him to close his eyes while his hands were being examined, for I knew by that stench what their appearance would be; but he would have none of it, and took a keen, almost clinical interest in the proceedings. The removal of the bandages revealed a sight so unpleasant that it is better not to attempt description. The top two joints of the second finger of the right hand had literally been chewed off, as had a slightly lesser portion of the same finger of the other hand. The local doctor had somehow contrived to stitch them on again, but now they were very dead indeed. Terry looked at them dispassionately: 'Chop 'em off, Doctor,' he said, 'that ruddy lot's no good to anyone.' Terry was only just fifteen; he never shed one tear either in pain or in self-pity.

The next day we drove to Glasgow, where his father had come to meet him, and he was installed in a nursing home. There he quickly became everybody's pet, and the ten days passed more quickly than he had expected.

When we drove back together to Camusfeàrna we had agreed upon deception for the time being – we were both frightened of the Press getting hold of the story (Edal was at the height of her fame), and also frightened of a local scandal, scandal that might end in her being killed. We owned a portable petrol-driven saw, and outside our circle it was to be given out that Terry had lost his fingers when the chain of this struck a nail in wood and flew off.

I had questioned Terry so closely that he had brought to light the knowledge of which he himself had been unaware – when Edal attacked him he had been wearing Caroline's sweater for the first time. Yet even with this partial solution to her behaviour, the savagery of the attack and the massiveness of the damage made it out of the question for her to meet anyone but Jimmy and myself in the future. It was plain that no amount of attachment to her could justify the risks inherent in her continuing to live in the house and being petted by visitors. If we were to keep her at all there was only one possible course to pursue, and having made the decision, we put it into action as quickly as possible. At the seaward side of Camusfeàrna cottage we would erect a prefabricated wooden house at right-angles to it, so that the two formed an L; this new house Edal would share with Jimmy, and through a hatch in its wall she would have permanent access to a spacious enclosure with two pools and every kind of waterworks we could devise. Her living conditions would not be greatly changed, for she could still share Jimmy's bed as was her wont, and she could be taken out for walks on any occasion that the coast (literally) was clear. As an insurance policy against Teko some day surprising us by a similar attack, I decided that he, too, must have a large pool adjoining his lean-to shed.

Jimmy's new house arrived by sea in half a gale of wind, and its unloading presented a weird spectacle as we poled ourselves about on its sections, steering them clear of the rocks and painfully hauling them above the tide's edge. My mind went back to the Island of Soay, and the building of the factory seventeen years earlier; I realized that once again, as if it were an inescapable pattern, I was in the initial stages of constructing and maintaining a complex organization on an almost impossibly remote site.

When the building was finally erected, decorated and furnished, it made an imposing room, thirty feet long by twelve feet wide, with eight large windows. The furthest ten feet were divided by a waist-high partition to form a bedroom for both Jimmy and Edal, and, since she was now to have permanent access to water and we could not dry her every time she emerged from it, we adopted the technique of an infra-red lamp hanging above a bed of towels just inside the hatch. This extremely practical idea had not, in fact, been ours in invention; it had been devised by one of the few other people in the British Isles who keep otters, Mr Jeremy Harris, and it ensured that the otter's bedding would always be dry whether or not there was a human in attendance.

At this point, while I am describing what may appear an excessive concern for Edal's comfort and well-being, I should perhaps explain my own attitude towards her in the light of all that had taken place. She had inflicted terrible damage on someone for whom I was responsible and of whom I was fond, but for several seemingly valid reasons I did not feel I could send her away. Any private home to which she went would be exposed to the same risk, and it seemed an act of wanton cruelty to send this house-living animal to a life sentence behind the prison bars of a zoo. She was extremely and affectionately attached to Jimmy and to myself; she had acted instinctively; moreover, it was in some sense to the exploitation of her person in print that I owed my present prosperity. There will, no doubt, be those who feel these loyalties to be misguided; I can only say that in our minds we had no option.

The prefabricated house was the easiest part of our plan to put into operation, though it involved much time, labour and expense; the installation of pools of the size we felt to be necessary was a very much more formidable task. In broad principle there are two main types of swimming-pool marketed for use in, say, suburban gardens; those which are circular, made of sectional steel sheeting standing upright upon the ground and holding a giant bag of waterproof material, and those which are rectangular, made of some such substance as fibreglass, designed to be sunk into a prepared pit of the same dimensions. Both are almost unbelievably costly, but of the two the sheet-metal-and-bag type is less so. This, in view of the general heavy outlay, decided us upon the wrong choice, and we ordered three, two of four yards diameter and one of six yards. One small and one large were to be installed at different levels, partially sunk, in Edal's new quarters, and the third was to be erected in a new enclosure surrounding Teko's house, in case he too should at some time in the future have to be treated with caution.

Teko's pool burst on the first day that it was filled with water, and, being immediately outside my ground-floor window, it flooded the house with all its four thousand gallons. It did more, for it laid flat the wooden paling of the enclosure, and had Terry, who was standing beside the pool, not seen the metal beginning to bulge, he might well have been killed. The containing wall of the pool burst on that side only, and I think my calculations are conservative when I say that the metal sheets must have been slammed down by not less than twenty tons of water. A week later we replaced the wreckage by a sunk fibreglass tank sixteen feet by eight by four-and-a-half feet deep. This object, looking like a giant's washing-up basin, arrived by the usual combination of rail and boat travel, and was delivered in Camusfeàrna south bay by a hired launch. (The *Polar Star* was absent, as so often that summer, undergoing some minor surgery to her fuel system.)

Edal's pools were partially sunk, and boarded outside to resemble huge vats; in their case there was no such disaster as had occurred with Teko's, but she began early to take a mischievous delight in ripping the PVC lining with her teeth, so that the level of the water could never be relied upon, and the complicated system of syphon and waterfall that we had devised was rarely in working order. We had, nevertheless, solved the problem of her continued existence at Camusfeàrna.

# 4

# The Wreck of the Polar Star

Saturday, 7th October 1961, began in a calm and orderly manner and ended in chaos. The events of the evening formed one of the chain of disasters, greater or lesser, that have punctuated the attempt to make Camusfeàrna, in all its isolation, a place of semi-permanent residence. At some time in the morning Miss Jean Alexander, who manages the Invermoriston Hotel, telephoned to say that she had staying with her Mr Lionel Edwards, known to several generations as a painter of hunting scenes, together with his daughter and son-in-law. Mr Edwards was particularly anxious to visit Camusfeàrna and see the otters, but he was by now a man in old age, and the long, steep track between Druimfiaclach and Camusfeàrna was beyond his capacity. The visit was possible only if we could take the *Polar Star* to the village pier four miles away and collect him there, returning him in the evening to the same place where his car would be waiting. There appeared no possible reason against this; the weather was flat calm with intermittent light rain and we had nothing on hand but the normal routine of the household. We arranged to collect Mr Edwards's party from the pier at about two-thirty.

Everything went smoothly until the visitors, who had lingered long watching Edal and Teko disporting themselves in their respective pools, began their homeward journey in the evening, and even then I was unaware of anything amiss. We cast off the *Polar Star*'s moorings at about a quarter past six; it was a dull grey evening with heavy rain hammering down on to a completely smooth sea, and there was not a whisper of wind from any quarter. There were some parcels to be fetched from the village, and it was dusk before Jimmy, Terry, and I set out again for home, the beginning of one of the worst nights I can remember.

215

The very high speed of the *Polar Star* reduces the time necessary for the journey to a little over ten minutes and we used all her speed because I thought that the very poor visibility might make it difficult to find our moorings; I was the more concerned when as we approached the Camusfeàrna islands I saw patches of dense grey mist. There was still no breath of wind to disperse them, and still the vertical rain streamed down and hissed into an unmoving sea; it was with real relief that I saw the big white buoy loom up through the mist no more than ten yards ahead. Jimmy and Terry lifted it aboard. I saw from their gestures that something was wrong, but the continuous rasping screech of the clear-glass circle in the windscreen made it impossible to hear their voice. Then Jimmy came down through the wheelhouse hatch. 'There's no dinghy on the moorings – just a cut end of rope!'

It was clear to me at once what had happened; I had been careless for the first time, and must have cut the rope with one of the *Polar Star*'s propellers as we left for the village. The full gravity of the situation did not immediately strike me; in that dead calm sea it seemed easy enough to calculate the drift of the dinghy during the hour of our absence and to recover her by one means or another. The only real trouble at this stage was the mist and the increasing darkness in a spot so strewn with rock and reef. The tide had been ebbing for nearly an hour and a half, which meant that in the absence of any wind the dinghy should have drifted southward and come ashore somewhere on the lighthouse island, whose dark bulk was by now only faintly discernible against the clouded night sky. The only point on the whole island where it might even theoretically be practicable to land one of the boys was at the lighthouse itself, where two L-shaped lengths of heavy-gauge piping led down into the water to form a rough-and-ready pier usable at any tide higher than three-quarter ebb springs. On one engine and minimum possible revs I crept cautiously round the north end of the island; the searchlight lit only a solid wall of rain, and as the lighthouse came into view its flashes seemed like torchlight shining on fountain spray, lighting nothing below them. We were no more than five yards from the pipes before I could make them out in the thin light of Terry's torch, and it was a tribute as much to his agility as to my manoeuvring that he contrived to scramble ashore while with enormous relief I put the engine astern. It was about then that I realized that this was the darkest night I had ever seen.

Terry's task was tough even for one who had not had two fingers amputated only a few weeks before. He was to search the northern shore of the island with its thousand weed-covered outcrops and treacherous crevices, and if he found the dinghy he was to bring it where we would lie at anchor as near to our moorings as we could judge. If he found nothing, he was to wait until nearly midnight, wade waist-deep to the next island in the chain, and so to Camusfeàrna south bay, where the tiny pram dinghy was drawn up on the sand beach. From there it would be a two-mile row right round the south side of the islands to reach where we lay at anchor, but at least the sea was so far in our favour. We had chosen Terry for this role because his hands made it difficult for him to handle anchor or rope, while his rowing was little affected.

Jimmy and I returned to the north side of the island and dropped anchor, though by now the darkness was so total that, with the lighthouse obscured by the headland, we had little real idea of our position. At first we thought we could make out the faint flicker of a torch from time to time on the island shore, but then everything was black outside the lit cockpit of the *Polar Star* and the only sound was that of the rain. So it was for an hour or more; then came the first whine of wind in the rigging of the wireless mast, and a little later the first slap of breaking water on the ship's side. The wind was southerly and we were lying in shelter; it was plain now that Terry's alternative course, to row the pram round the lee shore of the islands in pitch darkness, would be little less than suicidal. Jimmy and I conferred, and decided to take the *Polar Star* round to the south bay and anchor her there, so that Terry, if he could launch the pram at all, would have but a short row out to us. It was then a little after half past nine.

We weighed anchor and very gingerly we set off again. It was as if one were deprived of all one's useful senses – the utter enveloping blackness and the deafening scream of the clear-glass combined to produce a sensation of claustrophobia such as I have never before experienced. I wanted to shout 'Let me out of here! Let me out of here!' We passed well to the west of the lighthouse and kept on southward for what I thought an amply safe distance before turning up for the south bay; but, no doubt subconsciously accustomed to the *Polar Star*'s normal high speed, I overestimated the distance we had covered. The lighthouse was obscured by the headland, and the only visible thing outside the wheelhouse was the intermittent pinprick of another lighthouse miles to the south-west.

I did have a split second of warning, but it was too brief to be of any value. The searchlight had shone only upon the unvarying wall of rain; now, only feet from our bows, I had a sickening camera-shutter image of solid rock. Then we struck and struck hard, and the bows reared. Both engines full astern produced only a hideous grinding sound, and after a few seconds we stopped them.

The worst of it was that we had no clear idea of our position, nor whether we were aground on an island or a reef. The whole of the area of the Camusfeàrna islands is a death-trap, even in daylight, to any boat unfamiliar with it; now, with more than four hours ebb tide, we might be on any one of fifty rocks. The *West Coast Pilot* with an inspired typographical slip, describes the south side of the islands as 'foul fround', and never had the fround seemed fouler than now with the *Polar Star* hard aground in the middle of a black night and a rising wind.

When I went aft I thought the hull was holed, for the floorboards were awash, but then I saw that the angle at which her bows had reared must have sent all the bilge water to the stern and that this might be no more than the accumulation of rainwater over many hours of downpour. We decided to try to explore our surroundings, and we clambered overboard, Jimmy holding the head rope and I the stern. The rock shelved steeply and it was slippery and weed-covered; feeling upward in the darkness there was only more weed. We did little speculation aloud as to our whereabouts, for the evidence so far pointed to a reef, and neither Jimmy nor I could swim. There was one life-jacket in the *Polar Star*, and Terry had the other.

The wind rose steadily and the waves came out of the dark and broke over us, and as they grew greater they broke, too, over the *Polar Star*'s starboard quarter, so that she began to ship green water into the after cockpit. Then she began to bump and slam upon the rock that was holding her, and it was clear that she would break up if she stayed where she was. We went back aboard her and tried the engines again; she would not move, but there seemed a faint chance that if we were both ashore on the rock we might push her off on the crest of a wave to take her chance of finding sand or gravel. We pumped her bilges, and for another despairing half hour we struggled in the slimy seaweed and the breaking waves until at length a slight veer in the wind did our work for us and suddenly she was free. All we had salvaged from her was a boat-hook. Our watches had stopped owing to immersion, but I think it was then about eleven o'clock. As the *Polar Star* drifted away from us we both felt very desolate.

We were surprised by how quickly her mast-light was obscured – no piece of rock formation that we could visualize could have hidden her so quickly, but by now it was almost dead low tide, and this was no guarantee that we were not on a reef. We could explore only by touch, for the blackness was utter and complete; passing one's hand before one's eyes they registered no faintest change of shade. Jimmy said: 'This is what it must be like to be blind, stone blind.'

The first thing seemed to be to get above the waves; this was no very logical process of reasoning, for we had no inch of dry clothing between us, and the rain was now lashing in on a force six southerly wind. The first ten feet were almost vertical and all weed-covered, and we could only raise ourselves almost inch by inch. More weed and more; I began to have a chilling certainty that we must be on a reef and not an island, and high tide would be before dawn. A small glow of hope warmed us when my hand touched the roughness of rock for the first time, but it was barnacles that I felt beneath my finger-tips. Jimmy found bare dry rock first, but it was smooth and sheer and he could find no fingerhold. He felt out to the left with his foot and there was nothing there; I did the same to my right and found nothing either. We were evidently climbing some sort of narrow buttress. I remember saying: 'There just isn't a piece of rock like this anywhere round Camusfeàrna.'

That first twenty or thirty feet until we came suddenly on rough, tussocky grass must have taken us more than half an hour. We went on climbing, grass, rock, then grass again. Jimmy said suddenly: 'There's only one piece of ground like this – we're at the gull colony on the south face of the Lighthouse Island. I bet that in another quarter of an hour we'll see the lighthouse.' We did, and we were safe, but our troubles had only begun.

Even in the best of daylight conditions, the traverse of the half-mile length of the Lighthouse Island is no easy matter, for it is one of the roughest, toughest pieces of ground that may be conceived. Its uneven, rocky shore is split by deep fissures many feet deep, and these are camouflaged, as are pitfall traps for wild animals, by a rank growth of heather and briar. Above the shoreline the surface is never even; it is as though a truddle of big boulders had been flung together by some giant and then roughly coated over with the coarsest vegetation available to the climate. There are patches of dense, waist-high scrub willow through which it is entirely impossible to force a passage; ankle-twisting areas of tussock grass where each football-sized clump is as hard at its base as a stone; rooty heather growing three feet and more from treacherous holes and gulleys; and, worst of all, bramble thickets like barbed-wire entanglements. When in summer we would come here to count the eider ducks' nests or harvest herring gull eggs we would pick our way with difficulty though this defensive jungle and often have to retrace our footsteps and seek a new path through the undergrowth; now we were confronted with the whole length of the island without even the use of our eyes. Also we were in a hurry now, both because of the urgency of calling salvage to the

*Polar Star*, and because soon the depth of water would increase between us and the next island of the chain.

We joined hands like children, and with Jimmy in the lead with the boat-hook we began to feel our way forward foot by foot. We stumbled and fell and swore, the briars tore at our legs and we bruised our shins and twisted our ankles among the rocks, and our teeth were chattering and all the time the rain came deluging in on the south wind; it ran in at our collars and trickled out into our shoes, and there was no speck of illumination in all the black night. Before each step forward Jimmy felt ahead of him with the boat-hook; it was fifteen feet long, but often it touched nothing and we had to skirt our way along the edge of a long rock-fissure only to find ourselves brought up short again by the density of undergrowth. At some point in this nightmare journey, we came into sight of a small white light that could only be the mast-light of the *Polar Star*; it seemed stationary, but we found it impossible to estimate the distance or judge whether she was on rock or soft beach. It must have taken us the best part of an hour to reach the north-eastern tip of the island, from which by wading we might gain the next, and by that time both of us were very near to the stage at which it seems simpler to lie down and give up. Of Terry we had heard nothing, and it would be superfluous to add that we had seen nothing.

The water between the islands was chest-high; sometimes, when our feet slipped deep among the weedy rocks, it was head-high and we were floundering. Jimmy led me on by the hand, feeling his way before him with the boat-hook, and it struck me what a bizarre spectacle we would present if some miracle could suddenly lift the darkness and leave us flooded with light.

'Even the weariest river winds somewhere safe to sea', and it was where the Camusfeàrna burn does this that there occurred the artistically climactic incident of the night. We had been on flat grassy ground for some minutes when I heard in front of us the familiar sound of the burn running over shingle and boulders; I forsook Jimmy's guiding hand, and shouting: 'We've done it! We're saved!', I stepped briskly forward. Never had pride a swifter fall; I had been at the very brink of the low sand cliff where the sand martins breed, and I stepped straight into space to fall ten feet and land on my head. For the first time that night I was truly unconscious for a little while, to be brought round by the full weight of Jimmy's boot on my face.

Terry reached the house perhaps half an hour after we did, and he had passed as bad a time or worse; for he had been for even longer without light. All hopes of finding the dinghy had ended abruptly and painfully after the first ten minutes, when a long slithering fall among the slimy rocks of the tide-line had smashed the torch and hurt the newly healed stumps of his fingers. He went on searching in the dark, hoping to stumble on the dinghy by accident, but he only stumbled on everything else. He saw us begin to move the *Polar Star* from where we had her anchored, and feeling the freshening wind he guessed our purpose. He began to cross the island to put his alternative plan into action, but without the aid of the boat-hook that had saved us from broken limbs, he fared worse and his progress was even slower than ours. When at last he was on the south side of the island he saw the mast-head light of the *Polar Star*, stationary perhaps a quarter of a mile from him, but no port or starboard lights. At first he could not bring himself to believe that she had been abandoned; then he tried to visualize her position, and realized that she must be aground. He had a life-jacket and he tried to swim to her, but he was exhausted and beginning to feel the effects of exposure, so he dragged himself ashore on the first piece of land he could reach. This was another island, if possible rougher and more inhospitable than the Lighthouse Island, and it took him some time to recognize where he was. By the time he reached Camusfeàrna he was far gone, but still as indomitably cheerful as his chattering teeth would permit him.

As soon as I had reached the house I had telephoned to Bruce Watt, who had long ago been skipper of my shark-fishing vessel, the *Sea Leopard*, and who now possessed three sizeable boats for the diversion of tourists. He was also coxswain of Mallaig lifeboat.

*

I do not know how Bruce effected the salvage, but at first light in the morning he had the *Polar Star* alongside his boat, *Western Isles*, on my moorings. He then removed *Polar Star* to Mallaig.

The dinghy was recovered 4½ miles N on the afternoon of the same day.

# 5

## Teko Revisited

It was well that we had given thought to the possibility, however improbable it appeared then, that the friendly, bouncing, affectionate Teko might one day commit the same outrage as had Edal, for by the time it did happen we were entirely prepared. He had his own heated house, his own enclosure and pool, and it had been planned in such a way that a dividing gate could exclude him from either one or the other. In emergency, he could be tended by the most timorous.

The emergency was not, in fact, long in coming. In November I became engaged to be married, and in December my future wife, Lavinia, and stepchildren Nicholas and Simon Renton came to Camusfeàrna for part of the Christmas holidays.

Terry was at that time still looking after Teko and taking him for his daily walk, in company with the deerhound Dirk. Dirk was a comparatively recent acquisition, a gigantic yearling standing nearly forty inches at the shoulder, and it had been a joy to discover that he and Teko regarded each other as natural playmates, Dirk making rings of dazzling speed around the otter, or leaping over him high in the air. Simon, then aged thirteen, had accompanied the party more than once, and Teko had given him more than a casual and friendly greeting as they set off.

As in the case of Edal and Caroline, the attack came without warning or apparent reason, and not long after they had left the house. They were on their way to the island beaches, and Simon was walking a little in front; the two animals, who had not yet begun to romp seriously, were walking sedately between him and Terry. Suddenly something detonated in Teko's brain – akin, I am certain, to Edal's past explosions of jealousy. He flew at Simon from behind, knocked him down (it must be remembered that Teko weighed little less than fifty pounds) and bit him savagely in the thigh. It was not just a single bite, it was a sustained attack, that might have been extremely serious had not Terry done a flying rugger tackle and pulled him off by the tail. It was the first of two rescues carried out by Terry after he had lost his own fingers. Teko responded instantly to Terry's authority; there was at no moment any sign of the attack changing direction from Simon to himself.

From what emotional rag-bag these outbursts are pulled it is impossible to say with any certainty, but I am convinced that the emotion is basically that which we describe as jealousy. To the otters, Caroline and Simon were interlopers; the otters sensed, if it is permissible to anthropomorphize so far, that something they had regarded as being their exclusive right was being shared with a stranger.

The immediate consequences of this incident were less grave than might have been feared, and were greatly helped toward this end by Simon's cavalier attitude to his injuries. He was unable to play football for a week after going back to school, and he will never lose the scars, but, like Terry, he shed no tear and made no complaint.

I left Camusfeàrna for London on 19th January, to be married on 1st February, and on the 22nd Teko attacked Jimmy. He and Terry had taken Teko and Dirk for a walk, and as usual the dog and the otter had indulged in wild games in and out of the sea. They had begun to walk home, Jimmy leading with Dirk and Terry following with Teko. Jimmy stopped for a moment to pat and caress the dog, and in that instant Teko flew at him from behind. The first deep bite was in the calf of the leg, but by the time Jimmy had realized that Teko's rage was too great to yield to any persuasion, he had received other severe bites in the shin and the foot. Jimmy did the only thing he could do; he ran for it, with Teko in close pursuit. Normally he would have outdistanced Teko quickly, but he was handicapped both by his injuries and by heavy boots, and he fell once, to realize as he recovered himself that Teko was almost upon him and that Terry was still some yards behind. By now this demoniac and breathless procession had reached a point immediately above the small sand cliff where the sand martins breed, the point from which I had fallen on the night we abandoned the *Polar Star*; and Jimmy, remembering that Teko had always evinced a dislike of heights, jumped from this cliff and floundered across the burn. The moment's pause that this manoeuvre had given Teko had been time enough for Terry to overtake him and attach his lead. Jimmy was in a state of virtual collapse at the other side of the burn.

All this was kept secret from me until my return to Camusfeàrna sixteen days later.

Terry is convinced that this disaster too was due to jealousy, that there existed some close bond between dog and otter, and that Teko saw this relationship threatened by Jimmy's apparent affection for the dog. It was Jimmy, in any case, who was in that situation the outsider; both Teko and Dirk were specifically under Terry's charge, and the three formed in some sense an independent unit.

Whatever the reason, I was faced on my return with a situation not easy of solution. I was to leave for North Africa in the near future; during my absence only Terry could look after Teko, and only Jimmy could look after Edal. If either of them were ill one otter would have to be treated as a zoo animal, tended without contact. I had become, and remain, the only person who trusted both otters and had no reason to fear either of them.

There have been times when, despite their consistently affectionate attitude to me, it has been difficult to forget the terrible injuries they have inflicted upon others. These moments have risen mainly with Teko. He has always possessed a genius for removing his harness and an intense dislike for having it refitted, which is in itself an exceedingly difficult task when the otter is uncooperative. Teko resists the operation with all his really enormous strength and eel-like sinuosity, accompanying his motor actions with vocalization calculated to intimidate the most courageous. His sound of displeasure is an essentially cockney vowel sound 'wow-wow-wow', each syllable prolonged and yelled out somewhere in the middle range of a tenor's voice; there have been times when I have almost expected this to change suddenly into the scream that accompanies an attack, but I have at no moment truly lost the sensation of mastery in which lies my salvation. The occasion when I have come nearest to doing so was in the autumn of 1962, when Terry, who had by that time given up looking after otters and was engaged entirely upon the construction of new buildings, came to tell me that Teko had a terrible wound. This proved not to be an exaggeration – it was an enormous incision that looked as if it could only have been made with a scalpel as a first stage to removing the limb, and it stretched from under the arm almost to the shoulder. Behind the elbow, where the forelimb joins the body, an otter has a great baggy fold of skin which becomes almost like a wing when the limb is extended forward; this had been cut right through to reveal not only flesh but sinew. The wound was at least three inches deep and, because a side-strap of the harness had sunk right into its depths, it was gaping four inches wide. Seen in profile as he stood on his hind legs, the whole animal looked as if he had virtually been cut in two.

The first task was clearly to remove the harness, and I was the only one of us who could attempt it. Knowing that Teko must be in great pain, and remembering how much he hated his harness being handled even without this added stimulus to anger, I thought it very probable that my moment had come; it was, however, impossible to leave him in his present condition. (It may be worth mentioning that no form of thigh-boot or glove provides any protection, as armour, against an otter that is attacking with serious intent.) It would clearly be impracticable to hold him in such a way as to undo the two buckles securing the harness, and the material itself was of extremely hard nylon so that I did not think it possible to cut through with a single stroke of any blade that I had; moreover, any sawing action would necessarily drag the strap deeper and deeper into the flesh. In the end I settled for the kitchen scissors, and I entered his enclosure trying consciously to repress the fear that I felt, for however the emotion of fear is communicated to an animal the fact of its communication is unquestionable and disastrous.

Teko stood up and put his forepaws against me – they reached almost to my hip – and whimpered. I put my face down to his and spoke consoling, caressing words to him while my hands were busy about his shoulder, trying to work the scissor blade under the nylon. It cut slowly, but it cut; after the first strap gave way there was a second, and then finally I had to pull the shoulder-strap out of the wound in which it was deeply embedded – throughout all this Teko made not one single angry sound.

For eight days thereafter I had to go into his house and treat the wound by blowing powder deep into the sulcus, and though my manipulations must have been exceedingly painful he made no demonstration of protest whatsoever. (As a further safeguard against infection we put an enormous hunk of rock salt in his pool; this fascinated him beyond measure, and at the end of the first hour he had somehow contrived to hoist the whole forty-pound lump to the surface and to manhandle it out of the water on to the bank. Then he put it back and repeated the performance.)

Whereas Teko always gives me delighted welcome when I return after absence from Camusfeàrna, repeating again and again his greeting sound of 'whack-o, whack-o', Edal would as invariably shrill her rebukes to myself or Jimmy for a desertion of even a day or two. (At first I was at a loss to interpret this phenomenon, and it was not until recently that I learnt that it is commonly recognized among human infants, the form of protest ranging between behaviour superficially akin to Edal's and enuresis; the rebuke, when it is not overtly expressed, is implicit.) Edal would wail and snarl and lie on her back scrabbling at the air with her hands, her voice a shrewish and feminine variation upon Teko's, lacking the consonant but retaining the cockney intonation, so that it emerges as 'ow-ow-ow', with a richness of disyllabic vowel-sound that might have baffled Professor Higgins had he encountered it in Eliza Doolittle. It was not until whichever of us had been absent had adequately apologized for his inconstancy that she would abandon her outraged attitude and seek the reassurance of caressing hands. What, one asks oneself, would Lovelace have felt had Lucasta's only reaction to his poem (and, after all, Edal enjoyed not only four brief verses but several

228

thousand words of prose) been 'ow-ow-ow' until he said it was all untrue and he was never going away again?

It is an appropriate moment to place on record an unpalatable opinion, in which I hope that I may be proved wrong. Whatever may be true of other species, I do not believe that any fully adult otter of that to which Edal and Teko belong is to be trusted completely with any human other than its acknowledged foster-parents. The emotions are too intense, the degree of affection accorded by the otter too profound. To achieve placidity, to enjoy to the full the company of one of these wholly fascinating creatures one would have perforce to live the life of a hermit, with only animal companionship.

Edal and Teko will not, I think, have forfeited final sympathy by the momentary violence that I have described. They acted instinctively and within the framework of their heritage, a framework in which violence was essential to survival and reproduction. It is not the existence of these explosions that should excite attention and comment, but that a carnivorous wild animal, never domesticated in the early history of mankind as were the wild dogs, should in the first generation of captivity or other association with man display so much that he finds acceptable and approvable.

# 6

# Accident, Fire and Flood

We had little use from the *Polar Star* during the autumn months; what time was not taken up by repairs after her wreck and the fitting of her new engines was filled, for the most part, by gales and heavy seas.

Meanwhile, before she could be brought ashore in February, we had to arrange the building of a cradle for her, for she could not be beached in the ordinary way without damage to her propeller-shafts. A wheeled cradle to carry a boat of nine tons deadweight is a substantial vehicle, costly to construct and exceedingly difficult to transport to a site as remote as Camusfeàrna. Ours was built on the Clyde, some 250 road miles to the south of us, and carried by heavy lorry to the village pier five miles away; from there we hired one of the semi-local car-ferry boats to bring the massive structure in sections to the south bay at low tide.

The cradle had then to be assembled in shallow water before the tide rose; the whole operation had to be timed with military precision, for the *Polar Star*, lying seventeen miles to the southward, was to be floated on to her cradle as the tide came up. The whole eleven tons we then intended to winch up the beach and on to the grass beside the house, using for this purpose our own Sahara Land Rover. The car was already at the house, for, after the narrative of *Ring of Bright Water* had been brought to a close, the proprietors of the estate on whose land Camusfeàrna lies had decided to bulldoze a track to a neighbouring bay, and we had paid for three extra days bulldozing to branch this track to Camusfeàrna. The result could hardly be called a road; in places, indeed, the bulldozer seemed to have succeeded merely in removing the floating crust from stretches of peat bog, but by

Land Rover the track was usable after a spell of dry weather, when its gradient of one in three was not mud-covered nor its flatter stretches reduced by rain to seemingly bottomless morass. The downward journey was usually practicable in theory, though the fording of the Camusfeàrna burn, which cut the upper section of the track, was difficult in spate; but to ascend in anything but the driest conditions we had become used to putting out anchors ahead of the Land Rover and hauling her up on her own winch. Certain sections of the track were by now littered with broken anchor flukes in evidence of past failure.

Our plans did not run with clockwork efficiency. The two-ton cradle came apart as it was dropped into the sea, and its massive metal parts proved very difficult to reassemble in the water. When Jimmy Watt in the Land Rover began to winch it to the position chosen for floating-on, the *Polar Star* was still on the horizon, but long before we were ready she was cruising impatiently round the bay. It was a further two hours before she settled solidly on to the heavy timbers of her cradle, and our work was only begun.

The Land Rover was able to move the whole eleven tons a hundred yards up the beach to the edge of the grass, but the step up from the shingle on to the field itself was beyond her capacity, and we succeeded only in burning out the clutch. For the completion of the work, and for the removal of the now useless Land Rover, we had two days later to hire a breakdown lorry from a garage twenty miles away. The lorry was able to winch the *Polar Star* on to the grass, but the removal of the reluctant Land Rover presented greater difficulties. At the end of three hours the cortège had progressed less than a hundred yards up the one in three gradient of the track, and it was some seven hours after the beginning of the operation when, after midnight, the exhausted pall-bearers reached the metalled road at Druimfiaclach. It is such frequent incidents as these that render life at Camusfeàrna more costly than that of many a great mansion house nearer to the amenities of civilization.

All this was after the great freeze-up. First had come tempests and hurricanes that knocked the fences flat, whisked the slates from the roof like leaves in autumn, blew dinghies about as if they were pieces of paper, while the surf fell upon the windows of the house and crusted them thick with salt. The gentle slope of the high sand-dunes to the sea became overnight a vertical cliff some ten feet high as the invading waves roared in and battered the dunes into a resistant wall; the racing torrent of the burn in spate undermined the roots of the alders and the trees fell; the length and breadth of the field, where the bent-grass itself lay flattened by the wind, was scattered with seaweed and flotsam from the beach. It had been impossible to watch the sea, for one could not stand upright without support, much less keep one's eyes open as the hurricane hurled mingled spume and sand landward at a hundred miles an hour.

When the days of tempest were over it began to snow, and – something I had only seen once before at Camusfeàrna – it lay right down to the sea's edge. Slowly it turned intensely cold; the burn froze over and then finally the waterfall itself. It froze solid, still in the form of a waterfall, so that only the lack of movement betrayed its sculptural substance. Giant icicles formed a fringe from the banks of the pool beneath it, icicles more than seven feet long and as thick as a man's arm, and the deep pool itself was solid for more than two feet. The snow fell as though it would never end. Flat on the field and down to the tide it lay nearly two feet deep, and on the margin of the sea itself floated a tinkling crust of ice. On the hill above us the road was blocked; there the snow lay evenly more than a yard deep, and there were drifts into which an elephant could have disappeared.

Everywhere the snow went on falling, but the days were for the most part bright and sunny and the sea blue, and the plantation of young firs on the hillside above us became a regiment of Christmas trees. We improvised a toboggan, to the huge delight of Teko, who would straddle it to be towed round at ever-increasing speed. He seemed to understand the idea very soon, and when we pulled the toboggan to the top of a slope he would climb on to it and wait with obvious impatience for someone to shove it off down the slope. As it began to slow he would kick with his hind legs to maintain the impetus, and when his chariot came to rest he would work angrily at the ropes with his teeth, as if by

so doing he could once more coax it into movement. We sent to London for a real toboggan, but by the time it arrived the snow had long gone and had given place to mud and quagmire.

The geese had left us, the wild grey geese that I had domesticated at Camusfeàrna two and a half years before. The day before the snow began they had taken wing, spiralled high above Druimfia-clach and made off southward at a great height. Of the eleven that left, only three came back in the spring; the rest, no doubt, suffered the common fate of wild creatures that have been taught to trust their worst enemy.

During all this time we had, as I have said, little use from the *Polar Star*, yet one glorious morning will always stand out in my memory. Since the roads were still blocked by snow when the time came for a visiting friend to return to Sicily, we could only reach the distant station by sea. The winter sun was just up in a bare blue sky, the shadows still long and blue upon the snow, and the great white hills all about us were salmon-pink above a smooth enamel sea of beetle-wing blue. On every side so little showed through the snow that the only colours of which one was aware were those of its varying tones, from shadows to sunlit brilliance, and the two blues of sea and sky. The *Polar Star* roared north between the frozen mountains, and her great leaping seething wake held the reflected light of the sun and the snows; to us on board her the racing boat seemed the only moving thing in a world of ice-cold colour, her speed the direct expression of human exhilaration.

In February 1962 Malcolm and Paula Macdonald, who had given Edal to me in the spring of 1959 came to Camusfeàrna to visit her after an absence of nearly three years. I had told them of all that had happened during the past six months, of her attack upon Terry and of her apparent hatred of women, and they both agreed that it would be inadvisable for Paula to meet Edal face to face. Malcolm would go into her room with Jimmy, and Paula would watch over the waist-high partition that separated Jimmy's sitting-room from Edal's quarters. We were in the living-room when we reached this sensible decision, and a moment or two later I was called to the telephone to take a long-distance call. The telephone conversation was prolonged, and it was some quarter of an hour later that I returned, to find the living-room empty. I went across to Jimmy's house, and as I entered his sitting-room I at first saw nobody. Then I heard voices from beyond Edal's partition, and hurried forward. Sitting on the bed were Jimmy, Malcolm and Paula, and to the last two Edal was making every demonstration of the profoundest welcome and affection. It might have been thought surprising that Edal should remember them at all after that long lapse of time and the mental and physical crises through which she had passed; this, however, was not a question of mere recognition but of positive joy. She squirmed and beamed and pushed her fingers into their mouths; then, as Paula talked to Edal the baby language to which she had been accustomed as an infant, Edal reverted to behaviour that she had not displayed for a full two years. When Paula had first brought her to Camusfeàrna Edal had a well-established and slightly inconvenient method of displaying her affection for her foster-parent, that of sucking and nibbling at Paula's neck. This she had reserved for Paula only, and had never transferred the pattern to Jimmy or myself; now she climbed up on Paula's lap and went into her old ritual as though it were days rather than years that Paula had been away.

It was, in some respects, a heart-rending reunion, for some six weeks before, the two West African otter cubs that Malcolm and Paula had brought back from Nigeria to replace Edal had been killed. These two were without exception the most domesticated and endearing otters I had ever seen, living totally free and behaving like very well brought-up but extremely playful dogs. A minister of the Church of Scotland, mooching along the foreshore with a shotgun, found them at play by the tide's edge and shot them. One was killed outright, the other died of her wounds in the water. The Lord gave man control over the beasts of the field, as this minister reminded a journalist.

In the course of that winter of 1961–62 we fortuitously acquired two more otters, and once again with the element of coincidence that would seem by now to have become a stereotype. First, a gamekeeper telephoned from the south of Scotland. That after-noon, he told me, he had been walking along a river bank when he had come unexpectedly upon a bitch otter with four very small cubs; one had been farther ashore than the others and found his route to the river blocked by a man and a dog. He just squatted and blinked, as though considering at leisure the correct course of action in these totally unfamiliar circumstances. Probably it was this certain gormlessness of personality which has to some extent characterized his existence ever since, that saved his life – for the gamekeeper, seeing this very small creature just sitting there and blinking hopelessly at him, threw a game-bag over it and picked it up. He took it home, put it in a box with some wire-netting over the top, and telephoned to me.

Despite the complications of the existing otter *ménage* at Camusfeàrna, I did not hesitate. I had always wanted a British otter, and had come near to realizing this ambition when in a previous summer a local keeper had brought me a small female cub that his terriers had caught, but alas she proved to have a double compound fracture of the lower jaw, and were it to remain unset she would for all her life have been unable to feed herself. Jimmy and I bottle-fed her and tended her wound for a few weeks, but when at last the necessary surgery was carried out in a distant town she died of post-operational shock. Now this completely undamaged cub was more than I could resist.

Transport, however, presented problems. As nobody knew whether or not the cub was weaned it clearly could not be sent unaccompanied on a long train journey; Jimmy was on holiday in the south, Terry was not yet old enough to drive a car, and I could not leave him in sole charge at Camusfeàrna. I hired a driver and my neighbour, Morag MacKinnon, volunteered to make the three hundred mile journey in my Land Rover.

When two days later I went up the hill to Druimfiaclach to meet them I carried on my back a wicker fishing creel, thinking this to be an ideal container for a small and possibly very active creature intent upon escape. This picture, however, proved entirely false. When I entered the kitchen at Druimfiaclach, Morag was sitting with the cub on her knee, and it looked remarkably domesticated if not particularly intelligent. I carried it down to Camusfeàrna inside my shirt, and it fed contentedly from a bottle immediately after arrival.

A few weeks later, after I had gone to London to be married, another unweaned cub arrived. The first had been a male, the second, to dot the i's of the coincidence, was a female. Jimmy received a telephone call from the Isle of Skye, to say that a bitch otter in milk had been shot a few days before and now a roadmender had found a tiny unweaned female cub in a ditch. Within three days the two were together in the upstairs room that Edal used to occupy.

The male we had named Mossy, after the earlier cub that died; the female was christened in my absence by the day of her arrival, Monday. How the characters of each of these two would have developed in the absence of the other, it is impossible to say. Mossy, certainly, would have demanded a great deal of patience. As long as he was kept in a large box and only lifted from it to take his bottle he appeared docile and promising, but when he was liberated in the room he did not display the confidence I had expected. I had to sleep on a mattress on the floor before he would consent to curl up in the crook of my knee as all my other otters had liked to do, and he would avoid being handled if he could. It took a fortnight of patience before he would allow us to begin to handle him again and before he started to play with such moving objects as a screwed-up ball of paper on the end of a string. Perhaps he would have developed into a truly dog-like creature had I not had to go south to London and had Monday not arrived a few days later, but I fancy that his IQ would always have remained noticeably low.

Monday, by contrast, was from the beginning utterly confident and of a very high degree of intelligence. She was visibly the younger of the two, being little larger than a big rat when she arrived. At the start Jimmy kept her separate from Mossy; she lived in a large basket by the kitchen fire, and if she had remained alone there can be no doubt that she would have become an apotheosis among domesticated otters. When, however, after a few days, she climbed from her basket, explored her new surroundings, and fell wolfishly upon a plate of roast mutton, Jimmy decided that the time had come to introduce her to her future mate.

Carried upstairs to Mossy's room she at first stayed quite still, while Mossy advanced and withdrew from her again and again. At last she followed him, a little uncertainly, as he moved away from her, and from that moment he took possession of her. He nuzzled her and climbed all over her, making a small, high wickering sound in the back of his throat, and when Jimmy went to pick her up Mossy made an angry dart at him with the explosive breathing noise in the cheeks that is his sound of aggression.

Every day Monday spent a little time in that room, before being returned to the kitchen, and each day Mossy became more possessive and more angry when she was removed. In less than a week she took up permanent quarters with him, and from then on Mossy took no interest in human beings except as purveyors of eel meat. Though Monday remained confiding, the two were self-sufficient. They indulged in endless mutual grooming, though in this as in all else Monday remained the subservient partner and Mossy retained his demanding male arrogance. A typical and oft-repeated tableau was that of Mossy lying at ease upon his back, preening, in a desultory way, his chest and forearms, while at the lower end of his body Monday performed for him services that afforded him the greatest evident delight. They slept much throughout the day, showing a preference for darkness; sometimes they would curl up together underneath a chest of drawers, but more often they appeared as a conspicuous and faintly stirring lump under the carpet. Towards evening they would awake and begin to play games that gathered tempo until from the living-room the noise above resembled nothing so much as a couple of toy trains running on the rimless spokes of their wheels. Round and round the bare boarding next to the walls they would race tirelessly, the thunder of their progress interrupted only by Mossy's inevitable catching of Monday, when the sounds of galloping feet would change to prolonged and concerted wickering. This wickering is extremely difficult to describe; it is a very rapidly repeated staccato but musical note of which the effect is almost of something mechanical. It is in the treble key; perhaps the nearest parallel would be the concept of a motor-mower whose voice had not yet broken, and the nearest approach to accurate reproduction is to rub a wetted finger-tip quickly to and fro over half an inch of glass surface.

Humans, in their role of providers, remained creatures of enormous importance to Mossy and Monday, and at the sound of a step on the stairway they would make a single competitive rush for the half-door that separated them from the landing. After the first few weeks we had removed the carpet until such time as outdoor quarters could be arranged for Mossy and Monday, so that by now there was nothing to deaden the patter, or thunder, of their tiny feet on bare linoleum. We tape-recorded the noise of this race from one corner of the room to that diagonally opposite, and the effect is that of a soundtrack deliberately speeded up, so that it becomes simply a solid roar, without perceptible impact of individual feet. At the end one can distinguish one single tap on the drum, so to speak – the sound of their forepaws hitting the door as they stood up against it in frenzied anticipation.

Sometimes Dirk the deerhound would accompany whoever went up to feed them; he would put his paws up on the half-door and gaze down with benign interest at the sharp little faces looking up at his.

At this time we fed Mossy and Monday by hand upon pieces of chopped eel, partly so that they could thus be forced daily into human contact and so retain some domesticity, but partly, also, in order to ensure that each received a due share; for Mossy, despite his possessiveness towards his consort, had proved himself an apostle of enlightened self-interest, and ungallant to the ultimate degree. Anything he could possibly snatch from her he did, and when we had first offered them whole eels he had contrived to carry the whole lot, in one journey to a distant corner, where while eating the first he snarlingly guarded the remainder. If during this display of anti-feminism one gave another eel to Monday, he would shoot across the room from his corner, whisk it away from her, and add it to his own defended store. There was no solution but to feed each with inch-long lengths of eel from a pair of tweezers; these were necessary because, while Monday took these bonbons with all the gentleness of a well-trained dog, Mossy was by instinct a grabber, and cared nothing whether or not his needle-sharp teeth enclosed more than a piece of eel. At the time I resented Mossy, and thought only what a rewarding animal to domesticate Monday would have been without him, for it was not until some three months later that we moved them outside and had all the unwearying joy of watching two wild otters at play in a glass tank.

Meanwhile both these otters had to receive the injections necessary to ensure their future health. The injections were in two doses at a fortnight's interval, and in this matter, too, Monday displayed most strikingly the quality of intelligence that Mossy lacked. Neither of them was handleable in the sense that they could be held still while being injected with a hypodermic needle; but to this problem the same resourceful vet, Donald MacLennan, who had saved Edal's life, had as always brought answers. He introduced us to an instrument I had never seen, a dog-catcher; a long metal tube from the distal end of which protrudes a noose that can be drawn tight from the butt. Neither animal being familiar with the function or potentialities of this device, the first injections produced no difficulty at all, and the work was completed in five minutes. We began with Monday, because she was the first to go into a corner where she could be walled off and confined by a piece of boarding some three feet high and four feet long. After that initial mistake on her part, she displayed, however, a cunning in avoiding the noose that no human brain in the same body could possibly have surpassed. She had, after all, only her jaws and her two forepaws at her disposal, for after the first quarter of an hour we had closed her in so completely that she had no room to manoeuvre. Again and again as the noose descended towards her head she would anticipate trouble by going to meet it - she would spring up and seize it between her teeth, worry it, and throw it back over her shoulder with a flick of the neck. More than once, when someone had momentarily succeeded in distracting her attention and we had the noose almost in position, she would get her paws inside it and pull it open with that extraordinary strength which even very small otters can display. It took three-quarters of an hour, and the cooperation of three people, before we finally secured her; it had been a hateful proceeding, and I dreaded its repetition with Mossy.

I need not have worried. While Monday had clearly retained an acute recollection of the noose – almost, one is tempted to write, an understanding of its mechanical principle – that great booby Mossy, although angry and blustering at being boarded off into a narrow corner of the room, had no more idea of how to avoid capture than he had shown on the river bank in his extreme infancy. With him it was all over in three minutes.

For both of them, in however varying degree, I felt that the experience must have been traumatic, and I expected that it would be a long time before they recovered their trust in us, even as providers of food. I thought it would be weeks before we again heard that rush of scampering feet at the sound of a boot on the stair. In fact it was less than an hour; neither seemed to bear us any ill-will for the outrages we had committed upon their persons.

They were, however, rapidly growing up, and both our own pressure upon the limited accommodation of the house and their increasing agility made it necessary to move them to outdoor quarters. It was, perhaps, the second factor that forced the decision upon us, for one incident made it evident that we could no longer ventilate the room by leaving the top of the window open without running the risk of their exit. We had removed a top drawer from the chest of drawers in order to sort through its contents, and immediately Mossy and Monday saw the resulting dark cavern as an ideal retreat from unwelcome human visitors. That this new den was some four feet from the ground troubled them not at all; the exact process by which they progressed from the floor to invisibility was too quick for the eye to follow, but the fact remained that the vertical distance was greater than that which they would have to ascend to reach the window. We made somewhat hasty preparations for their removal to an enclosure immediately outside the living-room window.

This was the autumn; both Lavinia and I were abroad during the early winter months, and we did not see Mossy and Monday again until the New Year of 1963.

Conventional insurance policies cover accident, fire and flood, and in a year of miscellaneous mishaps which included the first and last of these items it would perhaps have been unreasonable to expect fire not to have been attracted to Camusfeàrna by its general aura of crisis and vulnerability. I was, of course, alone in the house when it happened. I had been rendering down a great quantity of beef fat; when I had finished I placed the very large basin of liquid fat on the kitchen floor, put a frying pan of water on the electric hotplate with the intention of cooking myself some kippers, and then went to answer the telephone. The conversation lasted some ten minutes; I had a mental eye on the frying pan of water, but I did not think that, starting from cold, it could have evaporated in that time.

Exactly as I put the receiver down there was a muffled but heavy explosion from the kitchen, heavy enough to send a shiver through the pine-panelling of the whole ground-floor. Tearing through into the living-room I looked aghast at the entrance to the small kitchen – the whole doorway was blotted out in a roaring mass of flames whose tongues were even now shooting along the living-room rafters and devouring small pendant objects in their progress. Just inside the main door of the house was a large new fire extinguisher; with this knowledge I felt quietly confident. I seized this impressive weapon rapidly, carried out the simple instructions printed upon it, advanced as near to the flames as the heat allowed me, and directed the nozzle toward the kitchen ceiling, for this, I thought, was the point from which the flames might take over the rest of the house.

The jet of extinguishing fluid lasted for something less than three seconds; then this pretentiously aggressive and brightly coloured instrument just began to dribble on to the floor. The only tap in the house lay beyond the wall of flames, and the nearest water out of doors was Teko's pool. I grabbed two buckets and raced for it; the bolt on his gate was stuck, and when I finally forced it open Teko was waiting to slip past me. By the time I had the two buckets full and the gate closed behind me I thought there was little chance of saving the house; for it is entirely lined with the ideal tinder of Oregon pine-panelling, and I was already considering what should be salvaged and how two irreconcilable otters might be rescued simultaneously with Mossy and Monday, whose room would be the first to go. The first buckets had little effect beyond a blinding cloud of steam; eight times I ran to and fro between the pool and the kitchen, throwing the water to the ceiling in cupped hands, and eight times Teko did all that he knew to make ingress or egress from his enclosure impossible. After the last of these nightmare journeys, I was amazed to see that no flame remained; the walls and ceiling of the kitchen, which had been repainted a week before, were blackened and charred, but no living spark was left.

The first thing to catch my eye among the dismal debris was the remains of something that looked like the casing of a small home-made bomb, the ragged strips of thin, twisted metal that result from an explosion within a container. There were a con-siderable number of these scattered round the room, and then quite suddenly I saw their origin. Embedded in the basin of fat, now congealed by many gallons of water, was the warhead – the upper half of a deodorant spray of popular make. This tin, evidently, had stood too close to the hotplate on which I had prepared to cook my kippers; it had exploded, and with awful accuracy of aim the upper portion had travelled eight feet to slam into the basin of liquid fat. The force of the impact had sprayed fat all over the walls and ceiling; enough had fallen on the hot plate to start the fire, and this had in turn detonated two more deodorant cans, several pieces of which had also found their way into the fat and given fresh impetus to the flames.

Accident, fire and flood. Not long after the fire came the plague of rats. We had known for some months that for the first time in the history of Camusfeàrna there were a few in the house, but they did not appear to multiply, and caused us little trouble. Now there was a sudden population explosion and, far from our being able to ignore the rats, they became our major preoccupation. Whether they really numbered thousands I do not know, but certainly they gave that impression. Sleep became impossible at night as behind the panelling, they fought and mated, played and ran races, rolling, it seemed, some kind of resonant ball at high speed and for hours on end; food disappeared from the most inaccessible places, and floors and furniture became full with rat dung; they gnawed through the panelling to allow themselves multiple entry to every room and chewed the upholstery of soft furniture in order to build themselves nests; and, worst outrage of them all, one of their number bit my head twice during one night. Possibly he too was in search of nesting material. To add to their other nauseous characteristics, they were cannibals by apparent preference, for if one of their number was caught in a trap he was invariably eaten before morning.

At first I was unwilling to use rat poison, for the memory of an experience long ago remained fresh in my mind. When I was an undergraduate at Oxford there was a small enclosure in the park containing ornamental waterfowl such as Mandarin and Carolina ducks and a few comparative rarities; every year these birds laid eggs and every year they were eaten by rats, insolently and in daylight before spectators. Waterfowl were in those days one of my major interests and I felt this to be a waste. The park keeper gave me permission to exterminate the rats and, full of youthful enthusiasm, I bought a packet of widely advertised and well known rat poison. On this packet were printed the words 'harmless to poultry and all domestic livestock'. I put poisoned bread and bran in the waterfowl enclosure, and the next morning every single bird in it was dead.

So at the beginning we tried every method of destruction other than poison. Outside, where we had refuse pits among the sand-dunes they had formed a honeycomb of interconnecting burrows having their entrances many yards apart; into these we poured large quantities of petrol and ignited it to form a heavy subterranean detonation. This certainly did kill a great number of rats but the birth rate evidently remained consistently higher than the death rate. We shot them with shotguns, rifles and pistols; we swiped at them with pokers, sticks and axes; we set for them snares and snap-traps and live-traps, but nothing made any impression upon their numbers.

The very first rat that we caught was in a live-trap on the living-room floor. None of us wanted the task of drowning it, and eventually it was left to me to carry the cage down to the stream. I submerged it immediately; the rat went on running round the cage as if it were in air and not water. No bubbles rose. After perhaps half a minute it put its paws up between the wire mesh of the trap and hung there, looking at me. It went on looking at me; it must have been a further minute or more before I realized that it was dead.

The live-traps were useless. The following day one trap held seven half-grown rats, and the day after there were another six; then no rat ever entered them again. By October the situation was unbearable and we consulted what the ungenteel used to call a rat-catcher, but is in fact a Rodent Operative.

There appeared to me to be only one possible poison, on grounds of safety, efficiency, and humanity, and even this, *War-farin*, could not completely be guaranteed harmless to the otters. The risk, however, was comparatively small, and in the event our judgement was wholly vindicated, for at the end of a week the otters were in excellent health and there was not a single remaining rat at Camusfeàrna.

In the course of the Rodent Operative's visit I learned much about rats that was strange to me. The common man, he said, tended to think of them as creatures of barnyard and building, in constant association with man; this was wholly fallacious and he would guarantee to find me rats on the pinnacles of the Cuillin Hills. As an example he cited the meteorological station on the summit of Ben Nevis; rats had arrived within a day or two of completion of the hutments, and it would be unreasonable to assume them to have climbed 4,000 feet from the rich refuses of Fort William. It was due to the perpetually wandering habits of the rat, he explained, that they had settled at Camusfeàrna; not a square yard of countryside was unvisited by some rats in the course of six months, and they would stop wherever they found food plentiful. An open refuse pit, which at Camusfeàrna was our only means of disposing of kitchen rubbish, was irresistible.

He also told me that I had been using the snap-traps, which were simply a larger version of the ordinary mousetrap, in a completely mistaken way. In my innocence I had asked him the best bait to use on these. 'None,' he replied. 'You don't bait them at all. I've never been able to understand why the makers put that little bait-peg on them – it gives people the wrong idea from the start.' He expounded his own method, which he said was foolproof. A rat in a room will at some time during the night run round the whole perimeter of the walls, and an unbaited snap-trap placed with the spring-platform against the wall was therefore infallible. But, he added, all traps became obsolete with the introduction of *Warfarin*, and rodents need no longer present a problem to anybody.

Accident, fire and flood. Dirk the deerhound broke his leg. Any dog with a broken tibia produces many problems; when the dog weighs something like a hundredweight and the leg is the better part of a yard long, the problems are disproportionately increased. It had become a stereotype that after any absence from Camusfeàrna I would inevitably return to find that some disaster had taken place while I was away, and Dirk's accident conformed precisely to that pattern. Lavinia and I had been visiting friends some fifteen sea miles or 120 road miles to the southward; we had travelled by car, and had formed an intricate plan by which both sea and road transport were available for other family projects. My stepson Nicholas and Jimmy Watt had been invited to fish a salmon river the following day, in the area where we had been staying; we therefore decided to leave the car at the fishing port there, where the *Polar Star* had been undergoing some adjustments to her gear-box, and return to Camusfeàrna in her. We could then immediately transport Nicholas and Jimmy to the port by boat, leaving them the use of the car and ourselves returning to Camusfeàrna in the *Polar Star*.

This plan, surprisingly, we carried through without inter- ference by weather or any of the many other factors that might have caused its dislocation, but when we dropped anchor in Camusfeàrna bay to take Nicholas and Jimmy on board, they brought the news that Dirk had broken his leg a few minutes before.

The dog had been in the house when Terry had announced that the *Polar Star* was on the horizon, and the whole party went out to watch her; Dirk, not in those days the best disciplined of dogs, had slipped out unnoticed and set out for a canter on the hill. No one was aware of his absence until a few minutes later, when a newly appointed estate manager who had been inspecting the forestry ground knocked at Camusfeàrna door and announced to Terry: 'Your dog's up there by the hill track, and he seems to have hurt himself pretty badly.'

Terry found Dirk at a distance of something like half a mile from the house, howling pitifully and unable to rise, each successive struggle causing him even intenser agony. It was obvious to Terry that Dirk had a fractured foreleg, and equally obvious to him that there was no way to get the dog home but to carry him, for to construct a stretcher would mean leaving Dirk for a long time in his present plight. It was fortunate that Terry, though past his sixteenth birthday by only four days, was constructed to the same Goliath specification as Dirk; two years at Camusfeàrna had transformed him from a pallid London child into a Hercules of six foot two and thirteen stone. Dirk has never been accurately weighed, but Dell's *The Scottish Deerhound* gives the weight of a dog standing thirty inches at the shoulders as 95 to 105 lb, and Dirk is very considerably over thirty inches. Terry simply picked him up, one hand under his chest and the other under his haunches, and carried him home.

The vet arrived soon after Lavinia and I had returned from our southward journey with the *Polar Star*, and in half an hour the dog's leg was set and plastered, but we were barely at the beginning of our troubles. Even an able-bodied dog of Dirk's proportions occupies a surprising amount of space in a cottage the size of Camusfeàrna; but only now, immobilized by his injury, did his vast extended frame reveal the enormity of his stature. In broad terms he occupies three feet by five, and the slightest attempt at movement of any kind caused him an agony so acute that he could not contain his voice, so that night and day became hideous with his screams. To move him out of doors so that he might relieve himself was the work of two men, carrying and manoeuvring through doorways his vast forequarters and thereafter supporting him in this helpless position until necessity overcame his inhibitions and he allowed his sphincters to relax. He required constant nursing night and day, and after the first two nights it was clear that we could not keep him at Camusfeàrna throughout his convalescence. We made arrangements for his reception at a hospital kennel in Inverness the following day and addressed ourselves to the problems of his transport. We spent the morning building a stretcher; this we covered with foam rubber cushioning and over it we nailed an army blanket, the free portion of which would be passed over the prostrate dog and in turn nailed down to hold him in position.

It was just after we had succeeded in carrying Dirk from the house and laying him on the stretcher that a party of unannounced visitors arrived. They were, they told Terry, friends of some people whom I had received earlier in the year, and who had told this party that they were sure I would not mind if they called. To the best of my recollection there were five or six of them, a comparatively modest invasion, for families holidaying in the West Highlands seemed often to consist of double that number.

I told Terry to explain that I could not see them at present, but that if they cared to go for a walk and return in an hour it was possible that the present crisis would be over. They did not choose to leave immediately, but stayed to annoy Teko by peering at him over the paling, thus adding his penetrating voice to Dirk's pathetic howls as we arranged his sprawling carcass upon the stretcher.

We manoeuvred the huge wooden structure though the rear door of the Land Rover with the greatest difficulty, for the door itself was narrow, and we had to tip the stretcher at an angle of forty-five degrees before it would pass through and lie flat across the seats. The nailed blanket, however, held Dirk from sliding, and the stretcher settled neatly into its position.

The Land Rover set off very slowly up the steep track. At the end of half an hour it had progressed less than two hundred yards, for the tyres found no grip upon the slippery mud of the steep gradient, and Jimmy and Terry were once more reduced to hauling the car up by her own winch.

At this point the visitors returned; my apologies for inability to receive them after all evoked no other response than unconcealed and boorish anger that they had been sent on a fruitless walk instead of being informed of the fact when they first arrived. The very gaucherie of their egregious presumption deprived me of words. They retired huffily to a neighbouring hilltop, from where they watched with sour satisfaction our struggles with the improvised ambulance.

When at length Jimmy and Terry reached the metalled road their real troubles began. The braking power of the Land Rover being greater than her acceleration, Dirk was perpetually shifted forward and downward on his stretcher; since he could use only his hind limbs in an effort to rise or readjust his position, their pushing movements only propelled him further towards the bulkhead between him and the driving cab. Each one of these movements pressed the strained blanket against his plastered foreleg. Jimmy remembers the eighty-mile journey as a nightmare, Dirk screaming and helplessly defecating where he lay, so that the stench in the car became almost as unbearable as the pitiful sounds of the dog's distress. A score of times they halted to rearrange him, and by the time they arrived at their distant destination both Dirk and his stretcher were anchored by a spider's web of string and rope to every stable object in the rear of the Land Rover. Accident, fire and flood.

# 7

## *The Tides Return*

I travelled in the autumn of 1962 to southern Europe and North Africa, and when I returned to Camusfeàrna I found much change. The house now had many of the amenities of civilization, including sanitation, a bath and showers, and the tiny kitchen was now all-electric. Every one of these innovations dependent upon water was, however, functionless, for at the date of my return the supply had been frozen for more than a month, and remains frozen at the time of writing five weeks later.

My arrival at the house had a curious, almost surrealistic flavour. During my absence a jeep had been added to the Camusfeàrna transport fleet, and in this we bucked and jolted in the dark down the frozen track whose mud mountains and ruts had become as hard as rock. At the house the headlights showed a single greylag goose standing outside the door, and Jimmy explained to me that of the five that we had imported in the late summer to replace those that had left us in July this was the sole survivor. Two had disappeared only a week ago, fallen prey, probably, to foxes or wildcats whose more usual sources of food supply were cut off by the snow and the cold. Now this single goose tried to push past us into the house, and having succeeded in entering the living-room tried immediately to jump up on to the sofa whose entire surface was occupied by the sprawling form of Dirk the deerhound. Deterred from this enterprise by Dirk's uncooperative spirit, the goose then hopped into an armchair. At no time in the past had the bird even tried to enter the house. We removed it to the bathroom, and Jimmy had just remarked that despite all the many inconveniences of the month-long freeze we could at least be thankful that there had never been even the briefest power cut, when all the lights went off. We had very little coal, very little paraffin, and no cut wood.

Thus it was sitting in overcoats by candlelight in the freezing living-room that I learned in detail of recent happenings at Camusfeàrna, happenings of which I had heard only in the barest outline.

Terry Nutkins had left Camusfeàrna to become a zoo keeper in London, and Jimmy was now in sole charge of an increasingly complicated *ménage*.

A few weeks before, a mate for Teko had arrived from Griqualand in South-East Africa. This otter proved to be an enormous animal, bigger than Teko himself, extremely domesticated and affectionate towards human beings, and her introduction to Teko had presented none of the problems we had anticipated. Placed in accommodation adjoining his, so that they might become accustomed to each other's voices and smells before closer acquaintance, she had brushed aside these formalities by climbing into his enclosure during the night, and in the morning they were curled up together in his bed. This happy and promising situation was cut short by her sudden and then unexplained death only two days before my homecoming. She had been healthy and in high spirits in the evening, and when Jimmy had gone in to her in the morning he had found her dead but still perceptibly warm, curled up in Teko's bed under the infra-red lamp, the tip of her tail in her mouth as though she had been sucking it – a habit, like that of Edal sucking her bib, that she had in life.

During the short weeks of her life with Teko, Mossy and

Monday had discovered their unrivalled powers of escape from any enclosure in which they might be confined, and on more than one occasion all four animals had been found together in Teko's pool. It would, perhaps be truer to say that Monday had discovered her powers of escape and had somehow coerced her moronic consort into cooperation in such matters as combining their strength to move heavy stones and taking alternate shifts in digging the long tunnels that she planned. Even then, owing to his greater size and absolute absence of initiative, Mossy often found himself left behind while she made her escape through some aperture too small to permit his passage. On this first evening of my return he was alone in the enclosure, but during the night she returned for him and from outside enlarged her latest tunnel until he could squeeze through. From then on, for the first three weeks of my stay, their capture and recapture became our major preoccupation, until at length I was forced to realize that nothing but a zoo cage could confine her, and I accepted defeat.

Monday could climb like a monkey, balance like a tight-rope walker, dig like a badger, move stones that were heavy to a human, jump like a squirrel, make herself thin as an eel or flat as a flounder; no device nor ingenuity of ours could make her once relent her first avowed intent to be a pilgrim. But most of all it was her brain, the systematic application of her many skills and her single-minded pertinacity, that convinced me of the uselessness of the struggle.

She had tasted freedom and she would have no more of prison. It was not, in the prevailing circumstances, an inviting prison or one calculated to lead to resignation; the glass tank frozen, all running water stopped, the small patch of ground now hard as rock and without vegetation. Outside were the sea and the islands with their many habitable lairs among the rocks and the bracken and the rooty heather; outside was the freedom of the waves and the white sands and the weedy rock pools. There was nothing I wanted more than to let her go free, but with the knowledge of all the other tame otters that because of their confidence in man had been shot or bludgeoned to death by the first strange human being they approached, I felt that I must confine her. It took three weeks to convince me that this was not only an impossibility but would be more cruel than any death she could meet in freedom.

One wall of their enclosure was formed by the Camusfeàrna house itself; the other three were of continuous, smooth, wooden paling five feet high. The only points at which the woodwork did present a completely smooth face were the right-angles formed by their own house, of the same height as the paling, and a further right-angle where a heavy straining-post had been boarded round. At the base of the fence we had sunk fine-mesh wire-netting into the ground, extending six inches vertically into the ground and then two and a half feet horizontally inwards. As a further safeguard against tunnelling, we had placed heavy stones along the greater part of the perimeter. This was the prison from which, during a time of bitter frost when the ground was frozen as hard as iron four feet underground, Monday escaped time and again with contemptuous ease.

At the beginning I thought naively that our only problem was to catch them, for I could not seriously believe in the impossibility of making the enclosure proof against escape. We constructed in the paling a foot-square drop-hatch that could be closed by the release of a string from an upper-storey window. I disposed a number of eels temptingly a yard or two inside the trap, and at dusk I sat down with the release-string in my hand to await developments. The otters arrived very soon after dark; they came and went between the eels and the hatch so that there was never a clear moment when both of them were inside simultaneously. Eventually I decided that to catch one was better than to catch neither, and I released the string when only Mossy was in the enclosure. I felt certain that Monday would come in to him during the night; in this I was right, but at the time I did not know that she would as certainly perform a rescue, and contrive somehow to extract her clottish companion from captivity before dawn.

During the night I could hear her whistling impatiently to him from outside and his peevish and fretful responses as he explained the patent impossibility of reaching her; at some time in the small hours these sounds ceased, and in my innocence I imagined her to have joined him in their house and settled down for the night.

In the morning they had both gone. She had indeed climbed into the enclosure, but only in order to move a few massive stones, tunnel under the wire-netting and liberate the captive.

The following night, having as I thought made all tunnelling projects impossible, I reset the trap and again sat at the window with the string in my hand. This time I had to wait much longer and it was Monday that I caught. The front door of the house, in temporary disuse, led directly into the enclosure, and I went out to her carrying peace offerings. She ran straight up to me, emitted a breathy, explosive sound of challenge, and gave my boot a sharp, symbolic nip. She then ran to the corner where the paling formed a convex right-angle, and began to shin rapidly up it with the powerful hunching movements of a bear climbing a tree. I had literally to push her down, while Jimmy ran for materials wherewith to form an unscaleable overhang at the top of this corner. In the end it looked as if it would challenge even a monkey's capacities.

The next morning she had gone again. I attached pieces of slippery Formica to the paling at the points where she was wont to climb. Miraculously they gave her no pause. Every night she came brazenly into the trap, insolently confident of her ability to overcome or undermine any obstacle that I might set in the way of her escape before morning. Every day my preparations became more elaborate, and every day she mocked me. The trap was by this time automatic; an ingenious system of strings ensured that when she pulled at eels the hatch would close itself and at the same time ring the ship's bell upon the gatepost. The whole of the area on which she had exercised her feats of climbing was covered by a great sheet of smooth metal, a relic of Teko's first ill-fated pool, and the night after the appearance of this fresh puzzle we caught both Mossy and Monday. They were still there in the morning, and all the day through they slept in their house. I had no doubt in my mind that they were now captive for as long as we wished them to remain so. Twenty-four hours later they had once more vanished, this time by an ambitious tunnelling scheme that involved the moving of a stone weighing some sixty or seventy pounds.

We made only one more attempt. The following evening, just

254

before dusk, Jimmy called to me that Monday had come in through the door of our new extension building and that he had closed it behind her. She came through into the living-room and began to explore, briskly and impatiently, ignoring us altogether, rather in the manner of a testy colonel inspecting company lines. Having exhausted the possibilities of floor-level she moved upwards, displaying a degree of acrobatic power that appeared hardly credible. In the same way that water finds its way downward between and around all obstacles by force of gravity, so she appeared to be borne upward by some like but contrary force concealed within her. High on the shelves she stepped daintily and gracefully amongst the bottles and tins and groceries; finding little to her liking, she returned to the floor with the same sinuously effortless movements, climbed on to the sofa and said something exceedingly rude to Dirk, and finally moved off to continue her researches in the new wing. When she entered the bathroom we closed the door behind her, intending to confine her there until we had secured Mossy. It was a sliding door; in less than three minutes she had discovered the principle of its operation and was back in the living-room.

We coaxed her back into the bathroom and this time secured the door so that there was no means of opening it.

Mossy did not return that night, and in the morning we found that Monday had chewed her way through the bathroom plasterboarding and had already got to work on the woodwork that lay beyond it. She was, however, still captive against her will, and for the first time.

In the evening we caught Mossy, and brought Monday through to join him in their enclosure, which I believed to be now proof against any attempt at escape. During the night there was much whistling and the sounds of heavy stones being moved; at dawn I looked out from my window and saw Monday doing a high rope-walk along the top of the paling. She had not climbed up from inside, but had contrived her escape at ground-level and was now returning for her consort. In a further five minutes they were both on their way to the sea.

It was at this point that I abandoned the struggle, as much on humanitarian grounds as in the knowledge that by one means or another she would always outwit me. I hoped, but with little conviction, that Mossy and Monday would remain in the vicinity of Camusfeàrna and its islands, where they would be at least relatively safe from death at human hands. It was not until several days later, and after Lavinia had joined me from London, that I discovered how little grudge they appeared to bear us for our determination to make them captive, for they had taken up permanent residence under the floor of the new wing.

Their entry to this improbable refuge was under the door that now formed the principal entrance to the house; here immediately below the threshold, was a small unboarded portion giving access to the space between floor and foundations. From this slit, some two feet long and four inches high, Lavinia found that she could call them at will to take food from her hand. The slit was divided in the middle by an upright plank; invariably at her call the two small faces, one blunt and one sharp, would peer out as though from letter boxes, and invariably it would be Mossy who was to the left of the upright and Monday to the right. This position they would assume at the first sound of her calling voice, and they remained completely indifferent to the tramp of human feet stepping over them to enter or leave the house.

Now that their freedom was established, it seemed to me that to encourage this unexpected domesticity we should take every possible step to make their self-elected quarters as luxurious as possible. Choosing a time at which they were both engaged with

Lavinia outside, we cut a rectangle in the wooden floor of the room beneath which they had chosen to set up house, and sunk between it and the foundations a well-bedded and draughtproof kennel whose roof was formed by a raisable hatch in the floor of the room. This, to my surprise, they took possession of immediately, but they did not accord a like approval to other arrangements we had made for their comfort. With the idea of protecting them from the prevailing sea-winds we had built up earthworks that covered all the seaward-facing space between the new wooden wing and its foundations, thus leaving the otters only one common entrance and exit. We had forgotten an otter's insistence upon alternative means of egress; the next morning earthworks had been efficiently tunnelled in two different places. The amount of labour that they had put into this work was, however, an encouragement to believe that they considered themselves to be perfecting otherwise ideal and permanent quarters.

At morning and before dusk they would, as I have said, come out to Lavinia's call and take food from her hand, but as to where they went at night we had no knowledge until she followed them. It was a season of bitter cold; the days were for the most part still and bright with winter sunshine, but the nights were Arctic, and the burn was frozen right down into its tidal reaches, with a layer of ice that capsized as the tide went out and floated up to form a new and thicker layer as it returned. A little before dusk one evening Lavinia, who had been down to the burn to break the ice and draw water, heard them calling to each other at some little distance from the house. Following Monday's small, urgent voice, she came upon them playing in a partly frozen pool, shooting under stretches of ice, and bobbing up where it ended, climbing on to it and rolling upon it, diving back and splashing as they sported together. Fearing that they would resent her intrusion, and read into it some further attempt at capture, Lavinia had approached them by stealth, crawling upon all-fours; only when they began to move on down the stream did she stand up and call to them, but they found in her presence no cause for any alarm. As they neared the tide she walked beside them, their heads now no more than silhouettes on a sea blanched by sunset colours, until suddenly a curlew rose before them with its rasping cry of warning, and in a panic they turned and raced back upstream and into the darkness. The next night again she followed them down the burn in the dusk, and lost them in the thickening darkness as they swam out towards the islands.

With the liberation of Mossy and Monday, something seemed to me restored to Camusfeàrna, something that had been lost for many months, for once again these were wild creatures free without fear of man and choosing to make their homes with him. As if to reinforce this mood, two of the wild geese suddenly returned after an absence of seven months; one of them was the great gander who had sired all the young of the previous year, and now on the very day of his arrival came straight up to us to take food from our hands. Somehow, with all this unwary confidence in mankind he had survived the autumn and the winter months and fallen prey to no wildfowler's gun; perhaps he had joined some vast flock of wild grey geese and during his long absence from Camusfeàrna had taken his reactions from them. It is sad that for the otters there is no such safety in numbers; sad to think that Monday's whole dynamic personality may be blotted out to appease momentarily the inner emptiness and frustration that causes the desire to kill.

Before me is a letter from Norway, telling of yet another pet otter done to death:

She was tame and she would follow me like a dog. The last days we used to go fishing in a nearby loch. She jumped about in the rowboat while I was pulling the oars. Now and again I left her alone in the loch, sure to pick her up again when I wanted her to stay at home. But this very morning a mason passing the loch on his way to work saw the kind and confident animal and gave her a kick with his heavy boot. I found her dead, resting on a pile of branches out in the water.

Destruction, empty and purposeless, unmitigated even by the strange intimacy that binds the archetypal hunter to his quarry. I hope that if ever again I write of Camusfeàrna the murder of Mossy and Monday may not mar the pages of my book.

# RAVEN SEEK
# THY BROTHER

# Foreword

This has been a difficult, sometimes painful, story to tell in its entirety, but I have done my best to be accurate both in fact and in date. Anyone who reads this will realize that the immediate sequel to *Ring of Bright Water*, *The Rocks Remain*, contained a certain amount of dissimulation which was unavoidable at that time, and which I hope to have dispelled by this full narrative. This is the history of Camusfeàrna and its satellite lighthouses during the past five years. It is easier, for many reasons, to write truthfully about animals than about human beings (and not only because the animals can't retort that they are misrepresented) but with the minimal reservations and reticences that are only decent to the human species, I have done my best to tell the whole story.

To avoid confusion I have retained the name Camusfeàrna throughout, though with the necessarily precise placing of the two other lighthouses of Ornsay and Kyleakin it will be obvious to any interested reader that Camusfeàrna is Sandaig, by Sandaig Lighthouse, on the mainland of Scotland some five miles south of Glenelg village. The real name of the house on the road a mile and more above my coastal cottage is not Druimfiaclach (which means 'the ridge of the teeth') but Tormor, and the family who used to live there was called MacLeod – John Donald and Mary MacLeod and their children. The MacLeods have gone now and their sons are children no more, married and with families of their own. With the dropping of these aliases there goes, so to speak, the last of the open secrets.

Lastly, I should like to say that, despite apparent and almost uncanny evidence to the contrary, no part of this book was written with hindsight from the events described in the brief epilogue. This actual paragraph, the epilogue itself, and the title of the last Chapter, are all that have been added since 20 January 1968.

Gavin Maxwell
*Kyleakin Lighthouse, July 1968*

# I

# *The Rowan Tree*

On a wild blustery afternoon in the late autumn of 1966 I stood on the steep hillside above the Highland seaboard cottage that I had written of in *Ring of Bright Water* as Camusfeàrna, and that had once been my home. The sky, the sea, and the white sand beaches between the islands half uncovered by the ebb tide, I recognized as from long ago, but only visually; they held for me nothing that I wanted to remember. The sharp, penetrating past images that knocked on the door of my conscious mind were almost wholly painful, and I tried hard to ignore them.

The sea was so dark a blue as to be almost black, the wave-crests short, white and vicious. A force nine wind was blowing in from the south-west, hustling great grey clouds that seemed to outrun each other so that they left between them gaps though which a bright white sunlight spotlit here a beach, here a hill, there an island. Across the Sound of Sleat, where a fishing boat was plunging deep with a high white foam about her bows, the foothills of Skye were dusted with snow, their summits dead-white against a dark grey sky. Gulls drifted on the wet wind, white too, but the air was too strong for them to pursue a steady course; they slanted, lifted, banked and wheeled, calling raucously to each other as the wind-blasts blew them about. Out in the Sound, foam amid foam, a small school of whales passed – little creatures perhaps thirty feet long. Once I would have been intent, interested to recognize their species, their scientific name. As I looked at them now they seemed no more than a passing disturbance in the water, almost an intrusion.

I was looking down upon Camusfeàrna, and I believed that I was saying goodbye to it after eighteen years. Suddenly there came a sharp flurry of hail, I pulled up the hood of my duffel

263

coat, and crouched back into the steep hillside. It gave no shelter; there was no shelter from any wind, and I knew it, suddenly and completely.

Abruptly a shaft of pallid but finely focused sunlight lit the house and the field below me; the house that I was leaving, as I thought, for ever. I tried, with a great effort, to remember it as I had first seen it – a weather-worn cottage within a stone's throw of the sea, standing unfenced upon a green grass field, only the low marram-grown dunes between it and the breaking waves. Untenanted, deserted, waiting. I remembered how I had first come to live there; relying for furniture upon fish boxes and all the extraordinary riches that the sea would throw up after a south-westerly gale. Then, there was no water supply to the house, no telephone, no electricity, no road. I was a mile and a half below my nearest neighbours on the single track road, the family whom I have called MacKinnon, at Druimfiaclach. Like everybody and everything else they had gone; their little house of green corrugated iron stood empty, the once carefully tended flower garden overgrown with weeds and nettles, and now there was no occupied human habitation within five miles of Camusfeàrna.

Many other external things had changed too. This used to be a bare moorland hillside, rough with rock and heather and bracken patches, naked and windswept and virgin; it was so when I first came to live at Camusfeàrna, with nothing but a Primus stove to cook on, nothing but a bucket to draw water from the little river a hundred yards from the house, nothing but the wood thrown up on the beach to fuel the fire in the desolate kitchen. Now there was a dense, dripping ten-year-old growth of sitka and larch at my back as I looked down upon the house, for the landlord had, after various unsuccessful experiments, decided to devote his ground to forestry.

For some unconnected reason, the once green field upon which the house of Camusfeàrna stood was now a jungle of rank rushes reaching almost to the walls of the cottage.

The house had changed too. When I first came to it Camusfeàrna had been a four-roomed cottage, two rooms upstairs and two down. Now, as I looked down upon it, I saw straggling pre-fabricated wings built with the ugliness born of what had seemed necessity and a strict regard for time. On the seaward side of the house stood two broken-down jeeps, whose stamina had not proved equal to the boulders and potholes that composed the two-mile track bulldozed four years before. Between these pieces of defeated machinery and the sea the motor launch *Polar Star* lay high and dry on her massive wheeled cradle, her bronze propellers glinting wetly on the grass below her stern.

Telegraph posts and wires descended the hill from one direction, electric conveyances from another. They converged upon Camusfeàrna, and around the house itself were high wooden palings confining two otters that had once been house-living pets. Each of them, more than three years before, had unpredictably produced reactions as savage as that of an untamed leopard; with dismay and with bitter remorse for wild creatures taken from their natural surroundings, I had recognized that I was the only human at Camusfeàrna who could still trust them, who in daily contact had always found them both friendly and affectionate, and I had constructed for them what I had thought of as being ideal zoo conditions. The massiveness of the damage they had inflicted upon other humans – the hysterical, almost manic, sustained attacks that characterize the mustelline family when the killer instinct is somehow aroused, precluded any possibility of allowing them liberty; the most I could do was occasionally to take them for a walk – separately, for they hated each other – and to employ staff to look after them, for I could not always be at Camusfeàrna.

Now, as I sat huddled into my duffel coat with the hail hitting me and melting so that the ice pellets became chill liquid and found their way through every broken fastening of my clothes, I was surveying what I had done to Camusfeàrna – what I had done to the animals and what I had done to myself.

For the past two years the upkeep of that cottage, centred around the otters, had been much like the maintenance of an Antarctic weather station. It had, in fact, cost more than £7,000 a year, whether I was there or in some distant country.

For the past week it had deluged with rain, it had snowed heavily and then thawed so that the mountain snows came cascading down every crevice of the hillsides, and then it had rained again, so that the Camusfeàrna burn had become a racing, surging white torrent, and flood water lay in wide pools all over the flat ground around the house. These glittered whenever the tearing clouds left the pale autumn sun momentarily uncovered; one in particular caught my attention because of its curious shape, a perfect figure of eight. It was in the otter enclosure at the northern end of the house, the pen occupied by Teko, the male otter who had been at Camusfeàrna for seven years. This was what was called a zoo pattern of behaviour, repetitive, compulsive action born of boredom and frustration; for hour after hour, day after day, he would walk this same track until it had become a pathway beaten bare of vegetation and deep enough to hold water. In time, I thought, it would be grass-grown again, and the fences would be pulled down, for they would have no further use. I had given up at last; Camusfeàrna was to be closed down, and both otters were to go to a zoo. I did not know where I should go to live myself.

A single raven swept by, high on the hustling wind, his deep guttural croaks almost muted by its force. I remembered how Wilfred Thesiger had once told me that when a camel caravan in Southern Arabia would sight a single raven overhead the Bedouin would attempt to annul the evil omen by calling to it, 'Raven, seek thy brother!' It seemed too late now for that invocation.

Between me and the forlorn watery pattern in Teko's enclosure stood the rowan tree, the magic tree that stands beside every old

Highland cottage, and round which is centred so much of Gaelic superstition and lore. The rowan is the guardian, the protecting power, the tree of life, infinitely malignant if harmed or disrespected; capable, too, of carrying within itself the good – or evil – wishes of those who have the power to commune with it. Few Highlanders will cut a rowan, even in the course of modern forestry operations, nor bring its bright berries into a dwelling, for they are the blood of the tree and it will curse those who shed its blood.

My rowan had shed its berries now, and the gales had stripped its branches of their scarlet leaves; but it held my attention, because I was seeing it with a new eye, and a strong, sudden, and recent recollection. Sitting there huddled against the gale on the wet hillside above Camusfeàrna my mind went back four months to the summer, to a garden on the shores of the Aegean. The sun was parching, the cicadas screeching in a heavy-laden fig tree, the flowers of morning glory that twined a trellised column beside my chair were shut tight against the brilliant butterflies that danced before them.

I sat reading the typescript of an unpublished autobiography, the life story of a poetess. I was reading with perhaps more than ordinary attention, for these pages concerned myself and painful happenings that had taken place many years before. And then suddenly a paragraph seemed to separate itself from the page and to hit up at me with an almost physical impact. Here was my rowan tree.

I cannot recall the words, the sentences, that composed that paragraph; only the shocking image with which they left me. We had quarrelled violently at Camusfeàrna, and as she left the door she had turned and said to me with a venom that utterly belied her words, 'May God forgive you', and I had replied, 'He will.' That short exchange was not on the page before me, but I was reading a sequel unknown to me, for it was years before we had met again, by chance in a London street, after my marriage to someone else.

She had always believed that she possessed great and terrible occult powers, and in that moment of hatred she had not doubted her ability to blight the years ahead of me. She had gone back to Camusfeàrna secretly by night – I pictured it now as a wild night of wind and sleet-storm, roaring surf, and a witch's moon – and she had put her hands upon the trunk of the rowan tree and with all the strength of her spirit she had cursed me, saying, 'Let him suffer here as I am suffering.' Then she had left, up over the bleak hillside.

I put down the manuscript and stared at the coarse dark-green grass of the Greek lawn, thinking how exactly the pattern of the last years had paralleled her blind desire for destruction. A little of this she must have known, for it was public knowledge, and I wondered if she had exulted; but there was much more that she could not know. She could not know, amongst much else, that by now I had already taken the bitter decision to send the otters to a zoo, to find homes for my dogs, and to leave Camusfeàrna. I bore her no ill-will now, whether or not her curse could have influenced events: I just did not understand how such love and hatred could coexist.

> Some say the world will end in fire
> And some in ice
> From what I've tasted of desire
> I hold with those who favour fire
> But if it had to perish twice
> I think I know enough of hate
> To say that ice is also great
> And would suffice.*

As I looked at the grass beyond my feet I saw a pale object about half the size of a matchstick moving spasmodically among the leaves. Sometimes it fluttered like a flag, sometimes it moved a few inches to the right or to the left, sometimes it advanced a little, sometimes retired. Leaning forward, I saw that it was a sliver of white, papery foliage being carried by an ant about a quarter of its size. The ant was trying to move it in my direction,

* Robert Frost, 'Fire and Ice'.

but constantly it jammed between the blades of grass as would a tree trunk carried horizontally through a forest. Then the ant would shuffle, sidestep and reverse, manoeuvre one end of its burden between the obstacles, and at length move an inch or two forward. I looked round me in search of its possible destination. Behind me, and to my right, forming the corner of a rectangle, was a rough brick wall perhaps five feet high, and at the top of the wall was a terrace that led away into parched and uncultivated ground. Perhaps, I thought, the ant's nest was somewhere in the wall, but this at its nearest point was still some twenty feet from the ant, and between the grass and the wall was a yard or so of empty herbaceous border, where the earth had been dug and lay in hard uneven lumps the size of a golf ball; whatever the ant's

destination it appeared patently impossible of achievement.

At the end of a quarter of an hour it had reached the manuscript that lay on the grass at my side. There, squarely on the typed words 'rowan tree', it paused to rest, shifting its burden between the mandibles as if to achieve a more balanced grip. I thought of Bruce and the spider; I became wholly and childishly absorbed, and the ant's adventure became mine.

The ant rested for a full minute upon the glaring white paper, its antennae waving slowly as if questing for knowledge of the hazards before it. Then, quite suddenly, as though at the fall of a starter's flag, it shot across the page at tremendous speed and plunged once more into the grass jungle between it and the wall. The same enormous but patient energy animated every movement; the same reversals and backward haulage, the same sidestepping and apparent understanding of mechanical principle, the same firm sense of direction – straight to the wall. When at length it had struggled free of the herbage and into the dry earth-cakes of the border, the enormity of the obstacles ahead seemed to cause no loss of heart; at the foot of each steep earth mountain – each, in ratio to the stature of the ant, several hundred feet high to a human – it would turn carefully, readjust its grip, and reverse up the slope. At the summit it would turn again to face forward and rush down the ensuing slope. The ant never once tried to avoid an obstacle in its path nor to circumvent the next, even when to the human eye this appeared easy; both the purpose and the direction were absolutes.

From the time at which I had first sighted with an abstracted eye the ant and the curious banner-like burden to which it appeared to attach so supreme an importance, almost half an hour had passed before it reached the foot of the wall. The bricks towered above the insect, rough and uneven; some sloped outward with vertiginous overhangs, and in their deep crevasses were dense meshes of whitish cobwebs, layer upon layer of them, like some elaborately contrived barricade.

The ant paused at the foot of the wall, the foremost pair of legs raised and feeling at it as though trying to assess the magnitude of the barrier in front. Then it turned, and began to reverse up the sheer surface at incredible speed, head downward with the prize clenched between its jaws. The first three bricks were easy; then the ant reached a ledge, backed on to it, and set off forwards again. At three feet from the ground the going became difficult, and a brick above leaned outward with a sharp overhang. The ant tried it forwards very slowly, all six feet testing every possible foothold. The length of its body now leaned outward from the perpendicular. It slipped back half an inch, miraculously recovered its hold, then slipped again. For a moment it hung by its two front feet only. There was a twisting of the body as the other legs reached frantically inward for foothold; then it fell, all the way to the rough baked earth at the foot of the wall. In our terms of relative measurement it was as if a human mountaineer had fallen an unbroken thousand feet.

For a moment the ant lay upon its back, quite motionless, the white papery object, which I now thought of as a message, still firmly held. The legs began to wave slowly, the ant righted itself, faced the wall, and rushed at it again as though in great anger.

The first high fall. I remembered mine; my marriage had been a misery for both partners. I had taken longer to recover than the ant.

At the second attempt the ant avoided, whether by chance or foresight, the brink from which it had fallen; it turned towards the corner of the wall, reached a point some inches higher than before, and found the spread canopy of cobwebs overhead. The message became enmeshed and, in a desperate scrambling struggle to loose it, the ant fell again. This time he took a little longer to recover, and when he did he was unconcerned with the wall; all that mattered was the search for what he had lost. He ran rapidly in small circles and tangents, pausing only momentarily to test the air with his antennae. At the end of several minutes he had not moved a foot from the spot on to which he had fallen.

The second fall. Marriage finished though not yet dissolved; the otters imprisoned as a public danger, Camusfeàrna mechanized and staffed and under siege by sightseers, the idyll over and the message lost somewhere in the fall. I had searched as the ant did, but I too had run in circles.

I leaned over, careful not to throw the shadow of my arm over the distraught ant, and dislodged the message from the spider's web. It fluttered down and landed six inches away from him, lying whitely in the pale, hard earth, hidden from him, I realized, by enormous mountain ridges. It was minutes before he found it. There was an almost visible triumph and satisfaction as he adjusted his posture, gripped it anew, and rushed at the wall. He was tired now, and the ascent was slower, more hesitating; he did not even regain his former height; when he fell he lay longer, and when he moved again there was evidence of injury; only five of his six agile legs remained functional. I did not think he would try again, but he did, because he still carried his message.

The third fall. The motor accident, the unrealized injury, hospital and helplessness, pain and dragging convalescence, the feeling of defeat, a slow fighting defection from everything that had made my life what it was, an unwilling return to an unwanting womb. The ant had certainly done better.

In all the ant fell six times, and each time his recovery took longer, but after the second fall he never lost what he carried.

The seventh time, incredibly, he scaled the wall, the whole five feet of it. It had taken him an hour and twenty minutes; he was injured and exhausted, but he was there. He stood on the brink of the terrace above, on the flat dust-covered path beyond which there was jungle. I stood up and stepped over to watch him. He did not seem to move at all, but having anthropomorphized him – (he must have been neuter, a worker, but my identification with him had made him male) – I thought of him as panting with great breaths, stretching and reassuring tortured muscles, secure in the knowledge of having overcome at last the most terrible part of his journey. He still held the message; sometimes he moved it slightly between his jaws.

He had remained so for perhaps two minutes when the climactic drama took place. From the other side of the yard-wide dust path, out of the uncultivated scrub beyond, came scurrying a smaller ant, redder than he was, appearing to be of a different species. It ran swiftly across the dust, as if orientated to a known destination. It seized the message from my ant's jaws, apparently encountering no resistance, and returned at enormous speed in the direction from which it had come, disappearing quickly into the undergrowth. My ant seemed unconscious of loss; for a moment the whole action seemed like a relay race in which each individual had fulfilled his role and played a faultless part. So,

too, it had seemed to me when I was weak and exhausted; a relay race in which, at the end of my course, I had nothing to do but pass on the baton and trust my successor to carry it home to the laurels. I had nothing to do, I thought, but to rest and recover.

But then, very suddenly, my ant appeared to realize that he was no longer holding anything between his jaws. He behaved as he had at the second fall, when the message had remained entangled in the spiders' webs; he ran violently in circles, with tremendous agitation, two of the six legs held high and no longer touching the ground. After perhaps half a minute he appeared to pick up a scent, and raced after his despoiler. Then he was lost to my sight among the high vegetation.

All this I remembered in a series of vivid visual images while I crouched shivering on the cold wet hillside above Camusfeàrna, looking down at the house that had been my home. The sun was beginning to set now, a cold glary sunset behind the jagged peaks of Skye, the clouds damp and muzzy with the south-westerly gale. I looked down at Camusfeàrna, trying to refocus my eyes which had been too long centred upon the slow heat of that Greek garden in July. There was water in my shoes and cold water running down my spine. The ant, I supposed, was dead now, but he remained a challenge. I was not dead yet.

I watched as a girl came out from the door of Camusfeàrna, carrying fish for the otters. She and her seven-year-old daughter were the only other human occupants of the house. There were more than a dozen dogs around her. Three of them were mine, two deerhounds and their six-months-old puppy. The rest varied in size from Great Danes to miniature poodles; I had no contact with any of these, no contact with Camusfeàrna any more.

I stood up and started to walk down to the house. It was dark now, and only lights showed, the lights of the house, of Isle Ornsay Lighthouse, and of a single fishing boat in the Sound, heading south for Mallaig. I was on a fleeting farewell visit to Camusfeàrna; everything had been arranged. The otters were going to a zoo, the remaining dogs to what good homes they might find. Gus, my favourite dog, the reputedly savage and untamable Pyrenean Mountain Dog, who in reality had been as soft and soppy as a spaniel, had been killed during my absence, hanged by his own choke chain while left out at night.

For the few short weeks of my visit to Camusfeàrna I had tried to avoid seeing the otters. Their end in a zoo was something to which I could never reconcile myself, the institutionalization of unwanted children; but there had seemed no alternative. I could not even earn the money to support them; though already I had received an uncountable number of letters from the public censuring my decision in the most unequivocal terms. What could they know of the impossibilities? Seven thousand pounds a year to keep Camusfeàrna alive but barren – how many of my correspondents could find that money, now or ever, to keep something beautiful even dimly alive in an oxygen mask? And for how long? I had known that it was over, done, finished; but still the unknown faces, unknown voices, had hammered at me to do the impossible, even the ridiculous. Some asked why I did not 'set them free'. As well to ask why one could not set free a dog that one had owned and cherished for seven years; these two otters, Edal and Teko, had been bottle-reared by humans from early infancy, had lived in human houses until the danger of the situation had become disastrously apparent, and they were used to having their meals provided at regular hours. They would not leave; and if, instead, one were oneself to leave they would neither be able to fend for themselves nor to withstand the rigours of the Scottish climate without the heated sleeping quarters to which they were accustomed. It had been a different matter with the various Scottish otters we had kept at Camusfeàrna; we did set them free, and miraculously they appeared to have survived, for years anyway, the peril inherent in a wild animal's trust of man. I saw them occasionally; more often, however, I received letters from English tourists visiting the West Highlands telling me that at some point which was always within fifteen miles or so of Camusfeàrna an otter had come out of the sea, and had approached them unafraid, and sniffed at their shoes. Was this, some of them asked, the normal behaviour of an otter? Each of these letters gave me a tremendous lift of heart, for they told me that the creatures we had taught to trust humans had not yet been murdered because of it.

But with Edal and Teko there could be no such simple solution, and I had made up my mind at last. To love animals as well as humans increases one's capacity for suffering; sometimes I have envied those who are indifferent to mammals of other species than their own, but perhaps it increases, too, a general perception and understanding, the compassion and tenderness that is all too latent in most of humanity – so latent that by now we threaten the survival even of our own species. These things which constituted my attitude towards the two otters made my decision the outcome of a painful struggle, more painful than I would care to describe. But the struggle was over, the decision made. The otters were going, Camusfeàrna would be closed; somewhere I would find a new life.

Nothing is ever as definite as that. If you love a human or an animal there are great ropes pulling you back to the object of that love, and the hands that haul upon the ropes are your own. But it was a little late for loving.

I started down the hill towards the lights of the house. In the darkness the night seemed wilder even than the dusk had been; the rain, driven in from the sea by a full gale, slashed and battered at my face. The tide had turned, and I could hear the roar and hiss of the incoming breakers pounding on the beach below the house. It was an apt enough setting for a long farewell.

*

I passed between the rowan tree, its form just visible against the hurrying nighted clouds, and Teko's enclosure. Teko would by now be in his sleeping quarters, the little lean-to slate-roofed outhouse built on the northerly wall of Camusfeàrna cottage. There he had an overhead infra-red lamp, a raised platform, and a bed consisting of a large lorry tyre filled with blankets. As I passed by, I visualized his sleeping form; I did not expect ever to see him again, because I did not think that I could have borne to visit him in a zoo.

A dog suddenly nuzzled at me in the dark. Something huge, at waist level. I put my hands down and recognized my deerhound bitch Hazel, wet and draggled like I was, but warm and welcoming. Since the Pyrenean Mountain Dog, Gus, had been killed, Hazel had been my familiar; her vast form sleeping on top of my bed, to our great mutual discomfort but to her great delight. Many people may think that I should be ashamed to write that at this, that seemed our last meeting, I was near to tears. She put her paws on my shoulders, and her head was a foot above mine, I said goodbye to her and I let her into the house to warm and dry.

I had said goodbye to Hazel, and now I wanted, obsessively, to say goodbye to Teko. For some minutes I stood there in the dark and the rain and the high wind, knowing that what I wanted to do could only make things worse; but perhaps with a subconscious knowledge of what was going to happen, with a subconscious will to change what was happening to Camusfeàrna and to change all decisions I had made, I turned and opened the high wooden gate to his little house. I closed the gate behind me and switched on the electric light in his sleeping quarters. He wasn't there – and small wonder. The gale had dislodged slates from his roof; the entire floor was under something like an inch of water; the blankets were soaking, and the infra-red lamp had fused. I called him, and he came through from the big enclosure which contained his swimming pool, wet and draggled and miserable.

He greeted me as might a castaway on a desert island greet his rescuing ship. All his language which I had come to know so well over seven years he employed in welcome, in rebuke, in renewed hope for the future. The mustelline access of emotion that may turn to such terrible violence was now all affection and desire for reassurance; he squirmed and writhed and put his fingers in my mouth and ears; he put his mouth to mine and sought the animal exchange of saliva.

I called at the top of my voice for dry towels and dry blankets; when these arrived he took pleasure in being dried as he had when he was an infant, and when I had furnished his tyre with warm blankets he entered it at my gesture and composed himself to sleep on his back, his head resting ludicrously upon my forearm, his mouth open and snoring slightly.

I disengaged myself and left him sleeping, knowing now that I could not send him to a zoo, and that somehow or other he must be taken again to the waterfall, to the rock pools, to the sea and the river, to roam free as he had once become accustomed long ago. I did not know how this might be achieved, but I knew that it must happen; that if it did not I would be a betrayer, and a betrayer of animal loyalties becomes a betrayer in human situations too.

I lacked courage; I asked someone else to telephone to the zoo to which Teko had been destined, saying that whereas Edal now appeared relatively independent of human company and might settle there, Teko would not, and I would keep him. I did not know how; I knew only the necessity. I had become committed. I wanted to spend the next summer giving back to this animal the joy and freedom that we had once shared in Camusfeàrna. My own future had become dim and blurred by multiple problems; his, at least, I could restore for a season.

So when I left Camusfeàrna for North Africa in December 1966 I was not saying a true farewell as I had planned and prepared. I was returning, come what might, hell and high water. I felt that by now I was acquainted with both.

# 2

# A Little Late for Loving

Some of the history of Camusfeàrna after the publication of *Ring of Bright Water* I tried to write of in *The Rocks Remain*, but it was necessarily an incomplete story, and I treated much of it in a semi-farcical vein that I should find difficult to do today. Then I saw the happenings as isolated and episodic, however bad the worst of them had been, rather than as part of a trend that was leading steadily toward the end of Camusfeàrna and all that it had stood for. With hindsight now each seems a logical step on a stairway of decline; though even with that hindsight only a few would have been avoidable.

In August 1961 the female otter, Edal, had almost literally chewed off two fingers from her keeper Terry Nutkins; in time even Jimmy Watt, who had known her for so long, lost his trust in her, and she was totally confined, as is any animal in a zoo. This in itself was a heavy enough hammer blow, but it was only the first, so that as time went on I came to expect nothing but blows.

In October of the same year there was the wreck of the *Polar Star*, a night such as I hope never to pass again.

In November I became engaged to be married, and in December the male otter, Teko, savagely attacked my fiancée's son Simon, then aged thirteen. In January 1962, while I was in London preparing for my wedding on 1 February, Teko attacked Jimmy Watt, and after that both otters became animals living under zoo conditions.

By the last months of that year the stresses of an incompatible marriage had become too great for me to write, and the sequel to *Ring of Bright Water*, which should by then have been completed, had hardly been begun. A friend offered to lend me an empty villa in a remote village of Majorca, and I went there meaning to shut myself off from all problems at home, and to concentrate upon working as I had never done in my life. On the day of my arrival my car was stolen from Palma dock, and within half an hour had been irreparably crashed. The whole of my time in Majorca was taken up by legal and police formalities, and by the time I returned to England the book was little further forward than before my departure.

When I came back I found that Terry Nutkins had left; Jimmy Watt was alone, and there were not enough hours in the day to deal with all the responsibilities that the management of Camusfeàrna now entailed. This was the beginning of a series of temporary assistants, nearly all of whom, each in his own way, brought the end of Camusfeàrna perceptibly nearer.

Some six weeks later my wife and I separated, though we were not divorced until July 1964. It is with the end of *The Rocks Remain*, in the spring of 1963, that I take up the story of Camus-feàrna – or perhaps some may choose to think of it as the story of the rowan tree.

On 24 June 1963 I left Camusfeàrna for the south. I was going to spend a fortnight at my brother's home in Greece. Normally I would have looked forward keenly to this visit, but now I did not want to leave my own home – or what little was left of it – for I was trying desperately to hold it together.

At the top of the hill I transferred my luggage from the jeep to the big Land Rover in which I was going to drive to Inverness to take the train south. This Land Rover was one which I had used in North Africa, and had a number of special features. Amongst others was one that a few minutes later probably saved my life – a BBC hard roof, designed to carry the weight of men and equipment. I remember that it was a sunny morning with no wind, and that the sea in the Sound of Sleat below me was brilliant blue. There were big white cumulus clouds high over the purple hills of Skye.

The first seventeen miles of road from Camusfeàrna is single-tracked, with passing places every two or three hundred yards, and for the first five miles to the village it is very narrow indeed. Barely wide enough, for example, for car and a bicycle to pass abreast.

I had driven half a mile or so, and I was going uphill at perhaps twenty miles an hour, when from behind a heathery knoll on my right a stag jumped across the road right under my wheels. I swerved instinctively and just missed the stag. He was bounding down the bank below me on my left and I was in the act of righting the steering wheel when a second stag followed him. I could not avoid this one, but I suppose I must have tried. I felt the dull thud of contact; then I felt the car lurch over, and I knew that I was overturning. My head hit the roof as the car completed her first somersault, then something heavy hit me in the ribs as she rolled over again.

If I lost consciousness at all it must have been for moments only. I was still in the driver's seat but I was lying on my right hand side, and grass and heather were pushing through the window into my neck and cheek. The engine was still running, but I could not reach the switch with my left hand because of a big suitcase that had been on the passenger's seat and was now pinning my left arm to my side. There were two full jerry cans of petrol on the front end of the Land Rover, besides a full tank; I was in no condition to assess rationally the likelihood of fire, but I knew that if it started while I was in this helpless position I should at the least be very badly burned. I struggled to get the suitcase off me, but I could only do this by half turning upward in my seat so as to be able to push with my left hand. This was made the more difficult because my left foot was somehow caught between the pedals, so that it would not turn with me and give me purchase. I struggled, squeezing my foot enough to hurt a little, but it would not move. Though I could not shift the suitcase I managed at last to worm my left arm through below it and reach the ignition switch. Then there was absolute silence, and I lay there getting my breath back.

I could move the suitcase only by butting it simultaneously with my head and left shoulder; at each butt it bounced, until one, stronger than the rest, toppled it over to lodge behind the gear lever, in the passenger's foot-well. Then I had both arms free, and I started to try to climb out. Because, like other Land Rovers, there were three seats in front, the door through which I had to make my escape seemed a very long way above me. I tried to haul myself up by the gear lever, and it was only then that I realized that my left foot was truly trapped and that it would not follow me. I writhed and squirmed and twisted it, but it was still held fast. At last I gave it one terrific jerk, which hurt only in the sense that a bad graze hurts, and I was free. I climbed awkwardly out of the horizontal passenger's door, jumped down to the ground and lit a cigarette.

There was hardly a mark on the visible portions of the car. There was no sign of the stags, though the second had left a big tuft of hair on the bumpers. There was no blood. It seemed to me as if neither the stag nor I had received serious injury. I was very wrong.

I did not understand then, and I have never understood since, the causes of that accident which had such far-reaching consequences, which changed, in fact, my life for years to come. To begin with, the stags had run downhill, straight at the forestry fence a bare thirty yards or so below the road, and a stag in summer would do this only if suddenly surprised from above by a human being. Even then they would have heard the noise of the Land Rover approaching. I climbed the knoll with a sort of anger, thinking that there really was someone up there, someone who had seen the car rolling over and over down the bank and had been too indifferent to help me while I lay there trapped and thinking that I was about to be roasted.

There was nothing; only the slot marks of the stags in soft black peat a few yards from the road, and, higher up, a few sheep grazing scattered and undisturbed. That ruled out the possibility of a dog, for the sheep would have bunched together. I began to walk back the way I had come.

When I reached Druimfiaclach, the cottage on the road above Camusfeàrna, I turned in to see my old friends the MacKinnons; I felt I could do with one of Morag's cups of tea before I started down the hill to telephone about having the Land Rover restored to the road. Calum Murdo was as puzzled as I was about the behaviour of the stags. 'It's not like the beasts at all,' he said. In fact I think he did not believe me until he saw the tufts of stag's hair in the joints of the bumpers.

While I was sitting in the MacKinnons' kitchen the doctor came in. She was comparatively new to the district, though it had been many years since the village had had a male doctor. She had seen the Land Rover as she passed; she had been puzzled, as anyone would have been, as to how the accident could have happened, and she had stopped at Druimfiaclach to ask if anyone had been hurt. I told her briefly of the sequence of events. 'And you're not hurt?' she asked.

'No, not at all.'

'You're sure?'

'Quite sure. Only a bruise or two, and a graze on one foot. I feel fine.' I believed this completely, so that when the symptoms of damage began to appear I did not at first connect them in any way with the accident.

'Well,' said Calum Murdo, 'I don't know whether to say you are lucky or not, Major' (my war-time rank had stuck to me in the district, despite every effort on my part to rid myself of it). 'You get away with driving that Mercedes at a hundred and fifty miles an hour and you and the population of the British Isles seem to survive it, and now you leave the road in a Land Rover doing less than twenty. They say the devil looks after his own; he's got a lot of different ways of doing it, and maybe he employs stags as well as special roofs built on to Land Rovers. Anyway one thing's certain, we none of us get it before our time – "I have a rendezvous with death at some disputed barricade" . . . You'll pardon me if I'm carried away by the exuberance of my own verbosity . . .'

Five days later I arrived at Athens airport. As I left the aircraft and began to walk down the gang-stairs the heat seemed almost to push one down into the ground. The passengers began to walk across the tarmac towards the airport buildings some two hundred yards distant, and after a quarter of the way I could feel the sweat trickling down every inch of my body. I was halfway when I became aware of a curious cramping pain starting in my left foot, a dull pain like the feeling of a bruise, but growing steadily in intensity. To my enormous surprise it became so bad that I had to stop. I put down my hand luggage and wriggled my foot about, thinking that perhaps I had sat for too long in one position in the aircraft. After perhaps a minute the pain receded, but it was back with me by the time I had reached the Customs. As soon as I was standing still – and there was nothing else to do for quite a long time – it wore off. My brother was there to meet me at the airport with his car; after that I had no more walking to do, and I forgot the episode completely.

My brother owned a yacht and two beautiful small villas, adjoining each other, on the island of Euboea, their brilliantly creepered and vine-trellised terraces a hundred feet or so above the sea. Throughout the whole of the summer he was in the habit of chartering the yacht with the larger of the two villas; only very occasionally, when, as now, there was a last-minute cancellation of a charter, did he have the use of the yacht for himself and his friends.

In a sense of format, set in a different climate, and a different, harder beauty, my brother's home at Katounia was curiously like my own at Camusfeàrna; the little seaside village five miles to the north; the port, the nearest shopping centre, seventeen miles to the south.

We drove from Athens to the port, Chalkis, where a bridge spans the narrow fast-flowing channel between the mainland and Euboea, and where the yacht was berthed to meet us. It was dark when we reached Chalkis, and my brother decided to spend the night there and sail in the morning. Again I had had no walking to do, and I had not given another thought to the curious behaviour of my foot at Athens airport.

We ate at a restaurant table on the waterfront, the narrow strip of water between us and the mainland bright with multicoloured slivers of reflected light that wriggled like eels on the running tide. We drank retsina and ate hot roasted crabs. Fortunately I had finished eating before I saw just how they were cooked; even then I was forced to move my chair so that I did not have to watch it any longer. A few yards from our table a girl, a gentle-faced little creature of ten or eleven years old, stood before a charcoal grill, and beside her was a big tray full of octopus arms and crabs. From time to time she would take a pair of tongs and place something new upon the grill in front of her. The grid on which she put them was surrounded on three sides by upright sheets of glass like a vivarium; I wondered idly why this should be so, and then I suddenly saw that the legs of the crab nearest to me on the grid were waving slowly, that the only completely motionless things on its whole surface were the octopus arms. After some minutes I realized that the crabs were being roasted alive, very, very slowly, but those that I was watching were in the later stages of cooking; lying there on their backs with the glowing coals below them, this protest of lingering life was all that was left to them. After a very long time all movement stopped, the girl inspected them and signalled to a waiter. He brought a tray, and to it with her tongs she transferred the hot crabs and octopus arms until the grid was bare of bodies. It was only then that I understood the significance of the glass sides. With her tongs she selected a fresh crab and placed it carefully, back downwards, upon the grid. For a few seconds it remained without movement; then, as the heat from the glowing coals penetrated through the carapace the crab suddenly twisted right side up and literally shot into the air. It struck the glass side, fell back on to the grid and began to scuttle around it at fantastic speed. One of its legs went through the grid, touched the embers and was burnt off. The girl caught the crab again with her tongs, and patiently replaced it on its back. She had to repeat this three times before only the legs waved helplessly and she could turn her attention to the next victim. This one actually scaled the glass with the force of its first leap and fell to the pavement where it scuttled about on scorched legs. Someone at the next table noticed it and laughed. Then I moved my chair so that I couldn't see the little girl any more, and there was only the delicious smell of hot crab coming from behind me.

Edal and Teko. 'We walked the two otters along the beach and about the field, always at a respectful distance from each other.'

'He and Teko regarded each other as natural playmates, Dirk making rings of dazzling speed around the otter.'

Gavin and Edal. 'She quickly became deeply affectionate and demonstrative.'

The shoreline.

Jimmy and the greylag geese.

# Terry and Teko

'Teko at that time was a weighty
ball of very soft dark brown fur
and fat and bonhomie.'

The *Polar Star* – 'As with so many other "bargains" she required an enormous amount of expenditure before at last she became both trustworthy and socially presentable.'

Isle Ornsay – 'The lighthouse, the cottage and the walled garden, all dazzlingly white-washed, stood on a small, rocky, tidal islet.'

'The beaches at Camusfeàrna are a treasure house for any man whose eye finds wealth at the sea's edge.'

The Kyleakin lighthouse on Eilean Ban – 'The lighthouse itself is an imposing structure, seventy feet high and connected to the mass of the island by a bridge.'

'At Kyleakin I felt as if I were coming home.'

When we sailed north in the morning the cares, the worries, the pressures and emotional strains of my life at home seemed to slip from me like a sloughed snakeskin. Here in the fresh breeze streaming south, ruffling the sea to the hue of dark lapis lazuli and striking miniature rainbows from the white upthrust of our bow wave, with the sun not yet too hot for a bare skin nor the deck planks too scorching for bare feet, I felt free and exhilarated as I had used to feel always at Camusfeàrna. Perhaps, I thought, the secret of keeping one's vision was always to be a nomad, never to remain long enough in one place to allow time for the deadly clouding of sight, the creeping cataract, that is composed of preoccupation with past mistakes and their present results. I felt the salt spray on my face and I was happy.

On our starboard bow the great pale mountain cliff of Candeli towered three thousand feet out of the sea, a pair of eagles wheeling in steep arcs on the hard blue sky above. Just beyond its foot was a little flat calm bay where the water was emerald green backed by wild flowering pink oleanders.

In the afternoon we took the small inflatable rubber speedboat called *Grishkin* and roared down the coast to the little calm bay I'd seen at the foot of Mount Candeli. We beached her there on the roasting hot pebble beach below the giant cliff, and I set off to cruise with a snorkel. I cannot swim without it, so that this is not only my favourite water sport but my only one; rarely indulged, because to me it is essentially a leisurely pastime, and the sea at Camusfeàrna never becomes warm enough for a swimmer to be leisurely.

I swam slowly, entranced as always by the shoals of bright, multicoloured fish, the waving weeds, the host of marine life that passed unobscured below the clear glass of the mask. I swam out to the edge of the shelf, the sea's floor so far no more than ten feet below my face, and looked down into the great dim murk where the shelf ended and the depth plunged down an unguessable distance. There were huge shadows moving down there, too indistinct for identification, but I thought they were tunny. I turned for the shore; there is no more reason for a snorkel to jam in a hundred fathoms than in one, but even strong swimmers tell me that they experience the same illogical fear when looking down suddenly into the shadowed mysteries of the sea's abyss.

When I came back into shallower water I saw the brilliant mother-of-pearl gleam of an angel shell lying open and empty between the black spines of two sea urchins on a rock. I was trying to dive for it when the same thing happened to my left foot as had happened at the airport, but this time it took place much more quickly. I was in real pain in less than a minute. I remained long enough to get the angel shell, then I headed for the shore as quickly as I could. I landed on a smooth rock and took off the snorkel. I sat down and examined the foot carefully; I looked at it and prodded it, but at first I was none the wiser. It looked the same as its fellow but for the scab of a long graze across the arch of the instep. There had been enough dried blood, I remembered, to make it necessary to soak the sock from the foot when I had got back to Camusfeàrna that day after the Land Rover accident. There had been a bluish bruise, too, but it had soon disappeared. This was the first time that I connected what was happening with the recollection of my foot jammed between the pedals of the car; something sinister and unseen must be taking place below the marks of that graze. The rock was so hot that I had to move my foot; and simultaneously I realized that the pain had stopped.

I had enough medical knowledge to grasp the implications. I had not emerged from that ridiculous accident unscathed; the blood supply to the foot was impaired. Heat caused a temporary alleviation, but the foot itself was in the very first stages of dying. Without supply of blood it could not live.

Even if I had acted then and there the situation was already beyond my control; I was probably right in wanting, for the duration of my brief holiday, to forget that something terrible and far-reaching had happened to me. I walked back to the speedboat, carrying my angel shell, and telling myself that this was a temporary obstruction that would clear itself. I could not bring myself to believe in any real sense that I might become a partial cripple; I had been too long used to strenuous physical exertion and the full use of my muscles and limbs, as a necessary part of my existence, to accept the idea of any change other than as a purely intellectual concept.

The next day we began a cruise of the Aegean islands, Skiaros, Skiathos, and Skopelos with its steep, chalk-white town and echoing marble sea-caves where the mud nests of a thousand swifts clung to the remote vaulted ceilings. By now the limitations of my physical activity had become exact and predictable – a hundred yards' slow walking before I had to rest and allow the pain to wear off, five minutes in the sea before I had to land and warm the foot on a hot stone until the cramp slackened.

When I got back from Greece to England I went at once to see a doctor about my foot. His opinion was somewhat vague, but generally encouraging. The temperature of the foot was considerably lower than that of the other, indicating a reduced circulation, but he did not think a natural cure impossible. He gave me pills to take, which were arterial dilators, and asked me to watch progress carefully. In the case of deterioration he advised me to see a specialist, and not to be content with only one opinion.

I returned to Camusfeàrna. Once there it was obvious that without the heat of a Greek summer sun upon a bare instep to aid circulation I was now virtually crippled, whether or not the crushed vessels might eventually re-channelize themselves naturally. I was scarcely able to walk at all, and when I sat writing at my desk I had to keep my left foot upon a hot water bottle to avoid the cramp setting in even without use of the muscles. All feeling of freedom had gone from Camusfeàrna now, and it was a wildly unsuitable place for someone in my condition to live, more than a mile from the road. I felt as much of a prisoner as the otters that were now confined to zoo conditions. I had always worked hard there, writing for long hours every day; now there was nothing for me to do when I had finished work, nothing to do but go on sitting at that desk and worry about the infinite problems that seemed to form the future of Camusfeàrna. The staff problem was acute. Jimmy Watt, who had then been with me for five years, had originally looked after one otter and a very small uncomplicated household; now he had under his charge the running and maintenance of two jeeps; a Land Rover; the forty-foot speedboat *Polar Star*; half a dozen dinghies and outboard engines; and our recent purchases, the two lighthouse cottages of Isle Ornsay and Kyleakin, besides two cottages I had bought near to the village. In varying degrees all four of these houses were in need of more or less extensive renovation or alteration, and if I was to go on writing the responsibility for every detail had to remain with him. A gale would blow up, and someone would have to go out to *Polar Star* at her ill-sheltered moorings north of the islands, nearly a mile away, to pump her bilges and secure her tarpaulins. Every so often someone had to take her seventeen miles south for refuelling. Someone had to order household stores and collect them and the mail from the road at the top of the hill. Assistants came and went, leaving behind them diverse trails of disaster, but it was plainly impossible to run this microscopic but infinitely complex empire without Jimmy and two assistants. An accountant's analysis had shown that, excluding wages – but taking into consideration all other expenses, such as light, heat, transport fuel, vehicle repairs, human and animal food, laundry, insurances and telephone – each human being at Camusfeàrna was costing nearly twenty pounds a week. Wages included, the total sum was well above a hundred pounds a week. Even at that comparatively early date the cottage of Camusfeàrna itself was costing five thousand pounds a year, and the only way in which to meet this charge was for me to forget all the joy that I had once found in its beauty and its freedom and to remain immured between the walls of my little bedroom-study and write day long. Casual visitors, often strangers who wanted to see the otters, could not be expected to understand this situation, and my work was constantly behind schedule.

The only freedom now lay in *Polar Star*, and on the days of holiday when all conditions were right and we would take her to visit the lighthouses or just cruise the long winding sea lochs that, like Norwegian fjords, fray the mainland coast between high hills, I experienced a feeling of liberation and exhilaration as complete as I had on my brother's boat in Greece. The glory of summer days on *Polar Star* is with me still; days when the sea was so utterly smooth that the groups of guillemots and razorbills would leave spreading circular ripples as they dived before our bows, and our foaming white wake lay like a furrow far astern of us; the deep, pulsing throb of engines almost inaudible in the forward wheelhouse; the pull and suck of the whirlpools in the tide race of the narrows at Kylerhea tugging at the rudders; the screaming, hovering, plunging hordes of gulls feeding upon fry forced up to the surface by great shoals of mackerel beneath them, and the fluttering pull of a darrow line on which danced a dozen or more fish as bright as fine blue and green enamel; storms when the ship would buck and slew in the waves like a bronco, and a terrifying white wall of water would pile up under her leeward bows so that she lay over to sixty degrees or so and I would be fighting not only with the wheel but with cold fear; all these, but perhaps most of all the quiet evenings when we returned her to her moorings at sunset and we would sit for long in the open after-cockpit. The sun going down behind the Cuillin of Skye, scarlet streamers of cloud reflected as a great path of blood across the Sound and staining the small wavelets that slapped lightly at the boat's side with a fluid changing mosaic of pale fire and jade. We would sit there until the hills had become black silhouettes against an apple-green afterglow, the only sounds the water lapping against the hull and crying of the seabirds, the colonies of gulls and of Arctic terns on the islands beside us. Those moments of peace and stillness at *Polar Star*'s moorings had come to represent to me what the waterfall once had, the waterfall now disfigured by pendant lines of black alkathene piping that carried the water supply to the house and to the otters' enclosures. Enclosures; the whole of Camusfeàrna by now seemed to me an enclosure, the sea the only freedom.

The house and its surroundings were as much a prison to me as to the otters confined behind fences.

As the weeks went by it was impossible to disguise from myself that the condition of my foot was deteriorating rapidly. But a sort of inertia, born perhaps of a subconscious fear of the future, blocked me from taking any positive action. By October, when the deep sunburn of Greece had worn away and the true colour of the foot was revealed, it was a cold bluish white, and a cratered ulcer had begun to form near the base of the big toe. One day the doctor called to visit another member of the household, and inspected my foot. She said, 'Now you've got to do something; you can't postpone it any longer, unless you're prepared to lose the foot. When I say that I mean that there is now a possibility of future gangrene and total amputation at the ankle. This is no place for you now.' It was indeed no place for me, physically or mentally; it seemed a dead-end, without even the peace and quiet associated with a cul-de-sac.

So in late November I went back to London and saw specialists. The first said that it might be possible to replace the crushed vessels with artificial ones; the second said that the vessels were too small to replace satisfactorily, and in all likelihood would anyway be cast off by the system in the course of a year or two. There was no alternative, he said, to lumbar sympathectomy (the removal of a nerve through an incision in the abdomen in order to permit a full flow of the blood supply to the lower limbs).

I said, 'How long have I got before this operation becomes urgent?'

'That is a very difficult question to answer. Prognosis is not always clairvoyant, you know. In my opinion not very long – two, three months, possibly four if you were lucky, judging by the present rate of deterioration. Have you ever seen gangrene?'

'Yes.' I had indeed; I remembered with sick horror Terry's fingers after they had been chewed off by Edal; the stench, the amputation, the realization that parts of a young human body had gone for ever, lying there blackened in an enamel basin, and that nothing in the world could ever restore them. In some way they had been to me more terrible to look at than a corpse.

'Then you realize that, after the initial onset, the progress of the condition may be very rapid. An emergency operation is always undesirable. I take it that you are now reconciled to the necessity of surgical interference?'

'Yes.' Reconciled was not quite the appropriate word, but this was no time to discuss finer shades of meaning. I did not feel then that I could ever be reconciled to any of these things that had so changed my life, even though I might recognize their menacing aura.

'I understand that you live in Scotland. Would you prefer to have the operation there or in London?'

The problems of Camusfeàrna babbled at me as I sat there in the calm, clinical atmosphere of the Harley Street consulting room with the muted rumble of traffic outside; I couldn't separate myself from them by five hundred miles. I said, 'Scotland.'

# 3
## The Third Fall

I was admitted to hospital on Boxing Day 1963. I was afraid, but I suppose I had by then come near to the consultant's adjective 'reconciled'. In fact the institution did not call itself a hospital; it was a vast nursing home, built, it seemed, with utter disregard for cost. I was slightly disconcerted to find a nun behind the reception desk, in a spacious hall where a notice requested visitors not to wear stiletto heels. I wondered just what a visitor so shod was expected to do after reading this. The pallid, wax-work nun took down the usual particulars with a chilling impersonality, and without once raising her eyes from the form that she was filling in. 'Next of kin? Religion?' Because my own beliefs are eclectic and personal, I suddenly found that I could not answer this question. I hesitated for so long that at last she did look up, and her expression was icy, her thin lips pressed together. 'Religion?' she repeated in her small expressionless voice. I knew there was a word for what I wanted to say, but I just could not find it. She laid down her pen and waited, while I felt like a prisoner of the Spanish Inquisition. I said, rather desperately, 'I'm afraid I don't subscribe to any orthodox religion.' 'Non-denominational,' she murmured, managing to convey an infinity of distaste in the words, and I watched her inscribe them in a handwriting as anonymous as her face and voice. Then she rang a push-button bell, and passed me on to another nun who was as human and welcoming as a well-greased cog wheel.

The procedure, which must of logical necessity be routine, seemed to me grotesque. I was put to bed, my temperature and pulse duly recorded, and I was told that in the absence of doctor's instructions I might not even walk across the passage to the lavatory. The nuns who were on duty had no knowledge whatsoever as to why I was there, and when I tried to explain to one of them that I was to undergo left lumbar sympathectomy resulting from an injury six months before, she merely replied, 'What is this operation you mentioned?' I tried to supply the information she lacked, but she said, 'That has nothing to do with me; I am not a surgical nurse.' Indeed, as I discovered later, she was not a qualified nurse at all; in common with the great majority of the nuns who helped in the huge building she was merely fulfilling a supposed vocation. In many cases the vocation was considerably less than obvious.

Later, a night nurse came on duty, who, although a Catholic, was not a nun. 'What a lot of nonsense!' she exclaimed; 'of course you can go to the lavatory, or walk up and down the corridor all night if you like. These nuns just stick to rigid rules that double the work for everyone. What's the sense in someone having to bring you bed-pans and things when you're quite capable of doing everything for yourself? After you've had the operation – that's a different matter, and a nurse's head would be up on a charger if she put a foot wrong that way. But now, when you've just been admitted for an op like that, it's crazy. They make me sick, the lot of them – they're just not human, and no one's going to tell me it does a patient any good to be treated like a corpse from the moment he gets into hospital. Would you like a cup of tea?'

'Well, just at the moment what I'd ask for if I wasn't in hospital would be a drink.'

'You mean the hard stuff? I can fix that for you too – but keep it out of sight. I'll be back in five minutes, and don't take more than ten drinking it, because I'll be back to take the glass away.'

Oh, hard stuff nurse – I shall remember you with gratitude and affection for the rest of my life. I hope you will accept this tribute and be proud of a truer vocation than was apparent to me in the Order.

The next morning the barber arrived, and after half an hour's very conscientious work left my body smooth and hairless as a baby's. He actually used a magnifying glass to make certain that the perfection of his work was unquestionable. It was strange, I thought, how the whole routine from the moment of admission could be taken by a stranger, some anthropologist observing a new tribal ritual and unfamiliar with its reasons, for a deliberate reduction to a dependent and infantile status of helplessness; this childish hairlessness the visible symbol of submission. Even the word 'nurse' was one belonging essentially to childhood; and here there were yet others added to the hierarchy of the nursery, the 'Reverend Mother' and the 'Mother Superior' . . . I was the patient inferior.

There was one curious thing about my subsequent convalescence while I was still in the hospital. I was working, as soon as I had recovered the energy and application necessary to work at all, on the autobiography of my childhood, which was published in 1965 under the title of *The House of Elrig*. I realized with absolute certainty that my helplessness and dependence, my hairless body, my reduction in middle age to a childhood status, had performed for me some miracle of time transposition, so that I was able to think as a child and to recall images and attitudes that would otherwise have been lost to me. In some sense I did really re-enter childhood, so that to write of it was not an effort of memory, but an actual reliving of those early years, because I was required now to conform to that distant authoritarian pattern. The re-creation was strangely complete; I had passed through the stage of acute illness, corresponding to the dependent infant years, and gone on to impatient and resentful convalescence which found its exact parallel in the intolerant protest of puberty and adolescence. In this way and because the sequence of the writing followed these stages faithfully but unintentionally, long lost scenes and feelings, dialogues and mental directions, became things of the present and not of the past. The images, I suppose, were random, but they were real and uncontrived. The dedication

> This book is for the house
> and all I kissed
> But greatly more than these
> For children like I was
> If they exist

was, in my mind, rhetorical; I did not really believe that they did exist, and I was genuinely amazed when many children's letters began to arrive telling me that they were exactly as I had been, that I had put their own thoughts and confusions into lucid words. It is a terrible indictment of parents or otherwise responsible adults that children should feel driven to seek the confidence, and by implication the absolution, of a total stranger. I know that I owe this inestimable compliment to the two stags who caused my trivial motor accident, and the crushing of my left foot. Perhaps even to the curse upon the Camusfeàrna rowan tree; historically, curses seem often to have back-fired, and if I had not written the story of my childhood as honestly as I was allowed I should not now have the host of vicarious sons and daughters that brighten my world.

# 4

## The Captive and the Free

When at last I was discharged from hospital the temperature of my left foot had been restored – indeed it was slightly higher than that of the undamaged one – but I seemed no nearer to being able to walk. The same cramp would come on after the same distance as it had before my operation; no one seemed to be prepared to say just when mobility might be regained, but I understood that it would be a few weeks at most. I left the hospital double crippled, because besides the cramp in my foot my wound had not healed and my belly felt as if it contained a collection of spiked golf balls that bounced at each hesitating step. My brother, who was home for a time from his house in Greece, came to fetch me. I remember the long drive to our family home, Monreith, in Wigtownshire, because it was the first time for weeks that I had seen anything but the hospital walls and the drab view of industrial brickwork from my ward window. Now there were green fields, and moorlands and budding trees, and air that smelled of them instead of disinfectants.

When at length I returned to Camusfeàrna in the late spring of 1964 I was completely helpless. I could not walk, and even to be driven in a jeep up the hill track with its rocks and potholes hurt my wound so much that I left the house as little as possible, and then almost always by boat. It was the beginning of a curious interaction between myself and those who staffed Camusfeàrna. Their solicitude and their desire to relieve me of every kind of task and responsibility, other than that of writing, worked upon me psychologically to increase my helplessness and dependence; at first I felt myself to be a cypher in my own household, and by degrees that is what I became. They were, the young and healthy, really and actually the masters; never had an adolescent rebellion so complete and satisfying a success with so small an expenditure of force. I could take no part in the activity of the others; I wrote for increasingly long hours every day, working simultaneously on *The House of Elrig* and *Lords of the Atlas*, but with an ever growing sense of frustration – and, I believe, a growing petulance and ill temper. At some unremembered stage of my upbringing I had been taught to believe that self-pity is one of the most despicable of human emotions, and no doubt my surliness and irritability were substitutes for the state of mind in which I really wanted to indulge. I felt like an aphis, immobile but solicitously kept alive in a cell by ants who tended me assiduously for my daily excretion of written words. Had my thoughts been less fogged by frustration I should have realized then that it was folly to try to perpetuate a mutant phase of Camusfeàrna that had proved in an evolutionary sense to be an unpleasant dead end, and instead of spending huge sums on the conversion of two isolated island lighthouse cottages I had bought in October 1963 I should have sold them and bought some house with a road to it, and thus minimized the effects of my crippledom. But those lighthouses became my chief distraction, both because I could reach them by boat, and because they seemed then to represent something emergent and hopeful in the general muddle of my personal situation.

The two otters Edal and Teko were, like myself, by now confined. The Scottish otters, Mossy and Monday, which we had liberated early in 1963, had lived for months under the floor of the house, but at length they had decided in favour of less noisy quarters. They had taken up residence on one of the nearby islands, and we saw them increasingly rarely. At some time during my convalescence at Monreith, however, there had arrived at Camusfeàrna one of the strangest otters in what was by then a long series.

It had become customary for anyone who had come into possession of an unwanted otter in Scotland – and sometimes very much further afield, even in South Africa – to communicate with us. Of the otters actually sent to us, owing sometimes to their extreme infancy and once to a malady carried from a far country, few survived.

This new otter, whose owner had named her Tibby, was the companion of a bachelor cripple who lived alone on the island of Eigg, and who was unable to move without crutches. His increasingly frequent visits to hospital made him anxious to secure Tibby's welfare in the future by finding her a permanent home where she could live free as she was accustomed, and he at once thought of Camusfeàrna. So Tibby had arrived, accompanied by her owner, during my absence. She was thought to be about a year old; she was small and friendly and domesticated, and in appearance almost indistinguishable from Monday at the time when she and Mossy lived under the coat-room floor.

Tibby's owner stayed at Camusfeàrna for a few days, and when he left Tibby was confined to the house for a week or two so that she might become accustomed to her new surroundings. At the end of that time she was placed in Teko's enclosure, for Teko had never displayed animosity towards any otter that had shared his premises either by chance or design. So that she should have some inviolable refuge from him if she wanted it, she was provided with a separate shed with an entrance so small as to preclude the passage of Teko's bulky form. This was the situation when I returned from Monreith to Camusfeàrna.

The arrangement worked well enough for a short time, but Tibby suddenly discovered, as Monday had before her, that stone walls do not a prison make nor iron bars a cage. Nor, she decided, would she take these for an hermitage. She simply climbed out, and having done so she did not head south-west towards the distant island of Eigg from which she had come, but north-east towards the village, the direction in which her master had left, unseen by her, weeks before. At that time a local resident, Alan MacDiarmaid, who had spent his childhood at Camusfeàrna before I ever came to it, was working for us before setting up as an independent builder and contractor in the neighbourhood. He lived now in the village, and drove his car every morning to Druimfiaclach, the cottage on the road a mile above Camusfeàrna, and walked down the track to us. On the first morning after

Tibby's disappearance he arrived with her trotting obediently at his heels. He had found her on the road near to the village, caught her without difficulty, and put her in the boot of his white Riley. Liberated at Druimfiaclach, she had followed him down the track to Camusfeàrna without question or demur. We found the place from which she had escaped and made it, as we thought, impregnable. Alan spent the whole day working on the enclosure, and when he had finished it seemed that not even Monday herself, that Houdini of the otter world, could have escaped from it.

Two days later Alan again arrived with Tibby bouncing along at his heels. Again he had found her near the village, caught her, put her in the boot, and driven her to Druimfiaclach. I can't remember how often this farce was repeated before Tibby made up her mind that she would not be caught again. She decided to remain at the village. She located the only man who resembled her late master, in that he too was a cripple on crutches, and she tried to attach herself to him. She carried up grass and began to build herself a nest under his house. Unfortunately he was not otter-minded, and viewed her proposal of partnership with less than enthusiasm. Repulsed and no doubt bewildered, she forsook the immediate area, and it was some long time before I had any real evidence that she was alive. A month or two later an apparently tame otter appeared on a rock by the pier of Kylerhea ferry, a mile or two from the village, and sat down unconcernedly to eat a fish within a few yards of a number of tourists who were waiting to cross the ferry with their cars, but this may as well have been Monday. Months later I received a telephone call from a slightly inebriated gentleman who informed me that he had caught a 'half-grown' female otter and would I like to buy it. As far as I could make out, the call came from a village some twenty miles to the north. I asked him how he had caught it. He had been gathering shellfish on the shore and it had come up to him and sniffed at his shoes so he had 'thrown his coat over it'. I pointed out that this could not be a wild otter, that it must be one of mine, and suggested that he set it free at once. But, he protested, otters were worth money – even the skin would fetch £4. I said that I would pay him double that sum to liberate her.

He demurred, and said that he would consider the question and telephone back after a few minutes. Half an hour later he informed me that all negotiations were now at an end, because the otter had vanished. As this power of evaporation was common to both Tibby and Monday I could not be certain which of them this had been, but I thought that Monday was by now far too wary to sniff at a stranger's feet.

The next time, however, there could be no possibility of doubt. The telephoner said he had actually been followed to his house by an otter. The otter had tried to come in, but he had been afraid and had driven her away. Acting on a sudden inspiration I asked, 'You don't by any chance use crutches, do you?' 'Yes,' he replied, with astonishment in his voice, 'but how in the world could you know that?' I told him the story of Tibby, and he promised to tell me if she came back, but I never heard from him again, and as I had not caught his name I could not enquire myself.

Perhaps if I had never had the operation, and had lost my left foot by amputation, I should have earned Tibby's allegiance for life.

Mossy and Monday, I am almost certain, brought up three cubs on the island off Camusfeàrna where, in earlier years, there had always been an otters' holt. Here some big boulders lay together in such a way that beneath them there were commodious but, to a human, inaccessible chambers. We knew that the holt had been untenanted during the time that Mossy and Monday had been first captive and then free but living under the house; we knew also that it became occupied once more at some time soon after they left us. In the late summer of 1964, while I was writing in my room at Camusfeàrna, I heard the extraordinarily penetrating sound, something between a whistle and a squeak, that a young otter makes when it is trying to regain contact with a lost parent. The sound came from the waterfall; I limped across the field and peered cautiously over the shrub-grown bank that screens it from the direction of the house. All I saw at first was Mossy, the male; no other otter, I thought, could look quite so stupid, so silly, so unaware of any intruder. He was sitting on a rock ledge at the side of the falling white water, below where a small holly bush grew from the steep bank at the water's side, and he was, as usual, doing nothing in particular. Then the penetrating call came again, nearer at hand, and below my line of vision. I raised my head a little more, and three very small cubs came into view, cubs of about the same size as Mossy and Monday were when they first came to us. One was on a stone in midstream below the waterfall, and the other two were on the long, smooth, steeply sloping rock that formed the opposite bank from that on which Mossy was sitting. As I watched, one of these half slid, half tumbled down into the water; splashed around for a moment, climbed back out again; and then, looking to the top of the waterfall, called again. I looked up too, just, but only just, in time to glimpse a small sharp face like Monday's peering round a rock at the lip of the fall where the water began to spill over in cascade. The inference was obvious; she had climbed the fall and the cubs could not follow; Mossy, as in all other situations in which I had known him, did not know what to do about it. I was reminded of a *New Yorker* cartoon, in which a family of rats were attempting to board a ship by means of its berthing rope, and had been brought up short by the huge disc of a rat-stop. The little rats were fussing about on the rope behind their parents, and the mother was looking at them over her shoulder and saying, 'Oh, do for heaven's sake stop chattering and let your father *think*.' Mossy was presumably thinking, but as usual without result.

I was determined to secure a photograph of the family; I did not think Monday had seen me, but in case she had, and decided to take her cubs downstream again before I could return with a camera, I fetched a length of net and stretched it across the stream at the wooden bridge below the house. Then I went back to the waterfall with a camera. As I crossed the field I realized that the calling had stopped before even I had laid the net, and when I peered over the bank again there were no otters and no otter cubs. I walked downstream to the net, but they had not passed that way, for there was soft sand at each side of the stream, and if they had bypassed the net on land they would have left their prints there.

It was foolish of me to think that I could outwit Monday, who had proved so often and so conclusively in the past that she was master of any situation I could devise. She must have seen me at once, and somehow contrived in the first minute or so after my departure to convey her cubs and her dumb spouse up over the waterfall and into the inaccessible reaches of the cliff-walled stream above it. Monday, with much experience of human ways, was free, and she intended that she and her cubs should remain so.

Yet two and a half years later, in the spring of 1967, she hobbled into Camusfeàrna kitchen with a foreleg broken by a gin trap, and remained in the house until it was healed and she was again on the point of giving birth. She trusted us in her trouble, the highest compliment a wild animal can pay to humans who have once been its captors, and that she trusted Camusfeàrna and no other house was evident by her survival during the absent years.

# 5

## *Bitter Spring*

I was away from Scotland for some months during which my mother died, after a protracted and distressing illness, and when I returned to Camusfeàrna in April it was with a feeling of deep foreboding. It would have been better if I had paid greater heed to this and closed Camusfeàrna then, but the desire to resist and to fight against misfortune was still strong in me.

There was only one encouragement, and it was brief. The wild grey geese came back to Camusfeàrna for the last time. Year after year, since we had brought a brood of unfledged goslings from the diminished flock on the great loch at Monreith, these and their progeny had been wont to return to us in the late spring; having wintered, miraculously unscathed by human hand, in some southerly region unknown to us.

Their origins went far back in my life, to the days before the war, when I had built up at Monreith a collection of the wild geese of the world; when snow geese from North America and bar-headed geese from Tibet grazed the grassy slope below the old castle and the garden itself held exotic rarities. There had been the little lesser whitefronts that I had myself brought back from Lapland the last summer before the war; they would answer to their names with a shrill clamour that reminded me of the vast tundra and of the shine of still lake water under the midnight sun, of the sour tang of reindeer grease and the smell of trout cooking over a camp fire.

There had been a Cape Barren goose, I remember, who would walk in through the open French windows of the library and squat in front of the fire, her delicate dove-grey argus-eyed plumage quivering with contentment, and at the hour of the evening flight the air would be full of the wild wings and the desolate music of the greylags and the snow geese from the loch. During the war, when all good grain was needed for human consumption, there had been terrible mortality among the rarer species, nearly half of their number dying in twenty-four hours of aspergillosis caused by a consignment of mouldy wheat. Despite this disaster, mine had been the only collection in Europe to survive the war somehow, and it was thus, though somewhat depleted, unique. By then I had transferred myself to the north-west of Scotland, and Peter Scott had decided upon Slimbridge as the perfect site for what is now the world famous Wildfowl Trust. He had acquired the site, but there were no very obvious means of acquiring quickly anything but the British-wintering species of wild geese to stock it. He came to Monreith and found some twenty species still surviving, three-quarters of them the sole representatives of their race upon the European continent. It would have been hard to resist his eagerness even if I had had any real reason for refusal, which I had not. So they went to Slimbridge – all, that is to say, but for the flock of full-winged breeding greylags, the descendants by many generations of birds that I had wing-tipped on Wigtown Bay in the days when I was an ardent wildfowler.

So the greylags were left, and they bred about the loch shore and on the island until the numbers which were grazing the agricultural land of the estate drew adverse attention. At times there were more than a hundred, though the flock may have been augmented by truly wild birds wintering on the estuary of the Cree and the Bladnoch rivers. Their fate, in any case, was the same; they were treated as vermin, and their comparative tameness made their destruction the easier. By the time that I brought the brood of unfledged goslings to Camusfeàrna there were only four breeding pairs left on the loch at Monreith, and now there are none.

In due course the greylags began to breed at Camusfeàrna, always on the little reedy lochan a mile above us, across the road from Druimfiaclach. Morag MacKinnon used to feed them and make much of them; she had names for them all, even when the original five had increased to thirteen. That was the highest number they ever reached; not only because there were always more geese than ganders, resulting in a proportion of infertile eggs, but because there was never a spring in which the whole flock returned from their unknown wintering haunt, and once we had to bring a fresh brood from Monreith to prevent our stock dying out. Some must inevitably have been shot; others, perhaps, remained with the flocks that had adopted them, and flew north in the spring to breed in the wild laval mountains of Iceland.

We had become used to waiting for their return to Camusfeàrna late in April or in May. It was always a dramatic event; someone, while we were about our usual tasks either in or outside the house, would suddenly call, 'I hear geese!', and we would gather together searching the sky for confirmation. Then the sound would come again, the wild, haunting call that seems to hold within it the image of vast windswept spaces, mountain and salt marsh and limitless sky, the very utterance of the north and of untamed places; a lone voice first, like a bugle on a falling cadence, then joined by others in a tumbling cascade of silver trumpets, and the small flock would come into focus still high and far off but with wings set for the long spiral glide down to the greensward of Camusfeàrna. Then they would circle the field low over the house, the great wings audibly fraying the air each time they passed; and at last with a great flurry of pinions beating as the flock braked steeply to alight, they stood again before our door, as unafraid as if they had never encountered a human hunter. One of us would go to the kitchen to bring them bread, and the old gander who was their leader, the one whom Morag used to call George, would ruffle out his plumage and advance towards us with his neck held low and parallel to the ground, setting up a great gabbling clamour before beginning to guzzle the bread from our hands.

It was thus that they returned for the last time in the late spring of 1965. We heard them far away, thin and clear at first, then fainter and buffeted by a stiff southerly breeze that drove before it big shapeless white clouds above an ink-dark sea beginning to break into a chop of short steep waves. The little flock of five passed high over Camusfeàrna, heading inland in a perfect V formation; they checked in answer to our call to them, but resumed and held their course, so that there was nothing but that brief hesitation in answer to our voices to tell us that these were the Camusfeàrna geese. They passed out of sight in the direction of Druimfiaclach; then, five minutes later, they came back in a single straight descent on stiff outstretched wings, slanting steeply down from the horizon hilltop above the house.

There were two ganders and three geese; the third goose, whom Morag had in previous years named Cinderella, was unpaired, and remained at some distance from the others; she had always been small and silly looking. There was nothing to show that this was the last time the wild geese would ever come back to Camusfeàrna; but their epoch, which had been part of the idyll, was over.

George and his mate took up residence, as they had in previous years, on the lochan at Druimfiaclach, and from there they paid us irregular but almost daily visits. The other pair flew further inland and we assumed that they were nesting on one of the many hill lochs above us. We never saw them again. Cinderella stayed alone about the Camusfeàrna beaches, until one day we came upon her remains, eaten by a fox or a wildcat.

Then one day, visiting Druimfiaclach to collect stores (the cottage was now empty and shuttered, the MacKinnons gone) we saw that George had a broken wing. It trailed out from him on the water as he swam, and he tried constantly, both by its own helpless musculature and by his beak, to put it back into position. We carried a small fibre-glass dinghy up to the lochan, and approached him closely enough to assess the damage. It seemed a simple fracture of the ulna, caused, I thought, by striking the telegraph wires in a half light, and I thought it would heal by itself. But it meant that George could sire no goslings that year, for the act of copulation takes place in water and requires the use of both wings to maintain balance.

In fact his female did not even lay, and a few weeks later I was told that George was dead, his carcass floating near to the edge of the reeds. We went up and launched the fibre-glass dinghy again and recovered his body. The wing had set perfectly and he had been able to fly, but there were twenty pellets of No. 5 shot in his neck and that was that. The concentration of shot showed that he had been killed from very close range, and since he had no fear of men this was in no way surprising. His mate lingered about the lochan for a week; then she too disappeared, and no wild goose ever came back to Camusfeàrna again. With their absence something, for me mystic, had gone for ever.

# 6

# Isle Ornsay Lighthouse

The two lighthouses, which had been my main focus of attention in all leisure moments since I was crippled, had become my property by curious coincidence. Camusfeàrna itself stands on the mainland shore of the Sound of Sleat, and from it leads north-westward a mile-long chain of small islands, some grassy and some heathery; on the furthest out of these, the largest, is a minor lighthouse erected in 1909. There was no house attached to this; the light was operated by gas cylinder, and tended by the occupant of Camusfeàrna croft, a shepherd; for the work was far from being a full time job. When, before my arrival, Camus-feàrna had stood empty, the light had become the responsibility of Druimfiaclach, the cottage on the road a mile up the hillside. When I came to the place in 1948 the incumbent was Calum Murdo MacKinnon, who was also the local roadmender, and he held the post until he and his wife Morag left the district in 1965.

Three miles away, W.S.W. across the Sound of Sleat, is Isle Ornsay Lighthouse, on the Isle of Skye; at night its signal, a double flash every seven seconds, were the only lights in sight from Camusfeàrna shore. This was a much larger lighthouse than the one on the Camusfeàrna island, built at the seaward extremity of a small green islet, and it possessed a big cottage to house two lighthouse keepers and their families. I had never landed at Ornsay Light, though one of the keepers was an acquaintance, for on calm evenings he would sometimes visit us after he had been fishing for mackerel. On one such still summer evening in 1963 when the peaceful evening light had lingered long on the hilltops, he came in at dusk, bringing a present of fish, and as we sat in the kitchen–living-room he said:

'I'm afraid this is the last dram I'll be taking with you –

Ornsay Lighthouse is to be made fully automatic, and I'm being transferred to Ardnamurchan. I'll be sorry to leave; I'd got kind of fond of the place, but in our job you have to go where you're sent. Anyway, I'm glad it's not Hyskeir or any other one of those rocks where there isn't room to stretch your legs if you step outside the house. They say Ardnamurchan is not a bad place at all, and it's certainly an important one, being the most westerly

point of the whole mainland of Scotland. Still, I'll miss Ornsay.'

I asked him what was going to happen to the house.

'Oh, the Northern Lighthouse Board will put it up for sale, no doubt, and it'll be a lucky man who gets it. They put a whole new roof on it a year or two back, and that cost them several thousand pounds. It's quite a big place too, built for two families, though I suppose anyone buying it would need to do a bit of alteration, because in a manner of speaking it's got two front doors and there's no connexion between the two halves of the house. There's a big walled garden, too, though we haven't done much with that for the last few years back, since tinned vegetables came into fashion.'

All this had touched off in me an immediate train of thought. I was a grace-and-favour tenant of Camusfeàrna, with no ultimate security of tenure; the terms of the lease stated specifically that there would be no compensation for improvements, and that at expiry the house must be left as I had found it. I had brought in the telephone and electric light – the latter at great cost – and during the time of my marriage a great deal of money had been spent in the way of extensions to the house: bathroom and sanitation (neither of which it had possessed before), deep-freezes, and other bulky and expensive electrical appliances. I had realized that if I were required to leave Camusfeàrna the removal of all these things by land would present insurmountable problems; they could only be taken out by sea, and even then only by a considerable number of journeys in *Polar Star*. All this added up to looking for an alternative cottage on the coast, and I had already found out that this simply did not exist. Isle Ornsay, only ten minutes distant from Camusfeàrna at *Polar Star*'s maximum speed, appeared an ideal insurance policy against possible future homelessness.

Anonymous enquiry to the Northern Lighthouse Board elicited three salient facts: that the prospective purchaser must meet with its approval; that the house would not necessarily go to the highest bidder; that, other factors being equal, preference would be given to someone who would also buy the houses of Kyleakin Lighthouse, eleven miles north of Camusfeàrna by sea. Kyleakin was a major lighthouse on a narrow shipping thoroughfare, connected by a causeway to a substantial hilly island of rock and heather in mid-channel between Skye and the mainland at Kyle of Lochalsh. The lighthouse keepers' cottage, also built for two families, stood high on this heathery island, with a fantastic view northwards to the Red Hills of Skye and southward right down Loch Duich to the hills called the Five Sisters of Kintail.

At that time my earned income was almost indecently large, so large that if for no other reason than fear of disbelief I shall not mention the sum. This strictly temporary affluence had not in any essential changed my way of life or thought, but it did mean that for those few short, foresightless and improvident years I just did not have to think about money at all. It is an interesting experience to have had once in a lifetime, even though the lack of foresight brought the disastrous consequences my *hubris* deserved. With this attitude of mind, which fully deserved the good Scots noun 'fecklessness', I should have bought the lighthouses even had the Northern Lighthouse Board asked from me a considerably larger sum than they did.

Each had an entirely different atmosphere and character. I went first to see Isle Ornsay, with Jimmy Watt and Alan MacDiarmaid. We took *Polar Star* across from Camusfeàrna on an early summer's day so glorious that even a grim Glasgow slum in the Gorbals would have seemed transfigured. At *Polar Star*'s moorings the still air was full of the sound of nesting sea birds, the white wheeling wings of the gulls patterning a blue and cloudless sky; the slender terns, the sea-swallows, with their dancing, ballet-like flight, screaming their disapproval of human intrusion in a series of swirling sallies from their breeding rock a hundred yards away. A big bull Atlantic seal showed his head above the smooth surface a stone's throw distant, stared, and submerged with a heavy splash. An eider duck and her brood of fluffy ducklings made a pattern of spreading ripples on the clear shiny water, and there were black and white oystercatchers with their brilliant red beaks piping from the weed-covered rocks at the sea's edge. All this was the essence of Camusfeàrna as I had known it in the early days of the idyll, before the clouds formed and the storm broke, before the days of disaster and diminished vision.

We found that it took twelve-and-a-half minutes to reach Isle Ornsay Lighthouse, keeping *Polar Star* at a high cruising speed but not at her maximum. We timed this carefully because with the engines burning nine gallons of diesel fuel an hour we wanted to estimate probable future expenses. We went to anchor a few hundred yards north-east of the lighthouse and rowed ashore in the dinghy. The lighthouse, the cottage and the walled garden, all dazzlingly white-washed, stood on a small, rocky, tidal islet, the very green grass grazed down to lawn length by black-faced sheep and their bleating lambs. We drew the dinghy up at a little concrete slipway, and began to walk up the short steep grass slope to the house; a sandpiper flew twittering from her nest of four eggs a yard from the pathway, and stood bobbing on a stone.

I had lived in the West Highlands and Islands for many years by then, but never, except perhaps at my very first sight of

Camusfeàrna sixteen years before, had any view affected me as strongly as the splendour and purity of the immense panorama spread before the islet. Looking eastward, directly across the Sound of Sleat, one could see far up Loch Hourn, its entrance guarded on the northerly side by the mighty conical peak of Ben Sgriol that rose behind Camusfeàrna, a vast scree slope plunging more than three thousand feet from its pinnacle into the sea, diminishing to doll size the tiny houses at its foot. On the southern side of Loch Hourn rose the great hills of Knoydart, Ladhar Bheinn, Ben Ghuiserein and Sgurr na Coire Choinneachain, huge and mysterious in the haze of summer heat; further to the south the huddled houses of Mallaig made a faint white blur above miles of sea as smooth as pale blue satin. Beyond Mallaig, dim in the still blue distance, was the point of Ardnamurchan. To the north of Loch Hourn, Camusfeàrna Lighthouse looked tiny and insignificant on its island that seemed no more than a promontory, dwarfed like all else by the vastness of the hills that formed its back-cloth.

It was as though I had found Camusfeàrna once again, the same sense of sudden freedom and elation, the same shedding of past mistakes and their perennial repercussions. Here, it seemed to me, where the rocks and the white stone buildings were the only solid things in a limitless bubble of blue water and blue air, one might be able to live at peace again, to recover a true vision long lost by now in the lives of other humans and in the strifes of far countries; here one might set back the clock and re-enter Eden.

Alan looked around him over the sea and the hills and the open sky and said, 'To think I've lived all my life just across there on the mainland and seen Isle Ornsay light flashing and never knew that this paradise was just across the Sound! Look, you've got another colony of terns on a rock a hundred yards away, and no big gulls to bother them. And seals too – just look at their heads coming up round the *Polar Star*. And if you wanted to have the otters here – look at that walled garden – plenty of space, and not even Monday could get out of that. This is a paradise right enough!'

It seemed paradise indeed; I did not know, though I was already in middle age, that you cannot buy paradise, for it disintegrates at the touch of money, and it is not composed solely of scenery. It is made of what many of us will never touch in a lifetime, and having touched it once there can be no second spring, no encore after the curtain falls. This is the core of our condition, that we do not know why nor at what point we squandered our heritage; we only know, too late always, that it cannot be recovered or restored. I did not know it then; this was paradise, and I was going to buy it for hard cash. But Isle Ornsay had no rowan tree, no guardian, only the four wild winds of heaven, no shelter. 'She had put her hands upon the trunk of the rowan tree and with all the strength of her spirit she had cursed me, saying, "Let him suffer here as I am suffering." Then she had left, up over the bleak hillside.' I had not known this when I bought Isle Ornsay, all unprotected, and if I had known I should not have been much disturbed.

> Because I see these mountains they are brought low,
> Because I drink these waters they are bitter,
> Because I tread these black rocks they are barren,
> Because I have found these islands they are lost;
> Upon seal and seabird dreaming their innocent world
> My shadow has fallen.

I remember the very first time that I ever landed at Isle Ornsay, and the first time that I was aware of the place other than as a lighthouse, twenty-four years ago as I write now. I had bought the Island of Soay and was preparing to start there the shark fishing industry which I believed would solve the problems of the island's small and isolated community. The factory, with its pier and slipway for hauling by steampower ten-ton carcasses on to a flensing yard like that of a whaling station, its oil-extraction units and fish meal plants and glue tanks, its salting vats and laboratory and all the other costly follies, consisted still of plans on paper; and in those days, at the war's end, all kinds of equipment were difficult or impossible to come by. I landed at

Isle Ornsay village from my little thirty-foot lobster boat, the *Gannet*, that gallant little craft that after the Island of Soay Shark Fisheries Ltd became fact rather than fantasy was the most successful harpoon-gun boat of them all, and killed nearly two hundred sharks of almost her own length. Isle Ornsay was a dead place by then, a few scattered cottages, the mansion house ruined and nettle-grown, the pier in need of repair; there was little enough to tell a visitor that this had once been a prosperous place; indeed I did not know myself that it had been a great port crowded with ships, the industrial centre of Skye and all the adjacent mainland coast.

Soon after I had landed, my predatory eye was caught by a large rusty hand winch standing near the head of the pier. I went over and examined it; it was intact though obviously in long disuse, and a little probing with a knife showed that the rust was not too deep for the winch to be restored as a functional item. At Soay I should need many winches, large and small, ranging from huge steam-driven things to little toys like this one. I looked around me for some sign of human life, and saw a middle-aged man in tattered oilskins sitting on the ground with his back against a wall. He was smoking a pipe and eyeing me with some curiosity; strange visitors to Isle Ornsay must have been a great rarity in those days of fuel restrictions and disrupted communications.

I went over to him and asked him if he knew to whom the winch belonged. He looked me up and down speculatively, without moving or taking the pipe from his mouth. Clearly I presented a problem; though I was dressed in a torn seaman's jersey and dirty old canvas trousers and had several days' stubble on my face, my voice must have told him that I wasn't a fisherman as he understood the term. Few West Highlanders will ever give a direct reply to a question as it is first put to them, any more than an Arab merchant will give the final price of his wares on first demand. Fact is something to be approached circuitously or tangentially, to go straight to the heart of the matter would be clumsy and unrefined. In this case my question about the winch had anyway to be subsidiary to his own as yet unspoken question as to my identity. So he looked me up and down from untidy head to shabby, patched rubber-booted toe and back up again, and then said, 'You'll be a scrap merchant?'

I said I wasn't a scrap merchant. I didn't want to elaborate, to tell him that I was the man who had bought Soay and whose projects for it had been widely reported in the newspapers, because if he chanced to be the owner of the winch this knowledge would send the price soaring. So I said I just happened to need a winch like this one, and could he tell me who it belonged to. After a long pause, and with patent mistrust, he replied, 'There hasn't been a scrap man here for a long time. There's some old iron lying near the beach in Camuscross down there, but I couldn't rightly say who owns it. It's been there as long as I can remember – but it wouldn't be easy to shift. The half of it's bedded down in that black mud, and you couldn't get your boat in there except at high springs, and then the iron would be under water. Ay, it would be a problem right enough.'

I gave up, and wandered away to explore the ruins of the mansion house. Early seventeenth century, I thought, with later additions; it must once have been magnificent, with a high-walled garden stretching away behind it, and a real curiosity of a lavatory – a beautiful little stone structure built on the rocks directly above the sea, so that no drainage system was necessary.

Unfortunately I found, among the nettles that flanked the old gateway to the mansion house, a pile of lorry tyres – another thing that it was difficult to obtain in those days, and which I badly needed as boat fenders for the big Stornaway drifter I had bought, the *Dove*. With resolution but not without misgiving I went back to the man with the pipe, who watched my approach out of the corner of his eye, without turning his head. I asked, diffident but defiant, about the tyres. He took his pipe from his mouth and looked me straight in the eye. At length he said:

'It is a scrap merchant you will be.' This time it was an order, not a statement; it sounded like an army directive.

I left Isle Ornsay empty-handed; the winch and the tyres were still there, in exactly the same positions, when I bought Isle Ornsay Lighthouse cottage just twenty years later. But by then the winch was rusted away, and I had no use for the tyres.

# 7

# Kyleakin Lighthouse

We went next to inspect Kyleakin Lighthouse, in the same splendid summer weather of cumulus clouds and calm seas; up the cliff coast and past Glenelg village on our starboard side, on into the narrows at Kylerhea where the spring tides run at nine knots, past the mouth of Loch Duich and into Loch Alsh. Only at two points does the Island of Skye almost touch the mainland of Scotland, at Kylerhea and at Kyleakin, and Kyleakin is very much the narrower of the two channels. Here a chain of shaggy, heathery islands reaches out from the mainland, so that the last and highest of them, on whose rocks the lighthouse was built, almost closes the channel, leaving less than three hundred yards of water between it and a high rocky promontory of Skye where Kyleakin House stands upon the summit sheltered by a crown of trees.

We came up Loch Alsh leaving Kyle on the starboard side, dodged between the crossing ferry boats, and came in slowly to the southern side of the island, where between steep rocks there was a bay at the foot of the slope. Here a runway on the beach had been cleared of boulders, and at its shoreward end a small shed for an outboard engine showed pale against the dark heather. We anchored the *Polar Star* clear of the tide's current and rowed the dinghy ashore.

Every new island or islet upon which I have ever landed for the first time holds a mystery of its own, a feeling of discovery that is some small echo of the wonder and anticipation with which the early navigators set foot upon greater unknown shores.

The lighthouse itself is an imposing structure, seventy feet high, and connected to the mass of the island by a bridge. From the bridge a steep path leads up to where the joined cottages are perched high on the south-east-facing slope of the island.

316

Deeply though I had been impressed by Isle Ornsay, I felt drawn to Kyleakin as I had to few places in my life – and this despite its nearness to the summer tourist scene. I have since tried to analyse this feeling of profound attraction; at first I thought it might be due to nothing more complex than the fact that Camusfeàrna, with all its echoes of past unhappiness and loss, was out of sight. But I think now that it was a far call back to childhood, for the long, rough heather, the briars and the outcrops of bare rock might have been those surrounding The House of Elrig where I was born, the house that obsessed my childhood and adolescence and came to represent for me the only refuge in a frightening and unfamiliar world. The land surrounding Elrig was a wilderness in which the close-cropped green turf of Isle Ornsay would have found no place, but at Kyleakin I felt as if I were coming home. It was here, I decided, that I would live if ever I left Camusfeàrna.

Even in the early years after the war, when I first came to live at Camusfeàrna, both Kyleakin on Skye and Kyle of Lochalsh on the mainland shore – from which the mail for our district used to arrive by a thirty-foot motor launch in every wind and weather – were very quiet little places, and seemed to retain much of an earlier flavour. Though the crossing was the only car ferry to Skye (for the Glenelg–Kylerhea ferry was not renewed until 1963, and the Mallaig–Armadale service carrying many cars at a time did not come into being until 1965) there was little tourist traffic, and correspondingly few shops and hotels. Those that there were had for the most part a modest, old-world atmosphere; in Kyle of Lochalsh, for example, the Pioneer Stores – which is now a sort of miniature Marks and Spencers, essentially of this decade – was a dim little premises run by two elderly ladies, and it smelled of Harris tweed and tallow and such homely things; it had an indefinable personality of its own, like the Post Office in Glenelg, which sold cheese as well as postage stamps. The Marine Stores, less massively equipped than it is today, had a sort of nostalgic quality crystallized for me by a pair of bellows which I bought there in 1952. Bellows were a necessity at Camusfeàrna, and I had none. There seemed to be only one pair in the Marine Stores, and they were, I remember, hanging from the ceiling; they were sturdily constructed of beechwood and leather, and ornamented with brass studs. When I asked how much they were the proprietor unhooked them from the ceiling and looked for a price-tag. An expression of mild surprise crossed his face as he saw what was plainly written on the smooth white board of one side – four shillings. 'Four shillings,' he said; 'that's pre-war stock left over from the good old days. It takes a thing like that to remind one what they were like.'

If one drove from Camusfeàrna to Kyle, a distance of almost forty miles by roads that were then entirely single tracked, one would meet hardly another vehicle, even in summer, and if one did it would be, as often as not, a local car or a lorry carrying sheep or Forestry Commission timber. Just when all this changed, just when Skye and the mainland coastline became a great summer holiday resort thronged with cars and caravans I find it impossible to remember accurately, but now that stretch of road – mercifully widened for at least a small section of its length – often carries a nose-to-tail procession of cars for miles on end, and the Kyle sea frontage has been modified to contain vast car parks for tourists awaiting their turn on the ferry. (Before these were constructed the queue of stationary vehicles would occasionally stretch for a quarter of a mile or more inland.) New shops and new hotels had sprung up at Kyleakin to deal with new demands, and though it is still a small fishing port, with the emphasis upon prawns and lobsters, the atmosphere in summer is that of a village geared primarily to touristic requirements.

But the lighthouse island was untouched by these changes, and it seemed to me an enchanted place. I bought both lighthouses in October 1963. In the Deed of Sale of Ornsay I was curious to notice a specific clause excluding mineral rights in the land purchased. I knew that the rocks were of hornblende schist, and contained large garnets and other crystals, but that was not the reason for the clause; a far more precious metal underlies that rock. There was no mention of anything invisible at Kyleakin.

Before describing in detail the ghosts that seem indisputably to haunt Kyleakin Lighthouse island they must be shown in perspective, separated from the great host of their more dubious and debatable relations common to the whole area of the West Highlands and Islands.

Superstitions of every kind – witches, the evil-eye, omens, mermaids, fairies, kelpies (water horses), sacred waters, trees and stones – were at the very core of the Skye man's life. There were propitious days to begin a task (Monday was the most favourable) and disastrous days (Saturday was the worst). All action had if possible to follow the sun's course, and a boat putting to sea would initially row sunwise no matter what its real destination. Fishermen would ensure a heavy catch of herring by walking three times sunwise round a sacred stone. Crops were planted and harvested by the phases of the moon – the sowing on the wax and the reaping on the wane. A waxing moon was held to communicate power of growth, so that sheep-shearing, and even a human haircut, could only take place during this phase. Anything that must dry, such as wood, peat, hay or corn, was cut only on a waning moon, so that it could not be re-vitalized by the moon's strength.

Among the old people, and not a few of the younger, the world of the 'supernatural' is accepted as unquestioningly as the 'natural'. Until very recently the belief in witches was universal. A witch could take the form of an animal at will, usually that of a hare or a cat, but sometimes horses, cows, or even whales, and whereas she could be killed only by a silver bullet any injury inflicted upon her while in animal shape left corresponding marks when she resumed her human identity. A hare would be shot at and wounded, and the next day some old woman would be found to have gunshot wounds in her legs or arms.

Many of these stories from the district are very detailed; these are samples. A Kyleakin man was troubled by a cat that consistently raided his kitchen. He succeeded at last in catching it, and cut off one of its ears; soon afterwards it was discovered that a local woman had lost an ear, and for the rest of her life she had to wear a shawl over her head to hide her shame.

A fishing family suffered from the attentions of a small whale that constantly tore their nets and freed the fish. At length one of the boat's crew armed himself with a sharpened three-pronged potato fork and hurled this at the whale as its back showed passing the boat. The whale sounded and did not reappear. The next day a woman, already believed to be a witch, died in great agony, calling down curses upon the name of the fisherman. An examination of her dead body showed three terrible wounds in her side, corresponding to the prongs of the fork. The whale was never seen again.

Kelpies were held to inhabit many lochs; they waylaid maidens by night and carried them down into the cold deep, so that they were seen no more. Loch na Beiste (Loch of the Beast) at Kyleakin is said to contain a creature that some describe as having a head covered with a mane, while others who claim to have seen it refuse utterly to give any description whatsoever. Two fishermen in a rowing boat were almost submerged by an unknown animal which they described as about twenty feet long, as thick as a man's thigh, and with a maned neck. The carcass of some apparently unknown creature with a mane is said to have been found in the Boom Defence Net off Camusfeàrna Lighthouse island during the Second World War, but no scientist ever examined it, and it remains a story.

The mermaids of Skye, called in Gaelic Maighdean Mara (sea maiden) or Maighdean na Tuinne (maiden of the waves), seem to be less frustrating to the male sex than the rest of their kind; instead of remaining fish from the waist down they become wholly human after their capture. A Skye man caught one in his nets and took her home. She shed her tail at once, and, delighted with this cooperative metamorphosis, he hid it in the rafters of the barn, and made the most of what had replaced it. She lived with him many years, and bore him children. At length one of these, playing in the barn, chanced upon the tail, and came running to his mother to ask what it was. 'It's my tail!' she cried in wild delight, 'my long lost tail!' and without a backward look she hurried down to the sea with it and was never seen again.

Most Skye men would laugh at such stories now, but I think there are few who would deny absolutely the existence of 'second sight', whose possessor is able, often most unwillingly, to see into the future – not all the future, but isolated happenings usually of a calamitous nature. A possessor of this ability is feared, but also fears his or her own powers, so that a ritual of exorcism was devised; at the very first vision the seer must recount all that he saw to an intimate friend who meanwhile holds a Bible before his face and turns the pages rapidly. However open a mind one may try to keep as to the possibility of 'second sight', the credibility of this as a remedy must rank with the mermaid's tail.

Whatever is foreseen, the image is said always to be of great detail, never a blurred impression. Often it is a funeral, and the face of every mourner is recognizable, together with knowledge of the time and the place; sometimes it is a photoflash, but of equal intensity and shock. One Skye woman, drinking a cup of tea with neighbours, suddenly fainted. When she was again conscious she at first refused any explanation, but under pressure she whispered that she had had a sudden and instant vision of the corpse of a boy whom she had seen ploughing in a nearby field. The boy died by drowning within a week.

A whole volume could be filled with such tales; they vary little, and for the most part concern simply the prophetic vision and its fulfilment.

Apart from the specific gift, or curse, of the 'second sight' any unexplained phenomenon is held to presage some event that is yet to come; the very opposite, if one may put it that way, of the more familiar European conception that a house is haunted by humans or happenings belonging to the past.

Two men were sitting talking in a shed on Kyleakin pier when from outside came the sound of a splintering crash as of two boats in collision. They ran out, but found nothing to explain the noise, nor had anyone else heard it. A few days later an old and partially deaf fisherman, an octogenarian, had his launch at anchor in the narrows, hand-lining mackerel, and failed to hear the approach of the MacBrayne Stornoway-to-Kyle steamer, the *Loch Ness*. When he turned and saw her bows towering over him he knew that he could do nothing, for he was too late to get his anchor up; he stood and waited without flinching. Just before the impact a rope was thrown to him from the forepeak of the *Loch Ness*, and as he caught it his boat was literally sliced in two. Old as he was he contrived to cling on to the lifeline for many minutes before he was finally hauled aboard, and his life was saved. It was accepted as being entirely natural that the sound of the collision should have been audible days before to anyone attuned to hear it.

All my life my own attitude toward what is popularly called the 'supernatural' had been cautious and strictly empirical. I had not once personally experienced anything that could not be rationalized and made to fit into the plainly minute and constricted framework of my own human experience and limited knowledge. I had recognized that what my senses could perceive and my brain understand was no more than a millionth, a billionth, part of even the human cosmos, but I was essentially of the faithless generation that waited for a sign. I had adopted a scientific approach which demanded unquestionable evidence before accepting and assimilating any new concept, and having read Spencer Brown on the theory of probability I had pigeon-holed several curious experiences under the temporary and pending label of 'coincidence'.

This broadly sceptical attitude changed in May 1964 with the undeniable arrival at Camusfeàrna of what is usually known as a poltergeist. It remained our guest – a very unconventional one – for two days, and when it departed I was disappointed, for I longed to go on studying those weird phenomena that were actually testable, though inexplicable, by my five senses.

They had begun one evening at about 10 p.m. There were three of us sitting in the kitchen–living room of Camusfeàrna. Along one wall there is a homemade sofa, above which are shelves holding groceries and tinned foods, like any small village store. I was sitting at the end of this sofa nearest to the actual kitchen, a small room whose door was on my left. In front of the fireplace, at forty-five degrees to my right, was an L-shaped sofa, also homemade. On the section facing and parallel to where I was sitting was a guest, Richard Frere, who later became the manager of Camusfeàrna and its small but complex dependencies. Richard is a mountaineer of distinction, an extremely practical man, little given to fantasy. Facing the fireplace, and in profile to both of us, was Jimmy Watt, then aged twenty.

Among the grocery stores above my head – tins of green vegetables, pickles, jam-jars and so on – I suddenly heard a scraping sound, but I only just had time to look upward before I saw an object flying outward from above my head. It landed about three feet in front of me; a glass marmalade jar smashed to pieces on the cement floor. It was curious that after a moment's pause Richard and I both said, simultaneously and somewhat disbelievingly, 'Poltergeist!'

I climbed up and examined the top shelf, a foot wide, from which the missile had launched itself. The woodwork was deep in dust, and the jar had been standing close against the back wall. From its original position there was a clean track of its own width, clear of dust, all the way to the edge of the shelf. There cannot have been more than half an inch between the jar and the wall, allowing no space for mechanical propulsion, yet somehow it had projected itself over a distance little less than six feet.

I was alone when the next incident took place, but unless I were to distrust my senses I must say that as far as I was concerned it really did happen. I was standing in the little kitchen waiting for a kettle to boil when I was aware of a curious rustling sound in the living-room behind me. I turned to look, and saw a stack of long-playing discs fanning themselves out like a pack of cards over the floor from where they had been piled under a little table supporting a record-player. They slid outward in an orderly movement, and came to rest covering more than a yard of the floor, each neatly overlapping the next. I replaced them as they had been, and tried to produce the same effect myself by mechanical principle. It wasn't possible; as in the case of the marmalade jar, there was not room between them and the wall for a hand or any human artifice to propel them outward.

Jimmy had been out; when he returned a little later I described to him what had happened, and was about to resume boiling the kettle to make coffee. We entered the little kitchen together, and as we did so something shot off a high shelf opposite to us, hit my face lightly, and fell to the floor. It was a baby's plastic feeding bottle with a rubber teat, relegated, like other things for which we had infrequent use (this we used occasionally for orphaned lambs in the spring) to the high shelf above the cooker. It had cleared the cooker by two or three feet, and, like the marmalade jar, it had left a dust-free trail in its passage. This time I had the subjective feeling that this object had definitely been aimed at me; whatever was throwing things about was, it seemed to me, no longer random in direction.

The kitchen door opened from the room in which we stood, a square hall or lobby hung with rows of coats and oilskins; on the floor below them were dog beds, and rows of rubber sea-boots. In the corner of the room diagonally opposite to the lavatory door a large empty laundry hamper stood on a low table.

The following day when I went through to the kitchen I did not close the door to this room behind me. I sat down, and there came a resounding crash from the lobby I had just left. I knew there were no dogs in the house, nothing animate that could have caused that noise.

I re-entered the coat room with a certain caution. It was not difficult to see what had produced the sound; the laundry hamper had been thrown from the table and flung more than halfway across the room. It lay upside down with its lid open, within a few feet of the lavatory door. It had evidently been propelled with considerable force, for it had sailed clean over two tall pairs of rubber thigh boots that stood in its path.

That, unfortunately, was the last manifestation of the Camus-feàrna poltergeist. I waited hopefully for the least sign of its continued presence, for I was profoundly fascinated by this first-hand evidence of an unknown world; but after that last splendid gesture of the laundry hamper it was years before anything ever happened again that was not capable of easy interpretation in normal terms. The brief visit had, however, broken through a lifelong barrier composed, if not of disbelief, at least of mild scepticism; and after that glimpse of the unguessed I could not, two years later, view the curse upon the rowan tree with the degree of scorn that I would probably have accorded it before.

It was soon after the lighthouse cottages became mine that a resident of Kyleakin, not born locally, said to me with a slight constraint in her voice, 'I suppose you know that the lighthouse island is haunted?' I said that I didn't, and she replied, 'Well, I was told about it in confidence, but as you've actually bought the place now I don't suppose there's any harm in telling you. There doesn't seem to be much doubt about it, anyway. You'd better talk to some past lighthouse keepers; I believe any of them can tell you all about it. It seems that it's not frightening, anyway, it's just there.'

I sought out the most easily available, and though he was a slow starter, as I should have been in the circumstances, he eventually gave me a wealth of detail that, coming from so clearly level-headed a source, left me with the conviction that there must be something on the island not explicable in ordinary terms. He referred not only to his own experiences, but to those of his former colleagues and his predecessors.

There have been experiences which must be classified as indi-vidual, but there has remained a standard, unvarying pattern common to all who have occupied the house. From somewhere just *outside* the walls, never seeming to be within them, comes the sound of low-pitched muttering voices, as though intentionally subdued, but rising and falling in intensity, as if in hurried argument. This may be preceded or succeeded by loud metallic clangs; these have been variously described as the sound made

325

by an iron poker raking out a stove, or, perhaps more fancifully, as the clash of claymores or broadswords. With one exception, which was after my ownership, these things have been puzzling but never frightening.

A keeper whom we may call MacLellan was on the island for seven years, and during that time became so accustomed to the voices and the metallic clang that he came simply to ignore them. He was a Gaelic speaker, and was certain that the language spoken bore no relation to Gaelic. He emphasized that the occurrence was always during the small hours of the morning. He told me, too, that a relief keeper who spent eighteen months there had followed the advice of a predecessor, with absolute success. If, on hearing the voices for the first time, one asked loudly, 'Who's there?' they would cease and never recur.

I daresay I should have paid little enough attention to these stories if I had not had more contemporary evidence. At first, having bought the lighthouse cottages, my idea was only to maintain them in good condition until I should need to occupy one or the other myself. This negative scheme developed, through the project of furnishing them minimally in order to obtain a minimal summer rent, to converting them completely into comfortable, even luxurious, houses which could avail themselves of the tourist boom in the West Highlands. There seemed to be no immediate prospect of my being required to leave Camusfeàrna, and here might be a source of income that did not necessitate my writing at a desk for eight hours a day. I went into this, as I always have with any new project, with enthusiasm.

I had recently made the acquaintance of Richard Frere. He had trained himself as a builder, a joiner, a mechanic, and much else. Work, physical or mental, was his food. When he offered to take over the structural conversion of the lighthouses, and his wife, a talented decorator, to make herself responsible for the interior décor of Ornsay, I had embarked on a programme that deserved better financial results for all of us.

This arrangement was infinitely more economical than I could have achieved from any contractor; for both of them it was a hobby, and by it I benefited enormously. On 15 May 1964 Richard and his wife Joan began the conversion of Isle Ornsay and finished early in August. By then it was a luxury house, though we continued alterations and improvements until April 1966.

In October 1964, Richard began a similar conversion at Kyleakin – to my own somewhat ambitious designs – at first with an assistant, and then alone for some weeks. (The first assistant was Terry Nutkins, who had temporarily returned to our employment, and who kept a pair of wildcats in the annexe building subsequently known as The Cat House.) Terry left in January and for some weeks Richard was alone at Kyleakin. I had regarded Richard as a test case for the existence of some unexplained phenomenon at Kyleakin, and had been careful to tell him nothing of the stories I had heard. If, I thought, so pre-eminently sane and level-headed a man were to experience anything unusual without preconditioning there would no longer be any doubt in my mind. Richard writes:

In January 1965 I returned [to the island] to spend the night and subsequent nights alone. I had my dog Hedda (Dalmatian bitch) with me, and she was never at any time worried by atmosphere or voices. I slept very soundly for the first three or four nights. At first, the weather was calm with frost; on the fourth night a southwesterly wind was blowing, which kept me awake until after midnight, and when I slept it was fitfully. I was awakened shortly after 3 a.m. by a sharp metallic clang. I heard the first voices a few minutes later. The wind had dropped, and it was raining. The voices, a curious disconnected muttering, rose and fell and seemed to be travelling down the north side of the house from west to east. So kindly was the atmosphere within the house that my only fear was that I should *become* afraid. *Nothing* would have made me go outside, but I was strangely prepared to lie and listen. It went on for about ten minutes, the clang being repeated two or three times. The voices suggested the passage of many people past the house, but I heard nothing of their movement. Believe it or not, I went to sleep again before it was entirely quiet; though, as I say, the very audible part continued for about ten minutes. This performance was repeated often, but never in stormy conditions; or, if it was, it was impossible to hear it. I always had the impression (if one can accept it to be some captive echo from the past) that here was a war-like party, arriving stealthily to deploy on the island preparatory to some battle or skirmish. By March it was all over.

Many lighthouse cottage occupants have heard the voices, and all accounts seem to agree that they are low-pitched and incoherent, but I myself have heard sharp sounds and expressions which would be meaningful if I knew the language.

There is one particular sentence in Richard's letter which ties up closely with my searching questions to a former lighthouse keeper. 'By March it was all over.' No one could remember having heard the voices during the spring and summer months; it appeared to be a seasonal haunting, limited to autumn and winter. Morag MacKinnon, who used to be my neighbour at Druimfiaclach above Camusfeàrna, went to live in the house for a few weeks early in 1966, in company with a boy who was preparing the adjoining island for a further project which I shall describe later. She wrote, 'I personally heard the voices only once. One Sunday morning at about 8.15, lying in bed, I heard what I thought was the wireless turned low, but I was puzzled that I had not heard the boy getting up. The voices were pitched quite low, alternately strengthening and fading, and were speaking in some foreign language. I got up and found that the wireless was not on and the boy still sleeping, and then I realized that the voices had stopped as soon as I had left my bedroom. Everyone else who has heard this had told me that it is not frightening, and having now heard it myself I agree, but at the same time I can't any longer doubt that voices *do* speak, and that it is not in English or Gaelic.' (Morag is bilingual in these two.) 'It certainly isn't just an old wives' tale like a lot of the ghost stories in these parts.'

Kyleakin is named after King Haco of Norway who, just seven hundred years before I bought the lighthouse cottage, anchored his invading fleet in the lee of the lighthouse preparatory to his last and disastrous attempt to conquer Scotland. He left his name to Kyleakin – the Narrows of Haco – and perhaps he left some ghosts as well, for the invisible inhabitants of the lighthouse island speak no tongue that is known in Scotland now.

I never heard the voices myself, because in all the time I have owned the house until now I have only spent two nights there, in July 1965, with a party of friends. I was still at the stage when I felt that I had all the time in the world; I loved Kyleakin and everything about it, and I planned to live in it later.

# 8

## Something Old and Something New

With the supreme need for some sort of regeneration that I felt after my return to Camusfeàrna as a cripple, it was perhaps not surprising that I looked at the lighthouse islands with a speculative eye, probing their possibilities for some new and improbable project. I had a plan for Isle Ornsay, but it was a distant and ambitious one, requiring more capital than I could outlay, even if the Northern Lighthouse Board were to grant their permission. I wanted, at some time in the future, to form there a porpoise pool, and to study captive porpoises as dolphins are being studied in the few great oceanariums of the world. There seemed every likelihood that the dolphins' extraordinary mental development and powers of communication were paralleled or even surpassed in the porpoise; yet, so far as I knew, the experiment had never been tried. The rock formations of Isle Ornsay lighthouse island lent themselves well to the construction of a spacious sea pool, but I recognized that this project must wait for a much later date and that it might be years before I could own talking porpoises.

For Kyleakin, however, I had conceived a much more immediate and practical scheme, something else that would be absolutely new. I intended to found an eider duck colony – or at least to establish whether or not it was possible to do so. If I succeeded I would have opened the way to a new industry for the crofting population of the West Highlands and Islands.

There will be some to whom the eider will require no introduction; to others, perhaps, who have no particular interest in ornithology, the connotation of the word will be limited to the eider-down (which rarely contains eider-down) used upon a bed in cold weather.

Eiders are somehow more like animals than birds; perhaps it is this impression of weight and compressed bulk, or their peculiarly unavian voices, or the way their massive bills ascend in a straight line to the top of their skulls without any 'scoop' in between. Or perhaps it is their curious and very individual smell, which seems as if it could have nothing to do with a bird. They hold, anyway, some strange fascination for most people who have had anything to do with them.

The drake in breeding plumage is a superb creation, suggesting the full dress uniform of some unknown navy's admiral. The first impression is of black and white, but at close quarters the black-capped head that looked simply white from far off seems like the texture of white velvet and shows feathers of pale scintillating electric green on the rear half of the cheek and on the nape; the breast, above the sharp dividing line from a black abdomen, is a pale gamboge, almost peach. From the white back the secondary wing feathers of the same colour sweep down in perfect scimitar curves over the black sides, adding immensely to the effect of a uniform designed for pomp and panache. The whole finery looks so formal that one has the impression that it must be uncomfortable, restricting, and the sureness and grace of all movement that is not on land is disconcerting. One would expect, too, that this essentially massive and masculine image would be incapable of anything but gruff and curt utterance, yet the mating call, uttered as the drake flings his splendid head far back on to his shoulders, is a woodwind sound, something between the lowest note of a flute and the highest of an oboe, a serenade so sweet and pure that it seems to become a part of the smooth, blue sea and the small jewelled tumble of wavelets upon white sand under a summer sky.

As with all the eiders, the female is dowdy by comparison, but in a way no less impressive. She is of a warm vermiculated brown all over, bulky and thick-necked, increasing the impression of lead-like weight; her voice is appropriately bass, whether in contentment or complaint. Above all she appears, with this voice and manner, competent to deal brusquely with any situation – but unfortunately this is not always true.

*

Eiders breed at Camusfeàrna, and over much of the north-west
coast of Scotland and its thousand islands. They do so, however,
in the most disastrous conditions, almost as if inviting the destruction of the species. They choose to make their nests where there
is the maximum commotion of other breeding species; and this
most often means that they lay in the very midst of their worst
enemies, the greater gulls. Thus at Camusfeàrna lighthouse island,
where there are some two or three hundred pairs of nesting
herring gulls and lesser black-backed gulls (to say nothing of a
dozen pairs of that great vulture of the sea, the greater black-
backed gull) some thirty or forty female eiders lay their eggs every
year. One would say that on that island there could be nothing
that they could desire – neither fresh water nor smooth beaches
for their toddling young, nor safety for their unhatched eggs. It
would appear a deliberately suicidal situation, since there are
adjacent islands with none of these disadvantages or hazards.
Yet the fact remains that they do limit their breeding territory to
this and similar islands throughout the area, despite the destruction by predators of at least three-quarters of their potential
offspring. Long before I had acquired Kyleakin Lighthouse this
fact had puzzled me; there was an inescapable conclusion that
the tumult and the shouting of other species, even if they were
proven enemies, provided some necessary stimulus to the eiders'
reproduction.

From the time that the female has completed her clutch of five eggs, laid in a carefully chosen site amongst heather, bracken, dwarf-willow or goose-grass, she begins to pluck her own breast of the fine down underlying the firm, springy feathers, and with this she surrounds her nest. The down serves a double purpose. When she leaves her nest to drink (she eats nothing during the four weeks of incubation) she arranges the down with her massive bill so that it covers the eggs; thus at the same time concealing them from robber gulls and maintaining their temperature until she returns. If unexpectedly disturbed from her nest she will (under extreme provocation, for female eiders are very tame while they are incubating, and will often allow themselves to be touched or even stroked) take off in a flurry, emitting as she does so a strong-smelling liquid which falls upon the eggs. This is not, as many people have thought, excreta; for, fasting, she has nothing to excrete. The inference is that when she has not time to cover her eggs she ejects this liquid as a deterrent to predators; to make the smell of her eggs noxious and unpalatable. It is a curious smell, very pungent, and resembling the smell of frying liver. For the few who may have smelled the cooking liver of a stag after the rut has begun the simile is almost exact. It is a warm, perhaps hot odour, suggesting its own colour of rich brown; most humans do not find it unpleasant, but feel that if it were increased to the least degree it would be nauseating.

Ever since the Gallgaels and the Norsemen had colonized Iceland, even long before King Haco had come and left his name to Kyleakin, they had realized the immense value of the eiders which bred in fantastic numbers in their new land; and, probably without recognition of the reasons, they had sensed that movement, noise and colour had something to do with the eiders' basic requirements. They lured the eiders away from the predator gull colonies, and for the wild white wings and raucous voices of the enemy they substituted an elaboration of fluttering flags, little wind-driven clacking propellers, and reeded wind instruments that would sigh, groan, or trumpet, according to the strength of the breeze. Over the centuries these traditional means became lore; and even without true scientific knowledge or controlled experiment they had been able to form colonies of several thousand pairs of eiders, and to harvest from the nests a great quantity of the down – at first only for local household use, but later as an important source of income from export.

The island immediately adjoining Kyleakin Lighthouse island, separated from it at low tide by only a few yards of water, was rough and heathery, and despite the presence of breeding greater black-backed gulls and hooded crows, both the very worst enemies of the eiders, there were already some twenty or more pairs nesting there; each probably raising to maturity a fifth of their potential offspring. From the lighthouse cottage this island could be kept under perpetual observation, and it appeared the ideal site for experiment. It was the property of the National Trust for Scotland, who gave their immediate and unqualified approval to my project.

Early in July 1965 Richard Frere had finished his massive work of conversion of the two Kyleakin cottages into one, his instal-lation of a generator and the electric wiring of the whole premises, and he left, warning me that a certain amount of tidying up would be necessary before my guests arrived the following week. These had been invited for a week's cruise on *Polar Star*, using first Isle Ornsay Lighthouse and then Kyleakin as a base. So the day after Richard's departure I set out from Camusfeàrna in *Polar Star*, carrying a work party to spend a full day preparing the house for its very first residential occupancy since I had bought it.

I was immensely proud of the house and its furnishings, for while the décor of Isle Ornsay had been largely the work of Richard's wife Joan, Kyleakin had been my particular project, my own unaided concept. Against the advice of both architects and friends, I had created, on the southern side of the house, a single room more than forty feet long, its windows looking down the long reach of Lochalsh and Loch Duich to the distant peaks of The Five Sisters of Kintail. In that loch lay perhaps the most spectacular piece of architecture surviving in Scotland, the ancient island stronghold of the Clan MacRae, Eilleann Donan Castle.

Because the room I planned would be little more than eleven

feet wide, all my advisers were unanimous in saying that it would look disproportionate, like a corridor, and that, furthermore, it would be impossible to heat adequately. I believed that the corridor effect could be obviated by using neutral-coloured furniture against the inner wall, the only strong colours being bright cushions which would draw the eye away from the four large windows, and one large wall mirror would reflect the sea and the ruin of Castle Moille. There were to be no pictures other than Michael Ayrton's vast and splendid, almost colourless wax of the falling Icarus, dominating the far end of the room as one entered it from the kitchen–dining-room. The heating problem I proposed to solve by two very wide open fireplaces, one under the Icarus and one at the near end of the room, against the inner wall; these would be supplemented if necessary by electric heating from the generator we had installed. I had made watercolour sketches of this room as I visualized it, and hoped that it would become, and all the furniture had been chosen to correspond as exactly as possible with these drawings.

The project had been entirely successful; I bought the furniture with great care in London and finally transhipped it to the island with a surprisingly small list of breakages. The house itself was now all and more than I had ever hoped for, and I had exact plans for the formation of a wild informal garden where flowering shrubs and rare honeysuckles would grow in the shelter of the rock crevices and buttresses on the northern side of the house.

# 9
# *The Struggle*

One day early in August, the local policeman called in the course of a routine check of firearms certificates. Any visit to Camusfeàrna from the outside world, no matter how official the visitor may be, becomes of necessity a social occasion, for the visitor has trudged all the weary distance down the hill from Druimfiaclach, and it would be inhospitable not to offer some refreshment before he starts the steep and boggy climb back to the road. So, our business done, we had a drink together, and sat talking for a while. After half an hour or so I was conscious of a pain in my stomach, but it was not a very severe pain, and I expected it to pass off. But by the time the constable had left it was steadily increasing in intensity, and it was something completely outside my personal experience. I had had a duodenal ulcer during the war, but it had never recurred, and it had not felt like this. I was alone in the house now, and I began to search with growing desperation for some antacid, but I could find nothing. It seemed the one item missing from the sizeable medicine chests I had carried with me in North Africa. I was determined to ride this out, because I was due in the very near future for a medical examination for life insurance, and if I were to call a doctor now I might as well forget the whole project. As well might a mouse determine to resist a tiger.

After an hour all possible question of surviving this storm by myself had gone. I was in such acute pain that I could hardly drag myself to the telephone. The village doctor was a new arrival and I had not yet met him; it was going to be, I thought as I dialled his number, doubled up with pain, a curious introduction. A friendly, cheerful and essentially competent voice answered me, and I said (with difficulty) a rehearsed speech, 'Doctor

Dunlop? You don't know me, but I'm in your practice – my name is Gavin Maxwell, and I live at Camusfeàrna, on the shore below Druimfiaclach.' 'Yes,' he said, 'I know just where you are – what can I do for you?'

I remember how long it seemed to take me to answer; I remember the litter of papers on the desk before me, which were all out of focus, because I am far-sighted, and during the past half hour I had somewhere lost my spectacles; I remember that through the window I could see against a blue sky a single raven circling high above the field, his guttural croaks timed to a rhythmic side-somersault. The pain seemed too great to speak.

The doctor's voice came again, calm but somehow unprofessional, as though we were old friends: 'Take your time, but try and tell me what's wrong.'

I said, 'I don't know for certain, but I think I've perforated a duodenal ulcer. I've had nothing to eat for eighteen hours, so perhaps there's no peritonitis – but I'm not thinking very clearly.'

'I'll be with you just as quick as I can. Lie down and try not to move until I get there.' He spoke as though he had no other patient, no other responsibilities nor worries of his own; as though the five mile drive and the long walk down the hill did not exist.

When he arrived he gave me morphia and said that he would return in four hours' time. This was my first meeting with Doctor Tony Dunlop, a young man, married and with small children, who had practised medicine in challenging countries such as West Africa, and had finally chosen a remote country practice where his exceptional personality and understanding of individual patients gave full scope for his powers. This was a man of wide and varied interests and broad learning, and I wished even then that our first meeting had been in more fortunate circumstances.

He returned at seven o'clock in the evening, and by then I was almost incapable of speech. The pain had become so acute that I was no longer a truly rational human being; the most I could summon up was 'Doctor, I would like to know whether this is likely to prove fatal, because if it is there are things I must do first – signing documents and so on.' He answered, 'No, I don't think so – at least I hope not, and I think I'm right. We've got to get you to hospital quickly. I'm going to give you some more morphia now, but that's the last I can give you, because the doctors in Inverness couldn't make a fair diagnosis if the symptoms were obliterated by pain-killers. Your staff has come home now, and they're constructing a stretcher. You'll go up the hill in your Land Rover on this stretcher, and at the village you'll be transferred to my car, whose seats fold back to make a bed. We've got eighty miles to go, and I've telephoned for an ambulance to meet us halfway, or wherever we happen to meet on the road – if you're lucky you'll be in hospital by midnight.'

So I was carried out on a home-made stretcher and driven – a journey I shall never forget – up the jolting jeep track to Druimfiaclach, empty and desolate then. At the village I was transferred as discreetly as possible from the Land Rover to the doctor's car. It was a long drive through the night; either the pain or the morphia or the combination of the two made me garrulous; for I remember talking a lot. I remember that the doctor drove very fast and with great skill. We met the ambulance some few miles west of Invermoriston. I asked for more morphia for the last leg of the journey but was gently and firmly refused. I arrived in hospital at Inverness at one in the morning.

Some thirty-six hours later the surgeon, a man of high reputation in his profession and great personal charm, showed me the X-ray plates. 'This,' he said, 'is an acute exacerbation of an ulcer probably of long standing. I want to put the alternatives clearly before you. The first, which is what I recommend, is for you to remain here and for me to operate after a short time, a partial gastrectomy which I will explain to you. The second choice is for you to remain here under treatment for about two months, without surgery. As you've explained to me that your life is very heavily committed until November, there is of course a third possible course of action, and that is for you, being fully aware of all the risks involved, to go home after a day or two's rest here, and to return and let me operate in November. If you choose this last course I should like to ask for your assurance that you really will come back in November.'

It seemed to me that this was the only possible thing to do,

338

and I said so, though I cringed before the idea of further abdominal surgery.

It was only a few hours after this conversation, and while I was still in hospital that I received a telephone call from London. There had been a board meeting of the company which had been formed to manage my affairs, a meeting which I had been due to attend. The caller, a co-director, was bleakly informative. It had come to light that owing to faulty internal accounting the company's finances were far from what we had imagined. The assets covered the liabilities, but little more, and at this meeting it was demonstrated that the maintenance of Camusfeàrna cottage and its otters was costing £7,000 a year. A new director, a retired businessman, recommended the immediate sale of all the company's assets, including the two lighthouses, and even – owing to a misconception of what was whose – some of my own.

This policy seemed to me to lack finesse; and, moreover, to be abandoning the battle before a blow had been struck, because the enemy's strength had been found to be almost equal to our own. For example, neither of the lighthouses, upon which we had lavished so much money, were mortgaged, and we had succeeded in letting them to holiday parties for as much as £65 a week each. (This sum may sound excessive, but it usually amounted to less than £10 a head each, with the use of boats and engines and a private island.) These were the things uppermost in my mind; though no doubt at a lower level of consciousness lay the realization that the loss of the lighthouses would mean the end of my cherished eider project, and at that time it seemed to me that my life held nothing to replace it.

So I replied that I was not in agreement; that I would return to Camusfeàrna the next day, and temporarily assume the function of managing director, in an effort to restore financial stability. The mouse and the tiger again.

When I came back and told the local doctor of my decision he said, 'Well, it's a novel treatment for a duodenal ulcer, certainly, but I've had ulcers myself and I found they did best on a diet of hot curries and plenty of alcohol, which is hardly the conventional treatment. I wish you good luck.'

It was in a spirit of challenge that I re-entered Camusfeàrna on 4 August – a double challenge, mental and physical. I was determined both to solve the company's finances while at the same time finishing my book *Lords of the Atlas* on schedule, and to regain the state of physical health and activity that I had possessed before the Land Rover accident. It was an ambitious programme, and one with obviously conflicting time-factors.

My first action as managing director was to try to raise mortgages on the lighthouses. Everyone with whom I spoke assured me that this would be easy, but it was not. Time and time again negotiations seemed to be almost complete when they fell through, and there were so many intermediaries that I could never satisfy myself as to which link in the chain had broken. The heart of the matter seemed to be that the houses, however solid and magnificently built, were on islands, and this, despite their desirability as holiday homes, was a major deterrent to any prospective mortgagee. Meanwhile I found that, bad though the position discovered at the board meeting had been, there was worse to come, for the list of creditors had been far from complete. More and more bills, of which the directors had then been ignorant, began to pour into Camusfeàrna, but even with this new avalanche the assets still held the balance on paper. I closed entirely the small office in London, which, however incredibly, had been revealed as responsible for an annual debit of £3,000. This gigantically disproportionate debit was transformed, by letting the premises for a few pounds a week, into a minor source of income. Having done this, and in order to gain time, I did an extremely foolish thing; I devoted the whole of my mother's legacy to the payment of pressing company creditors. I was in fact a minority shareholder in the company, and this was the very first capital I had owned since the demise of the Island of Soay Shark Fisheries eighteen years earlier. Ever since then I had been a hand-to-mouth earner, first as a portrait painter and then as a writer, unable to budget because there had been no fixed income. But now, because the company was registered in my own name rather than in the decent obscurity and anonymity of some word unconnected with me, I felt that I had no alternative but to use my own money to pay its debts. I have since been told that this action demonstrated a lack of rudimentary business sense, but I can only repeat that I felt, and still feel, that I had no choice. The result, however, was to add personal poverty to company difficulties; nor did the company creditors appear to appreciate that I had acted from a sense of moral responsibility. For the greater part of them money was all that counted, and where it came from was immaterial. I know for a fact that many believed my personal resources to be almost inexhaustible, and that my failure to pay every company creditor immediately was wilful parsimony on my part. Thus, anyway, I lost the last capital that I am ever likely to possess, and the fault was nobody's but my own.

At Camusfeàrna itself I began studying its economy, and realized that the questions of transport and communication lay at the heart of all our problems. To buy in bulk and to store in bulk was the only possible solution. Food, whether for humans or otters, was costing us many times its face value because of the necessity to buy hurriedly and in small quantities, often from great distances. I have used the simile earlier; it would apparently cost little to live in an Antarctic weather station - but, living there, the moment one tried to establish daily or even weekly contact with the outside world the cost of living would be greater than that at any five-star hotel. Because practically every telephone call necessary to my function as managing director of a company in distress was a trunk call, and often a protracted one, and because some of our temporary employees would often hold interminable conversations with their girlfriends hundreds of miles distant, the telephone bill itself became a major problem, and one which I could do little to solve; if the employees were denied the right to use the telephone they would leave, and if they left I should not have time to write.

But on the transport and supply side there was an obvious remedy and I began by buying deep freezes that could contain enough food both for animals and humans for months at a time. This, though it represented an almost final drain upon my private resources, did temporarily solve a major problem.

341

It is perhaps worth mentioning, for any improbable others who might somehow find themselves in the same situation that, though at Camusfeàrna we were surrounded by natural food of all kinds – shellfish ranging through cockles and mussels to oysters; fish of many species; edible fungi and much else – the average adolescent will not eat any food to which he has not been brought up. The situation is almost parallel to that obtaining in primitive Muslim cultures, in which, for reasons long forgotten, some birds, beasts and fishes are 'unclean', while others, so alike as to be almost indistinguishable, are lawful food. I remember being sent out in the marshes of Southern Iraq to shoot for the pot because we had nothing to eat; the majority of birds that passed my way were of a species of wader called godwit, and I shot as many as I could. When I returned with my bag it was sharply and vocally divided into clean and unclean; there were two species, the bar-tailed godwit and the black-tailed godwit, and one (I forget which) was not clean food. The extremely unpalatable pigmy cormorants and African darters, were, on the other hand, clean, and I was reproached for not having killed them.

Time and time again I tried to explain to some new temporary employee at Camusfeàrna that when he had been new born he had liked only his mother's milk and subsequently what food she served him after he was weaned; that to survive in the world one had to adapt oneself to new foods that were habitual to the people among whom one was living, but always to no avail. Food had to be 'as mother made it' (usually, it turned out, from tins) and its provision at Camusfeàrna was extremely expensive. Gastronomically, the adventurous spirit attributed to the British was completely lacking; we were surrounded by free food that no one would eat, but which would have been very costly in more sophisticated society. (I remember a Greek sailor on my brother's yacht being offered a little vol-au-vent of caviare and being asked what he thought of it. He replied that the pastry was excellent, but he didn't like the 'black stuff in the middle'.)

All this struggle was paper and telephone work; the physical target I had set myself, some sort of rejuvenescence – and above all the exhilaration of contact with the elements and the natural world, that had formed so great a part of my life – was steadily receding, for there just did not seem to be time for physical exercise. I was losing the battle on both fronts, although like Queen Victoria I was not interested in the possibility of defeat; I believed that it simply did not exist.

I had my minor trivial triumphs in the economic field. Because our mail was not delivered to Camusfeàrna but to a wooden box on the roadside at Druimfiaclach, two and a half miles away from us by jeep track, the daily collection of letters was costing us a small fortune in petrol and mechanical deterioration – a mild word to use of, say, broken axles and half-shafts. I applied to the Post Office for subsidy, and was refused. I, in turn, refused to take no for an answer, and at the end of an impassioned correspondence I was awarded £100 annually for collection of mail for Camusfeàrna and for the old croft across the field. With this and many other economies effected in the whole management of the establishment I had no real doubt that I could make the place viable once more.

But I felt the absolute necessity of occasionally getting far away from that desk at which I sat for something like twelve hours every day, trying to give six to the writing of a book and six to company management, eating snack meals and ending each day too tired to talk. Though the sporting tradition and the blood-thirstiness of my youth had largely deserted me (why is fishing so widely considered a respectable blood-sport and shooting in any form so despicable? – I suspect here an identification with weapons used against man, and that if man-hooking was part of warfare there would be an equal outcry against the patient angler) I accepted in October an invitation to stalk at a distant deer forest. This had been one of my major hobbies in the past, and I felt that – if I were still physically capable of the tremendous effort involved – it might prove to be the tonic I so badly needed.

It was. The days that I spent on the hill, in worse weather conditions than it is easy to visualize, gave to me a feeling of complete and utter release, of a unity with nature that I had long lacked at Camusfeàrna.

One afternoon especially, though it was bloodless enough to satisfy the most squeamish, is fresh in my memory as I write.

From where I stood on the hilltop, with the wet wind tearing in great gusts at my face and sodden clothing, I could see no further than a radius of twenty yards into the surrounding mist. The abyss below me to my left, a two thousand foot fall of scree and rock-face and straggling heather, was filled with moving grey-white cloud; here on the bare summit of the huge ridge, where all that grew underfoot was lichen and mosses amid granite chips, small ragged clouds, darker than the mist that covered all the hilltop, came streaming up out of the great blanketed gulf; they sailed by swiftly and low overhead and were gone into the dimness that covered all. The only sound was the rushing of the wind as it broke and scattered the drops of ever-falling rain.

Suddenly, from far away, from the hidden hill-face beyond the gulf, borne thin and clear on the wind, wild and elemental, came the sound that during all the many years I have spent among the red deer of Scotland, in their aloof tempestuous territory of rock and mist, has never lost its fascination for me – the voice of the stag in rut. It begins low and throaty like a bull's roar, then hollows out to a higher, dying cadence, that seems to hold at the same time challenge, despair and frustration. I stirred to that

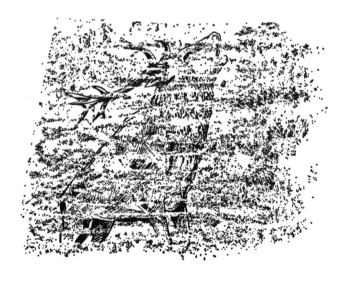

desolate music as I stirred to the whip of wind and rain, to the ice-cold cling of my drenched clothing, to the hard ache of long unused muscles that had climbed from the infinitely distant floor of the glen below. With the water running down my neck and spine all the way to water-logged shoes, with the cold so bitter that I was conscious of my own shivering, I felt an actual buoyancy, an uplift of spirit. This was my world, the cradle of my species, shared with the wild creatures; it was the only world I wanted, and I felt that I had no place at a writing desk.

In these primeval situations man the hunter reacts to unexpected sound as does man the hunted – instantaneously. Suddenly, from no more than fifty yards away, from just inside the encircling mist, came the same wild voice, magnified by my loss of vision to a nearness, an immediacy, that set my heart hammering and my eyes straining; the instant drop to a prone position was atavistic. (There is, I have always found, something revitalizing, re-energizing, in this contact between hands and body and the small growth of the mountain earth.) Wind and cloud whined past my face, but borne on them now was the strange, elusive, pungent smell, musky and sour-sweet, of the rutting stag.

In the edge of the mist shapes without apparent context formed and re-formed. A tuft of heather, only yards away, assumed the aspect of a far-off wooded crest, a whitened, weather-worn double heather-stem took on the shape of the distant antlers of an archetypal stag.

I began to crawl forward, wet belly to wet heather that changed after a few yards to soft black peat, relic of vegetation rotted a million years ago, and the dark paste was thickly packed beneath my finger nails. The smell of the stag grew stronger.

With tremendous impact now his voice came again, so near to me that it was I who was afraid, returning in that moment to the dim red dawn of our race when man was both hunter and hunted. In exactly the same instant I saw his horns before me, indistinct but twenty times the size of the impostor heather stems, and from the corner of my right eye I saw simultaneously the ears of a hind, blurred by the mist, but so near to me that I could have touched them with a fishing rod. I was right in among the deer,

345

and the wet, stinging wind was whipping at my left cheek, so that my scent must have missed the hind's nostrils by inches rather than by feet, but she was still unaware of my presence. The cloud which lay on the hilltop began to thicken and whiten, and the stag's horns became intermittently invisible, but when he roared again the sound seemed even nearer than before. I slipped the leather foresight protector from my rifle, and lay with my chin pressed to the ground, the wet woodwork clammy in my palms and my teeth beginning to chatter.

The small, tattered black clouds still raced by low overhead, forming a ceiling, so that one felt as if in a small fog-filled room, crowded with invisible inhabitants. Then, driven by the wind, an eagle swept low out of the speeding clouds, so low that as he saw me the rasp of air between the great pinion feathers of his wings as he sheered off was audible even above the din of the gale and the rain. He tilted upwards and away from me and was at once lost in the clouds. But the violent sweep of those vast wings as they banked not ten feet above me must have set up some momentary shift in the direction of wind current, for the hind was suddenly towering dimly over me. She was not more than fifteen feet away, but she looked as though seen through frosted glass. She gave one grunting, exhaling bark, and faded quickly into the murk.

With the deer gone, I was left upon the clouded hilltop with the light going, soaked and with the almost horizontal rain cutting to my ribs, and five miles to walk home in the dusk, but I was content. Here, perhaps, I was beyond the range of the rowan tree.

# 10

# *Hounds and Hares*

I went back to the paper war at Camusfeàrna, and in November I returned to hospital at Inverness for the abdominal operation I dreaded so much. I left Camusfeàrna with a reasonably calm mind, for my literary commitments were fulfilled, the lighthouse mortgages now seemed certain, and the deep freezes were full of food for dogs and humans and fish for otters.

I was back at Camusfeàrna within forty-eight hours. The X-rays had shown the ulcer to be completely healed, and the surgeon said he could find no excuse whatsoever for operating. At that moment I felt that the tide had turned on both battle fronts, and that victory was in sight.

Although paper work had now become my daily routine, I had one more venture that autumn into the outdoor world that meant so much to me. For three years I had owned a vast deerhound called Dirk (the replacement of a predecessor by the same name, who had met a tragic death by drinking petrol) and in September I bought for him a mate, a bitch called Hazel. Both were, by deerhound standards, past their prime, for they are a short-lived race – past their prime, that is to say, either for coursing or for breeding, and by purists the former is considered the criterion. However, when I bought Hazel I was invited to join that select body the Deerhound Club, and to bring both hounds to the annual coursing meeting in the central Highlands.

I accepted, and entered Dirk and Hazel; not that either of them could be expected to put up much of a performance, Dirk because he was completely inexperienced, and Hazel because as a bitch who had already borne several litters of puppies she was seemingly already too old for speed. But I was, apart from anything else, intensely curious to see for myself this sport, about whose unthinkable brutality I had received so many circulars from anti-blood sport bodies and individuals. Hares, I had been told, were literally torn slowly in half, screaming the while, by the coursing couple of hounds that overtook them. Hares do scream when in pain, and that voice is horrifying like the wailing of a distressed human infant, producing in all but the most hardened and impervious observer a feeling of identification that is nauseating. I had heard it often, not only in the man-made situations of the shooting party, but from hares taken by foxes and eagles, whose predatory instincts could patently not be banned without still further blood-letting by man. No hare can ever die of old age – and very rarely indeed does any other non-predator do so – so that the killing of a hare by a man-controlled dog rather than by fox or eagle (or by the wolf exterminated in Scotland by man) seemed to me nearer to the ecological normal than the undoubted horrors of the battery farm and the fat-stock slaughterhouse. The predators, on the other hand, do quite often die what for some curious reason we call 'natural' deaths – that is death from old age or disease – as opposed to violent and painful death at the hands of some species other than man.

If these 'natural' deaths (and both categories must surely be accepted as natural to anyone who deplores man's intervention on the scene) are for some reason less regrettable than the normal bloody deaths of the non-predators, then it appeared to me that the anti-blood sport societies should confine their energies to the carnivores; who, without man's pursuit, might die of malnutrition and exposure. Most of all I felt this in the case of otter-hunting, the only blood sport (other than bull-fighting) in which the animal has virtually no chance of survival – because, unlike fox-hunting, the whole 'field' of human followers is actively combined with the hounds to make impossible the escape of a harmless predator that is actually beneficial to man. The fact that otters do somehow survive in otter-hunting territories, in however decreasing numbers, is a tribute to their exceptional mental abilities, which sometimes prove superior (if the animal is adult) to those of a large group of humans and hounds trained in their pursuit.

*

The quarry at this coursing meeting was the blue or mountain hare, which turns white in winter, and before describing those days I ought perhaps to say at the outset that although I saw some thirty or forty hares killed I did not see one that did not die instantly – 'chopped' by the hound's jaws so that its neck was broken, and not once did I hear a hare utter a sound. This is in marked contrast to a hare taken by fox or eagle, and the fact merits some consideration by those who condemn the sport as I have seen it.

This was a mixed meeting for deerhounds and salukis, and the large and comfortable hotel where the members stayed was considerably fuller of dogs than of humans. In the morning the long procession of cars drove some miles to an old farm house high on bare moorland. It was bitterly cold weather; snow lay everywhere in patches, and from a dull sky it blew in, fine and powdery, on a keen east wind. Under the orders of the red-coated judge (I am not certain whether the convention of calling red 'pink' extends beyond fox-hunting circles) the party spread out in a long line across the moor, each owner leading his or her hound or hounds. Jimmy Watt led Hazel and I led Dirk. Some thirty yards ahead of the line walked the slipper, attired as the judge, his two selected dogs on a special coupled leash that could be slipped at the pull of a finger. The judge had to be extremely active, for points were awarded to each hound not only for his pure speed and stamina, but for his contribution to the kill by cooperation with his partner; thus in the case of a long course over broken ground the judge must keep hounds and hare in view, and with the aid of binoculars be in a position to observe the details of the kill and the part each hound has played.

The first two hounds in the slips were salukis, their delicate, slim, silk-soft grace and feathery coats somehow making them appear far too gentle to kill even a mouse. Both were experienced; though they came from different kennels they adapted their movements to each other on the coupling leash, and though they strained lightly upon it they were not dragging their handler behind them.

The first hare, pure white, started from a patch of snow-free

349

heather some twenty yards ahead of them. I was surprised that the hounds were not immediately slipped, for I had never seen salukis in action, and I was totally unprepared for their perform-ance. The slipper allowed the hare a full sixty yards' start before he unleashed the now wildly straining hounds. The speed of their take-off was breath-taking, unimaginable; it did not seem possible that any living creature could possess that ferocious acceleration. A fine spray of powdered snow rose in the wake of their flying forms as, running neck and neck at unguessable speed, they relentlessly overhauled the fleeing hare. He had been running straight, *ventre à terre*, but when after a quarter of a mile the hounds were no more than twenty yards behind him he changed tactics and began to dodge and to twist. It was here that the extraordinary teamwork of the two hounds became apparent; neither rushed in to the kill, each headed the hare as it turned until the moment came when one hound had the perfect opportu-nity. Then there was one swift chop of those long and deceptively slender jaws, and the hare was dead. It was a striking display of speed, skill and precision, and the salukis had certainly killed more cleanly than would the hare's natural enemies.

The next pair in the slips were deerhounds. We were on higher and harder ground now, near to the crest of a long rounded ridge where the snow lay thinly among scattered stumps of burned heather. This time the hare started nearly eighty yards ahead, and the hounds were slipped on the instant. If the salukis' take-off had been amazing, that of the deerhounds was positively awe-inspiring. Their great backs arched, their mighty thigh muscles thrusting, their long necks straining forward, they came racing diagonally across my front at something like fifty miles an hour, and the thunder of their flying feet hitting the hard ground was like the sound of furiously galloping horses. Their speed seemed to me even greater than that of the salukis, and to have a quality of irresistible impetus, like the sweeping downward rush of a stooping eagle.

It was only when they began to close on the hare that I realized how the deerhounds were handicapped by comparison with the salukis. This couple were as clever a combination as their predecessors, and manoeuvred the zig-zagging hare with the same perfection of timing, but their great height was against them. Time and time again the hare would have been within jaws' range of one or the other, but in the split second that it took to reach down a yard and more the hare had tacked again. That hare escaped, as did many others, both from salukis and deerhounds, sometimes simply by outrunning the hounds, sometimes by tactics, and sometimes by slipping into a hole or a hillside crevice.

When Hazel's turn came she astonished me as much as she did her previous owners, who were present. She showed an astounding turn of speed for a middle-aged matron; on her first course she outran her younger partner, and, with complete disregard for team spirit, killed the hare single-handed. During the two days she was slipped four times and killed three hares, but only once did she make the least attempt to cooperate with the other hound, and on her final slipping, seeing the hare running up a steep slope, she gave up after three hundred yards and came walking quietly back with a reproachful expression on her face. She clearly felt that too much was being demanded from a woman of her age, more especially under the prevailing weather conditions. The bitter, biting east wind never ceased, and bore upon it flurries of fine fluttering snow. Hazel wanted to be stretched out, as was her wont, on a sofa before a log fire; her killer instinct, like my own, had diminished with age, though she had remained an exhibitionist, and had satisfactorily demonstrated that she was still worthy of admiration in the physical field.

At length it was Dirk's turn. I had been prepared for failure, but not for farce. He was coupled with another, younger, deerhound, and from the first moment he seemed unable to coordinate his movements with those of the hound to which he was linked. When the hare was started and the couple slipped, Dirk simply did not see the quarry. His partner shot off in pursuit, and he seemed mildly puzzled by this; he followed for a few yards and then turned back and began to prance and gambol in an aimless, amiable way up and down the waiting line. He appeared particularly fascinated by the female humans who were being literally dragged helter-skelter across the moor by uncontrollable couples of his own species who had sighted the hare and would answer to no word of command. Overt laughter from all sides prompted me to apologize to the judge, who replied, 'Well, if he has no other function he is at least the perfect court jester.'

The second time, he was coupled with a very beautiful blonde saluki bitch. He was clearly anxious to make closer acquaintance with her than their parallel position in the slips permitted. When the hare was started she was far faster off the mark than he, and, being left behind in the first twenty yards, he suddenly seemed to have no further doubts as to what this sport was about. It was quite clearly a competitive sport – to see whether a deerhound dog could catch an attractive saluki bitch and reap his reward. At first he never even saw the hare, and when he did he ignored it; it had nothing to do with him – the bitch was his business. He had the heels of her, and after a couple of hundred yards they were nose to tail – his nose, that is to say, remaining jammed under her tail, while both were racing at forty or fifty miles an hour. The bitch completely ignored this intimate and inappropriate contact, and contrived to kill the hare on her own, despite these whirlwind attentions from her unwanted partner. When she returned, trotting quietly with the dead hare in her jaws, Dirk came prancing back beside her, patently proud of her prowess, but in human eyes in deep disgrace mitigated only by his powerful potential for comedy.

After this second farce, I apologized again to the judge who said, 'If he's ever going to course at all he'll have to learn now. He's got the strength and the speed, but he thinks it's just a bitch hunt. From now on you have my permission to slip him at any hare in reasonable range, no matter what other hounds are officially in the slips. That's the only way he can learn what he's supposed to do.'

The long line began to move again, wheeling across a vast boggy flat where the snow clustered thick in the heather tufts, and the inch-deep water crackled and crunched underfoot as the ice splintered among the sphagnum moss. Far away from me hares were started and killed by other hounds, too far away for me to slip Dirk and risk a further farce. Low in the wind, beating their way against the finely falling snow, came a herd of whooper swans, dazzlingly white against the deep blue-grey sky, the golden bugles of their voices lingering long on the bitter air. Grouse whirred up from the heather, cackling as they lifted and let themselves be swept away on the wind in a great curving arc, but as yet there was no hare at which I dared slip Dirk. My foot was periodically painful, and I began to wish that this were all over, and like Hazel, that I could return to some cheerful fireside away from the chilling cold and miserable physical discomfort of this bleak and wintery moorland.

Then, as we left the frozen flat bog and began to ascend a slope, I saw before me a patch of long heather, sharply and darkly distant from the bare snow-dusted ground surrounding it, and I was instantly certain that it held a hare. I readjusted the rope through Dirk's collar and prepared it for instant release. The hare started twenty yards ahead, pure white against the background of dark heather, and for the first time Dirk really saw it and knew what was required of him; it was my fault that I snarled the rope and delayed his pursuit. He took off like a meteor while the hare was still in sight, mounting an horizon slope, and it was seven long minutes before we saw him again. The line stood still, awaiting word from the judge, and when at last they reappeared, the hare leading and Dirk a panting thirty yards behind, both were heading straight back for the line of hounds. Both hare and hound were exhausted, and any fresh hound unleashed could have killed in seconds, but the judge called to me to take in my hound and the hare went free as he deserved. He passed through the line of straining predators, crossed a deep peat-bog ditch, and was finally lost to sight in a flurry of snowstorm. But Dirk's reputation was restored; he had pursued a long course without flagging, and he lost the name of Court Jester.

The day after the meeting was over the snow began to fall in earnest, big white flakes drifting down from a still and silent sky, and we crept slowly back towards Camusfeàrna, the Land Rover rescuing en route, with her winch, a number of cars that had become helpless in a pale frozen white world.

It was not until after our return that I realized that the mortgaging of the lighthouses had become a mirage, and that only a miracle could now save Camusfeàrna from closure.

# II

# *So Far From Home*

That was the autumn of 1965; the final, decisive blow came early in the New Year of 1966. Jimmy Watt, who had been in charge of the whole changing household and its ever-increasing ramifications for eight long years, decided, not unreasonably, that he must now leave us and make some life for himself elsewhere. Having made this difficult decision he was generous enough to give five months' notice, and was thus prepared to remain in charge of Camusfeàrna and its tiny but complex empire until May 1966.

This was the death-knell of the old Camusfeàrna. Nobody but Jimmy, with his long experience of all our practical problems, and his unique ability to tackle them with a supreme and well-justified self-confidence – problems ranging through household supplies from distant towns to maintenance of buildings and of boats of all types and sizes, vehicles of many sorts, the management of otters, dogs and humans – could have kept the place alive. I recognized his own absolute necessity, as a young man of exceptional talent, to form a creative life of his own; but I recognized, too, that I had allowed him to become irreplaceable. (I remembered, too late, an incident long ago during the war. I had been pleading with my commanding officer to retain a specialist assistant who had received posting orders to another establishment. My commanding officer appeared to give the matter serious thought and kindly consideration. He doodled on his blotter for a minute or so, and then said, 'You mean he's literally indispensable to you in your branch of our work?' I fell instantly into the trap, and said, 'Yes, Sir, just that.' He replied, 'Then he must certainly go. We can't afford to allow anyone to become indispensable in SOE.' But, I protested, I was in the present

355

circumstances myself indispensable, and had personally trained my assistant. 'Then we must certainly take immediate steps to see that all your knowledge is committed to paper. I shall inform HQ and ask for a typist and two trainees. I appreciate that this will mean extra work for you, but I have no alternative.') Unfortunately I had failed to learn that lesson, that now returned after so many years to put an unequivocal end to all my plans and projects. It would mean finding zoo homes for the otters, and the final closure of the place as it had been, for the house could not stand without its corner-stone.

When I had assimilated the facts I visualized this weary task as being difficult but not impossible; I thought in my innocence that the right homes could somehow be found for all the animals; and that, however painful after eighteen years, I could transfer my loyalties and my interests from Camusfeàrna to somewhere else, perhaps to Kyleakin Lighthouse island, and make for myself a new life, with the eider experiment as a temporary focus of interest. Much of my zest, however, had gone with the knowledge that the Camusfeàrna epoch was over.

With research still necessary to complete details of *Lords of the Atlas*, I left Scotland for North Africa in February 1966. Two employees, under the nominal supervision of Jimmy Watt, were to prepare the Kyleakin island for the eider experiment; the creation of freshwater pools, flat beaches made from concrete, nesting boxes on the Icelandic plan, and the erection of flag-poles and bunting. Both employees left before my return and with their work incomplete, so the eider experiment was never attempted. The magic that had once glossed the world of Camusfeàrna had been wearing thin for a long time; now only the base metal of mistakes showed through, bare and ugly.

When I left Camusfeàrna in February 1966 there were, as I have said, still three employees – Jimmy, and the two temporary assistants working at Kyleakin. During my absence in Morocco the three were joined at Camusfeàrna by a young lady who had previously typed some of my manuscripts, and who now wanted temporary asylum in Scotland from personal problems. She came there in the spring of 1966, while I was abroad, with her seven-year-old daughter and an unimaginable host of wholly unexpected livestock (donkeys; ponies; miniature poodles and Great Danes; cats and geese; and a curious and enchanting breed of dogs which was the result of crossing the great woolly Old English sheepdog with the slim, silky, slender and shy Shetland sheepdog) and the casual copulations of this curious community resulted in a spectacular population explosion. At one moment there were, to say nothing of other species, twenty-six dogs. Camusfeàrna became an Animal Farm, where the four-legged ruled with an exigent and destructive dictatorship; the house had entered upon a new and more visible phase of its decline.

At first I learned of all this at second hand, because when I came back to England in May I could not face an immediate return to my home and all that it now entailed. I remained in London and continued my fruitless and increasingly febrile attempts to mortgage the lighthouses. At length I abandoned the idea and put them both up for sale as furnished houses. It seemed that fortune could never come my way again; every piece of news from day to day was of delay, disaster, or death. In the course of forty-eight hours, I remember, I learned of the death of my Pyrenean mountain dog at Camusfeàrna and of a white barb stallion I had bought in Morocco. The dog died because he had been left out all night, tied by a chain to a running line on the field; it was a wild night, and in his efforts to find shelter the dog strangled himself while trying to cross a wire fence. The superb white stallion, who could dance and rear at command, and who loved human beings for themselves, died of neglect and ill-treatment in a squalid *foundouk* in Marrakech, while in charge of an Arab whom I had trusted implicitly. He died perhaps the worst death an animal can die, and I do not want now to recall the details of an event that made me physically sick. (I was sent, by an English observer, not only a detailed description but coloured photographs.)

Financial survival now called for full but orderly retreat, and I began to sell our small possessions. I sold the cine-camera (which had cost us almost a thousand pounds) with which we had visualized making a series of documentary films in the Highlands and Islands, for little more than a third of what we had paid for it. This seemed a particular symbol, the first outward acknowledgement of the epoch's end. The only project left was to close Camusfeàrna as decently as possible.

I delayed my return to Scotland as long as I possibly could, and it was not until August that I went back to Camusfeàrna and tried to make sick-hearted preparations for the transfer of the otters to a zoo. Jimmy had gone, and there was no employee left at Camusfeàrna; only the young lady and her daughter and her incredible animal *ménage*.

Richard Frere, who had accomplished the conversion of the lighthouse cottages, had taken over the management both of the company and of my own personal affairs when Jimmy had left in May – because, he said, he liked challenges, and he could scarcely have found a greater one than this. He foresaw clearly the part he would have to play, that of the commander of a desperate rearguard action against insolvency until we could find buyers for Isle Ornsay and Kyleakin. He entered upon the task with the same spirit of enthusiasm that he would have embarked upon the climbing of some cliff previously considered unscalable, and with no illusions as to its difficulties and hardships.

Camusfeàrna seemed a sad place then and one already greatly changed, but in that sunny late September of 1966 I had one last memorable day in *Polar Star*, which I had decided should be moved the following year to Loch Ness to serve the tourist trade. We had had a week of gales and hurricanes which were about the worst I can remember in all the Camusfeàrna years. Anything that could blow away did so, and my worst fear was that the wooden paling enclosing the otters would fall before the tempest and liberate the otters among the great milling miscellany of undisciplined livestock to which Camusfeàrna was now playing temporary host. The fences held, however, and when the storm subsided it went, as so often, into a flat calm and a cloudless blue sky. Alan MacDiarmaid had returned to our employment for a fortnight, since I was by now the only male at Camusfeàrna, and we had various odd jobs to do at Kyleakin Lighthouse and Kyle of Lochalsh.

When we left the moorings in the morning I was immediately aware that something was amiss. Both engines started evenly, but the starboard motor appeared to have no transmission to its propeller. On opening the throttle the revolutions rose on the counter, but there was no increase in speed. From inside the boat we were able to establish that the hydraulic transmission from the engine was in order, and we assumed that there must be a dislocation at the propeller shaft. We started north on one engine.

It wasn't until we tied up alongside the pier at Kyle of Lochalsh that we found out that the starboard propeller wasn't there at all; somehow the tremendous punishment the boat had taken during the prolonged storm, the perpetual pitching on the high waves at her moorings, had found a weakness in the work of whoever had fitted that propeller, and it now lay in several fathoms of water below the mooring buoy. (Immediately after our return we began a search for the costly rubber skin-diving suit that we kept at Camusfeàrna against such emergencies. But it was no longer there; it had disappeared, together with much else, and despite lengthy police investigations it was never traced.)

So, in the afternoon, we returned from Kyle on one engine. This gave us eleven or twelve knots; enough, anyway to confront the north-running flood tide in the narrows of Kylerhea. We came down past Glenelg, and a mile or two north of *Polar Star*'s moorings, close in under the huge cliffs, we saw mackerel 'rushing' at the surface. This happens when their great shoals have pushed up their prey, the fry of their own and other species – called in this part of the world 'soil' – to the absolute limit, so that the pursuit is taking place almost above water. The effect to the onlooker is that of an intermittent moving flurry of white spray, often iridescent, and to those who depend upon fish for food, it holds an irresistible and intrinsic excitement.

This was the first evidence we had had that the mackerel were still in the area; they arrive in June or early July and leave, with the tourists, in early or late September, according to weather conditions. Apart from salmon heads and tails, and leaving aside a staple diet of eels, mackerel were the favourite food of the otters, and since the mackerel were still there, and I had invested in deep freezes, I had obviously to make the most of this opportunity.

We had two 'darrow' lines aboard (thirty fathoms of line, with a tail of twenty hooks on cat-gut, baited with dyed hens' feathers) and we set to work to take what mackerel we might from that shoal that was possibly the last of the season – so that the deep freezes would be full for the winter.

The results of that twenty minutes' fishing were little short of fantastic. There were moments when we lost the shoal, but always we found it again after a slow quartering of the ground, and time and time again we hauled in a wildly gyrating darrow holding between ten and nineteen (this was Alan's, and, I think, a Camus-feàrna record) flipping, flapping, fish whose coloured bars of lapis lazuli blue and emerald green took me back to my childhood in Galloway, where we trolled for these same fish with a single bait and a day's catch of thirty was worthy of note. Now we were sometimes taking in thirty mackerel in one minute, and by the time we were finished and had finally lost the shoal we had more than a hundredweight of fish.

We started off on our one engine for the mile-distant moorings of *Polar Star*. About halfway we found a fulmar petrel in our path on the still sea, and he seemed unable to rise. He paddled awkwardly away from the *Polar Star*'s course, but seemed incapable of taking wing. I said to Alan that we ought to rescue this derelict, and he set off in pursuit of it in an inflatable rubber dinghy while I stood off with *Polar Star*. It was, by any standards, a comic performance; no matter how closely the rubber dinghy could approach the fulmar, the bird could turn quicker than the boat and I could hear Alan's rich flow of invective across the few hundred yards of smooth sea that separated us. But in this situation, as in all others, Alan would not accept defeat, and after a quarter of an hour he was back on board *Polar Star* with the helpless but protesting fulmar. Protest, with fulmars, is direct and unequivocal – they shoot out from their mouths a liquid so nauseating and noxious in smell as to deter all but the most hardened ornithologist or would-be helper. While I was tying the bird's legs and wings he ejected a liberal dose of this hideous substance both over me and over the seat cushions of *Polar Star*'s cabin, but at length I had him secured in a cardboard box, and we headed home for our moorings.

We had more than a hundredweight of fish on board, and no very obvious means of carrying them to Camusfeàrna, a distance of half a mile by dinghy and half a mile on foot. I had a canvas yachting smock, and apart from my trousers that was all. We knotted the sleeves and the neck, slithered the great mass of fish inside this brimming receptacle and set off for Camusfeàrna, Alan carrying the fish on his heavily bowed shoulders, and I hugging tenderly to my breast the cardboard box containing the fulmar.

We were less than fifty yards from the house, passing over the sand dunes, when Alan said, 'Well, this certainly is an odd day – just look at that!' Almost at our feet, shuffling helplessly among the rank bent grass of the dunes, was a Manx shearwater, the enormous scimitar wings appropriate to the long glide and wave-swoop of the albatross family to which both the shearwater and the fulmar belonged used now as a means of terrestrial locomotion. 'Blown ashore,' said Alan, 'and they can't take off except either from water or a height. Better take him in too, until we can let them both go in decent condition.'

So we arrived, that evening at Camusfeàrna, with a fulmar in a cardboard box, and a Manx shearwater held in greaseproof paper (for the contact of human hand can remove the 'water-proofness' of a seabird's plumage, so that it remains sodden after the bath it so ardently yearns for).

We put them both in the bathroom, the shearwater in the shower compartment, and the fulmar at liberty. It was a very messy performance, the fulmar excreting, it seemed, far more than it ingested, and to the human nurses it was a painful one too. To start with, neither bird would eat of its own freewill; both were force fed, while one person held the beak open the other crammed in food and forced it down into the unwilling crop. The diet I had selected for each was different; I gave the fulmar fish and fish-liver and great quantities of bacon fat (remembering from the past how they had swarmed round sharks' and whales' livers and any fatty substance available) and the shearwater I fed upon mussels, fish-liver, and the black proteinous heads of limpets. We avoided all direct contact between their plumage and human hands, but despite this they refused to become waterproof. (A situation of shock or trauma is often responsible for this condition.) The fulmar – awkward, gauche, clumsy, and entirely without fear – would bathe with relish, stamping about in the water and making ritualistic gestures towards total submersion, but emerged completely sodden and draggled. The shearwater had forcibly to be bathed, appearing to loathe the water and everything to do with it; but they shared one characteristic in common – their twice-daily feeding was extremely painful. As the human fingers withdrew from the bird's crop, the hooked, parrot-bill tips of their beaks would snap to with an entirely unexpected force, more than enough to draw blood, before one could snatch one's hand away, and at the end of the first week my right hand was covered with innumerable scars.

Since these two ocean-living birds were rarely if ever seen by the zoo-frequenting public, I suggested to a Scottish zoo that they should now take over from us until the birds were fit for liberation. The reply was that they might be prepared to take the fulmar for a time, but not the shearwater, as they were impossible to keep alive in captivity. At length we found an RSPCA official who was prepared to try; by that time we were apparently the only people to have kept a shearwater in good and increasing health for more than three weeks. In our case, too, both birds had to be defended from all the other predatory livestock at Camus-feàrna, and they added their own problems to a household that had become nothing less than an ill-ordered menagerie. We drove the birds 200 miles to the RSPCA in Aberdeen.

Seaweed in the bathroom, banked up so that the fulmar's breast could rest against it as he preferred, great sploshy, white, slimy bird-droppings between oneself and the bath, scattered fragments of fish liver underfoot, the stamping clumsy gait of the fulmar whenever he felt like moving; these are my recollections of the two birds whose triumphal release by the RSPCA a few weeks later was perhaps a vindication of all we had suffered on their behalf.

The animal situation, with the added presence of these birds in the bathroom, was really extraordinary. There were so many creatures that one just couldn't move. Any opened door was an automatic invitation to a vast and vocal avalanche of dogs, of all sizes and shapes, but with patently conflicting desires. The fantastic fertility of the household was crystallized for me by the discovery one day, previously unknown to anyone, of a litter of weaned kittens living in the loft above the lobby.

With the necessity to make immediate and practical plans for the few animals that were my own, I circularized a short list of zoos with the following letter, every word I wrote rending me, for this was the overt end of Camusfeàrna:

Dear X

I am writing to you because it seems likely that this autumn I shall have to find a home for my two otters Edal and Teko, and I should like to donate them to a zoo which would keep them in the style to which they are accustomed.

I suppose that, since the lioness Elsa's death, Edal (of *Ring of Bright Water*) is probably the most famous living individual animal, and she would no doubt be a considerable draw to any zoo that owned her. Teko, also, has a very considerable fan public. Edal is *Aonyx Capensis* from Nigeria: Teko, from Sierra Leone, would appear to be of some unrecognized sub-species. They are not mated, and have to be kept separately.

I am naturally anxious to secure ideal conditions for them. This means, basically, what they have now – indoor quarters heated with overhead infra-red lamps, and extensive and varied water-works outside. They are not happy with only static water, and require some system of fountains, waterfalls, etc. to keep them content, besides deep water to dive in. As these things are not easy for everyone to provide, I am writing now to a short list of zoos to find out who would be keen to try.

Teko is fed mainly on fish and a few eels, though he is almost omnivorous; Edal will not eat sea fish other than mackerel, and is fed mainly on live eels. Though Teko is now the more playful of the two, they will both play for hours with any suitable object presented to them.

I should be most grateful for your first reactions to the idea, so that I may narrow the field.

The response to this circular was enthusiastic, and in August 1966 I chose a zoo whose council, I understood, had undertaken to provide completely suitable accommodation for the two otters Edal and Teko. This was to include a fountain in each pool, and numerous other amenities that would safeguard both the public and the otters. It seemed to me then that, even if this solution was distressing, I had solved the problem of how to close Camus-feàrna and ensure the welfare of the animals. These two things were by now my only targets, and I wanted to do them efficiently and cleanly.

At first the zoo asked for the otters at the end of September; then, owing to labour difficulties, the date was postponed until mid-October. I left Camusfeàrna, and went to live within an hour's drive of the zoo. In October the date was again postponed for a month, for the same reasons. It was December before I realized that the project had finally broken down.

A zoo committee, I was now informed, had cancelled the expenditure necessary to construct even one fountain. I was also made aware for the first time that our original understanding that Edal would be 'deposited' for six months and then donated if she had settled into contentment in this new environment, was not acceptable to the zoo, who would now only take her as a direct and immediate donation, despite the entirely inadequate accommodation provided. Originally this was not a decision of the council but an untimely inspiration on the part of an official. It represented, anyway, a deadlock, and for me a peculiarly unpleasant one; I had screwed myself up to the point of parting with Edal after years of mutual esteem, and now I had to unwind on the instant like a broken watch spring.

I did not feel that I had any choice other than to cancel all our arrangements, and to postpone the question of the otters' future home for a further year. Only my absolute faith in Richard Frere's ability to fight a financial rearguard action made this possible. The young lady, who, with her daughter and her uncountable

animals, was in tumultuous occupation of Camusfeàrna, con-
sented to tend the otters until some satisfactory and permanent
alternative had been achieved; they were thus still at Camusfeàrna
when I came back in August 1967.

# 12

# Return of Mossy and Monday

The otters were to remain at Camusfeàrna until some true solution had been found; it was on this unhappy but temporarily reassuring note that I left what little remained of the old Camusfeàrna in December 1966. So far I have written this factual narrative thousands of miles from the centre of its subject; living alone and abroad in a town previously unknown to me I have tried to reassemble in sequence the happenings that led to the disintegration of the Camusfeàrna myth, and, at the same time, to my determination to return to there at least for a last summer; to restore for a little while the situation as it once had been.

In late April of 1967, far from the focus of my story, I received two telegrams from Camusfeàrna. The first read 'Monday came home with the dogs today let me know what to do'; and the second, two days later, 'Feeding female indoors pink spots nose injured by trap feeding male under lobby Alan [Alan MacDiarmaid, who had looked after Tibby] does not recognize stop confinement unnecessary writing.'

She wrote, three times, but changes of address and postal uncertainties to a distant country made her narrative tantalizingly fragmentary; the first of her letters, describing the miraculous return after four years of two of our liberated indigenous otters, did not reach me.

So it was with a sense of unreality that I read the second, as one might read an isolated serial of a detective story whose beginning one has missed.

I often see them over at the islands and in the river estuary. The strange thing about them is that they are so active by day, return to

366

the house at night to eat and to sleep. How wonderful it is to see
them swimming and playing naturally in the sea and dashing
around with each other quite free. Monday is always the leader.
One good thing is that I think she would be far too clever to be
caught in a trap for a second time . . . I have persuaded the owner
of the trap at the lochan by Druimfiaclach to have it removed;
which is as well, because the otters often go fishing in that loch.
Her leg is quite healed now – only a small lump on the bone where
it was broken. They have been like phantom otters for the last two
weeks. I had a guest staying, and they only came to the bathroom
at night for the fish. But after the guest left Monday came back to
sleep, and on Sunday morning I got up very early and found her
still sleeping in the shower compartment of the bathroom, on her
back like Edal does. AND her belly was moving – I thought she was
pregnant before, but now I am certain. I don't think she will have
her cubs in the shower now, because there have been so many
people about, and also I don't think that the male (which we think
is Mossy) would go in there to her, but I am hoping she will have
them under the coatroom floor, where they spend a lot of time, but
I do not know if they are using that box. [Four years before, we
had cut a hatch in the coatroom floor and constructed below it a
box for their benefit.] I dare not lift the hatch to see, in case they
feel that I am invading their privacy.

Monday eats as much fish as she wants in the bathroom, and
then drags the rest out to Mossy. He is a bit of a glutton; he didn't
feed her when her leg was broken by the trap and she couldn't fend

for herself. Now she makes sure of her share; she eats hers first, taking no notice of us watching, and then drags the remains of a fish almost as big as herself across the linoleum, out of the door and then through the hole under it that leads to her quarters below the floor . . .

Besides the tantalizing speculations as to what the first and missing letter might have contained (beyond the lines quoted above there were hints that Druimfiaclach was no longer untenanted, and that there had been a further and even more spectacular population explosion among dogs and donkeys at Camusfeàrna), I read this letter with mixed feelings, because about halfway through it I began to realize that the implications were far-reaching and contrary to the policy that I had formed with difficulty – the policy of spending one last summer at Camusfeàrna and then closing it completely, with the two original otters Edal and Teko as well provided for by a public institution as I was able to contrive. Now I was faced with the possibility that the returned and wounded wanderer, Monday, had come back to Camusfeàrna, still unafraid of man, with the intention of giving birth to her cubs in what had once been her home and shelter before she was even weaned – a home which I had intended to vacate with all its animals and leave to the wild winds of heaven. If a further race of domesticated otters, unafraid of their worst enemy, were to be reared there, I could not shed this aftermath of a past responsibility and leave them to be slaughtered for their skins as they assuredly would be. It seemed that Camusfeàrna would not let me go.

In response to a telegram, a substitute for the missing letter arrived:

The female otter arrived on the afternoon of Tuesday, April 18. The coatroom door to the field was open, and also the connecting door from the coatroom to the living room. Two of my dogs were coming and going, and the otter just walked in with them. I hurriedly fetched two omelettes which I had already cooked for

Edal and Teko, and shut the doors. Then I sent you a cable to find out what you wanted done.

[I had replied, 'Please encourage and feed but make no attempt confine.']

I enticed her into the bathroom with a fish, and made her a bed in the shower compartment. She took up residence in this bed, and drank water from a bowl I held out to her. She was quite tame and unafraid; she allowed me to touch her, and I managed to put some chloromycetin cream on a large pus-discharging swelling on her right foreleg.

Later that evening when I was outside I saw another otter's head looking out from under the coatroom doorway. I went in and checked, but the female was still asleep in the shower compartment in the bathroom. The second otter couldn't be tempted to come into the house but he (it was a male) was tame enough to take food from the hand. Now that there were two I at first thought I should open the bathroom door and let the female out, but on second thoughts I felt that her leg might require more attention, and I saw that her mate would not leave the house while she was inside. When I got your cable I did let her out, but she just ate her fish as usual and then went back to sleep. She seemed completely unconcerned about her mate. She would go to the bathroom door and look out and then push it shut before retiring to bed – from which I had the impression that she had used it before.

[She had indeed; it is a sliding door, and during my efforts to confine her four years earlier she had learned its difficult mechanism by heart.]

It was difficult to get her to swim in the bath. All other enticements having failed, I got her to get her teeth firmly into a fish and just lifted her in by it. She immediately found herself facing the big mirror above the bath, and was fascinated by the otter she saw reflected there. She moved from side to side and chattered her teeth with annoyance when the other otter she saw did the same thing; then she started patting the glass with her hands. She seemed to have very definite ideas about how an otter hotel should be run. When she messed on the floor she would keep on tapping at the edge of it until, looking up at me and chattering her teeth, she persuaded me to clean it up.

369

When she is well fed and contented she lies on her back and nibbles and sucks her 'bib', the loose skin on her throat, like Edal does and which you photographed so successfully in your previous books about the otters at Camusfeàrna. Then she goes to sleep on her back, with her legs in the air. Whatever has happened, she seems to consider herself a member of the household by right.

Having a bath has been very difficult, because she has a habit of nipping one's toes; not, I think, from aggression but from mischief – so I go into the bathroom only in Wellington boots. Having undressed down to these, one removes one boot and puts that foot in the bath. Have you ever tried balancing on one leg in a bathful of hot water trying to get an uncooperative boot off the other foot? It's an experience only equalled by trying to get out of the bath afterwards.

It was not until she had been in the bathroom for four days that she seemed to wake up to her surroundings and began a tour of inspection. By this time she had put on a lot of weight, and she was much stronger and remarkably agile. She started by climbing up and throwing everything off the shelves, trying everything with her teeth and then scrutinizing it before disdainfully discarding it. Her face when she bit into a cake of soap is something I shall always remember.

Her *tour de force* was her assault on the mirror-fronted cupboard above the washhand basin. Having got on to the basin, she paused for quite a long time to examine the new otter face confronting her, apparently comparing it with the other otter face she had seen in the mirror above the bath. Then, finding that it smelt of nothing ottery, she opened the cupboard door. She held on to one of the shelves with her left hand, and used her right to throw out all the contents on to the floor. She wore the expression of a small child, who, strapped into a pram, throws out all its toys to see what effect it will have.

Nothing would make her leave the bathroom, and she seemed frightened of going out, so I cut a hole in the wall [plaster board and wood] so that she could come and go without fear of being shut out. For the next two weeks, that is up till now, she and her mate have been away all of each day, returning at night – she to the bathroom and he to his quarters under the floor.

It was some time before I found out how she had come to be wounded. I had suspected that she had been caught in a trap, but I didn't know anything definite until I was having a cup of coffee with the new people at Druimfiaclach. The lady of the house told me about an otter that her son had trapped. He had set a trap at the edge of the lochan below the house, and one day they saw something moving in it. Her son went down to investigate, and found that it was an otter. As soon as he opened the trap, instead of trying to run away she flew at him, and he fought her off with a stick. She returned to the attack, and again he defended himself with the stick. Then she made off, but turned round several times, as if trying to make up her mind whether to have another go at him. All this was five days before she arrived at Camusfeàrna, and she must have been unable to fend for herself all that time, because the trapper said that when he saw her she was in good condition, but she was very thin when she got here. How lucky that she remembered where to go in time of trouble, and that I was here to look after her.

It was, as nearly as I can calculate, just four years since either Monday or Mossy had visited Camusfeàrna house or come within sighting distance of it – for that brief appearance at the waterfall in the summer of 1964 had clearly been contrary to Monday's intentions – but the description contained in this letter left me in no possible doubt that these were the same two otters that I described in detail in *The Rocks Remain*. Mossy, with his stupid, timorous, egotistical nature; Monday with her miraculous powers of climbing and her apparent comprehension of all basic mechanical principles. In the very last sentence of that book I had written, 'If I ever again write of Camusfeàrna, I hope that I shall not have to write of the death of Monday, her whole dynamic personality wiped out as a result of the inner emptiness that is the desire to kill.' I have not, at least, had to do that. Injured and unable to fend for herself she had remembered and returned; she must have recalled that besides the free fish and the affection there had been prolonged and forcible confinement to fight against, but in seeking the sanctuary of Camusfeàrna in her present distress she had perhaps remembered also how constantly and contemptuously she had outwitted us, and felt confident of doing so again should the necessity arise.

So far away from Camusfeàrna, the last paragraph of the letter gave me a deep nostalgia for what I had once known. 'Camusfeàrna is more beautiful than ever now; there are great banks of primroses, bluebells, violets, and a great profusion of wild flowers everywhere.'

But the letter had a PS. 'A poltergeist has come here; yesterday it broke two windows; one while I was sitting on the corner of the sofa you yourself normally occupy, and one in the kitchen while I was washing up.'

Watchman, what of the rowan tree?

# 13

# *Many Maladies*

I came back to England on 18 June 1967, having engaged by correspondence only and without interview a temporary employee to help me at Camusfeàrna during my final summer there with the otters. This was Andrew Scot, a boy who had written to us periodically over the past five years, but whom I had never met, and who was now leaving school at the age of seventeen. Meanwhile I had to wait in London while the young lady who had been occupying Camusfeàrna arranged to move with her small daughter and her innumerable livestock (which now included two female donkeys said to be in foal – or is it in hinny? – to her pony which had been erroneously believed to be a gelding) to a house near to the village.

I began immediately to attack the problem of a final home for the otters, for the experiences of the previous year, and the final collapse of arrangements with the chosen zoo, had taught me that time could not, in this respect, be treated as expendable. I thought that Camusfeàrna as a household must be closed before the onset of winter, and negotiations must be begun at once.

I had given many hours of thought to this while I was still abroad, and I had returned with the outline of a plan. I did not now believe any zoo to be the answer; the great majority suffer from space restriction, and even with the sum of money voted by that council it would be difficult anywhere to secure what I would regard as ideal conditions. So I ruled out all zoos, and I had simultaneously to dismiss the possibility of a private home, for the necessary type of eccentric millionaire just did not exist.

This seemed to leave me with one possibility only – someone who would invest money in giving the animals perfect living conditions because they would earn him high dividends which would be immediately calculable – unlike a zoo, in which it is of necessity difficult to assess the earning value of any particular animal exhibited.

Lord Bath's lions at Longleat . . . the Duke of Bedford's great park at Woburn – but what had Woburn in the animal line that could really compete with Longleat's lions? I doubted whether the Longleat lions would have been so great a draw had not the public become lion-conscious through the story of Joy Adamson's lioness Elsa and after all, Edal had come near to outselling Elsa, and Edal was still alive whereas Elsa was dead. True there were very great rarities at Woburn – European bison and almost the whole world's population of the otherwise extinct Père David's deer, but these were not individually famous animals with a fan public of thousands as were Edal and Teko.

So I came home with the half-formed plan of approaching Woburn, a plan strongly reinforced by two happenings during my first few days in England. The first was being told of a cartoon in a daily paper showing two vans arriving at Woburn, one labelled 'lions' and the other 'Christians', with the caption 'Anything Bath can do Bedford can do better'. The second was the discovery that an acquaintance, Michael Alexander, held certain concessions, specifically to do with animals, at Woburn, and that there was at least a chance of these concessions being extended.

Michael was enthusiastic, and he drove me down to Woburn little more than a week after I had returned from abroad. He led me through Pets' Corner, where an improbable miscellany of animals both wild and domestic – but all sublimely ignoring the public who threaded their way between them – were brooded over by a benign and motionless vulture perched majestically upon the wooden railings of a small central enclosure. Three glorious macaws, free and untrammelled, flew from tree to tree above us or around us, the fantastic splendour of their plumage lit by a bright afternoon sun. We passed through Pets' Corner and out beyond it to an undeveloped site that Michael had visualized as a possible home for the otters. The moment I saw it I knew that here, if it was obtainable, could be the otters' paradise. We were looking out over a small lake, heavily overgrown with waterlilies, a roundish but not quite round lake perhaps 65 yards one way by 50 the other. The water, I was told, was some twelve feet deep in the middle, shelving to five feet at the edges. There was plainly a water system of inlet and outlet somewhere, for among the waterlilies near to us I caught sight of a golden orfe, and further out there were some small fish jumping, too far away for identification. We were standing in a colonnade of wooden pillars and arches, decorated in the Chinese manner, that stretched round almost half the lake's circumference, an ornamental covered passageway separated from the lake by a few feet of grass bank. The official name of this spectacular 'folly' was the Chinese Dairy, built in spacious days of long ago, as a separate jewel in the Bedford coronet; and just behind us where we stood a large room opened off the colonnade. Here was the perfect situation in which even the most cautious businessman would surely feel justified in a lavish outlay, because the otters would be an isolated exhibit which the public would pay individually to see. It was only unfortunate that the incompatibility of Edal and Teko presented its own problem, for the lake would have to be divided in two.

We planned artificial islands and fountains, the position of the heated sleeping quarters; in fact, though this was no more than a reconnaissance, we covered almost every detail. It remained for Michael to acquire concessions over this part of the estate that was not at the moment earning any significant money.

Having reached the stage at which there was little left to discuss, Michael took me on one of his safari trips through the great park. This vast and magnificently unspoilt piece of countryside, 3,000 acres enclosed by no less than thirteen miles of high brick wall, contained ten species of deer, living in a completely wild state in beautiful surroundings – to say nothing of both European and American bison, wallabies, llamas, alpacas, guanacos, breeding pairs of the ostrich-like rhea, and sarus cranes. The running of safari trips in huge four-wheel drive vehicles, so that the public could see all these splendours at close quarters, much as they might do in an African game reserve, had been Michael's earliest venture at Woburn, and met with a richly deserved popularity.

I felt as though I were slipping back into an earlier century, a century before the beginning of industrialization, when much of England must have been like this, great sweeps of grassland with noble oaks and herds of grazing deer. Robin Hood and his green-clad men would have seemed no more out of place here than the deer themselves. Apart from the fascination of the animals, many allowing the safari car to approach within a few yards of them, it was the lack of any carving up of this great piece of land that held its own exhilaration – that and its silence; and I could well understand how even those with no intrinsic interest in animals could find in a half-hour's safari tour a magic world in complete contrast to the wasteland of brick and stone and mechanical noise in which so many are condemned to live. On my return from the safari through that green parkland of quiet and peaceful animals, I felt that even though this was basically a commercial enterprise it was also a deeply-needed public service.

Meanwhile I had begun to produce a succession of curious and alarming physical disorders. Not long after my return from North Africa I sat down at my desk one morning to make some telephone calls. When the first number answered I was astonished to find that, with no premonitory symptoms, I had literally no voice at all; I could not even whisper. The next day I felt thoroughly ill, with headache and sickness and digestive troubles. I began to treat myself with antibiotics, but when after five days Ledermycin had proved ineffective I sent for the doctor. While he was examining me I noticed that he spent a great deal of time over my left lung, and when he had finished he said, 'I've no doubt that a change of antibiotic will soon clear up the general condition, but there are some crepitations from the base of your left lung and I think you have an early pneumonia. I should like an X-ray report as soon as possible.'

I replied, 'Well, I suppose I'm a classic for lung cancer; I'm the right age, and I smoke eighty cigarettes a day.'

He said, 'I'd like to make an appointment with the chest clinic by telephone now.' He did so, but he could not obtain one until

Friday, and it would be the following Tuesday before he would know the results. I asked him what was the worst that the X-ray could reveal, and he answered, 'Well, just what you said yourself.' Pressed upon the probability of this finding he would say neither that it was unlikely nor likely, but when I asked him whether he would tell me the absolute truth after the results were in his hands, he replied, 'Yes – you are one of my patients with whom I should feel that to be the right course of action.'

The time between Wednesday and Friday passed very slowly indeed, and during those two days I became absolutely convinced in myself that the findings would be positive. I was, as I had said to the doctor, a classic case for the disease, and now that the idea was in my mind I recognized that I had many of the textbook symptoms. Millions of people have been through this time of suspense and for very much longer periods than I, but I have never seen any subjective account of it, so it is perhaps worth recording my own reactions. Primarily, I felt it impossible to see or to talk to anyone who was not or had not been a cancer patient – this seemed a private, shut-off world that would be bewildering and frightening to anyone who had not shared it. To a few people whom it might affect I told the bare facts, but I did not feel able to discuss them. Because of this feeling of being outside and shut off from the normal world I cancelled all engagements until after the following Tuesday, when I should know the details and the prognosis. Unexpectedly, a complete resignation, one which I suppose might well have proved temporary, came very early on; I was concerned less with the fact that I had cancer (as I had convinced myself beyond all reasonable doubt) than with the alterations to plan and programme that this would involve; how Camusfeàrna would be run until the otters were moved to Woburn; who would move them; the general ordering of my affairs. Fear and despair would, I suppose, have come later, but during those forty-eight hours I felt neither.

At half past one on Friday afternoon I presented myself at the chest clinic, and after the X-ray photographs had been taken I was on the point of leaving when the radiologist said, 'Normally speaking you would have to wait for the findings until next week, when you would receive them from your own doctor. But that would keep you in suspense for another four days, so if you would care to wait for a while we may be able to tell you something today. That is if you would prefer it.'

I said that I would certainly prefer it and that I was very grateful indeed, which was an understatement. I sat in the waiting room reading back numbers of *Punch*; most of them contained political jokes whose significance was unintelligible to me, for I had been unable to follow home news during my six months in North Africa. There was a 'No Smoking' sign; I very much wanted a cigarette, arguing to myself that if I had cancer of the lung one more could not make any difference, and if I had not the same applied. But to walk even as far as the door to the street might mean that I missed the news when it came, and I sat on. As I considered my position I realized that only in the case of a negative result would the clinic be likely to tell me anything; if it were positive, it seemed to me, they would somehow arrange matters so that the news was broken to me by my own doctor. In this case, therefore, no news would be bad news. At the end of half an hour nothing had happened. There were three other patients in the room; looking at them I tried to determine from their demeanours whether they too were waiting for news all-important to them, but their faces told me nothing. I hoped that mine was as impassive.

After a little more than three-quarters of an hour a nurse came in and looked questioningly round. 'Mr Maxwell?' I stood up and she beckoned me into the corridor.

'Doctor said to tell you that your X-ray plates are perfectly satisfactory.'

There was a Delphic quality to this utterance, and I was desperate for certainty.

'Does he mean,' I said carefully, trying very hard to keep my voice to a casual tone, 'that the quality of the plates is satisfactory, or that my condition is satisfactory?'

She beamed at me from behind heavy horn-rimmed spectacles. 'He means that he can find no trace of any pathological condition. In other words, there's nothing wrong with you.

378

I resisted the temptation to hug her or to do a jig where I stood. I thanked her, and walked out into the summer sunshine and the streets busy with people into whose world I seemed suddenly to have re-entered.

# 14

## Return to Camusfeàrna

Coming back to Camusfeàrna after so long I was conscious of two impressions, though by their very nature one was very much quicker to register than the second.

It did not take long for me to realize that in the nineteen years of my occupancy I had never seen the house and its surrounds in such a state of damage and dereliction. An unusually wild and wet winter had combined with the presence of the host of livestock to leave hardly a single sheet of plaster boarding intact in the rooms we had built on to the old pine-panelled cottage, and even there the woodwork was in places deeply scarred by the marks of petulant paws. The plaster boarding was studded with actual holes, as though it had been under shell fire; only the claw and tooth marks surrounding these apertures showed that, by some curious feat of engineering difficult to comprehend, they too could be ascribed only to the drilling of determined dogs. The bathroom ceiling had collapsed under the weight of a cache of poodles temporarily stored in the loft above it; there were ten broken window panes and twelve broken window catches; not only the keys to all three outside doors were missing, but even those of the bathroom and the lavatory. Carpets and rugs had been so fouled that they had to be burnt; it was as though some omnivorous locust swarm had passed through the house on a mission of destruction.

Outside, the situation was little better. The sea winds had whipped the white walls to a dirty grey, grown over in places with a powdery green fungus; the white post-and-rail fence in front of the house was broken in a score of places, and all along the dunes between the house and the sea lay rubbish dumps of rusty cans and bottles, exposed, perhaps, by the wind's lifting of the sand that had originally covered our deep-dug pits. It had been a long time, too, since Camusfeàrna had housed a lusty male capable of digging one of those great graves for the unburnable detritus of the tinned food era. Worse, much worse, was a horror to which I am even more susceptible than most people – a remembered nausea going back over the long years to the Soay Shark Fishery and the day we discovered that sixteen tons of salted shark flesh had turned rotten in the closed brine tank. Here at Camusfeàrna someone had switched off the electric current to the largest of our deep freezes, and the fish inside were putrescent. In a final analysis I know now that it would take a finer olfactory sense than mine to distinguish between sixteen tons of rotten shark flesh and eight hundredweight of rotten haddock.

A visible touch of squalor was added by the presence and activities, both excremental and by 'footwork', of some forty head of heavy black cattle, great gravid creatures who trampled every soft piece of ground into a squelchy mire of dung and mud. They forced the flimsy gates protecting our tiny enclave and munched the few remaining gladioli that persisted among the weeds of once orderly flower beds below the windows; they leaned or scratched themselves upon everything that could – and did – give way beneath their weight; they, or something equally heavy, had broken the timbers of the bridge that spanned the burn; they escaped into the surrounding forestry ground, so that Andrew Scot spent the great part of his time rounding them up and ejecting them. Camusfeàrna was in a mess, and the prevailing images were of mud, rust, and decay.

So pervasive were these depressing pigments that it was some days before I began to see that there were others, completely conflicting with this scene, that could form quite another picture. By engaging, at a distance of thousands of miles, a temporary assistant whom I had neither interviewed nor even met, I had somehow stumbled upon perhaps the one person who could confront the whole situation not only without dismay but with confidence and even relish. Andrew Scot, whose letters over five years had been filed under the heading of 'juvenile fan' (they had not differed greatly in content from others whose authors I now know would have proved patently unsuitable) began to take shape as the ideal rescuer of Camusfeàrna in its sickness. The wild weather and the wet and the wind; the living conditions that had by now returned to the primitive; the absence of cinemas and social life; the enormously hard and often unpleasant work that every day involved; the daily weary plod up the steep hill path to Druimfiaclach, often ankle deep in mud and water, to collect our mail and heavy stores ordered from the village shop; the search for firewood along the desolate and chilling beaches in driving rain – these things were meat and drink to him, and never once did he complain or suggest that he might be happier elsewhere. To him everything seemed easy.

Nor was this all. Despite his detailed knowledge of the terrible injuries that both Edal and Teko had inflicted upon people in the past, and the obvious risk to himself, his aim and desire was to be able to handle them, to take them for walks, to be on terms with them that would not be those of a zoo-keeper in charge of dangerous animals. This knowledge came to me by a then not unexpected, but still disconcerting question: 'When do I start taking the otters out for walks?' I replied, 'Never, as far as I'm concerned – I'm the only person they've never threatened and has no fear of them. I'm not going to expose anyone else to what might be terrible injury.'

But he wouldn't take no for an answer; in fact he fought to achieve a situation of grave potential danger. He won his parents' permission, and the only remaining obstacle was my own. In the end I too had to give it.

It was eight months since I had had any personal contact with either Edal or Teko, and I myself was far from certain of my reception. I began with Teko; because, as I described very early in this book, I had a strange and reassuring momentary reunion with him in November 1966. So after the first few days at Camusfeàrna, days devoted to reorganizing my forces after the multiple mishaps of the past weeks, I went out one blustery but sunny morning to re-establish contact with Teko.

He was not visible in his enclosure, so I knew that he must be asleep in his house. I opened the gate and called him, and an answering, welcoming chirrup came from the darkness beyond his half-closed door. I waited and called again, and after a minute or so he walked out a little uncertainly into the unconfined world that he had not seen for more than four years. The right hand side of his face was swollen and his right eye completely closed; he looked a sick animal, unhealthily fat, and plainly suffering from an exacerbation of one of the tooth socket infections that had periodically bedevilled the lives of both these West African otters. He appeared bewildered and lost, but as he came nearer and caught my smell he began talking again – the little joyful, affectionate cries that I had not heard for so long. I bent down and put out my hands to him, and a moment later he was nuzzling my face with his wet nose and bristly whiskers, pushing his little monkey fingers into my ears and nose, and redoubling his cries of love and joy. I responded to him emotionally; what, I thought, had I done to deserve this warmth of continuing trust and devotion. I had confined him for four years; I had deprived him of the human society to which as a baby he had been conditioned by no will of his own; I had even at one point determined to send him to a zoo and into the possibly unloving care of strangers. I had betrayed him, and because our common language was so limited I had not even been able to explain to him the reasons for which I had done all these things.

This, our first walk together for so long, was a sad and guilt-ridden half-hour. Teko, clearly in pain with something akin to acute toothache as we know it, was confused and bewildered by the half-remembered outside world, and would hardly stray from my feet. Every few yards he would stop me to seek fresh reassurance, fresh loving conversation; he would not swim nor take delight in any of his old haunts, whether still, placid pools to explore or the stimulus of white water in cataract. At that moment it was me he needed and me only, and all else was subordinate. When I took him home to his house his only concern was that I should not leave him alone again. What torture the human species inflict upon their 'pets'.

In any other community it might seem strange to call upon a distinguished doctor to advise upon the condition and treatment of an animal, but this would be to ignore the personality of Dr Dunlop. Our local (fifty miles by road and sea-ferry) vet, Donald MacLennan, who had tended the otters with such miraculous skill for eight years, was on holiday, and so it was the doctor whom I consulted. He made a characteristically quick and accurate decision as to the antibiotic to be used, and in five days Teko was once more a healthy and active otter with an interest in all around him.

Thus my second walk with him was very different from the first. True, he stayed closer to me than he had once been used to do, but he remembered his old haunts and he made for them, he chased fish and porpoised in the calm reaches of the river, emerging every few minutes to stand up against me and apparently thank me with squeaks of pleasure, depositing a heavy skin-load of water on my already soaking trousers.

It was only when I brought him back to the house that difficulties began. It was a conflict of wills, and one that took me more than an hour to resolve. Teko simply would not re-enter his enclosure. He was tired, having taken more exercise than he had done for four years, and it was plain that he wanted nothing more than to curl up in his blankets under the infra-red lamp, but he would not voluntarily become a captive again. Time and time again he would come to the gate in the wooden paling and put his face in, talking all the time in low whimpering tones either to himself or to me, but nothing I could do would persuade him to come far enough in for the gate to be closed behind him. Gone were the days of harnesses and of leads; nothing could succeed but cajolery, and cajole I did, using every ruse I knew. Every time that I called to him he answered, with a small variation on his usual welcoming note, a variation I had not heard before, and which registered as plainly as articulate speech both protest and reproof. Just outside the gate he rolled and rubbed himself in the grass, movements that had always been a prelude to sleep, while I called and called, and Andrew Scot, sitting as sentinel on the steep hillside above us, was driven almost demented by devouring hordes of midges.

Some change of tactics was clearly a necessity; I stopped calling, went into his house and sat down on his bed below the heating lamp. After a few minutes the initiative had significantly changed; now it was he who was calling to me with increasing urgency, and I would not answer. His voice changed to the note, between a whistle and a squeak, with which an otter cub calls for parents whom it cannot find. It came nearer and nearer, and it held an audible and anxious question mark. I remained obstinately silent, and suddenly his face looked round the door. Instead of retreating again now that he had established my whereabouts, as I had half feared, he came bouncing across the floor, chattering with pleasure, and climbed up beside me, going through all his rituals of love and affection as though it were months since he had seen me. I fell in with his mood, and gave the full repertoire of reassurance that he had known in the distant days when he was a cub; blowing into his fur as though it were a woollen glove on a white winter's day; taking the tips of his little monkey fingers between my lips; responding to his nose against my mouth by an exchange of saliva. All very well, I thought, as his heavy, shiny body squirmed and wriggled all over me, but how was I to get myself out without employing some trick that would destroy his confidence in me. But I had completely misjudged the situation; he was like a child who, scarcely stifling its yawns, protests that it is far too early to go to bed, but who will when tucked up by a parent figure fall instantly asleep. Teko was in bed, he had received his equivalent of being tucked up and kissed goodnight, and I doubt whether I could have called him out again had I tried. My cautious, stealthy attempt to leave unnoticed was wholly unnecessary; he was occupied only with the question of finding

385

the most comfortable position for sleep, and he had found it before ever I closed the gate behind me.

I had achieved at least part of what I had dreamed of on that wild autumn evening the year before; I had restored at least a measure of freedom and contentment to this creature that had once been a companion at Camusfeàrna, and neither he nor I were captives any longer. From that day on, as I took him up to the waterfall or out to the island beaches of white sand, watching him swim and dive in the glass-clear water of the ebb tide, some of the colour of the Camusfeàrna landscape began to come back for me.

Within a week of this total reunion with Teko I began to realize that my own image of Camusfeàrna could not be truly re-created without a similar restoration of my relationship with Edal. I did not know whether this was possible, but I was prepared to risk much to find out. For five and a half years no human being had touched her, for five and a half years she had not seen beyond the confines of her small enclosure. No one understood what had caused the explosions of rage and violence that had periodically punctuated her record of affection and good humour. Yet the facts were there; she had inflicted terrible injuries, and had at last, early in 1962, broken even Jimmy Watt's nerve, by chasing him into the rafters of his own room and holding him there, screaming her rage at every attempt he made to move. From then on the history of Camusfeàrna with all its vicissitudes and its multiple occupants, had left me no opportunity to try to re-establish contact with her myself; and if I am to be honest I must confess that I think that when Jimmy became afraid of her I did too, because I knew that in all other things but this one Jimmy feared so little. But I knew, too, that she had never given me, personally, any cause to fear her, and I knew clearly that I could not respect myself or see Camusfeàrna whole again if I did not try to do for her what I had succeeded in doing for Teko. Both had, by the human killing of their parents when they were infants, been conditioned to unnatural dependence upon humans and their company, and both had been deprived of it because when they became adult they had behaved like wild animals instead of like well brought up Pekinese dogs. If their behaviour had been bewildering to us, ours must have been even more so to them; they had both received life sentences for actions, which by the very hysteria that characterized them, were probably unremembered.

I thought about all this, and I saw that if I postponed from day to day any positive action towards restoring her old status the project would become part of the pervading decline, the atmosphere of business unfinished and abandoned, that had stained the whole Camusfeàrna picture over the past five years. So on Sunday 10 September I determined to take her out the next day.

The decision may have been compulsive, but I think the preparations and safeguards showed an adequate degree of foresight. It would have been irresponsible, in view of her history, to risk her meeting strangers on the beaches, so we arranged that Andrew should sit on the hillside in a position to command visually both approaches to the Camusfeàrna bay and warn any unexpected visitors that there was a potentially dangerous animal loose on the beaches. He was to follow my progress with binoculars, and in the event of my receiving any gross injury he was to regain the house and telephone to the doctor at the village five miles away. For my own safety I laid out dressings, including surgical needle and thread, on the bathroom table. As an afterthought I added a hypodermic syringe and cocaine solution. As an emergency measure, that proved so mercifully unnecessary, I equipped myself with an item which I cannot understand why we never thought of before – a pot of pepper. Any attacking animal of Edal's size could, I thought, be rendered completely helpless by this means.

There were three ways to take Edal from her quarters into the outside world. One, which was out of the question because of the amount of objects that could be destroyed by an interested and inquisitive otter, was through the long prefabricated room that had been Jimmy's, and which led into the lobby. The second led directly into the lobby itself, and thence to the open air. The third was a new gate in the wooden paling, leading out on to the sand dunes, which Alan MacDiarmaid had made a few days before – while I was bringing myself to the boil, as it were, about the liberation of Edal.

When Andrew was positioned and the moment came to open this gate and call her out I remembered what Malcolm and Paula Macdonald had said to me when Edal first came to Camusfeàrna eight long, wild years before: 'Let her come to you; don't force yourself on her. Just ignore her, and she'll make friends with you.'

So I opened the gate to the dunes and called her as I had used to long ago – 'Whee-ee! Ee-eedal! Whee-ee!' There was a pattering of paws in the tunnel that protected her sleeping quarters from the wind, and suddenly she was there beside me – but much more interested in the mechanism of the gate than in me. She felt all around the hinges with her hands, went inside again to investigate them from another angle, and then suddenly set off on a tour of inspection of the premises of the house. Everything was new to her, everything had to be investigated with the thoroughness and attention to detail of an insurance company's detective. After only a few yards she arrived at the broken down jeep standing at the end of the work shed. She went underneath it and remained there for a long time, feeling everything with her fingers as if she were about to prepare a report on the condition of the vehicle. It must have been five minutes before she emerged, emitting one of her refined and lady-like sneezes (often *actually* stifled by the hand), and climbed up into the driver's seat. She fumbled with switches, descended to the floor to insert her fingers round the shafts of the brake and clutch pedals, and suddenly appeared standing on the driver's seat, her hands on the steering wheel, peering over the bonnet as if to test visibility. She left the car with an expression that suggested the words, 'Make a note to censure whoever was in charge of that one', and went on to an upturned dinghy that had suffered damage to several planks during a winter storm. She disappeared underneath it and was out of sight for several minutes; only an occasional probing finger appeared to be testing damaged woodwork. At last she emerged, climbed up, and made her way along the keel ridge, using both fingers and face to assess the situation. Satisfied anew that someone had blundered, she left the dinghy and began to follow me toward the sea, but suddenly she turned back. The work shed itself, which she had never even seen, demanded a full survey.

Besides a litter of tools and mechanical equipment, the shed at that moment contained the two deerhounds, Dirk and Hazel. They were awaiting transfer to their new home in Perthshire (for despite my determination to restore the otters to partial liberty I was at Camusfeàrna essentially to close it down as a house which required staff) and for this occasion they had been shut in. The key to the shed, like all other keys, had disappeared, and so we had, as part of our preparations, jammed the door shut with a diagonal piece of angle iron, bolstered at its ground end by two heavy stones.

Edal was obviously fascinated by this situation. Over months and years she had become accustomed to the smell of the deerhounds, and here they were shut up in a way that was a challenge to her ingenuity. She started to work on the piece of angle iron; she pulled at it with her hands, and finding that it would not yield she rolled over on to her back and tried to yank it downward. Discovering that this did not pay off, she walked round the construction several times and then deliberately set to work on the stones that jammed it in position. By this time I was becoming alarmed, because I could not visualize with anything but dismay what might happen if she set the deerhounds free. I walked away towards the sea, and, mercifully, she followed as I called.

Between her and the tide stood the massive form of *Polar Star* on her wheeled cradle, and this also demanded a lengthy and detailed appraisal – axles, wheels, everything that could be investigated to the full by an otter bent on factual knowledge. When we left *Polar Star* for the exposed sands of the ebb tide she came with me, but in a physical sense she ignored me; she was about her own business, and she did not acknowledge that this included me. In the shallows of the sand-ribs where the sea was no more than perhaps three feet deep she chased dabs and caught one; she was plainly happy, and I no longer felt afraid of her; nor, I think, did she in any way mistrust me.

But to take both otters out (they could never, as I have explained, be allowed to meet) brought us back to a situation that had its origin in 1959, when Terry Nutkins had been engaged as assistant otter keeper to Jimmy Watt. Obviously I could not exercise both animals and at the same time do my own work of writing. Andrew remained insistent upon complete contact; granted this absolute aim on his part and his parents' permission to try, there was no logical alternative for either of us.

It was, in brief, that if Andrew could achieve his goal of a trusting relationship with both animals he should not regard his present position as merely that of a temporary assistant in the closing down of Camusfeàrna, but should accompany the otters to Woburn and remain in charge of them there, responsible directly to myself. This project, which he regarded with an enthusiasm second only to the unfortunately impracticable notion of remaining with the otters at Camusfeàrna for ever, took a great weight from my mind. It meant that they might be tended by someone in whom I had already learned to place much confidence, someone who knew them, understood them and was fond of them, someone who might handle them in ill health when a stranger might be helpless. It meant, too, that the human contact re-established after so desperately long an interval need not be broken – and to this I attached great importance, for I believed that the present splendid condition of both animals was due at least in part to a psychological rejuvenescence.

Andrew himself was already taking a much deeper interest in the future of the otters than he himself realized. During my convalescence with Richard and Joan Frere I had begun a scale model of the complex new otter premises at Woburn, and when I had finally arrived at Camusfeàrna I had brought this with me and worked on it daily. Literally hundreds of man hours had by now gone into the model, in an effort to combine four almost irreconcilable principles – the Chinese decorative motif, so that the appearance of the Dairy Lake should not suffer; the well-being and comfort of the animals in the space at disposal; the convenience of their keeper, so that every part should be accessible for cleaning without the necessity to crawl on all-fours; and, finally, the ability of the public to view, so that the large capital outlay for this ambitious scheme should not be lost to that inveterate optimist Michael Alexander.

All these problems had by now been resolved as nearly as they might be, but from a welter of different proposals put forward both by Michael's side and my own we had not yet reached agreement on how to divide the lake in such a way as to keep Edal and Teko safely apart. Diagrams and drawings, samples of material, involved mathematical calculations and costings littered my table, but the whole subject was still in dispute by mid-September.

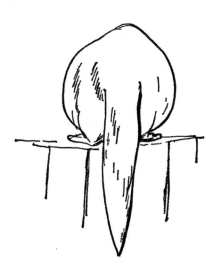

# 15

## *Peace Before Nightfall*

Andrew put to me again the question whose reply was causing me continued conflict – 'When do I start taking Teko out?' The issue could no more be postponed than my own self-demanded question about Edal, and I realized that this time I must make a firm decision, however difficult it might be. I could no longer make excuses on the grounds of the hazards inherent in the presence of other livestock; the five poodles had gone at last; the huge white Roman gander had followed a few days later, sitting grotesquely but majestically on the passenger's seat of the Land Rover in a sack tied at his neck; and finally we had at last succeeded in catching – not without many scratches, a querulous and highly vocal cat, elusive as a will o' the wisp, that haunted the premises long after the rest of the menagerie was remembered only by the mighty havoc it had wrought on the house and surroundings.

This was a Monday, and there were genuine reasons for postponing the experiment for several days. On the other hand Andrew, though not dreading the day with the same cold fear as I, was plainly mustering all his nervous energy for an ordeal of suspense. I decided to fix the day as Saturday, and then to spring the request upon him at five minutes' notice on Thursday, so that he should have no time to lose his confidence during a possibly sleepless night on Friday.

Meanwhile I rehearsed him carefully in the behaviour best calculated to produce a calm attitude in Teko's mind. Throughout the world of animals and birds, and of human infants, it had long been apparent to me that repetitive, sing-song sounds represent an attitude of amiability and thus of reassurance; conversely, a single note, especially if harsh in tone, invariably means alarm or challenge. This I am convinced, is the unconscious motive underlying human 'baby talk', which tends to a distortion of words, rendering them rhythmic, lending them a cadence, a rise and fall, that has its counterpart throughout much of the animal kingdom. As a single instance one may contrast the contented chattering of jackdaws with the harsh, drawn-out alarm note announcing the presence of danger.

For these reasons, and not only because the otters had become conditioned to it before ever they came to me, I had always been accustomed to speak to them in a sing-song baby language, an iambic rhythm, to which they had responded with calm and affection. (When, in the autumn of 1966, I had been on the point of sending them to a zoo, it had been an acute embarrassment to me to make a lengthy tape recording of these humanly ridiculous sounds for the benefit of their future keepers – who would, in all likelihood, never have used them. Fortunately, since the otters did not go to the zoo, the compact little spool of potential ridicule remained safely in my possession.)

Andrew had none of the inhibitions that might be expected towards chanting my silly words and phrases, even though I advised him to do this continuously throughout his walks with Teko; in this as in all other matters he displayed a wisdom and sanity far beyond his years, qualities that might well have saved Camusfeàrna had he arrived upon the scene long before he did, for he seemed born for the life.

On Thursday morning, as he finished the washing up, I remarked that it was a fine, sunny day, and asked whether he would like to take Teko out at once. He looked only slightly startled, and replied at once, 'Certainly I'd like to.'

He did not like being equipped with the pot of pepper, but I insisted. Now that it had come to the moment he was to all appearances completely confident, and it was I who had to exert all my reserves of self control to conceal my agitation.

The window situation at Camusfeàrna – what in educational documents perused with R. F. Mackenzie, Headmaster of Brae-head School, I have so often seen with wonderment referred to as 'fenestration' – is as inadequate for all round observation as educational authorities tend to find it for health reasons in every building genuinely suitable as a base for an exploratory outdoor life. Camusfeàrna was built with its back to the prevailing south-westerly winds, a lesson learnt from its predecessor some seventy yards across the field, whose occupants were driven to escape from a tempest-driven sea by a single tiny window on the sheltered, landward, side of the house. I had added only two windows to the original cottage of Camusfeàrna as I had found it, portholes from HMS *Vanguard* when she was broken up at a Clydeside shipyard. Both were upstairs; one looked north-east directly over Teko's enclosure, the other south-west to Camusfeàrna bay and the long reach of sea beyond it to the far islands of Eigg and Muick. Thus there was no single window from which I could follow the progress of the first experimental contact between a possibly dangerous animal and a courageous boy. I would have to begin by sticking my head out of the north-easterly porthole, set far back in the thickness of the house wall, and then move from room to room as the two progressed, as I hoped they would, towards the sea.

Andrew showed no sign of nervousness as, carrying a plate of Teko's favourite delicacy, tinned pilchards, he went to Teko's closed gate and called to him in a fair imitation of my own chanting language. With my head through the porthole and my shoulders jammed into the alcove that gave access to it, I watched as Teko lingered in his house and made no response. Andrew was wearing my clothes so that he should smell of security (a dubious policy, this, and one that might have led to the animal treating the human as an impostor to be punished) and at length

Teko caught the scent and emerged. He appeared confused to find that it was not I who awaited him; he refused the pilchards and returned to his house. His gate to the outside world was still closed, and knowing for an absolute certainty that sooner or later Andrew was going to open it I was conscious of a steadily mounting nervous tension. After a minute or so Teko came back to the gate, and while Andrew was opening it Teko grabbed the edge with his hands and emerged with force; he was talking, but in a language I understood imperfectly, a muted variation upon his 'wow-wow-wow' that could mean moderate anger, satisfaction in possession of interesting food (and presumably defence of it), or what I can only describe as aggressive affection. Then he rolled on his back, which in all the mustellines can be either a gesture of defence preceding violence or one of submission to dominance in a hierarchy; I simply did not know which of the two this was, and I began literally to sweat. Then I saw Andrew bend down and put a finger in one of Teko's paws, as one does to a baby whose grasp is still unsure; I saw the little monkey fingers close upon it, and suddenly I knew that all was well, that even if a complete and intimate accord might be postponed for a little the basis for it was already there.

As Andrew walked away toward the sea with Teko at his heel, a sea lying light and bare, milky below a pale sky, the dark rocks and seaweed shining in the low glint of an autumn sun, time once again shut up like an old, well-oiled telescope, and I was watching Jimmy or Terry setting out with one or other otter for their routine morning walk so many years before. Life, in the sense that I understood life, had returned to the house and its occupants.

I moved from room to room, trying to keep the two in sight as – after an exploration of unfamiliar objects less minute and conscientious than Edal's – Teko accompanied Andrew over the dunes and down to the estuary of the little river. At length I lost sight of them, and went out on to the dunes, so that I could follow and if necessary direct their progress along the beach. After an hour they were back within a hundred yards of the house, and to spare Andrew the weary business of re-confining an animal that had so amply demonstrated his intransigent attitude on this point, I went into his house and acted as a vocal bait to which Teko responded immediately.

The suspense was over, and I felt certain now that Teko would not harm Andrew; though, judging by the aloof way the animal had ignored the human except in the role of some sort of official guide to the terrain, I thought it might be a long time before they established any closer contact between each other. I thought Teko's affections were fixed on me, but I flattered myself. It was only four days later, at the end of their third walk, that the almost unbelievable happened. It was a grey day, with gusts of wet wind blowing in off the sea, and almost continuous small rain. Andrew and Teko had been away for some two hours or more when from my writing desk I noticed them across the field, Andrew calling unavailingly to Teko, who was pottering about the first steep slope of the jeep track and occasionally disappearing into the bushes at its side, where a little hidden stream flowed down deep between sheer sides. It was raining harder now, and I went to fetch an anorak before going out to lure Teko home. When I had put it on I looked out of the window to see Andrew and Teko rolling and romping together on the soaking grass of the field, and Teko's voice of greeting and pleasure came to me even through the closed window. Flat on his back Andrew lay in the drenched grass while Teko clambered over his chest and nuzzled his face and ears with ecstatic squeaks of delight; I saw Andrew blow into his fur as I did myself, and Teko nuzzling under his jacket; I saw Andrew's expression of deep delight, and I was full of wonder. The two were like long-lost, intimate friends who have suddenly rediscovered each other; and I wondered how much and by what means Andrew's desire for this rapport had communicated itself to the animal. How very small is our knowledge.

The relationship never looked back, though it was a further week before Andrew was able to rehouse Teko unaided. The following day he was determined to try it himself, but after the pair had lapped the house in patient procession more than thirty times, sometimes the one leading and sometimes the other, all in the pouring rain, I felt it only humane to come to the rescue.

*

It was only a few days after this that I myself achieved a full restoration of my old relationship with Edal. It was one of those rare autumn days when there was no breath of wind, and the sun shone upon the gold and russet and red of turning leaf on the steep hillside above the house. The tide was far, far out, and the still, cerulean sea broke only with a tiny white lather of foam upon the sculptured sands; the hues were so delicate, so finely contrasted, as to give the whole scene an air almost of fragility, as if at any moment it might burst like a soap bubble and leave the onlooker in a colourless vacuum.

I took Edal out to the island beaches and the white coral sands; she herself was in some way elated by the sunshine and the stillness, and she scampered about with a greater display of speed and enthusiasm than I had yet seen. When we had crossed the island bar and came to the bay called Traigh a Ghuirabain, I saw that the tide was lower than I ever remembered seeing it; the great stems and rubbery brown leaves of umbrella weed stood naked and glistening on the beach of sand and scattered stone, and further out still they showed ranked above the flat water like the canopied fronds of some primeval forest. I found some big clams exposed near to the shrunken tide's edge, and I began to wade out in search of more. The water was so clear that even when it was above my knees I could see every minute detail of the bottom; the multi-coloured fan shells and mussels; the mother-of-pearl top-shells; the chalk-white hieroglyphics, like some forgotten alphabet, left by the serpulid tube-worms upon shell and stone alike; the fine tracery in crimson and white of little fern-like weeds. I was absorbed in looking at these things beneath the surface, and had momentarily forgotten Edal, who, when I had last seen her, had been porpoising at high speed some hundred yards away. Now I felt a sudden nudge at my leg from behind, and turned to find her touching me, 'corkscrewing'; revolving at enormous speed, that is to say, like a chicken-spit gone demented. I remembered suddenly how she had been used to do this when she was small; an expression, it seemed, of immense delight in her surroundings, something more than a feeling of well-being; almost, it seemed, one of ecstasy. I remembered another thing long forgotten, how I would take her by the tail and swoosh her round in circles by it until a human would have become giddy, and how she would respond with a vacuous expression of happiness and contentment. Now, if ever, was the moment to restore these little rituals of rapport; I took her by the tail and began to swing her round by it faster and faster, and she let herself go limp as I did so, her face wearing that same long forgotten look of fulfilment. When I let her go she went shooting away in the clear water, and as I watched her I wondered which had restored most to the other. To me the sky and the sea and the mountains looked brighter, more real, the shallow sea's floor more brilliant than before, for an enduring mist of guilt had been lifted from them all. I was content now to let the future resolve itself, for I knew that I could no longer break the trust of animal friendship.

As we went home Edal paused upon a mound of heather and grass and began to roll and polish herself upon its surface. I sat down a few yards away from her, determined not to destroy this recovered confidence by intrusion, and lit a cigarette. During the past few years I suppose I had experienced these sights and sounds before – Ben Sgriol with its first cap of lace-like snow against a pale blue autumn sky, the distant roaring of stags upon the slopes of the Skye shore, the rowan berries scarlet, and the river running ice-cold into the calm Camusfeàrna bay, fringed everywhere by the fallen leaves of autumn; but they had meant little to me – the impact had been sensory only, for I had been no longer part of them, and in an ecological sense I had already become an outsider. Now I reached out towards this once familiar world, as out of nothing Andrew and Teko had reached out to each other, and I felt at one with all that my senses could perceive. High above me, wheeling in taut arcs, two buzzards mewed like kittens, and a single wild goose flew northwards over the Sound – a Pinkfoot, calling continuously, lost, as I had been lost for so long.

Foot by foot Edal squirmed nearer to me, now wriggling upon her back, now ostentatiously polishing her chest and throat. Her fur had a sheen that I had not seen for years, and her eyes were bright, in place of the dull, existent look to which I had become long accustomed. Down the slope she pushed herself, for the most part upon her back, with arms and monkey fingers waving, until at last her nose was in contact with my thigh. I still did not know how much liberty I could take with her on land, but then and there the feeling of unity, of shared pleasure and joy, took absolute control. I treated her as I had when she was a cub, in the days when everything was taken for granted and antipathy was out of the question; I took her by the shoulders and pulled her to me and stroked her and blew into her fur and rolled her over and tickled her toes and whiskers, and she responded as Teko had done, with little snuffles of affection and squirming movements to make closer contact. When we started home Edal and Teko had between them given back to me the land in which I lived, the vision that I had lost.

# *Epilogue*

Exactly one year, to a day, after the breakdown of our negotiations with the zoo in December 1966, I received a telephone call from Woburn to say that it had proved impossible to adapt the Chinese Dairy Lake for our requirements. The Comptroller offered alternative sites, and I travelled south in Arctic conditions to view the white and frozen ponds that were available. None was, to my mind, suitable; and furthermore our otter quarters had been constructed to stand under the cover of a colonnade.

The future was uncertain but the present contented; Teko was restored to the old puppy-like situation in which he would spend hours playing in the living room, chasing a torch beam with his tail and romping with his human playmates. Edal was once more a friend of whom we were unafraid, and I felt that we had truly reached our goal.

In the small hours of 20 January fire swept through Camusfeàrna, gutting the house and destroying everything that was within it. No human life was lost, and Teko was saved, but Edal died with the house, and she is buried at the foot of the rowan tree. On the rock above her are cut the words 'Edal, the otter of Ring of Bright Water, 1958–1968. Whatever joy she gave to you, give back to nature.'

Tonight at the last sentence of a dream I stand in thought before the Camusfeàrna door. Someone someday perhaps may build again upon that site, but there is much that cannot ever be rebuilt.

# Afterword by Virginia McKenna

I am at Camusfeàrna on 11 August, the afternoon of the eclipse. This morning, just before 11 a.m. the light greyed, and there was a stillness – apart from the heightened activity of the midges who appeared to think dusk had fallen, and it was time to begin their rounds of torment.

Now the midges have departed, the sun burns in a blue sky, huge white cloud-galleons slowly sail out to sea and the occasional cry of a gull pierces the silence.

In barely one month's time it will be the 30th anniversary of Gavin Maxwell's death, and almost forty years since his masterpiece *Ring of Bright Water* was published. A story of a man and his human and otter friends. What was it that made this book so special, so loved, so important to its thousands of readers and to English literature? There is no doubt that it touched our hearts, awoke in us a longing for that seemingly idyllic existence at Camusfeàrna, gave birth to a deep and lasting fascination for otters, gave us, as a casket of jewels, passages of descriptive writing about nature unequalled until now.

Yet Gavin Maxwell himself professed to be surprised at the book's success, considering it to be something on the lines of a personal diary, no more. And perhaps this was the key. *Ring of Bright Water* and its two *Ring* sequels are very personal stories. He was not afraid to tell us of his heartaches, disappointments, his conflicts, to reveal to us many darker aspects of his nature. It is not a simplistic tale of a man romping with otters on the wild beautiful beach of Camusfeàrna; bathing in the pools of the waterfall near his house, whose tumbling cascades sparkled like so many brilliants in between the shadows of the trees. It is much more than that.

All dreams must end and the idyllic life he sought and found on the west coast of Scotland inevitably changed as his increasing fame compromised his solitary way of life, and visitors from far and wide stumbled down the track to the Bay of Alders and his home.

Re-reading the three books I have been struck quite forcibly by what seems to be his almost unconscious ability to attract disaster. Dramatic events, tragic incidents, injury, fire, loss – more challenges to overcome than most of us will ever face in our lifetime.

And yet – and this is the wonder of it – what do we, his readers, his audience, remember? It is the beauty of the writing, the relationship with the otters, the joy of their life and grief at their death; the warmth and clutter of the 'pitch-pine panelled kitchen–living room'; the sunshine and storms that beat upon the shells and shingle of the sandy beach; the glistening sea; distant islands and mountains of Skye which met his gaze each day; the journeys (often disastrous) in his boat *Polar Star*; the greylag geese – his wild friends who returned each summer, their poignant cry signalling their approach.

In 1968 a film was made, based on *Ring of Bright Water*. My husband Bill Travers and I were in that production and the letter Bill had from Gavin Maxwell a year later when he saw the completed film was one of his most prized possessions. Gavin invited us to meet him but to our lasting regret this was not to be as he died that same year.

By a strange, extraordinary twist of fate, or whatever one likes to call it, three years ago in 1996 the Born Free Foundation (an animal welfare charity founded by Bill, myself and our eldest son Will) heard that Eilean Ban, the little 6-acre island between Kyle of Lochalsh and Kyleakin was to be sold by public auction.

Eilean Ban was Gavin Maxwell's last home, the place he moved to when his house at Camusfeàrna was destroyed by fire. Following his death it had a series of owners and, finally, it was bought by the Scottish Office prior to the construction of the Skye Bridge, under whose soaring arc the Eilean Ban house and lighthouse now nestle.

My son and I swung into action. We instinctively knew that we must save this little piece of history – for the local communities, for the wildlife that frequented its shores and habitat, and for Gavin Maxwell himself, so that his work and memory should remain an undiminished part of the nation's culture.

This 'twist of fate' or coincidence has been followed by others – the ultimate one being the timing of the publication of this trilogy and the opening of the Eilean Ban project – which includes the Brightwater Visitors Centre in Kyleakin. People will be able to come to Eilean Ban by boat, marvel at the breath-taking views, enter Gavin Maxwell's house and the Stevenson lighthouse and imagine, for a moment, what it must have been like to live there.

The inscription on Edal's grave at Camusfeàrna reads: 'Edal, the otter of Ring of Bright Water, 1958–1968. Whatever joy she gave to you, give back to nature.'

That is what we hope to do with Eilean Ban, but with a deep sense of gratitude to Gavin Maxwell himself who has allowed us to enter his all-embracing ring.

As I sit here in the now late afternoon sun at Camusfeàrna and look across the gleaming sea down to the Highland cattle on the beach, across to Edal's grave, to the memorial stone set on the site of Gavin Maxwell's house and under which his ashes are buried, I feel suspended in a time warp. A great sense of peace and gratitude pervades. Yes, things change and some things end, but here the presence of Gavin Maxwell and his otters is alive and well, the waterfall's beauty is as vibrant as ever, the gulls cry and the people who come to this glorious and wonderful place treasure its remoteness and simplicity as much as he did, when he first came down the track and 'turned the key in Camusfeàrna door for the first time'.

May it remain so always.

*11 August 1999*